LIVERPOOL
A STORY OF BRITAIN

Sam Wetherell is a Senior Lecturer in the History of Britain and the World at the University of York, specialising in urban and economic history. He is the author of *Foundations: How the Built Environment Made Twentieth-Century Britain*, and has published articles for academic and popular audiences about the history of community arts, the development of urban policy, contemporary politics, climate change, deindustrialisation and football.

ALSO BY SAM WETHERELL

Foundations: How the Built Environment Made Twentieth-Century Britain

SAM WETHERELL

LIVERPOOL

A STORY OF BRITAIN

HEAD of ZEUS

An Apollo Book

First published as *Liverpool and the Unmaking of Britain*
in the UK in 2025 by Head of Zeus Ltd

This paperback edition first published in 2026 by Head of Zeus Ltd,
part of Bloomsbury Publishing Plc

9 7 5 3 1 2 4 6 8

A catalogue record for this book is available from the British Library.

ISBN (PB): 9781035927661
ISBN (eBook): 9781035927678

Printed and bound in Great Britain by Clays Ltd, Elcograf S.p.A.

MIX
Paper | Supporting responsible forestry
FSC® C018072

Bloomsbury Publishing Plc
50 Bedford Square, London, WC1B 3DP, UK
Bloomsbury Publishing Ireland Limited
29 Earlsfort Terrace, Dublin 2, D02 AY28, Ireland

HEAD OF ZEUS LTD
5–8 Hardwick Street
London EC1R 4RG

To find out more about our authors and books
visit www.headofzeus.com
For product safety related questions contact productsafety@bloomsbury.com

For Hannah

While it is easy to move money, masonry is more permanent. The axes of trade have shifted. Liverpool is no longer one of the centres of the world. Liverpool is an unwanted mausoleum of an imperialist past.

Tony Lane, 'The City of Harder Times to Come', 1978

Oh, the future said, this train can go faster
than this track can withstand

Jorie Graham, 'Before', 2023

Contents

Introduction

From the window of an elevated railway overlooking the docks, Frank Shaw thought he could see the future of Liverpool, and, by extension, the world. Shaw was a retired naval captain who had stewarded cargo ships from Liverpool through the Mediterranean bound for East Asia. On a typical route these ships would sail from Liverpool's docks out of the mouth of the Mersey and into the Irish Sea. They would then turn south, passing through Gibraltar and into the Mediterranean to the Suez Canal. From there they would continue into the Indian Ocean and eventually out into the Malacca Strait to Penang and Singapore, and sometimes onwards to Hong Kong and Shanghai. Looking down from his carriage over the vast conglomeration of moored ships, warehouses, pubs, canteens, call stands, repair stations, blacksmiths and travel agents that clustered along the banks of the river, Shaw saw a world that was in thrall to Liverpool: 'every dock represented a fresh point in the compass… the world's oceans held no secrets from these [ships] resting between adventures, gathering fresh reserves of power to flaunt the smoke-sullied Red Ensign wherever the sun rises and sets.' For the retired captain, the future beat a path out into the sea via an imperial maritime order that touched the face of every continent on earth. Empire and commerce were inextricable, and Liverpool would continue to be at the command centre of both. 'The whole waste of savagery', he wrote, was 'tamed and made seemly by British enterprise.'[1]

Shaw was writing in 1952. In less than thirty years, the future he envisaged would come spectacularly undone. If he had lived to witness the same dockland panorama in 1980, he would have been in awe at the vertiginous pace of historical change. By then, the enormous chain of Victorian docks, most of which were still standing, were empty and eerily quiet – a jagged and nonsensical jumble of iron, brick and broken glass. The river itself, untreated and underused, had become a shallow patina concealing an underwater massif of sand and silt shot through with human faeces that occasionally and sickeningly bobbed into view. The Blue Funnell Line, the shipping company whose ships Shaw had directed, would have been unrecognisable and greatly diminished. Struggling to compete with the shipping lines launched by new post-colonial nations, the company gradually disbanded, moving its headquarters from Liverpool to London in 1980. The imperial waystations navigated by Shaw's ships – Suez, Aden, Malaysia, Singapore – were no longer a part of the British world. Even the distinctive elevated railway from which he had surveyed the city's riverfront was gone, dismantled and replaced with a chain of bus stops. Shaw's imperious vantage-point, the line of sight that permitted his pompous yet not entirely outlandish fantasy about the future of a world made, in part, by Liverpool, had itself been annulled.

Liverpool had outlasted the historical forces that conjured it into being and its future was now uncertain. By the beginning of the 1980s, the city was facing a concatenation of crises. Its population was in freefall, almost halving between 1930 and the millennium. Decolonisation, technological revolutions in cargo shipping and Britain's changing geographies of trade laid waste to Liverpool's docks. Between 1957 and 1983, seven out of every eight docking jobs disappeared from the city.[2] In 1971, the last commercial trans-Atlantic liner set sail from Liverpool to Montreal, never to return. The hundreds of light industrial enterprises that had been hastily erected in the mid-twentieth century to compensate for the city's shrinking maritime economy – car plants, food processing works, small electronics factories – were steadily gutted by the recessions of the 1970s and 1980s. Between 1979 and 1982, Merseyside saw an astonishing 384 factories close for good, taking with them more than 25,000 jobs.[3] Throughout the 1980s, between 15 and 20 per cent of the city remained permanently unemployed. The engines of industry and trade that had once made Liverpool a wealthy city of almost a million people had sputtered and died.

For the city's Black population, most of whom were descended from West African workers who had been employed as cheap labour on inter-continental ships, economic misery was compounded by police brutality. They had been effectively excluded from the tides of welfare and social mobility that had carried so many of their white fellow city dwellers away from the slums and out to the suburbs. In the early 1980s, the unemployment rate in parts of Toxteth, a neighbourhood that had seen the highest concentration of post-war Black settlement in the city, was estimated to be as high as 73 per cent.[4] In 1981, the residents of Toxteth, workless, brutalised by the state and subjugated by a racially unequal society that Liverpool's elites had helped impose on the wider world, launched a spectacular insurrection against the police. After three days the city was on the brink of martial law. The uprising culminated with the police indiscriminately firing tear gas at protestors from specialist shotguns with the express permission of the Home Secretary – a dramatic show of force from Liverpool's beleaguered Chief Constable. While tear gas had been used to quell uprisings across the empire in the twentieth century, this was the first and, to date, only time that the weapon had been used in mainland Britain. The violence of the British imperial state, meted out in Egypt, in Malaya, in Kenya and in Northern Ireland, had arrived on the streets of Liverpool.[5]

A few weeks after the Toxteth uprising, in a notorious top-secret memo addressed to Margaret Thatcher, Geoffrey Howe, the Chancellor of the Exchequer, argued that Liverpool's crisis was unsolvable. He warned the Prime Minister, who was entering her second full year of office, that plans to rescue the city 'might be sown on relatively stony ground'. He compared the funding of infrastructure, employment and care in the city to 'trying to make water flow uphill'. Howe suggested to Thatcher that the city could instead be guided towards a process of 'managed decline'.[6] In the eyes of the government, Liverpool and its population had become obsolete.

This book is about Liverpool's past and what it might tell us about Britain's future. In focusing on a single place, its aim is to give order to the cacophony of narratives, the diversity of experiences and the parade of individuals that make up Britain's recent history. It allows us to see how some of the different pieces of the post-war era – deindustrialisation, decolonisation and the rise of a new kind of neoliberal economy – tessellated, working together to transform the lives of everyday people.[7]

At first glance, Liverpool seems like an unusual place from which to tell a story about Britain as a whole. The city has often been seen as a place apart, its history at odds with the rest of the country. It occupies an insurgent, contrarian and almost otherworldly place within Britain's body politic, patronised, ignored, misunderstood and in some cases brazenly hated. For this reason, the city has often been an object of curiosity. Its economy dominated by trade rather than industry, its politics shaped by Irish nationalism and Trotskyist entryism, its society home to some of the oldest and most established Black and Chinese communities in Europe, the city has long been seen as an outlier to the rest of Britain.[8]

So why Liverpool? I argue that Liverpool's history is a prophecy. It is where we need to look to understand our present moment; a moment that is characterised by stalling wage growth, collapsing health systems, widespread homelessness, shrinking political horizons, emboldened far-right movements and new demands for Black civil rights from London to St Louis. With inequality widening and climate change accelerating, the crises of surplus labour, surplus buildings and surplus people will become ever more urgent. One of the tasks of the historian is to comb through the historical darkness in search of the connecting threads between then and now. This is the history that Britain's impending future demands we tell. The history that this book describes might be coming for us all.

It is time to establish a new way of thinking about Britain's recent history, one that is better suited for our multiple overlapping crises, as well as the crises to come. The old stories we tell about post-war Britain – the rise and fall of the 'welfare state', Thatcherism, permissiveness and decline – were told by historians working in, and in many instances benefitting from, different political and economic conditions – different climates (in both meanings of that word). They may seem increasingly marginal as the alarm bells begin to sound for our coming century. We need histories of worklessness rather than labour, of environmental ruin rather than planning, of policing rather than welfare, of disintegration rather than hegemony. We also need hopeful stories of joy and resistance unburdened by the heavy-handed moralism and withered political imagination of recent electoral high-politics. We need precedents that confront rather than enable the far-right political violence erupting on Britain's streets. We need, in other words, to see Liverpool's history as a prophecy.

This book does not intend to be comprehensive. There are neighbourhoods, communities, stories and powerful individuals that do not feature at all here. It is a historical argument rather than a local survey, a narrative rather than a textbook. After all, Liverpool is a city that has produced more history than it can consume locally.[9] Almost all Britons will be familiar with some of the stories in this book, and readers hoping to be immersed in the city's explosive, dramatic and tragic history will not be disappointed by what follows, whether it's the sudden emergence of the most successful rock band the world has ever known, the collapse of the docks, the pitched battles in Toxteth in 1981, the city's fiscal brinksmanship and near bankruptcy under a Militant Trotskyist regime, the Disney-like regeneration of the city's waterfront, the extraordinary success of its two football teams and the unforgivable catastrophe of Hillsborough. But there are many other stories too, such as the secret deportation of parts of the city's Chinese community, the flooding of a Welsh village to secure the city's water supply, the co-ordinated destruction of much of the city's public transportation, the mass rent strikes in the suburbs, the Conservative experiments in lawless free-market planning imported to Liverpool via Hong Kong, the radical feminist support networks founded to help Irish women arriving via boat to access abortions and the city's pioneering response to the AIDS crisis.

What does it mean to be rendered obsolete by historical change, to inhabit somewhere that has outlasted its purpose and yet continues to exist? In Liverpool as well as in Britain and many other places in the global north, historical time appears to have glitched and stalled. The past has accumulated and congealed in the streets, heavy and burdensome. In the words of Svetlana Alexievich, 'the future is not where it ought to be. Our time comes to us secondhand.'[10] Britons are all, to some degree, the detritus left behind by historical forces that have long since expired. Like many others across the former industrial world, we live in or among vast settlements conjured from the earth in previous centuries to service trade routes and export markets that no longer exist or raw materials that are no longer in use.

Throughout this book, I use the term obsolescence to make sense of what happened in post-war Liverpool. I expand the meaning of the concept, beyond the narrow technical use that we are most familiar with, using it to encompass multiple different features of life in the city.[11] First, it refers to the accumulated ruins of a built environment falling into disuse. By the 1970s and 1980s, Liverpool's waterfront was littered with gigantic, abandoned warehouses, empty silos and crumbling jetties, damp with seawater, fringed by grass and weeds – reclaimed by ungovernable nature. Its halo of suburbs and satellite towns was speckled with abandoned factories. The exodus of the city's population had left its inner-city neighbourhoods pockmarked with cratered lots and abandoned houses, many with leaking gas mains, others with dogs trapped inside to deter copper thieves.

Whether it was Friedrich Engels writing about Manchester in the 1840s, Charles Baudelaire writing about Paris in the late nineteenth century or the Chinese documentary-maker Cao Fei commenting on Guangzhou in the early twenty-first, observers of cities in the first flushes of rapid growth have expressed wonder at how built environments can be suddenly transformed, leaving few traces of the past behind. Henry James returned to New York after a spell in Europe in 1904 and was astonished at how the Manhattan of his childhood had changed beyond recognition in just a few years. New York, he wrote, was 'a provisional city', one that was 'crowned not only with no history, but with no credible possibility of time for history', and was ventilated only by a 'dreadful chill of change'.[12] In late twentieth-century Liverpool these sentiments had been turned on their head. Here, the mystifying tendency for the spaces of everyday life to be dissolved and re-made by capital had stalled. Buildings that had outlived their use remained in place, either derelict or vacant. Karl Marx's famous adage about the boundless creative and destructive powers of capitalism, 'all that is solid melts into air', had been inverted. Jobs and money had melted into air, but jetties, warehouses and uninhabitable terraced houses remained stubbornly solid.[13]

Second, obsolescence was also the fate of many of the people who were left in the wake of Liverpool's unravelling economy. At first, this meant those who had arrived in Liverpool via Britain's imperial circulatory systems and whose presence in the city was no longer wanted – Chinese and Black merchant sailors and their descendants, who were brutally policed and sometimes deported. Eventually, however, by the end of the century, large swathes of the rest of the city's working class would also come to be demonised, over-policed and rendered surplus. Obsolescence would come for the city's tens of thousands of long-term unemployed – dock workers, skilled engineers, merchant sailors, construction workers, women and men who scrubbed chickens and built cars on electrical assembly lines – people whose productive energies were no longer required. To be deemed obsolete was a contagious condition that burned through Liverpool's social order.

Obsolescence and its attendant fates of intensive policing, grinding poverty and cultural denigration only make sense in a world where people and places are crudely instrumentalised.

Contrary to the view of politicians, employers and journalists who are quick to reduce the worth of a person's life to their labour power, I will argue that being made obsolete should not mean being disposable. Alternatively, under the right political conditions, it could even be a type of freedom, a pre-requisite, perhaps, for imagining a better world.

Finally, I am not interested in exhuming the exhausted arguments about whether Britain 'declined' in the twentieth century. As a framework, 'obsolescence' avoids this debate, which is often parochial, moralistic and imbued with sentiment and nostalgia.[14] Liverpool's obsolescence was compatible with, and made possible by, enormous concentrations of wealth elsewhere in the country and had little to do with Britain's relative standing in the league tables of other developed economies. Inequality has fractured these shared national communities of redistribution to the point where all-encompassing pronouncements of 'decline' or revival are increasingly meaningless.[15] Nor is the object of this book to celebrate what came before Britain's obsolescence. The centuries that preceded it have cast long and terrible shadows: the enslavement and social murder of millions of Black Africans, the decimation of indigenous populations, the exclusion of women from dignified well-paid work and the birth of a carbon economy whose emissions fill the skies above.

There is no city in mainland Britain whose history was shaped more by empire than Liverpool. The story of Liverpool's obsolescence is the story of the collapse of the city's imperial maritime economy. In the early twentieth century, the city was at the helm of a world-spanning network of trade and movement patched together by steamships, many of which were manned by West African, Chinese, Malaysian and Somalian sailors with transient and global lives. After long, lonely voyages skirting deserts, rainforests and equatorial storms, these ships arrived in Liverpool to be serviced by tens of thousands of dock workers, many of whom lived and died within walking distance of the banks of the Mersey. Beginning in the middle of the twentieth century, Liverpool's mighty imperial nexus came spectacularly undone. As early as the 1930s, Britain's falling share in world trade began to corrode the city's networks of trade and influence. After the war, post-colonial nation states founded rival shipping companies that disrupted monopolies and disorganised trade. Meanwhile, Britain's entry into what would become the European Union reorientated the nation's trade away from its empire and towards the continent to its east, leaving Liverpool, in the words of one writer, 'marooned on the wrong side of the country'.[16] Finally, the adoption of shipping containers that rolled seamlessly from ships to trucks sent mortal shocks through the city's remaining trade routes, removing the necessity of most dockside labour and, eventually, bankrupting the port.

The unravelling of Liverpool's imperial maritime economy had profoundly different consequences for the various inhabitants of its planetary web. The city's dock workers and many of the thousands of other onshore workers who made their living in jobs associated with shipping and trade, almost all of whom were white, were offered life rafts by trade unions, activist local governments and state planners. In the early twentieth century, dock workers in Liverpool, like those across the country, had lived casual and uncertain lives, fighting for scraps of work each day with no job security and no guarantees. In 1947, the post-war Labour government introduced a system of registration and job security that undid more than a century of precarity and, in Liverpool, mitigated the downward pressure on wages caused by the reduction in trade. Meanwhile, between the 1930s and the 1960s, various arms of the state subsidised the creation of tens of thousands of new industrial jobs to absorb those who had been cut loose from the city's contracting maritime economy. These new jobs were underwritten by thousands of new homes, public and private, built in suburban coils around the city's ring roads and in the expanding new towns of Kirkby, Runcorn and Skelmersdale.

However, while white workers were temporarily rescued, the people of colour who also made a living from this oceanic system were quietly abandoned. Black sailors and their descendants, most of whom lived in cheap hostels by the docks or in rented slum housing, struggled to gain access to new industrial jobs or new council homes. In the 1930s, their lives were scrutinised and pathologised by academics at Liverpool University, at that time a leading centre for eugenics and race science. In 1948, the Black community was subject to an outburst of violence instigated by a white mob. In the 1950s, many were deported with the collusion of the shipping companies they had worked for. Most notoriously, the end of the war also saw more than a thousand Chinese merchant sailors who had settled in Liverpool deported in secret, many of whom were detained by the police in midnight raids and had British families who never knew their fate.

We can follow the consequences of this divergent response to the collapse of Liverpool's maritime economy into the 1960s, 1970s and 1980s. As job opportunities contracted and German bombs tore through the hinterlands of the docks, Liverpool's Black seafarers and their descendants moved inland to Toxteth. There, in crumbling terraced homes and ill-kept Victorian mansions hastily subdivided by rapacious landlords, their lives were circumscribed by unemployment, police violence and exclusion from all but the worst public and private housing. At the same time, many seafarers whose lives had been divided between Liverpool and cities in the decolonising world found themselves cut adrift, trapped behind the new immigration restrictions of the 1960s and 1970s.

Meanwhile, by the last third of the twentieth century, the machinery of welfare, industrial policy and economic growth that had rescued many of Liverpool's white dock workers was already falling apart. In the space of a few years, containerisation and the abandonment of the city's centuries-old network of Victorian docks eviscerated the post-war job protection scheme for dock workers. Its final abolition by Margaret Thatcher in 1989 plunged the city's small cohort of remaining dock workers back into precarious, insecure work. At the same time, the global economic turmoil of the 1970s and early 1980s saw the car assembly plants and small factories, once imagined to be the future of Liverpool's economy, either shrink their workforces or close for good. Without work, life in the city's new peripheral communities, places like Kirkby and Speke, came to feel like an indefinite incarceration where diminishing welfare payments were recycled to pay for increasing rents and where heroin came to plug the gaps left by insecurity and the broken promises of social mobility.[17] By the 1980s, many white people had become subjected to the same kinds of insecurity, downward social mobility, environmental ruin and police violence that had marked the lives of people of colour in the city for generations. To be racialised and to be made obsolete were overlapping processes.

The combined social and material effects of the city's obsolescence require us to think, therefore, about the ways that British capitalism was shaped by racial inequalities, inequalities that were themselves forged by the expansion and contraction of its empire. Many historians have long been aware of how Britain's economic prosperity was inseparable from colonial violence perpetrated in myriad forms overseas.[18] Indeed, this book is heavily influenced by a tradition of Black scholarship on both sides of the Atlantic that argues that racialisation – the ceaseless and brutal process of producing and justifying social difference – has been a process internal to the history of capitalism.[19] However, most theorists of what has come to be called 'racial capitalism' have studied these twin processes of racialisation and economic development in motion, from the slave plantation to the assembly line to the call centre.[20] Instead, obsolescence is what's left after these grand historical forces slowly grind to a halt. It is the study of a society that has outlived the productive forces that have called it into being.[21]

The shattered remains of Liverpool's imperial maritime economy were scattered across the city and the wider world. Contrary to many accounts of post-war Liverpool, which focus on a narrow segment of the city's working class, this book argues that the city's economic crisis intersected with and recast a post-imperial society that was structured by race at every level.[22] The implicit coding of Britain's working class as white is a fragile and cynical rhetorical move, one that is laundered through one-sided and parochial accounts of deindustrialisation. It is a claim that burns up swiftly on entering the atmosphere of Liverpool's recent history.

What was to be done about Liverpool's crisis? By the end of the twentieth century, the city had become an open-air laboratory for solutions to the problem of obsolescence. In the 1980s and 1990s, successive governments dreamed up various schemes for putting unemployed people to work and for repurposing surplus buildings for uses that would have been unimaginable for their original architects.

From the early 1980s, Margaret Thatcher's government used Liverpool as a testing ground for some of the neoliberal policies that her government was hoping to introduce on a national scale. In 1981, her government created the Merseyside Development Corporation (MDC), a shadowy body whose board was directly appointed by Westminster and which had the power to buy, sell and redevelop land, superseding the power of the democratically elected local government. A few months later, this was followed by an 'enterprise zone' in the city's southern fringes. Only a few hundred acres in size, the zone was a low-tax libertarian fantasy world layered over a landscape of abandoned factories and car assembly plants. Inspired by the laissez-faire economy of imperial Hong Kong, the zone was designed to showcase a new kind of low-tax, deregulated economy, one that, as Conservative politicians noted in secret memos, would soon be rolled out across the country. Liverpool's new urban economy demanded retrofitting and redeveloping the city's obsolete buildings. In 1984, the Herculaneum Dock was transformed into the first of five National Garden Festivals, a fantastical temporary garden show, attended by millions and intended to attract private property speculators back into the city. In 1988, parts of the Albert Dock were re-made into Tate Liverpool, a signal that the intangible forces of creativity and culture might halt Liverpool's downward spiral.

These different policies had a single guiding logic. The city would be re-made in order to compete on a global scale for money, tourists and jobs. Taxes would be lowered, buildings would be scrubbed clean and the city's history would be sanitised. Where Liverpool's docks had once processed textiles, guns and enslaved people, it was now incumbent on the newly expanded and renamed John Lennon Airport to import tourists and export culture in the form of football and the Beatles. Shorn of its imperial networks, the city was re-globalised in the 1980s and 1990s. This new international orientation welcomed the mobility of capital and tourists at the same time as Britain's border regime intensified, even for its former imperial subjects and their descendants. As Britain decolonised, new legislation in 1962, 1968, 1971 and 1981 tightened its borders, sealing the country off from its former empire and securing its social infrastructure from the claims of former colonial subjects.[23] The Black, unemployed and heavily policed residents of Toxteth, or what remained of the city's Chinese community after deportation drives in the 1940s, were not the beneficiaries or the imagined protagonists of this new cosmopolitanism. While Geoffrey Howe's notorious 1981 memo calling for the city's 'managed decline' was not spoken of again in the top levels of government, this book will argue that each of these measures in their own way was exactly that. Although some of the strategies deployed since 1980 were briefly successful on their own terms, Liverpool's continued purpose was never fully resolved.

Fortunately, these were not the only solutions to Liverpool's obsolescence. Immediately after the war, the city's fraying maritime networks meant that Liverpool became a hub for anti-colonial resistance movements that set out to abolish the imperial inequalities that sustained its economy. The city became a place where different visions of the post-colonial world were hotly debated by striking sailors, pan-Africanist intellectuals, eccentric preachers and future post-colonial leaders. Later, as Liverpool's Black community moved inland, it developed its own distinctive formation, organised through music, sport and radical forms of resistance. This was an expansive cultural and political Blackness forged in the furnace of white racism and police violence and organised through groups such as the Liverpool Black Caucus, the Liverpool 8 Defence Committee and the Liverpool 8 Law Centre, who were instrumental in staking a claim for Black people in the city and contesting police brutality in the streets and in the courtroom.[24] The uprising in Toxteth in 1981, a multi-racial insurrection against decades of police brutality, took the city's culture of resistance to its violent and combustible limit.

In other areas, too, Liverpool's residents refused to submit to the terms of their obsolescence. Perhaps most famously, the city elected a Trotskyist Militant Labour council in 1983 that waged war against Thatcher, refusing to implement savage cuts to municipal jobs and services entailed by reduced fiscal support from her government. In politicising the city's budget, the Council seized on widespread yet inchoate feelings of abandonment and despair and wielded them into a compelling new story about Liverpool's obsolescence. They were, however, resolutely uninterested in the social order of the post-colonial city that they ruled. Their mechanistic and parochial theory of politics meant that the Council refused to address the ongoing exclusion of the city's Black residents from the new homes and jobs that were created under its reign, while doubling down on their support for the police. Just like the job and housing creation drives of the mid-twentieth century, the Trotskyist insurgency amounted to a deficit-funded redevelopment programme whose spoils were largely reserved for the city's white population. Their programme was insufficiently rather than excessively imaginative. Liverpool's great political tragedy is that the Black abolitionists who duelled with police in 1981 and the white socialist politicians who squared off against government ministers in Westminster meeting rooms failed to find a common language during the city's greatest crisis. As late as the 1980s, the two vestigial halves of Liverpool's extinct imperial maritime economy were unable to meet across the political void.

Resistance flourished in other areas too. On the docks and on the factory floor, workers went on strike, organised sit-ins, slowed the pace of assembly lines and ridiculed their overseers. In the 1960s and 1970s, the sudden arrival of second wave feminism saw the founding of bookshops and reading groups, intimate spaces of discussion and dissent that opened new terrains of political struggle. Meanwhile, working-class women who were trapped in the workless new town of Kirkby organised rent strikes and were early pioneers of the 'Wages for Housework' campaign, which attempted to reconceive cleaning, caring and parenting as labour deserving remuneration. Black women, meanwhile, organised to re-imagine the provision of care, refusing to submit to the patronising and carceral way that Black people had been treated by medical and social services in Liverpool. Finally, during the AIDS crisis, radical health activists worked with heroin addicts and sex workers to establish a safe needle exchange programme, one of the first in the country. At the same time, and in the wake of a clumsy and hostile state response to the epidemic, gay men took it upon themselves to deinstitutionalise care, looking after each other, sharing resources, tending bedsides and memorialising the dead.

As the theorist Ruth Wilson Gilmore put it, those who have been abandoned by capital do also 'abandon themselves'.[25] Anti-colonial freedom fighters, mutual aid groups, activist lawyers, consciousness-raising circles, tenant associations and uncompromising unions all crafted solidarities that ran below the surface of formal politics like underground streams beneath limestone beds, shaping, recasting and opening up spaces for new futures. These inchoate and contradictory responses might be maps for how we should navigate through the storms of the coming century.

Prelude

The World that Liverpool Made

This book opens in 1945, just as Liverpool was exiting the stage of world history. Before we begin with Liverpool's obsolescence, we must first briefly review the events that led up to its spectacular decline. In a recent interview, the former Shadow Chancellor of the Exchequer John McDonnell argued that we need more local histories of British cities. Using Liverpool as an example, McDonnell argued that such histories could catalyse a revival in working-class politics and culture.[1] To write a truly comprehensive 'local' history of Liverpool, however, would require a visit to almost every continent on earth. The community of people whose lives have been shaped by Liverpool is a global one that stretches far beyond the city's present boundaries. Liverpool's local history, in other words, is the history of the world.

While Liverpool had been a regional centre for farming, fishing and short-distance trade since at least the thirteenth century, we can date its modern history to 1648, with the arrival of thirty tonnes of tobacco, the first cargo shipped from the Americas to the city. These new long-distance networks for trading tropical commodities grown in the distant frontiers of Britain's nascent empire transformed the fortunes of a city whose horizons had previously extended only to Wales and Ireland. In 1715, Liverpool opened the first commercial 'wet dock' in the world, a sophisticated system of gates and basins that protected ships from the tides and turbulent waters of the River Mersey. By this time, Liverpool had established itself as the third biggest seaport in Britain after London and Bristol. Within a hundred years of opening the wet dock, 40 per cent of the world's trade would pass through the city. The scale of this rise can be briefly shown by looking at five different places, each thousands of miles apart.

We might begin with the George's Plain sugar plantation in Westmoreland, Jamaica, a wide semicircle of flat land ringed by hills on the island's west coast where, in 1832, 350 African enslaved people worked. Liverpool was a relative latecomer to the slave trade, set back by the London-based Royal African Company, whose monopoly on the trade lasted until 1698. Beginning in the first decade of the eighteenth century, ships financed and owned by Liverpool merchants set sail from the city to West Africa. There, finished goods were traded for hundreds of people, who were incarcerated in suffocating holds for the long, perilous journey to the Caribbean or North America. By the end of the eighteenth century, this trade had come to dominate Liverpool's economy. Before 1800, no port in the world was more involved in the slave trade than Liverpool and, by the abolition of the trade in 1807, more than 1.1 million enslaved people had been transported by Liverpool ships.[2] George's Plain was purchased in 1769 by a merchant and slave trader named Richard Watt, who was born near Wigan but grew up in Liverpool. Watt was heavily involved in the trading of people between West Africa and the Caribbean on Liverpool ships and invested in multiple Liverpool-based firms that imported slave-made tropical goods into the city. In 1782, Watt, along with his vast fortune, returned to Liverpool and in 1795 he purchased Speke Hall estate to the south of the city, parts of which are now the site of Liverpool's John Lennon Airport.[3] In 1834, when slavery was abolished across the British empire, the inhabitants of George's Plain were freed, and Richard Watt's great nephew and heir was awarded £4,485 in compensation for the loss of his 'property'.[4]

Next, we might travel to Opobo, a small town on the delta of the Niger river in the far east of Nigeria, not far from its present-day border with Cameroon. When the slave trade was abolished in 1807, Liverpool re-purposed its trans-Atlantic and West African shipping networks to trade new commodities that were becoming central to Britain's industrial economy. Among these was palm oil, made from crushing the kernels of palm trees indigenous to West Africa, a central ingredient in soap manufacture as well as an industrial lubricant.[5] Opobo was one of many waystations for this trade. For much of the nineteenth century, the town and its hinterland were under the rule of King Jaja of Opobo, a powerful local leader who co-ordinated the harvesting of groundnuts up and down the river and brokered their shipping to European traders, mostly from Liverpool. In 1885, after refusing to cede his land to the British empire, Jaja was arrested by British authorities, deposed and deported to Barbados. In the early twentieth century, Opobo became a battleground between the Liverpool shipping company Elder Dempster and the Wirral-based soap manufacturer Lever Brothers, who attempted to build their own palm oil refineries along the Opobo coast. The Lever Brothers were forced out of the enterprise by Elder Dempster, who wanted to preserve their monopoly in the area.[6] Currently, Opobo is a sleepy backwater. Gone are the steamships and refineries. All that remains of Liverpool's imperial footprint is a memorial in the town square to the deposed King Jaja.

Switching back across the Atlantic, our next port of call is New Orleans. In the nineteenth century, Liverpool and New Orleans were bound together by threads of cotton. In the first half of the nineteenth century, the US South had been upended by a dizzying boom in cotton production. Planters were turning enormous tracts of former indigenous land in newly created southern states into gigantic, deforested monocultures worked by Black enslaved people. This explosion in cotton production was tied to the industrial revolution in Britain, a central part of which had been the mechanisation of textile production. During these years, the former French colonial outpost of New Orleans, purchased by the United States in 1803, became a bustling entrepôt where cotton was warehoused and exported across the world, chiefly to Liverpool. At the same time, New Orleans became one of the largest and most efficiently organised slave markets the world has ever seen.[7] In the middle of the nineteenth century, cotton accounted for almost half of Liverpool's trade. By this time, powerful and increasingly well-organised merchants in Liverpool set the commodity's global price. Operating from the Cotton Exchange built near the docks in 1808, these merchants acted as conduits between profoundly different capitalist regimes at different ends of the same supply chain – connecting the tropical agricultural labour of African American enslaved people with that of working-class men and women in factories in Manchester. In doing so, they set the pace at which native Americans were expropriated and enslaved people exploited in the fields of Alabama, Mississippi and Louisiana.[8] When the US Civil War erupted over the issue of slavery in 1861, Liverpool's elites sided with the pro-slavery Confederate south, sending warships and military supplies to ports that were under military blockade to support their doomed war effort.[9]

Meanwhile, on another side of the world, we find the small village of San Tin in Hong Kong's New Territories, nestled in a hilly stretch of farmland a few miles south of the present border with mainland China. We tend to think of Hong Kong as a dense bustling entrepôt, but much of the colony's land was, and remains, rural. Britain had acquired ownership over Hong Kong Island and parts of the Kowloon peninsula in 1842 after the Treaty of Nanjing following the First Opium War and in 1898 had extended its reach north to cover the sparsely populated New Territories. Meanwhile, in the late nineteenth century, Liverpool had complemented its ties to the Americas, India and West Africa with extensive trading routes to East Asia. It was in Hong Kong's New Territories, among other places, that locals were recruited to work as low-paid seamen on merchant vessels owned by companies such as the Blue Funnell Line, which travelled to and from Liverpool. In San Tin, shipping companies hoovered up the surplus men who were unable to find work in the village's subsistence economy. An anthropologist who surveyed the village in 1975 found that a third of households had a male who had worked as a seaman between 1900 and 1940 and that 15 per cent of those who had left either died at sea or were never heard from again.[10]

Finally, we might return to Liverpool and visit Scotland Road, a neighbourhood immediately north of the city's centre. While Liverpool re-made parts of the wider world, Scotland Road was where the world had come to Liverpool. In the nineteenth century, five million people emigrated from Ireland, many of whom were refugees from the catastrophic famine of 1845–52 and its aftermath. As the biggest port on the Irish Sea, untold numbers of these refugees passed through Liverpool, and while most departed on trains to London, Manchester or Birmingham or boarded ships to the United States or parts of Britain's empire, tens of thousands remained in the city, permanently altering its politics and society.[11] Many Irish refugees who made this journey passed through or settled in Scotland Road, a dense warren of tenements and slum houses that was demolished in the middle of the twentieth century. Famously chronicled in the memoirs of the Irish novelist Pat O'Mara, who grew up there at the turn of the twentieth century, Scotland Road was a site of desperate, rootless poverty. At its core was Paddy's Market where, as O'Mara put it, 'the refuse of the Empire is bought and sold', including second-hand clothes, trinkets from across the world and the services of sex workers whose clientele were the sailors for whom Liverpool was just one brief stop on world-spanning journeys.[12] As a result of these migrations Liverpool became a hub for anti-colonial Irish nationalism. In 1916, fifty volunteers, some of whom had never set foot in Ireland, left from Liverpool to fight in the doomed Easter Rising in Dublin. Meanwhile, Scotland Road was the only constituency in mainland Britain to elect an Irish Nationalist MP, T. P. O'Connor, who represented the neighbourhood between 1885 and 1929.

By 1910, Liverpool was larger and richer than any English city other than London. That year, the Royal Liver Building was nearing completion on the city's waterfront. The building, with its vast scale, elegant façade and modern construction methods, resembled the early skyscrapers of Manhattan or Chicago, reflecting the city's imperious pomp and world-making aspirations. Its twin spires were crowned with two sculptures of mythical liver birds, the ancient symbol of the city. The two birds, named Bertie and Bella, were made from copper and were eighteen feet tall with a wingspan of twenty-four feet. To this day, there is a legend that, if either were to fly away, Liverpool would be doomed. The Liver Building was also topped by two huge clocks, which, city boosters bragged, were two and a half feet wider than the clockface of Big Ben. Shortly before their installation, the directors of the Royal Liver Company squeezed around one of the clocks to eat lunch off its face.[13] It is hard to imagine a more fitting image for a city whose fortunes were living on borrowed time.

The history of Liverpool's emergence as one of the most significant command centres of the British empire is not the subject of this book. Instead, we begin in 1945 when, battered by two world wars and a great depression, Liverpool's centuries of growth were already coming undone.

The directors of the Royal Liver Company eat lunch off the face of the Liver Building's clock, shortly before its installation in 1911.

I

Departures

On a rainy Tuesday afternoon in May 1945, thousands gathered outside Liverpool Town Hall to hear news of the unconditional surrender of the German army. The announcement prompted an explosion of sound and light in a city that had spent much of the past six years trying its best to be invisible from the air. Bells rang out in churches and public buildings, the sound mingling with the blasts of fog horns from boats in the Mersey and the whistles from trains and trams. Licensing laws were effectively suspended, and many pubs remained open until they were drunk dry. An effigy of Hitler was subjected, in the words of one reporter, to 'an ignominious destruction'. The docks ground to a halt for forty-eight hours, with workers given two days off to celebrate. Illegal bonfires, many of which were assembled on the cratered ruins of buildings destroyed by German bombs, blazed long into the night, sending coils of smoke into the patchwork of clouds over the sky.[1]

Liverpool had been re-made by world war. The city had been at the centre of a vast global vortex of material and people. Its docks played a vital role in keeping open trans-Atlantic and imperial supply lines of food and weapons, at a time when eastern ports were too exposed to enemy attack. The city's streets had been scarred by German bombs, which had killed 4,000 people and left 100,000 homeless. During these years, the world had come to Liverpool. Almost five million people – mostly soldiers but also refugees, prisoners, students and emergency workers – passed through the city, creating, in places, a wild and frenetic cosmopolitanism.[2] To help integrate this makeshift international community, the Foreign Office sponsored the creation of the Allied Centre, a handful of dormitories and function rooms on Basnett Street that offered education, logistical help and a rich social world of entertainment for foreign visitors. The Centre held almost daily events for refugees from Europe, soldiers from different corners of Britain's empire and US servicemen. At any given time, visitors could find groups of sailors celebrating Greek Independence Day, a fundraising event for the Polish Red Cross, a tea party for Javanese seamen or lavish receptions for heads of state in exile including Charles de Gaulle and the King of Norway.

The paternalistic internationalism of the Allied Centre in Liverpool, however, belied what was taking place in the streets outside, where hasty attempts were being made to dispose of surplus workers who had been drafted into the war effort from overseas and whose labour was no longer required. The same month that the Centre hosted a dinner for Russian sailors, English classes for the children of the Panamanian Consul, a concert for Yugoslavian sailors and a meeting of the Canadian Wives Club, police cars were roaming the streets of Liverpool, raiding boarding houses, pubs and laundrettes to arrest and deport hundreds of Chinese merchant sailors who had been living in the city, some for many years.[3]

This book begins with what happened to Liverpool's unwanted populations in the immediate months and years after the end of the war. The first people deemed to be obsolete in post-war Liverpool were people of colour who were tied to Liverpool's imperial maritime history: Chinese seamen, West Indian migrant workers, African sailors and the mixed-race children fathered by Black American servicemen. The end of the war marked the beginning of a long process of ordering and sorting. Across the world, millions of demobilised soldiers, refugees and prisoners of war either returned to their place of origin or found new homes. What we think of as Britain's post-war 'welfare state' was forged against the backdrop of an extraordinary racist backlash in Liverpool, a backlash that included secret deportation drives, instances of street violence, police harassment and everyday discrimination in workplaces, nightclubs and boarding houses.[4] At the same time, however, at the twilight of Britain's empire, Black activists and intellectuals had other ideas. In the post-war years, Liverpool also became a stage for showcasing alternative visions of race relations on an imperial and global scale.

A few hours before dawn broke over Liverpool on 8 December 1945, a group of police and immigration officers were gathered at the city's port. Nearby, the SS *Diomed* was preparing to depart. Unlike the thousands of merchant ships that had docked in Liverpool during the previous years with supplies from across the Allied world to sustain Britain's war effort, the *Diomed* had been stripped of its cargo, its hold fitted instead with bunkbeds. After an hour had passed, to the relief of the officials, a hundred men emerged from the night. The men were Chinese merchant seamen, mostly from Shanghai, who had lived and worked in Liverpool, some for many years. They were searched by customs officials, who found nothing more suspicious than small amounts of currency, which the men were allowed to keep, and boarded the ship. As dawn broke, the *Diomed* slipped away down the Mersey and out into the Irish Sea bound, eventually, for Singapore.[5] These were the first of thousands of Chinese workers to be deported from Liverpool over the coming months, many of whom were rounded up and detained in night-time raids of lodging houses, restaurant kitchens and laundrettes by the police. Many left behind British wives and children who would never know their fate.

By 1945, Liverpool's Chinese community was already a hundred years old. From the mid-nineteenth century, the invention of steamshipping and the aggressive expansion of the British empire into ports such as Shanghai and Hong Kong had displaced tens of millions of Chinese migrants. The Opium Wars, fought in the 1840s and 1850s, had forced China to integrate into the global economy on unequal terms, triggering widespread famine and upheaval.

Some of this displaced population was recruited by the British empire as indentured servants, unpaid workers on fixed contracts who were dragooned into working on infrastructure projects in East Africa, Malaya and the Caribbean. Others found their way to Australia, New Zealand, South Africa and California to work on gold fields or build railways.[6]

Some of the extraordinary global movement of people that was unleashed by British imperial expansion into Chinese ports ended up in Liverpool. From 1866, Chinese sailors began to be recruited by the Ocean Steam Ship Company (which would later become the Blue Funnell Line), the first company to operate a regular steamshipping line from Liverpool to Shanghai and Hong Kong. Due to the transient nature of merchant shipping work, exact numbers are hard to pin down, but the number of Chinese settlers in Liverpool increased from the late nineteenth century, peaking at a few thousand during the First World War. Immigration restrictions in 1919 and 1925 later restricted numbers to a little over 500 in 1931.[7]

In the early twentieth century, this small population formed something close to a recognisable 'Chinatown' along Pitt Street and Frederick Street near the docks, arguably the oldest sustained Chinese settlement in Europe. These streets hosted a handful of cramped boarding houses, emigration agents, tobacconists and a local pub called The Nook, where one resident, Lai Fook, and his wife Edie made a living selling fried fish balls with orange peel and chilli sauce. Two Chinese food shops, Low Tow and Low Chung, could be found next door to each other on Pitt Street, selling tofu cakes (known by locals as 'white jelly' cakes), dried Chinese plums, gue tow (a kind of pickle), black jam cakes and dried shrimp. This community lived precarious and impoverished lives. Seamen who signed on for work in China earned between a third and a fifth of the wages of white British seamen doing the same job.[8]

Most Chinese seamen spent their time onshore living in a network of extremely basic and crowded lodging houses in Chinatown. Residents slept multiple men to a room in stacked bunkbeds and ate simple meals on long, shared tables, sometimes collectively organising the labour of cooking in basic kitchens. The better boarding houses had large urns of Chinese tea kept warm on the stove. Toilets were in the backyard. With their cramped quarters, communal rotas and routinised schedules, these boarding houses bore a resemblance to the living conditions aboard the ships on which they worked.[9] The boarding house keepers often played a direct role in disciplining and supplying labour for shipping companies and had been known to confiscate much of their guests' wages.[10] Meanwhile, Chinese settlers who were able to escape the perilous world of merchant shipping and put down roots in Liverpool beyond the immediate vicinity of the docks mostly worked in family-run laundrettes, which operated out of terraced houses across the city. These houses had been transformed into industrialised washing facilities with sleeping areas, often shared, carved out of back rooms. According to one estimate there were nearly a hundred Chinese-owned laundries in Liverpool in 1945.[11]

A man scrubs the floor of a lodging house for Chinese sailors in Liverpool in 1942.

The fact that Chinese settlers were almost entirely male meant that relationships and marriages with local women were common. According to interviews conducted by the historian Maria Wong in the 1980s with white women who married Chinese seamen, it was widely believed that Chinese men exuded a different type of masculinity to their white counterparts, more liberated from the alcoholism and violence common among some working-class families at the time. The continued low rates of pay for Chinese workers meant that women who married Chinese men sometimes had to find part-time work, often while also bearing the sole burden of domestic labour and childcare. This problem was particularly acute when their husbands were called up for long periods at sea, when wives were often forced into pawning possessions or subletting rooms as a strategy for survival.[12]

Although they were small, fledgling Chinese communities in Liverpool as well as in London were a source of intense fascination and at times cultural and moral panic in the inter-war period. Popular mystery novels by Agatha Christie, Sax Rohmer and Thomas Burke featured sinister Chinese villains with connections to city docks. These were in part inspired by a series of lurid, sensationalised drugs scandals with connections to London's Chinatown immediately after the First World War, such as the death of the actress Billie Carleton from a cocaine overdose in the Savoy Hotel in 1918, a scandal that resulted in the imprisonment of her drug dealer, Ada Song Ping You, a woman married to a Chinese man who had reportedly introduced her to opium.[13] This fascination drew on nineteenth-century associations of Chinese sailors with opium, gambling and organised crime, initially popularised by writers like Charles Dickens, Thomas De Quincey and Oscar Wilde. In Liverpool, these panics, coupled with anxieties that Chinese seamen were undercutting white wages, had a long history stretching back to the beginning of the twentieth century, with vivid articles about gambling and opium smuggling common in the local press.[14]

These various fictitious concerns about the morally 'undesirable' nature of the Chinese presence in cities such as Liverpool laid some of the groundwork for the deportation drives of the immediate post-war months. After the outbreak of war, as Liverpool became a crucial node in British global supply lines, the numbers of Chinese merchant seamen increased dramatically, with thousands of new workers, mostly from Shanghai, moving to Liverpool to increase the capacity of Liverpool's docks. As many as 20,000 Chinese seamen may have passed through Liverpool during these years.[15] Despite a reputation for strike-breaking and political quiescence, this new pool of Chinese labour militantly contested the fact that they were paid substantially less than their white counterparts. In 1942, Chinese seamen went on strike, eventually winning a substantial pay increase and a war-risk bonus that had been paid to white workers as a compensation for the dangers of their work. Others resorted to subtler and less organised forms of resistance. It was common, for example, for seamen to register with one of the worker pools to renew their legal standing in Britain, only to hide from sight when a ship arrived that needed to be worked.[16] In the late 1930s, a small number of seamen from rural villages in the Hong Kong New Territories were given certificates of nationality by the Home Office to allow shipping companies to take advantage of special subsidies for employing British subjects.[17] These were the minority, however. Most Chinese workers had little or no access to any kind of documentation that secured legal standing in Britain.

By early 1945, with the end of the war in sight, shipping companies and government officials became concerned that Chinese seamen were increasingly established in the city, finding forms of employment outside of the shipping pool and in some cases going underground. In May 1945, it was even suggested that the Chinese government, then in the midst of a civil war, dispatch military officers to Liverpool to discipline the labour pools.[18] One official referred vaguely to 'gambling and opium dens' and noted that 'I cannot imagine the Chief Constable of any town welcoming an undesirable Chinaman.'[19] Like previous generations of merchant seamen, many war-workers had also married local women, with one official estimating that there had been 117 such marriages in Liverpool during the war.[20] By the summer of 1945, many Chinese seamen with British wives and children started refusing to sign articles of work that would 'close' in the Far East without assurances that they would be allowed to return to Britain. These marriages were derided by officials, with one customs officer noting that 'many of them are not the choicest individuals… (nor, for that matter, are some of the wives), and it is felt that quite a number of the marriages have been contracted merely in order that the husband may make a claim to take up domicile here'.[21]

As summer turned to autumn and the war with Japan ended, re-opening supply routes to the Far East, shipping companies proceeded with the plan to employ Chinese settlers in Liverpool on articles of work that would entail a one-way trip back to China. On 19 October 1945, in a secret meeting that included officials from the Home Office, the Foreign Office, the Ministry of War Transport and Herbert Winstanley, the Chief Constable of Liverpool City Police, it was agreed that those who avoided the labour pool would be detained and forcibly deported. The group estimated the number of remaining Chinese seamen to be close to 2,000, and cited opium smoking, gambling, venereal disease and a desire to free up temporary housing in the city as the grounds for this extraordinary intervention. In order to make these steps comply with the law, the landing cards of seamen were 'varied' or altered, requiring them to leave the country by a specific date, and to justify deportation in the case of non-compliance. The officials agreed to present Chinese seamen with a false shipping date, two days in advance of the real date that their assigned ship would set sail. Anyone who refused to turn up for the 'theoretical sailing date' could be apprehended before the actual departure, maximising the use of space on the ships. Once again, the issue of married seamen was raised and then dismissed with a note that 'many of the wives were of the prostitute class and would not wish to accompany their husbands to China'.[22]

Beginning on 8 December, ships with modified cargo hulls to house dozens of deportees began to leave Liverpool and set sail for the Far East, initially to Singapore. The voyages were usually preceded by night-time raids of boarding houses, restaurant kitchens and laundries.[23] The ships, all named after figures from Greek mythology, left at dawn. By the end of March 1946, 800 men had been deported, and a further 1,993 had signed on for shipping articles that 'closed' in the Far East. Of the 800 deportees, 231 had required 'special rounding up' by the police and immigration officials.[24] Within the space of a few months, a considerable part of Liverpool's Chinese population had been made to disappear.

Despite a forensic campaign of recovery led by the wives and descendants of many of the men who were deported, exact details from these months remain murky and a comprehensive list of names of those forced to return has never been found.[25] Many of the wives of men who were deported would never know the fate of their husbands, believing, for the rest of their lives, that they and their children had been abandoned. Yvonne Foley, who was born in 1946, learned in 1957 that her real father had been a seaman from Shanghai. Foley spent years searching in vain for her father in Shanghai and began advocating for those in a similar situation. Peter Foo, another child of a deported seaman, was abandoned in Liverpool by his mother and step-father when he was fourteen and was left to be raised by his grandmother. Foo learned the truth about his father's deportation as an adult, and in a recent interview said that the racism and precarity he faced during his own childhood and adolescence had left him unsurprised. 'In a way I wasn't shocked… I've had to put up with racism all my life… I've never talked about compensation… I just want an apology.'[26]

In 2006, Foley organised for a memorial plaque to be installed in the Liverpool docks, facing out to sea. Its inscription reads: 'To the many Chinese merchant seamen who after both world wars were required to leave. For their wives and partners who were left in ignorance of what happened to their men. For the children who never knew their fathers. This is a small reminder of what took place. We hope nothing like it will ever happen again.'

The events of October 1945 to March 1946 are a remarkable and bleak chapter in the history of Liverpool and Britain more broadly. Here was an instance of racialised state violence, initiated under a Labour government, that was drowned out by the chaos and upheaval of war's end, but painfully remembered by the families who would be separated by two oceans for the rest of their lives. Most Britons are familiar with the arrival at Tilbury Docks of the *Empire Windrush* from Jamaica in 1948 with hundreds of Caribbean migrants onboard, a moment that has become symbolic of the beginnings of substantial Commonwealth migration. The arrival of the *Windrush* is often cited as an origin-point for a multi-racial, post-colonial country.[27] What would happen, though, if we instead told a story about Britain that took as its starting point the *Diomed*, sailing in the opposite direction, less than three years earlier? This voyage was a premonition of the border controls, privatised detention centres and deportations that would characterise Britain's relationship with its former imperial subjects in the years after decolonisation and beyond.

In the middle of the twentieth century, Liverpool sat at the heart of a vast, world-spanning circulatory system of steam-powered commodity shipping whose labour force was primarily structured by race. As we have already seen, one major artery of this imperial circulation system was commanded by the Blue Funnell Line and patched together with Chinese labour. A second, equally consequential artery was controlled by the shipping company Elder Dempster and stretched south to West Africa. Elder Dempster was founded in 1868 and used steamships to trade with Sierra Leone, Nigeria, the Gold Coast and other places. Initially trading tropical goods such as palm oil, groundnuts, mahogany and cocoa, Elder Dempster scaled up pre-existing networks that had developed to compensate for the abolition of the slave trade in 1807. The company's ships would set out from Liverpool roughly every ten days, sail to Dakar in Senegal and then work their way down the West African coast, stopping at more than thirty ports before finishing in Nigeria.[28]

The ships that moved between Liverpool and Africa were like mini-factories, with complex divisions of labour and gradations of skill and status. For most of its existence, Elder Dempster hired West Africans to do some of this onboard work. Aboard the company's ships, Black workers occupied the lowest rung of a racially structured hierarchy, tending to work below deck stoking coal fires, with prolonged exposure to smoke and extreme temperatures. It was usually the case that a small number of white workers would occupy the positions of captain, boatswain, chief steward and chief engineer while Black Africans worked as stokers, oilers, junior stewards and cooks. Black workers were hired for these jobs partly on the assumption that they were better able to withstand high temperatures and exposure to tropical diseases. As with Chinese merchant seamen, however, probably the most important factor driving the recruitment of African labour was the assumption that they could be paid significantly less than white workers. During the Second World War, Black sailors who were hired by Elder Dempster in Sierra Leone to work in engine rooms were paid £6 a month while white sailors hired in Liverpool were paid £16. Even when hired in Liverpool itself, Black workers were paid £12 a month, 20 per cent less than white sailors hired at the same port.[29] These low wages were worked out with the tacit agreement of the colonial governments of Sierra Leone and Nigeria. In the 1940s, Elder Dempster justified their policy to the British government on the grounds that higher rates of pay could threaten the stability of colonial rule in West Africa.[30]

Seafarers from West Africa formed the core of Liverpool's substantial Black population from the late nineteenth century. Although Liverpool's eighteenth- and early nineteenth-century history as a centre for the slave trade had resulted in small numbers of Black settlers before this time, it was only from the late nineteenth century that people of African descent began to settle in the city in any significant number. Exact numbers are difficult to come by, as Britain's census did not include race or ethnicity records until much later in the twentieth century. However, in 1943, the head of the Colonial Office's Welfare Department estimated Liverpool's Black population to be about 5,000.[31]

Many of these settlers lived a short walk south of the docks around Paradise Street and Parliament Street with hostels for

Black seamen on Warwick Street and Stanhope Street, an area that by 1919 was being referred to by the local press as 'darktown'.[32] In 1919, Liverpool's Black population had been subject to a spree of violent attacks from white sailors, culminating in the lynching of a Bermudan sailor, Charles Wooten, by a white mob. These attacks also occurred in other port cities with small Black, Arab and South Asian populations such as Cardiff, Glasgow and South Shields. In 1925, Stanley Baldwin's government introduced the Coloured Alien Seamen Order, which attempted to restrict the rights of non-white sailors to live and work in British ports.[33] As with merchant sailors from China, Liverpool's early twentieth-century Black population was made up almost entirely of young men. Many African seamen in Liverpool had wives and families in Freetown or Lagos who were supported by money sent home, while others began relationships and started families with local women.

In the 1930s, the presence of mixed-race couples and their children became a source of anxiety and fascination for eugenicists and racial scientists affiliated with Liverpool University's Department of Social Sciences. The university's role as one of the leading centres of British eugenics began with the appointment in 1923 of Alexander Carr-Saunders, a high-profile theorist of fertility rates and population studies.[34] In 1927, the department called a meeting to discuss what they saw as the problem of mixed-race children in Liverpool, a meeting attended by representatives from the police as well as from the University Settlement, a social reform group founded in 1908 that embedded university workers in the wider community.

At the meeting it was agreed to form a new body called the Liverpool Association for the Welfare of Half-Caste Children, which commissioned an explosive report by a former Liverpool University probation officer named Muriel Fletcher. The 'Fletcher Report', as it came to be known, was published in 1930 and called for the substitution of all Black labour on Liverpool's ships with white workers and for stringent enforcement of border controls.[35] The Report is widely credited with popularising the racist term 'half-caste' to refer to the children of mixed-race couples. It was based on a tiny data set – less than 3 per cent of the estimated number of mixed-race families in Liverpool – and only investigated those who had already been marked out for poor relief.[36] Nevertheless, Fletcher concluded that mixed-race families were an unwanted presence, incapable of assimilation: 'The coloured families have a low standard of life, morally and economically. It is practically impossible for half-caste children to be absorbed into our industrial life and this leads to grave moral results.'[37] As well as detailed pseudo-scientific analyses of the head shapes and skin colours of mixed-race children, it also denigrated the 'mentally weak' white women who formed relationships with Black men, suggesting that such relationships could only be the outcome of moral and sexual depravity. The Report argued that such women 'almost invariably regret their alliance with a coloured man, and realising they have chosen a life which is repugnant, become extremely sensitive about their position' and that 'the sexual demands [of the men] imply continual strain'.[38]

By the outbreak of the Second World War, then, Liverpool had an established Black population that was becoming ever more vulnerable, having suffered decades of violence and scrutiny from white mobs, the police and from philanthropic social researchers. During the war, this community was also becoming increasingly heterogenous, with the temporary stationing of soldiers and war-workers from across the British empire along with Black US servicemen adding to the small numbers of East African and Somali settlers. Black residents from Jamaica, Alabama or Sierra Leone had little in common other than the fact that their lives had been shaped by what the sociologist Paul Gilroy has called the 'Black Atlantic', a loose historical formation that Liverpool's eighteenth-century history of slave trading had helped to shape.[39] Indeed, since the end of the First World War, Arab, Somali, Egyptian and South Asian seamen and migrants had also been classified as 'Negroes' by immigration officials in the city and subjected to immigration restrictions on the grounds of race.[40] This was a group segmented by language, culture, nationality, religion and class, which included students at the University of

Liverpool, skilled technicians, political leaders and poor manual labourers.

Liverpool's war-time and post-war Black population also included a cohort of 345 West Indian technicians recruited by the Colonial Office and the Ministry of Labour in 1941 and 1942 with the aim of solving war-time labour shortages and mitigating the unemployment crisis in Britain's Caribbean empire. The men were housed in two government-run hostels, on Chatham Street and Bedford Street, and their day-to-day lives were overseen by a famous former West Indian cricketer, Learie Constantine, who was employed as a welfare officer.[41] From the start, this group were a source of fascination for politicians in Britain and the West Indies, with the Colonial Office hoping that their presence would be a public relations coup for the colonial war effort. One official quietly noted that 'one of the problems was to make such arrangements for the social life of these Jamaicans as would prevent their becoming "contaminated" by the rather unsatisfactory West African seamen population in Liverpool'.[42] Subsequently, the experiences of this group are well documented and shed light on the precarious and fraught lives of Black settlers in mid-twentieth-century Liverpool. In one of the earliest texts of the emerging science of domestic British 'race relations', the sociologist Anthony Richmond monitored the lives of these workers over the course of ten years, publishing his findings in 1954.[43]

Based on his interviews, it is clear how the ability of these men to find and maintain decent and dignified jobs was circumscribed by race. When the war ended, West Indian workers were often the first to be made unemployed. Richmond estimated that, by 1950, Black unemployment on Merseyside was close to 17 per cent, compared with 5 per cent for the region as a whole. While many employers who refused to hire Black workers cited 'bitter experience [of] bad behaviour', others blamed their white workers, claiming they would strike if confronted with Black co-workers. Those who were able to find work frequently complained that, despite their comparable levels of skill, they were given the worst and most degrading work to do in war-time factories. One interviewer said that he and his Black co-worker were given 'the worst kinds of work' while 'the white men are given the cream'. Meanwhile, responses from white workers to the West Indian technicians varied from bafflement to outright hostility, 'one worker asked in all seriousness where he kept his tail, another asked if women in Jamaica wore grass skirts and Jamaican workers frequently noted that they were complemented on their English'. Others had stories of their white colleagues being impressed by their levels of skill. One worker said, 'I remember the first day I started at the factory. I was put on a machine I was quite familiar with… before long I had a crowd of spectators around me all of them wide-eyed! One chap asked, "Where did you learn to do that?" I told him that I learned it all in a factory in Kingston. Everyone was very surprised that we knew anything about machines at all.'[44]

It was inevitable that these day-to-day racial antagonisms would produce a kind of political consciousness among the workers, some of whom saw their position through the lens of the deep historical inequalities forged by empire. One worker, while confronting a white colleague after a dispute over pay, claimed to have told him: 'What I am earning is merely a part of what has been taken from us in Africa, where people have been plundered and their belongings taken here to build your Empire.' The engineers who were able to find good work during these years were keenly aware of their role as ambassadors for Black people as a whole, with one worker noting, 'I feel I have a big responsibility to do my job well and to behave properly, because other people do not just judge me by what I do, but all the coloured people as well.'[45]

The same cohort of West Indian engineers also struggled to find stable and affordable housing in Liverpool. Many of the men left the government hostels, where, according to an early report, 'there was an atmosphere of discontent and unrest', and tried to find housing on the private rental market.[46] One of Richmond's informants describes the difficulties that this entailed:

> Two friends and myself scoured every street… without any luck. At that time we were working a 77-hour week and we

> had to tramp the streets after that; we were dog tired. The hostel only had hard bunks very close to the floor and I had not slept a wink for nights; it was terribly cold. Everywhere we went someone would come to the door, usually a lady; when she saw a black face… she gasped with surprise and either slammed the door in our face or called out to somebody to come quickly.[47]

When some of the technicians were able to find housing with some of the few landlords who permitted Black tenants, problems continued. Some informants described having to eat meals with dirty forks off dirty plates as landladies refused to wash up for their tenants between meals. For others, being a lodger meant an unwelcome crash-course in British cuisine, with one interviewer gratefully accepting 'black pudding' from his landlady, expecting 'a dark Christmas pudding', only to find 'stuff made from pigs' blood and fat' that made him 'sick to look at it'.[48]

The technicians were young, mostly unmarried men and many began relationships with local women. With war-time factory employment for young women relatively common, many of these relationships began in the workplace. While many women were happy to date or become friends with West Indian workers in the factory, it was often reported that they would refuse to acknowledge the same men if they ran into them on the street and would often turn down invitations to public dates for fear of judgement from their family. Women who started relationships with Black men were, in the words of one interviewee, 'marked at once' and in some instances presumed to be sex workers: 'If I was seen walking down Lime Street with the Queen of England and nobody recognised who she was, it would be assumed that she was a street girl.'[49] Mixed-race couples faced perpetual danger in public. On 17 October 1941, not long after arriving in Britain, one of the technicians, Cebert Lewis, was walking with his white girlfriend outside a cinema on Prescott Street in the town centre when they were stopped by a police officer. The officer took Lewis aside and started escorting the woman away down the street. According to Lewis' letter of complaint to the police, when he interjected the police officer rounded on him and started pushing him, saying, 'Move on and keep moving... You black n****r, what right have you to be going with a white woman?'[50]

At home, at work and in the streets in between, Liverpool's West Indian technicians suffered many of the problems of housing discrimination, workplace hostility and police brutality that would also shape the early experiences of the 'Windrush' generation after 1948. When the Colonial Office's employment scheme ended in 1946, the workers lost their special status in the eyes of the Ministry of Labour. At this point the men were given the option of enrolling in training schemes as students (training schemes that, for the most part, were unnecessary given their high levels of skill) or returning to the West Indies. Leaving would entail trying to find work in the midst of an economic crisis that had seen unemployment rates higher than 25 per cent in Jamaica. Anticipating being forced to return, thirteen technicians wrote a joint letter to the Welfare Department to no avail, urging that they should 'not be sent [to] the fields of unemployment... with distress and poverty... due to the patriotic sacrifices we have made'.[51]

While many succeeded in staying in Liverpool, some for the rest of their lives, many of those who returned struggled to adapt to life back in Jamaica and were left feeling bitter about their experiences. In letters written to those who remained in Liverpool, the returnees lamented their new situation. One technician wrote, 'The climate is lovely, yes, but to speak of anything else isn't worth the time. Since we returned home, it's as if we are being penalised for offering our services.' Another despaired, 'after the shock of existing conditions here it's a wonder I am capable of writing at all; to be quite frank I expected things to be bad, but not in my wildest dreams could I imagine anything as bad. We had a little chat... before I left England, I don't know if you remember; but bad as I told you then what conditions were, it was paradise compared to now.'[52]

While Black workers from either the West Indies or West Africa were never subjected to the same kinds of organised deportation drives as those from China, by the 1940s the government were also implementing subtle measures to reduce the numbers of Black merchant sailors in Liverpool. Officials were becoming increasingly concerned that significant numbers of West African sailors were unemployed and were thus a drain on Britain's expanding welfare state. In 1950, the Ministry of Transport were urged to enforce strict mandatory repatriation clauses in the contracts of African workers and that all workers, when signing on, should be informed 'of the virtual impossibility of finding regular sea employment in the United Kingdom'.[53]

Meanwhile, the Advisory Committee of the Colonial Welfare Department in Liverpool approved the purging of roughly a quarter of all seamen from the shipping register, depriving them of their source of income, with the hope of forcing Black workers into leaving the city. The purges were fiercely resisted by Black organisations in the city, including the Colonial People's Defence Association, who called on the local government to hire some of the sailors who were about to be made unemployed to do municipal work in the city. These demands were quickly shot down by the Transport and General Workers' Union, who claimed that its white members wouldn't stand for such a job creation scheme for unemployed Black workers.[54] Just as the Blue Funnell Line had willingly provided ships for the deportation of Chinese seamen, Elder Dempster co-operated with the government by stowing returning unemployed workers on their ships at the lowest possible cost. The shipping company was subsequently reimbursed by the government for their services, with one Ministry of Transport official confessing that 'so many West African candidates for repatriation are, for the most part, not the sort of people shipping companies seek in fare paying passengers'.[55]

Like the Chinese merchant seamen, many Black workers, including those who had been recruited from the empire to contribute to Britain's war effort in Liverpool, had found themselves suddenly obsolete. When the war ended, many struggled to forge lives in a city where their presence was unwanted, and many others were hastily and carelessly disposed of.

*

On any given morning in the 1930s or 1940s, children walking to St Patrick's School in Toxteth would likely have seen the strange sight of a Nigerian pastor, wearing a Kufi cap, with a patchy white beard, dressed neatly in somewhat worn clothing, asking them if they had had breakfast. If any of the children said no, the pastor, named Daniels Ekarte, would invite them into a pair of roughly knocked together terraced houses for some toast. This was the African Churches Mission, founded by Ekarte in 1931, which, for thirty years, was a centre for Christian philanthropy, community development and radical Black politics in Liverpool. Inside, the children may have seen a billiard room with a table for playing dominos, a hostel for the homeless and a reading room. They may even have caught a glimpse of the likes of Kwame Nkrumah, the anti-colonial leader and future first Prime Minister of post-colonial Ghana, Jomo Kenyatta, the future first Prime Minister of post-colonial Kenya, the pan-African writer and communist George Padmore or the actor and singer Paul Robeson, all of whom visited this strange address at different times.[56]

When picturing a map of the world, we are used to thinking of a spiderweb of borders drawn over every major continent marking out hundreds of sovereign and nominally equal nation states. The map we are familiar with is largely a product of a burst of decolonisation during the first two decades after the Second World War. At the outset of this process, however, in the 1940s and early 1950s, the exact contours of the post-war world were still to be decided, and not all would have predicted the shattering of Europe's empires into hundreds of small nations. Pan-Africanists, such as Kwame Nkrumah and the South African dissident Robert Sobukwe, hoped that Africa might instead become a gigantic integrated polity, a counterweight to other global superpowers. Others, such as the historian of slavery and first Prime Minister of Trinidad and Tobago Eric Williams, advocated for and briefly witnessed the creation of a West Indian Federation that would unite the post-colonial Caribbean, preventing any one nation from being dependent on Europe or the United States. Many in the Communist Party during this period imagined a more radical post-colonial internationalism, hoping to see the inversion of power relations both between and within nations and the eventual dissolution of borders.[57]

The political theorist Adom Getachew has referred to these different projects as experiments in 'world-making', attempts to imagine more radical, more democratic post-colonial futures beyond the creation of hundreds of nominally independent nation states.[58] Rather than gradually scale up the theory of sovereign nationhood that had slowly emerged in Europe since the seventeenth century to cover the globe, these world-makers sought to invert the inequalities of race and capital that structured the global order. Liverpool was a stage on which some of these different visions for the future were thought through and contested in the 1940s. Just as the city helped forge Britain's empire, some in Liverpool were eagerly anticipating its undoing at the dawn of the post-war world.

Many of the details of Daniels Ekarte's early life are unknown. He was likely born in Calabar in eastern Nigeria in 1896 or 1897. Following an early conversion by the celebrity Scottish missionary Mary Slessor, he worked his way to Liverpool as a sailor, probably working below deck in an Elder Dempster steamer and arriving shortly after the First World War. Ekarte was also a prolific gambler during this period and was associated with organised crime. He once claimed that he purchased a gun with the intention of returning to Calabar to 'shoot all missionaries, black and white'. Many of these stories are embellished and some are impossible to verify. For much of the 1920s, Ekarte worked in a sugar refinery by the docks and, following a second conversion experience in 1922, began honing his skills as an itinerant minister, preaching on street corners. By 1931, Ekarte had raised enough money from the Church of Scotland's missions committee to buy two adjacent houses, 122 and 124 Hill Street, and turn them into the African Churches Mission to serve the growing Black community.[59]

By all accounts, Ekarte was an enigmatic, magical but also frequently infuriating figure. St Clair Drake, the Black American sociologist who spent some time with Ekarte in Liverpool, wrote that even his closest supporters were 'continually bewildered and exasperated by him. They admire his "selflessness" on the one hand but deplore his "irresponsibility" [which] consists of occasionally using high status names in money raising campaigns without securing precise permission.'[60] As a working-class migrant with a little education who spent much of his life in poverty, Ekarte cut a striking figure amidst the circles of white middle-class philanthropists and elite Black intellectuals and politicians in which he moved.

Ekarte's first foray into politics came in 1940, as an advocate for the Black workers of two Elder Dempster ships who went on strike in Liverpool, the *Accra* and *Abosso*. In a series of bombastic letters to different branches of government, Ekarte accused Elder Dempster of underpaying Black workers, confiscating passports and running hostels in Liverpool whose conditions resembled 'slave camps'.[61] He was rebuffed by the Colonial Office and by Elder Dempster, who attempted to get MI5 to investigate the pastor for 'subversive activity' with a possible desire to see him deported.[62]

Ekarte's real calling came, however, with the 130,000 Black American servicemen who passed through Britain between 1942 and 1945.[63] On Merseyside, the arrival of Black US troops prompted some nightclubs in the area, with the support of local police, to introduce whites-only policies. These included the Rialto Ballroom on Upper Parliament Street, the Grafton Rooms on West Derby Road, the Aintree Institute in Walton, Burton Chambers near Stanley Park and Vale House in Sefton.[64] In making no distinction between Black US soldiers, West African seamen, the children of mixed-race couples or the technicians hired from the West Indies, these 'colour bars' helped establish race as one of the clearest markers of social difference in the city. Meanwhile, in Liverpool and across Britain it was common for US servicemen to start relationships and father children with local women. American soldiers who fell in love with British women had to receive permission from their commanding officers to get married, permission which was invariably refused to Black GIs from an officer corps that was almost entirely white.[65] When the war ended, the presence of illegitimate mixed-race children prompted a minor cultural panic on both sides of the Atlantic with reports circulating of 10,000 'brown babies' in Britain (the number was likely much lower, fewer than 2,000 according to a more conservative estimate).[66] Fearing social disgrace, many single parents of mixed-race children left their children to care homes and some local authorities hatched plans to deport mixed-race children to the United States.[67]

For Ekarte, these mixed-race children would form the basis for a radical world-making project. The pastor had long supported the Black nationalist and pan-Africanist politics of earlier twentieth-century politicians and writers such as Marcus Garvey and George Padmore, the latter of whom he had hosted in Liverpool. These thinkers called for the creation of a new, separatist homeland in Africa to which Black people across the world, but particularly those living in the Caribbean and the United States, should migrate, reversing the centuries-old Atlantic diaspora forged by European slavery. Building on the ideas of these thinkers, Ekarte imagined that this Black homeland would be modelled on Britain's white Dominion colonies of Canada, Australia and New Zealand.

In 1945, Ekarte announced his intention to house the mixed-race children in a new care home in Liverpool named after the US Black separatist Booker T. Washington. He hoped that these orphaned mixed-race children could be trained for service in new separatist states in Africa, to which they would be transported as teenagers. In an interview with St Clair Drake, Ekarte outlined this vision: 'The Englishman trains his children for emigration to Canada and Australia. We should train ours to redeem Africa. Garvey had the right idea but he was no leader… If white people can be trained to emigrate; why not black?'[68] Ekarte's plan to train hundreds, possibly thousands, of mixed-race children to become the foot-soldiers for a new Black homeland may well have dated back to his creation, in the late 1930s, of an all-Black boy scouts' troop in Toxteth that he called the Liverpool Africans.[69] It was a vision that had the support of leading British pan-Africanists including T. Ras Makonnen, the Guyanese activist and founder of a number of restaurants and nightclubs in Manchester for Black American servicemen.[70]

Ekarte's plans, however, immediately ran afoul of an alternative vision for Black liberation, that of the League of Coloured Peoples, a group founded in London in 1931. The League had been the primary advocate for Black civil rights in Britain and had close connections with the National Association for the Advancement of Coloured People (NAACP) in the United States. The body was founded and led for most of its short history by the Jamaican physician Harold Moody.[71] It was difficult to imagine two figures more different than Moody and Ekarte. While the effervescent and bombastic Ekarte had lived a working-class life, shaped by poverty, industrial work and an absence of formal education, the rational and calculated Moody was the child of middle-class parents and had trained as a doctor at King's College London. Moody and the League were, from the outset, firmly opposed to Ekarte's separatist politics. Instead, with something akin to a colourblind universalism, the League called for the long-term integration of Black and mixed-race residents into British society.[72] In 1943, the League held their annual meeting in Liverpool's Grand Central Hall, a recognition that, outside of London, mid-century Liverpool was at the forefront of Black British culture and politics. Material circulated in advance of the meeting implicitly rebuked the Black separatism championed by Ekarte: 'We must make it quite clear that we are not planning to build up Harlems, either in Liverpool or in Cardiff or anywhere else. We are not aiming at segregation in any form whatsoever. Our one aim is to remove completely the Colour Bar and any stigma at present attached to our people.'[73]

Meanwhile, in 1947, Ekarte was searching desperately for funding for his scheme and was on the verge of a breakthrough. Reports of the 'brown baby crisis' had garnered considerable attention in the United States. A group of Black women in Chicago formed a Brown Babies Organising Committee that sent £3,000 in donations to Liverpool. The African Churches Mission had been featured in glowing terms in *Ebony* and *Liberty*, two of the leading 1940s African American newspapers.[74] In January,

Ekarte sent a local activist and nightclub owner Edwin Duplan to New York to try and raise £100,000 for the centre and a series of high-profile events were planned for the coming year, with the rumoured support of Eleanor Roosevelt. Shortly after Duplan's visit, however, Moody himself arrived in New York and torpedoed Ekarte's plan. Moody urged local NAACP leaders not to support the pastor and warned that any money raised would not be well spent. Support for Ekarte among New York's Black elite quickly dried up.[75] What's more, it also seems likely that Duplan – a man known to the police for conning Black sailors out of money – had been stringing Ekarte along for profit.[76] Although donations from the Organising Committee in Chicago continued, these were deterred the following year by a sensational article in the *Chicago Defender* impugning Ekarte's operation as a 'swindle'.[77]

Despite these setbacks, Ekarte continued to house mixed-race children in Liverpool. At any given time, there were between eight and twelve children staying in his Mission building in Toxteth. The pastor also claimed to be paying for a further twenty-one children to be put up in private homes, eleven in Liverpool and the rest scattered around the country.[78] Without funding, the conditions in Ekarte's makeshift children's home deteriorated. In 1949, finding broken windows and not enough chairs for the children to sit on, the Home Office gave him twenty-eight days to close. Just four days later, before Ekarte had time to lodge an appeal, his Mission was raided at dawn and the children seized while the pastor was locked in his own office.[79]

While Ekarte's fostered children led impoverished and turbulent lives, their fate was marginally better than the mixed-race children housed at Rainbow Homes in Birkenhead on the other side of the Mersey. The Rainbow Homes project was the brainchild of a wealthy white middle-aged couple, Mr and Mrs Russell, and had the cautious support of the League. Within just a few months of the home's opening in November 1946, however, the Russells were overwhelmed and running out of money to support the twenty-four children they had agreed to house. An infant protection visitor found 'conditions very unsatisfactory... the kitchen and pantry are filthy, the house is bitterly cold'. By February, twenty of the children were ill with gastroenteritis and in April a horrified Home Office visitor found children who were emaciated, with little sign of any heat, food or proper clothing. Thirteen of the children had to be hospitalised and two died. By the summer the house had also been forced to close.[80]

Through this story we can see contrasting visions for the future place of race and empire in the post-war order. Despite his poverty, Ekarte developed his own vernacular brand of pan-Africanism, influenced by living in a city that was at the heart of the imperial world order and by engaging with some of the foremost world-makers of this time. At the core of this dispute was the question of how to manage the instability and violence that characterised mid-twentieth-century Black life in Liverpool. For Ekarte, as for Makonnen and Padmore, the solution was to retreat to a separate homeland, a Black Commonwealth in a future post-colonial Africa. In Ekarte's words 'The future holds nothing for [a mixed-race child] in this country; if it did one could console oneself with the reflection that although there is nothing today, tomorrow might bring something. But it is not so.'[81] For figures like Harold Moody and the League, however, the task was instead for people of colour to remain in Liverpool (or in London, New York or Kingston) and fight for equality and integration. Caught in the swells of these intellectual currents were the mixed-race children left behind by the upheavals of war. Their awful fate reveals some of the many ways that Blackness and disposability went hand in hand in mid-twentieth-century Liverpool.

On the night of 2 August 1948, a white crowd gathered outside Colsea House, a hostel run by the Colonial Office mostly for Black sailors employed by Elder Dempster. The crowd, numbering several hundred, began pelting the building with bricks and bottles until every window in its three-storey façade was broken. Some breached the building and began smashing furniture inside. This was the mid-point of three nights of unrest in the city, an explosion of violence referred to, somewhat obliquely, by contemporaries as 'the Liverpool Disturbances'. Across the city, fights broke out between white and Black workers on the docks and Black-owned cafés were targeted. In a large-scale confrontation on Upper Parliament Street, both white and Black antagonists brandished knives and iron bars.[82] Despite overwhelming evidence that the violence was instigated by a white mob, the police arrested roughly fifty Black and only ten white participants.[83] These events, fuelled by a contracting labour market, were reminiscent of the attacks on Black sailors in 1919, and prefigured the more destructive and more well-known upheavals in Nottingham and Notting Hill in 1958.

The 'disturbances' were further evidence, if any more was needed, that Liverpool's Black population would have to fight to justify its future existence in the city. T. Ras Makonnen responded to the violence by developing a precocious theory of domestic British racism. Makonnen's understanding of racism was institutional and state-sanctioned rather than inter-personal:

> African resentment is seething against the Police for their part in aggravating a small incident into a major offensive. Opinion is united in declaring that the Police gave active encouragement to lawless gangs of European hooligans and made the resulting violence a pretext to descend on African clubs and homes, to assault with brutality the people they found there… Relations between Africans and Europeans in the district have returned to normal, but an augmented police force remains – and with it mounting tension. This flaunting of police authority can serve only to increase the irritation of the African community among whom the feeling is general that the Police are not there to protect them from further outrage, but to intimidate them into silence… Today it is Liverpool, tomorrow… where?[84]

Not for the last time in Liverpool's history, many Black residents began to donate money in legal aid to those that were arrested.[85]

After the war, Liverpool's heterogenous communities of colour – Chinese merchant seamen, Black sailors from West Africa, West Indian technicians and the mixed-race children of Black American servicemen – were deemed to be obsolete. In the late 1940s, the Labour government, the police and shipping companies colluded in the creation of an ad hoc semi-privatised system of border restrictions and deportations in the city. While many British cities became increasingly racially diverse after the war, hosting substantial communities of Black and Asian migrants, particularly those who arrived during the brief 'Windrush' window between the 1948 Nationality Act and the 1962 Commonwealth Immigration Act, which effectively suspended border controls with the Commonwealth, Liverpool stood still. In the mid-twentieth century, Liverpool had been one of the most cosmopolitan cities in Britain, but, by the beginning of the twenty-first century, the city was whiter than the nation as a whole, its rich Black and Chinese histories having been sutured at a crucial moment in their formation.[86]

2

The Rescue Mission

In 1934, the sociologist David Caradog Jones claimed, with surprising precision, that there were exactly 74,010 too many people living on Merseyside. At just 24 years old, Caradog Jones was a rising star in Liverpool University's Department of Social Science, which was fast becoming one of the most important centres in Britain for eugenics and racial science. He made this claim in his vast, three-volume *Social Survey of Merseyside*, which attempted to gather data on every type of industry in the region. By comparing Merseyside's industrial capacity to that of London, Caradog Jones despaired that it was 'beyond any reasonable hope' that the region would ever again be able to provide enough jobs for the people who lived there. The sociologist expressed concerns that this permanent surplus population would lead to the moral and racial degeneration of Liverpool's working class. His nightmare was that the residents of poorer neighbourhoods, places which he associated with 'blindness and deafness, mental defect and epilepsy, tubercular disease and physical deformity, immorality, criminality, alcoholism and chronic destitution', would have children at higher rates than elsewhere, depreciating 'the quality of the people from whom… society is increasingly recruited'. While his colleagues in the same university department were founding the Liverpool Association for the Welfare of Half-Caste Children, which monitored and pathologised mixed-race families, Caradog Jones was making a similar argument about the eugenic stock of the rest of Liverpool's working class.[1]

The *Social Survey* was written while Liverpool was suffering through a major economic crisis, perhaps the biggest in the city's history at that time. The inter-war decades took a terrible toll on regions such as Merseyside, Tyneside and South Wales. Britain's falling share of world trade led to a contraction in the export-orientated industries that had underpinned nineteenth-century industrial urbanisation in these places, such as shipbuilding, textile manufacturing, coal mining and steel-making. The location of jobs and wealth along with the nature of work itself were changing. Light industries in which small goods such as radios, cigarettes and razors were mass produced for a domestic market by electrical assembly lines boomed in the Midlands, the South-East and the London suburbs while places such as Merseyside were entering a period of decline. On Merseyside, the biggest disaster during these decades occurred on the docks. While Liverpool had been involved in almost a third of all British trade in 1914, this fell to just over a fifth by 1938. By the beginning of the Second World War, close to one in five workers on Merseyside were unemployed.[2]

This chapter is about what became of the 'surplus labour' that so concerned Caradog Jones in the two decades after the end of the Second World War. During these years, large parts of Liverpool's working class were rescued from this presumed obsolescence. In the last chapter, we saw how Liverpool's Black and Chinese residents who were deemed to be obsolete after the war were deported and punished. During the same period, white 'surplus labour' was provided with jobs, housing and welfare. The story begins with the extraordinary transformation of the city's docks. What was once seasonal and unreliable work was reorganised by the post-war Labour government into a highly regulated semi-nationalised system that aimed to rescue dock workers from the insecurity that had characterised their labour for more than a century. This story is important, not just because the docks were where more people were employed than anywhere else in the city, but also because it reveals the heady mix of security, discipline and masculinity that was characteristic of many workplaces in mid-twentieth-century Britain.

Meanwhile, Liverpool's wider economic base was re-made by government intervention, as thousands of new industrial jobs were created through targeted subsidies in the 1940s and 1950s. Factories were channelled into new suburbs that ringed the outskirts of the city, housing hundreds of thousands and fixing in place a once transient urban population. In a decolonising world, as dock work continued to decline, these jobs had the short-term effect of protecting Liverpool's working population from the volatility of global trade, sealing the city off from the wider world to which it had once been inextricably connected.

Herbert Crosbie, who worked on Liverpool's docks shortly after the war, claimed that he could tell where a ship had arrived from just by its smell. The Elder Dempster steamships bringing cocoa beans and obeche timber would smell of West African rainforests. Ships from Malaya would arrive with the leathery smell of teak wood mixed with the acrid scent of freshly harvested rubber.[3] For the last forty years, most finished goods have moved across the world in identical steel shipping containers, transported between specially designed container ports at a remove from large urban centres. But, before the widespread use of shipping containers, dock work had been a tactile and sensory endeavour that involved tens of thousands of workers who laboured in the centre of urban ports. In order to understand how a substantial part of Liverpool's working class were rescued from the insecurity and superfluousness derided by social scientists like Caradog Jones, we must first understand what it was like to work on the docks in the mid-twentieth century and how this work radically changed in the years during and immediately after the Second World War.

In the early 1950s, 16,500 people worked in Liverpool's seven-and-a-half-mile complex of dockland, which stretched along the banks of the Mersey estuary.[4] Liverpool's docks were once a vital lynchpin in Britain's globalised free trade economy, importing food and other raw materials from across the empire and exporting the industrial wares produced in nearby Lancashire. The city once had the largest grain silo and the largest warehouses of any kind in the world.[5] Since the construction of a deep-water port in 1715, dock work had been Liverpool's *raison d'être*, fuelling the city's transformation from a small, early modern town into one of the biggest cities in Britain.

For much of Liverpool's history, working at the docks had been an inherently unreliable and precarious endeavour. Dock workers had no permanent employers. They would leave for work not knowing if they would be hired or if they would return empty-handed. Each day they would have to compete for multiple half-day-long shifts with no guarantees, jostling for attention from foremen side by side with chancers who had turned up that day looking for some extra cash. Dock work was governed by the rhythms of nature, its tempo set by far-away storms and droughts or the freezing and thawing of distant sea-ice.[6]

From the late nineteenth century in Liverpool, London and other large port cities, the casual and insecure nature of dock work had been a source of concern for trade unions, liberal economists and middle-class social reformers. Dock workers were often seen as a dangerous underclass, a social 'residuum' who were incapable of being disciplined by secure labour. That many Liverpool dock workers were Irish migrants or their descendants further exacerbated the extent to which they were seen as an alien presence.[7] For much of the early twentieth century, Liverpool's docks had been carefully segmented by faith and many dockside jobs were reserved for either Protestants or Irish Catholics. Carters, for example, who were responsible for moving goods around the docks, were overwhelmingly Protestant. As a rule, the docks north of Pier Head were controlled by Irish Catholic migrants and their descendants and those to the south were worked by Protestants.[8] Shipping companies, meanwhile, would know better than to hire a mix of Protestant and Irish Catholic workers to do the same job. In this context, symbols were important. One retired dock worker remembered his father, a Protestant foreman, threatening to fire a subordinate who came to work in a green tee-shirt.[9]

Despite the fleeting, competitive and sectarian nature of their work, dock workers developed an unusually high degree of solidarity. In the 1880s, London dock workers were among the pioneers of a new type of unionism that organised low-skilled workers, founding the Dock, Wharf, Riverside and General Labourers' Union in 1887. The union brought together a range of different trades and organised a successful strike of 100,000 workers in London in 1889, one of the most high-profile and consequential industrial actions of the nineteenth century.[10] Workers achieved an early victory in the fight for job security in Liverpool in 1912, when the Board of Trade approved a scheme for a centralised register of dock workers. Approved workers would be given a thin strip of metal called a 'tally', which qualified them to be prioritised for shifts and allowed them to receive weekly payments, meaning that dockers were no longer competing against anyone who turned up looking for a day's work. In practice, registration did little to alleviate the precarity of dock work in Liverpool. Initially, 31,300 tallies were issued, 4,000 more than the estimated total number of workers needed to service the docks (a figure that was already deemed to be over-inflated).[11]

The fight for job security was profoundly shaped by the long career of Ernest Bevin. Perhaps no national politician had as much impact on the lives of mid-twentieth-century Liverpool workers as Bevin, who rose through the ranks of the Dock, Wharf, Riverside and General Labourers' Union as a lorry driver in Bristol before the First World War. Bevin's obsession as a union leader and later as a Labour politician was to end casual labour on the docks, which, in his words, was nothing more than 'the liberty to go home with nothing'.[12] He became famous in 1920 for his marathon eleven-hour deposition to the Shaw Inquiry, a high-profile legal investigation into dock workers' pay. Bevin's performance culminated in an extraordinary moment of theatre. Responding to claims that dock workers could live comfortably on £2 8s 4½d a week, Bevin confronted business owners with plate after plate of the recommended diet, asking if they could survive on portions that would better suit 'a mousetrap, not a man'.[13]

For Bevin, this was a civilising mission, one of redemption, that would end the lingering reputation of dock workers as belonging to a despised underclass. Job security would, Bevin believed, elevate dock workers into the realms of working-class respectability, incorporating them back into the national community from which they had been rejected. During his eleven-hour deposition he argued that the disposability of dock workers was threatening Britain's social peace and went against the principles of national development: 'I do not believe that civilisation built upon this is worth having... If you refuse this claim [for security of employment]... you must go to the Minister of Education and tell him to close our schools... because to create aspirations in our minds, to create the love of the beautiful and then at the same time to deny us the wherewithal to obtain it is a false policy... Better keep us in dark ignorance.'[14]

While the outcome of the Shaw Inquiry was the extension of Liverpool's registration scheme across the country, employers refused to accept Bevin's proposal for a permanent maintenance payment that would ensure that pay would remain the same regardless of short-term fluctuations in trade. It wasn't until 1940 that Bevin's opportunity would finally come. That year, he was appointed Minister of Labour by Winston Churchill's new wartime coalition government. He inherited the job during a rare moment when docks were facing a shortage rather than a surplus of labour due to the demands of war. Using emergency powers, Bevin swiftly introduced a compulsory registration scheme for dock workers across the country and made every dock worker in the strategically important western coastal ports (including Liverpool) an employee of the Ministry of War Transport. Under these measures, Liverpool dock workers became a permanent workforce, paid a minimum weekly wage.[15]

By the end of the war, this emergency system had become entrenched, and the only question was how this newfound job security would be made to work in peacetime. There followed two years of complex negotiations between employers who wanted a privatised and decentralised system, with full control of the register of approved workers, and the union, which wanted a fully nationalised scheme with all payments coming from a single fund pooled among all ports. The National Dock Labour Board (NDLB) was finally created by the post-war Labour government in 1947 and was a hard-fought compromise between these two positions. The Board consisted of ten members, four from each side of the industry and an independent chair and vice-chair. Local boards were created across the country, also with a joint management structure, and were responsible for training, discipline, welfare and paid holidays. Every dock worker in the country became an employee of the NDLB. Registered dock workers who regularly showed up for work were paid a minimum weekly wage of £4 and 8s. On top of this, they would be paid 5s for each shift they worked after they had earned out their guarantee and any weekend or bank holiday earnings were paid on top of the weekly wage.[16]

Liverpool dock workers unloading a ship on the Gladstone Dock in 1949 shortly after the creation of the National Dock Labour Board.

The register of approved workers was tightly controlled by local boards and, given the gradual contraction of the industry, it was extremely difficult for new workers to gain entry. Despite the physical challenges of the work, the system had the effect of protecting older workers and shutting out new entrants. In 1949, the average age of a registered dock worker was 47 and almost a fifth of all workers on the register were over the age of 60.[17] New openings tended to be kept within families and passed down through male bloodlines. For this reason, dock work remained an almost entirely white enterprise in a city with high levels of Black unemployment.[18] The restricted register and the ageing profile of dock workers was also a particular problem given that Liverpool's unemployment crisis was skewed towards younger workers, with almost half of Liverpool's unemployed under the age of 35 during the Depression.[19] When openings on the register did appear, applicants had to complete an extensive training course that, in Liverpool, included lectures about the history of the port, practical demonstrations and officious talks from shipping companies about the high costs of operating.[20] This was a radical change from the days when anyone, regardless of experience, could arrive at the docks and be hired for a shift.

From interviews with dozens of dockers during this period collected in the 1980s, we can reconstruct a typical day for workers under this system.[21] The day would begin at 7.30am. By that time, workers would be arriving by foot (or by overhead railway, tram, bus or by bike if they lived further inland) at one of a dozen 'call stands' that were scattered throughout the miles-long dock complex that fronted the Mersey estuary. The call stands varied in size and quality, but each took the form of a large, enclosed room, in some cases regulated by a turnstile. Indoor stands were a modern feature of the docks, introduced in Liverpool only during the Second World War by what would become the NDLB. Before then, those seeking work that day gathered outside, often sheltered underneath the overhead railway that traversed the waterfront.[22] At 7.50am the gates to the stands were locked. What followed was a complex and awkward social process in which the supply of labour was matched to the volatile demands of shipping companies. By this time, the foreman would have received requests from shipping companies who were expecting arrivals that day for a 'berth' (meaning space) at the docks and an exact number of workers of different types to service the ship. He then selected workers from the assembled crowd, often trying to satisfy the desires of employers for work gangs with specific types of experience.

In this frenetic, competitive and face-to-face labour market, it was common for workers to employ an array of different tactics to get selected for 'good ships' (those that required relatively light work such as loading steam locomotives or work that had the possibility of overtime) and avoid bad assignments (such as handling heavy or complicated shipments or work with little prospect of overtime). Through skill, patronage or sometimes outright bribery ('putting half a crown on your shoulder' as it was referred to in the pre-war system), workers would attempt to win the favour of a foreman or a firm. These favoured workers were known colloquially as 'blue eyes'.[23] Many of those who weren't 'blue eyes' would try and stand as close as possible to someone who had obtained that status during the call. It was common, particularly before the war when hiring was less tightly regulated, for workers to give themselves memorable and outlandish nicknames to get noticed and remembered by the foreman. One docker, Frank Dooley, went by the name 'Rigamortis'.[24] Alternatively, jostling too hard and too ruthlessly during the call was also viewed as unseemly. In the 1950s and 1960s, it was still common to hear complaints that an over-zealous worker 'would take your ear off with his tally' during the call, referring to the metal tallies that dockers were issued in the inter-war years.[25]

After the call had ended, those who had been assigned work would set out with their gang to their assignment, while those who had struck out would either be distributed to a different stand or would wait around until the 1pm call later that day. There were many circumstances in which not being selected was preferable. Workers who had worked for the first four days of the week, for example, were eligible for their guaranteed weekly pay regardless of whether they were selected on Friday or Saturday (working these extra days with no increase in pay was known as 'working for the Queen' and was to be avoided at all costs).[26] The weekly minimum wage was preferable to some undesirable shifts, although dock workers, if selected by the foreman, had no choice other than to work their shift. One of the reasons the doors to the call stands were locked was to prevent workers from slipping out if it looked like bad assignments were imminent. If the work was completed early, employers were allowed to assign the gang to other tasks until the end of their designated shift, but once the shift was over the same group could only be re-hired via the exchange.

The work of loading and unloading ships varied in both time and difficulty depending on the ship's contents, and often required intimate physical contact with commodities from different parts of the world. Workers at the Queen's Dock would often encounter boats filled with fruit and vegetables, including Danish potatoes, bananas from the Canary Islands, oranges from Israel and grapes from Greece, which one docker remembered being so fresh 'you could almost wash your face in them'. Smaller boats would deliver bottles of wine from Bordeaux to the Albert Dock. The same dock also received tobacco arriving in wooden casks from Southern Africa, Turkey or the United States, which had to be unloaded, weighed, sampled by customs officers and then distributed into smaller bags. These tactile encounters with traded goods were often unpleasant. Loose sugar could corrode boots. Shipments of peanuts not properly treated could be infested with weevils, which ate through coats. Beef from Argentina or lamb from New Zealand would arrive in refrigerated holds where dockers had to limit their time due to the intense cold. Coils of pig iron exported to the United States would tear dockers' hands to shreds. According to one docker, 'if you get hold of a piece of it at the end of the day you couldn't hold a cup of tea'. Meanwhile, specialist jobs on the docks took on certain reputations. Ballast gangs, responsible for stabilising ships with wet sand, were remembered by one docker as being the roughest workers: 'some of them ate like pigs, drank like swine and looked like Mr. Universe'.[27] One docker vividly remembered the unpleasant sensory landscape of mid-twentieth-century work:

> Humping beef in a fridge ship 23 degrees freezing one day, sweating in a hold full of sugar – sweat and sugar acting as sandpaper on your back – a back covered in blood – coughing and spitting with cement and paper. Working your fingers to the bone on ingots of lead and copper – discharging wet hides and smelling to high heaven – going home smothered with lamp black, red ochre and oil.[28]

These working conditions led to high accident rates. As late as 1969, one in seven dock workers in Britain reported a personal injury at work.[29]

While a dock worker's day ended at different times depending on which shift they worked, many would have gravitated to the pubs along the waterfront such as The Duke's Crown by Canning Dock, which was rumoured to have an underground pipe connected directly to the shipments of Guinness that would come into the dock from Ireland, and where one docker remembered, 'if you went in on a Saturday night… the men got a pig's trotter and the women got some kind of corned beef salad sandwich'.[30] The NDLB, meanwhile, sought to cultivate and institutionalise the social lives of its tens of thousands of employees. The Board organised football games between different call stands, as well as competitive billiards games, rifle shooting, cricket and baseball matches. In 1952, it purchased a former greyhound track, Breck Park, and turned it into a sports ground. The Board also organised first aid classes for interested workers at Burton Manor industrial college in the Wirral and grants for dock workers to study at Liverpool University. A network of canteens built by the NDLB and overseen by the Ministry of Food were built along the docks where men could kill time between shifts.[31]

This system left ample space both for outright and more subtle methods of workplace resistance. We have already seen how dockers attempted to avoid undesirable ships and manipulate the shift system to claim the minimum wage with the least amount of work. Another means by which workers exercised their power was through a practice called the 'welt', which was reluctantly tolerated by employers. The welt was a system where half of a shift gang worked while the other half rested. As well as maintaining staffing levels at a time when jobs were diminishing, the welt was a way to ensure safety when equipment was scarce. As one docker remembered, when it came to unloading coal ships: 'Ship owners would try to make everyone go down there with no safety equipment... with just fuckin' bags around their shoes. Well, we would have none of that, and so we'd share the safety gear in shifts.'[32] Furthermore, in a world where goods were not entombed within steel shipping containers, minor theft was possible. One docker described carrying a hot water bottle under his shirt, which he would use to syphon imported rum (risking a forty-shilling fine if caught). A warning tale, probably apocryphal, concerned a docker who was caught stealing an alarm clock because it started ringing under his clothes.[33]

Workers also engaged in more formal and confrontational forms of resistance. Although the Transport and General Workers' Union, which represented the interests of workers in the NDLB, authorised no strikes in the 1940s and 1950s, unofficial or wildcat strikes were extremely common. These ranged from small gangs refusing to work under certain conditions to massive, nationwide shutdowns. Between 1947 and 1955, docks across the country saw an average of 441,700 days lost due to strikes each year.[34] Some of these, such as the Canadian Seamen Strike in 1949, showed an extraordinary global horizon of solidarity. The strike was in protest at the use of scab labour to service Canadian ships and saw the military deployed by the Labour government to unload ships in Bristol.[35] Beginning in 1954, many Liverpool workers, frustrated with the conservatism and disciplinary apparatus of the Transport and General Workers' Union, joined a more radical dissenting union, the National Amalgamated Stevedores and Dock Workers, known colloquially as the 'blue union' for the colour of its membership cards. In 1955, a two-day strike successfully overturned an attempt by the Board to limit registration solely to members of the Transport and General Workers' Union.[36]

Much of the first few years of Liverpool's local board was spent on enforcing discipline, with members of the Board frequently exasperated at the willingness of dock workers to go on strike without their union's permission. Across the country in the early 1950s, 15,000 dockers, roughly 18 per cent of the total workforce, were appearing annually before disciplinary committees.[37] In 1950, Liverpool's Board released a statement to the local press lambasting its own workers for striking over pay in Birkenhead, with the notice complaining of 'a small group of persons... prepared to interfere and cause labour troubles on the slightest pretext to harm the reputation of the port and... upset the economy of the country'.[38] A year later, the deputy chairman complained to the Minister of Labour that 'many of the men had not accepted the responsibilities which went with the benefits' of the scheme.[39] By 1952, the Board was processing thirty to forty disciplinary hearings each week, for offences including 'evading employment', 'pilfering', 'bad timekeeping', 'altering record sheets', 'negligence at work', 'using threatening language' and being 'under the influence of alcohol'. In 1954, forty workers were disciplined in one day for refusing to continue to work in a rainstorm.[40] Job security on the docks came with new types of discipline that would have been alien to the workers who had experienced the relative autonomy of the pre-war system.

In an interview in 1985, a former Liverpool dock worker confidently asserted that women 'had absolutely nothing to do with dockwork'.[41] The interview was conducted by a women's adult education group who spent two years collecting the memories of women who worked in and around the docks for much of the twentieth century. Contrary to the claims of this interviewee, the smooth functioning of Liverpool's docks was dependent on women's waged labour, labour that was often invisible, not least to the male dock workers with whom they worked side by side.

Superfluity, precarity and low levels of skills were problems that affected women's as well as men's labour between the wars. In many parts of Britain, new forms of light industrial and clerical work had expanded job opportunities for young, unmarried women in the 1920s and 1930s, a development that had seen autonomous working women becoming symbols of modernity and freedom.[42] With its economy dominated by the docks, however, these trends were less pronounced in Liverpool. While a handful of new jobs were created by department stores and the offices of shipping and marine insurance companies for salesclerks and typists, the domestic service jobs that had dominated women's work in the city since the nineteenth century continued to be their largest employer.

By the beginning of the Second World War, many of Liverpool's working women had already lived through the experiences of mechanisation and obsolescence that would face the male workforce later in the century. The case of tobacco workers is illustrative. For a brief period either side of the First World War, cigar-making, a trade that required a seven-year apprenticeship, had employed thousands of skilled women workers. In the 1920s and 1930s, however, mechanisation drove hundreds of women out of the trade and back into domestic service. Mechanisation had a similar effect on garment-making in Liverpool during the same years.[43] In the twentieth century, the docks supported a small handful of job opportunities for mostly unmarried women, which, unlike the jobs of their male counterparts, continued to be poorly paid and insecure in the post-war period. For the most part, these fell into four categories: clerical work, food and drink service, nursing and cleaning.

The new scheme for managing dock work required a massive amount of paperwork. When the NDLB began in 1947, Liverpool's local board employed more than seventy clerical staff, the overwhelming majority of whom were unmarried women. While male dock workers laboured in the open air at the heart of the city, these women were concealed inside the Board's offices on the ninth and tenth floors of an austere classical 1930s building in central Liverpool.[44] Their tasks ranged from typing and working telephones to operating Hollerith punch card machines – complex proto-computers that were used to organise the intricate new system of minimum weekly payments. This was a period when low-paid women were at the forefront of computing, a legacy of the idea that women were especially suited for dexterous types of light industrial work.[45] In 1948, junior punch card operators working for Liverpool's board earned between £120 and £210 a year. Despite the high levels of skill involved in their work, this was less than the dock workers' minimum weekly guarantee, which amounted to £220 a year, and substantially less than the dock workers' national average wage, which in the early years of the scheme was more than £350 a year.[46]

Women were also employed in the dozens of canteens that surrounded the docks, where workers could eat and kill time between shifts, many of which were directly overseen by the NDLB. Like domestic service, canteen work was a logical extension of the domestic labour that was expected of women in the home. In the words of one male dock worker, 'better to have a woman serving you food than a man. Seems right.' Canteen workers faced the difficult task of managing resources during a period of rationing and scarcity. Catherine Tipping remembered what she described as a 'big knob' from the Ministry of Food visiting her canteen and trying to demonstrate to her how many sandwiches could be made with a loaf of bread. At peak times this was a high-pressure environment. One former customer remembered a canteen with a makeshift conveyor belt of bread that passed under a grill while being continuously buttered.[47] Florence Martinfield worked as the manager of a dockside canteen between 1945 and 1950, working from 7.30am to 5.30pm each day. Her canteen was so close to the docks that, she remembered, when boats arrived with imported sulphur, all of the cutlery would turn black. She employed three women and was responsible for ordering and managing the food and overseeing the canteen's budget. Martinfield made £175 a year, which amounted to less than 80 per cent of a docker's minimum annual income. Canteen workers also had to negotiate complex and sometimes antagonistic relationships with their customers. One woman, Mrs Redmond, who worked in a canteen in the 1950s, said that part of her job was ignoring dirty jokes from the dock workers. Nora McGrady, who started working in a canteen aged 17, remembered scraping the mould off the underside of cakes each morning and tipping the dock workers she liked about which ones to avoid.[48]

Meanwhile, women who tended the bars of the countless pubs that lined the waterfront, and in some cases owned them, had to negotiate an even more fraught workplace. Many of these women, by necessity, developed tough personas to manage the mostly male clientele. Nell Flanegan, the licensee of the Custom House Hotel, for example, was known as the Duchess of Canning Place and would refuse to serve anyone she didn't like while doling out free drinks to her favourite customers. The licensee of one pub, meanwhile, was perpetually at war with both her staff and her customers, personally removing fighting men from her pub and firing one of her barmaids for speaking back to a customer who made sexist comments.[49]

While dock work, narrowly defined, was an almost entirely male endeavour, women found more openings in seafaring. From the late nineteenth century, small numbers of women were employed as stewardesses on the cruise-liners that crossed the Atlantic. This was, again, a logical extension of the forms of unwaged domestic and emotional labour expected of women at home.[50] Less glamorous was the work of cleaning the ships that docked in Liverpool's port, work that was performed almost exclusively by women. While the NDLB provided dock workers with equipment and protective clothing, cleaners in the 1950s had to source their own supplies. This was back-breaking work and women would return with cracked and bleeding hands from the chemicals they worked with. Mary Malloy, who worked as a ship's cleaner between 1941 and 1951 on Gladstone Dock to support her husband who was too ill to work, remembered the scene:

> Water boilers were on the quay and the cleaners carried water up and down steep gangways, stairs and so on. The ships were in a dreadful state after the voyage and everywhere had

> to be scrubbed and scoured several times to get the required finish. The women would stand in a line while work was inspected. The younger women did what were considered to be the heavier jobs, with a lot of climbing, using ladders and planks to clean 'deckets' [ceilings].

Like canteen workers and pub servers, cleaners often had to deal with harassment from the dock workers who were servicing nearby ships. One cleaner remembers a colleague being so incensed by a comment from one of the dock workers that she hit the man in the mouth with her scrubbing brush. She also remembered a similar incident in which a cleaner upended a bottle of filthy cleaning water onto one of the dock workers' heads.[51]

As with the unloading of ships, cleaning was unreliable and varied due to weather, season and downturns in trade. While male dock workers had won the security of a minimum weekly wage to compensate for these fluctuations, cleaners had no such guarantee, and their work was as casual and insecure as the dock workers of the early twentieth century. One woman, who worked as a cleaner between 1959 and 1961 before the uncertainty drove her back into tobacco manufacturing, remembered that 'the money couldn't be depended upon. You might have one-or-two-weeks' work, but then be off for about six weeks with nothing.' Mary Malloy spoke of the difficulty of managing irregular shifts while caring for two young children, remembering that she would depend on her eldest son to take her youngest to day-care while she worked.[52]

The historians who worked for the project from which some of the above accounts are drawn asked many of the women they interviewed, from cleaners to canteen workers to stewardesses, if they had ever been in a union.[53] All of the women who were asked said they hadn't, and that no union had ever approached them. Women working on the docks were excluded from the cocoons of job security and high pay that emerged to envelop many of Liverpool's male workers after the war. During what is remembered as a period of high employment, upward social mobility and industrial modernism, hundreds of British women were scraping by on the margins, computing, typing, cooking, caring and cleaning for low pay and little recognition.

In 1921, Adelaide Watt died childless after living alone for almost forty years in Speke Hall, her spacious sixteenth-century rural estate on the southern fringes of Liverpool. Watt was the last surviving heir of Richard Watt, the self-made slave trader and plantation owner who we last encountered in this book's prelude. Adelaide Watt had worked to develop a small farm on her estate, all the time worried about the expanding city, which loomed over her northern horizon. In 1928, seven years after her death, the Liverpool Corporation, the city's organ of local government, purchased her land for £200,000. Over the next twenty years, the land, named Speke, formed the basis of an experimental attempt to re-make Liverpool's economy, one that would shape the future development of Merseyside.

Liverpool's modern economy had always been an outlier. Unlike other industrial cities that rapidly expanded in the nineteenth century, Liverpool specialised in transporting rather than producing goods. To the extent that the city had a manufacturing base in the 1920s and 1930s, it was mostly clustered close to the docks and mainly involved the processing of imported goods – turning sugar and cocoa into chocolate, tobacco into cigarettes, timber into matches and palm oil into soap. One exception was the shipbuilding industry across the river in Birkenhead, which employed tens of thousands before 1914, when British yards produced two-thirds of all the world's merchant ships.[54]

The region's over-dependence on trade rather than production was cruelly exposed during the 1920s when Britain began to lose its dominance of world markets, and again in the 1930s when global commerce slumped due to the Depression. Unemployment levels hovered around 20 per cent for almost the entire inter-war period, peaking at 28 per cent in 1932. More than half of the unemployed had originally worked in transport, shipbuilding and distribution, trades that employed twice as many people in Liverpool than in the rest of the country.[55] As exports from Lancashire slowed, dock work took a significant hit. Between 1919 and 1939, Liverpool lost 1 per cent of its trade each year to other British ports, particularly London, where handling costs were cheaper and imports found a larger market.[56] Birkenhead's shipbuilders fared even worse. Cammell Laird, one of the country's biggest shipbuilders and one of the region's biggest employers, saw employment halve between 1929 and 1932. While Cammell Laird was eventually bailed out by Second World War defence contacts, in 1933 the company's output was less than 3 per cent of what it had been five years earlier.[57]

While Merseyside's economy was being battered by the economic turbulence of the inter-war years, other parts of the country were booming. New types of light industry powered by electricity and orientated towards domestic rather than global markets were thriving, particularly in the Midlands and in the South-East, bouncing back quickly from the Depression. Between 1924 and 1935, Greater London's share of national net output rose by 38.5 per cent at the expense of places like Merseyside, the North-East and South Wales.[58] By the 1930s, it was becoming clear to local leaders that, for Merseyside to resolve its unemployment crisis, the region had to find a way to turn unemployed dock workers and shipyard engineers into toymakers and gramophone assemblers.

Speke was one of the first and most spectacular battles in Liverpool's decades-long war to diversify its economy. Beginning in 1936, with unique permission from Parliament, the city cleared its newly purchased land and carpeted it with a grid of roads fronted by empty low-rise factories that were available to rent. In taking the unusual step of becoming an industrial landlord, Liverpool Corporation hoped to attract footloose capitalists looking to plug their operations into ready-made grids of transportation and energy and turn on a tap of cheap local labour. Although many of the prosperous 'new' industries in the south of England had been heavily reliant on women workers, the Corporation sought to limit applications to industries that would commit to hiring unskilled men. It undertook a similar project in Fazakerley, a patch of Lancashire farmland to the city's north, also beginning in 1936.

The two new industrial estates had low-rise factories designed to make goods for domestic consumption: paint, sweets, paper, clocks, drums and safes, for example.[59] With their minimalist, flexible structures, these estates were intended to mitigate the risk of obsolescence that faced other kinds of capital-intensive industrial developments by being able to house multiple different types of industry over their lifespan.

Crucially, Speke Industrial Estate was also ringed with thousands of new suburban homes that were built before and after the war. These were mostly council housing reserved for families that had been uprooted from the city's intensive slum clearance operations during these years. They were planned by Lancelot Keay, Liverpool's visionary director of housing between 1926 and 1948, who hoped that Speke would become an entirely self-sufficient community, with churches, libraries, schools, swimming baths, cinemas and sports grounds. While Keay is probably best remembered for designing elegant multi-storey blocks of flats in the city's heart – developments such as Gerard Gardens off Scotland Road or St Andrew's Gardens near Lime Street – his most consequential legacy was the construction of more than 30,000 low-rise suburban homes orbiting the Queen's Drive ring-road that once marked the boundary of the city and in satellite communities such as Speke.[60]

At the same time, Liverpool was also eyeing a patch of land near a village called Kirkby to its north-west, with plans to build an even larger complex of factories and housing. Much of Kirkby's land was owned by Hugh Molyneaux, the Earl of Sefton, a minor aristocrat and racehorse enthusiast whose family had held extensive landholdings in Lancashire for centuries. The Corporation's plans were temporarily set back by the outbreak of war, and the land was used instead by the Ministry of Supply to employ 20,000 people in a hastily erected munitions factory. In 1947, Liverpool Corporation inherited the factory grounds, purchased 4,000 acres of surrounding land and went ahead with the next phase of its expansion. Kirkby would become a gigantic industrial estate, at one point the biggest in Britain, employing more than 22,000. Like in Speke and Fazakerley, work and housing were part of the same deal, and 1,100 builders were mobilised to construct more than 47,500 homes in Kirkby over the course of the 1950s and 1960s.[61]

These new developments were a blueprint for Liverpool's post-war future. Developments such as Speke and Kirkby showed how workers that were deemed to be obsolete could be evacuated from the deteriorating inner city and provided with jobs and houses in the suburbs. This was the conclusion of the official 1944 Merseyside Plan, commissioned by the government and authored by the town planner Francis Longstreth-Thompson, which argued that there were still too many people in Liverpool and too few jobs. The plan argued that Merseyside should be thought of as one vast interconnected totality of people, jobs and infrastructure that could be reorganised in ways that were more prosperous and productive. The solution was for Liverpool to expand into its hinterland, transferring more than 250,000 people into new suburbs and dormitory towns that would radiate outwards from the banks of the Mersey into the interior of the country and south through the Wirral peninsula, separated by wedges of open farmland.[62]

By the 1950s, this transformation was already underway. The middle of the century saw an extraordinary reshuffling of Merseyside's population. Between 1911 and 1951, the neighbourhoods immediately inland from the docks almost halved in population, while southern and eastern suburbs saw their populations increase fivefold.[63] Between 1921 and 1961, Speke's population rose from just 366 to 27,000. Kirkby's expansion was even more dramatic. Between 1952, when the first new house was completed, and the 1961 census, Kirkby's population rose from 3,000 to 52,000.[64] As we will see later, these upheavals had the effect of reorganising the city's politics. While Liverpool's inner slums tended to be segregated along confessional lines, slum clearance broke up the tight communities of Irish Catholic or Protestant working-class residents.[65] Alongside newfound workplace security on the docks and in new factories, housing was an important means by which Irish Catholics were incorporated into Liverpool's social order and vested with a shared sense of whiteness that came to transcend the fierce political and religious battles of the earlier twentieth century.

The suburban frontier: new houses hastily erected on the outskirts of Kirkby.

Interviews with the first generation to leave their inner-city homes and move to Liverpool's suburbs reveal a profound disorientation.[66] At first, many lived remote, frontier lives. Roads on the new estates were unpaved and marked out by wooden planks laid out over mud. Property lines were demarcated by coils of wire. The houses, not yet connected to the electricity grid, were lit by candles. One interviewee said it was like being 'sent to Outer Mongolia'. Those with jobs in the city centre would have to walk to the nearest tram stop, sometimes at significant distance, to commute into work every day, while those who couldn't afford the tram would cycle or even walk, a round trip of sometimes more than a dozen miles. These new neighbourhoods had few other amenities at first. The building of pubs was restricted on puritanical grounds by the Corporation. One woman remembered residents complaining that 'the pubs were so far away that by the time they walked home they had sobered up'.[67] Another resident remembered being perpetually lost among the identical streets of new houses and being afraid to leave the house after dark in case they couldn't find their way home.[68]

The relative opulence of the new two-storey houses with indoor bathrooms, gardens and gas and electric fittings was in stark contrast with the extreme poverty of some of the new tenants, particularly during the Depression. These were not the middle-class, 'meanly decent' suburbs bemoaned by inter-war writers such as George Orwell and John Betjeman, who were mainly writing about the south of England.[69] One tenant in Liverpool remembered burning some of her old clothes on the fire to boil the kettle because she couldn't afford to use the gas. One first generation tenant, whose father was made unemployed, remembered her brothers scouring building sites of the half-built new houses at night trying to find wood to burn for heat. Another resident of a two-storey house with a garden in Knotty Ash remembered feeding her family with a single meal a day and stuffing her children's leaking shoes with newspaper.[70]

The new suburban houses were designed to be spaces for male-breadwinner families, with amenities for the streamlining of domestic labour performed by women.[71] Lancelot Keay, Liverpool's housing officer, advertised his homes by starring in a short informational film in which a Liverpool housewife looked to the camera and explained: 'Cooking is quick and easy with a modern gas cooker, I can set it at any speed and leave the meal preparing knowing it will be perfectly cooked while I am carrying out some other work.'[72] Despite this, many suburban women continued to work out of necessity. When one woman's husband lost his job, she toured the nearby estate offering to do others' washing for extra money. Other women found enterprising ways to capitalise on the remoteness of these new communities, with one group of women creating an ad hoc fish and chip shop for their neighbours, cooking the fish using one of their gas cookers and selling them out of their back door. Others struggled to use, understand or afford the new amenities, continuing to cook food on the fire rather than the gas stove and confessing, in one instance, that they were afraid of using the electricity.[73]

Moving into public housing also entailed new forms of discipline. Tenants were subjected to repeated visits from inspectors, who would check the beds for vermin and the baths to make sure they were being properly used. Subletting was strictly prohibited, which must have been particularly onerous to tenants who were suddenly space rich but cash poor. Any kind of alterations to the homes were banned and tenants were prohibited from keeping chickens or pigeons in their gardens. Before moving to their new homes, tenants' furniture was fumigated to kill bed bugs in large, specialised vans. Fumigating the property of tens of thousands of residents was an enormous endeavour costing Liverpool Corporation £19,000 a year.[74] As we have already seen on the docks, the arrival of job and housing security did not emancipate its beneficiaries from hard work, ill-health, coercion and relative poverty.

The movement of Liverpool's surplus population into suburbs that orbited new factory complexes chimed with some of the attempts made by the post-war Labour government to restructure Britain's economy on a national scale. In 1944, the Barlow Report, which along with the Beveridge Report would become one of the foundational documents of post-war life, highlighted the glaring unevenness of Britain's economic development. A century of rapid industrialisation and urbanisation had resulted in an indelible accumulation of people, factories and infrastructure in parts of the country where they were no longer needed. When the war ended, the challenge would be figuring out how to retrofit an economy built around road transport, electricity and domestic light industry into a national landscape dominated by railways, steam power and capital-intensive, export-orientated forms of production. The Report repeatedly cited Speke as a positive example of how local government intervention could attract new kinds of work.[75]

One of the first, serious legislative answers to the questions raised by the Report was the 1945 Distribution of Industry Act and the 1947 Town and Country Planning Act, which sought to restrict the development of new industries, channelling jobs to areas of the country with high unemployment. The Acts stipulated that all new factories of a certain size must be vetted by the Board of Trade and, if possible, encouraged to move to one of six 'Development Areas'. These areas included South Wales, the North-East, Cumberland and parts of western Scotland and southern Lancashire, places that were once the heartland of Britain's industrial economy, but which had been in decline for more than a generation.[76] As a port rather than a traditional centre of production, Merseyside was initially excluded from these measures. However, by 1948, unemployment in the region had risen to 6.5 per cent. Although this figure was much lower than the rates of 20 per cent that were common in the inter-war period, this was still twice the national average. In 1949, the future Prime Minister Harold Wilson and MP for the Liverpool suburb of Huyton, who was then head of the Board of Trade, included the region in this experimental scheme to rebalance Britain's economy.[77]

The Development Area irrigated Liverpool's new industrial zones with jobs. The new state of affairs meant that an industrialist in London or Coventry hoping to start a new factory in Britain would have to apply for an 'industrial development certificate' from the Board of Trade. After 1949, the Board of Trade had the power, if appropriate, to approve the factory on the condition that it opened in Speke, Aintree, Kirkby or any of the factory complexes in Liverpool's expanding hinterlands, where the Corporation had ready-made structures and a pool of labour waiting to be activated. By the 1950s, the provision of new jobs in a desperate bid to diversify Liverpool's industry became a complex numbers game. That decade, thanks in part to the Development Area, the region attracted 28,731 new manual jobs in factories with more than ten workers. However, during the same years, the region also lost 18,657 jobs, resulting in a net gain of just 10,074.[78] Re-making Liverpool's industrial base turned out to be like trying to fill a leaking bucket with water. It didn't help that when Merseyside was awarded Development Area status industrial policy was already in retreat in Britain. While more than half of all new industrial developments had been sent to depressed areas between 1945 and 1947, enthusiasm was waning by the end of that decade and the deployment of industrial development certificates to force new industries into moving was being used less and less by the Board of Trade.[79] It was only in the 1960s, when the machinery of industrial planning began to move car-manufacturing jobs into Liverpool's suburbs, that employment began to stabilise, albeit temporarily, a story that will be told in the next chapter.

In the middle of the twentieth century, Liverpool's white underclass, once deemed by philanthropists and social scientists to be precarious, obsolete and morally contagious, were temporarily rescued by state intervention. In the years after 1945, two different approaches to the city's 'surplus' labour emerged. On the one hand, thousands of Chinese merchant seamen, Black African seafarers and West Indian technicians were deported, policed or incarcerated in shabby hostels or crumbling rented homes. On the other hand, white dock workers were given job security and unemployed white workers were given housing and work in the city's expanding suburbs. The creation of a nominally universal 'welfare state', by ending the distinction between 'deserving' and 'undeserving' forms of poverty, saved Britain's white working class from the eugenicist derision of social investigators such as Caradog Jones.[80] This newly redeemed white working class would emerge after the war in Liverpool as well-paid dock workers, as engineers on electrical assembly lines on new industrial estates and as the tenants of mile after mile of newly built two-storey homes with gardens, gas kitchens and indoor bathrooms. That parts of Liverpool's working class were saved from obsolescence also meant, however, that they were subjected to new and often demeaning forms of discipline, coercion and atomisation at work and at home.

Liverpool's docks and the ships that served them reveal how pay and security were structured by hierarchies of gender and race. From this seven-and-a-half-mile stretch of land and water we can tell two stories. One is a triumphant story of warfare followed by welfare, of slum clearance and social mobility, a rescue mission launched to save parts of Liverpool's working class from obsolescence. Its heroes are the union leader and politician Ernest Bevin and the architect and technocrat Lancelot Keay. The other is a tragedy, a story of dispossession, exploitation, insecurity and the limits of workplace solidarity facing women and people of colour. Its heroes are the Black leaders and organisers George Moody or Daniels Ekarte, or the activist historian Yvonne Foley fighting to save the thousands of deported Chinese seafarers from historical oblivion. Its villains (in the case of the missing Chinese and Black seafarers) are the politicians in Britain's post-war Labour government, such as the same Ernest Bevin, who, by the time of the deportation drives of the immediate post-war years, was Foreign Secretary. Liverpool's first post-war decade teaches us that we should think of these two stories as interrelated threads of the same historical fabric.

3

Britain's Detroit

One of the most famous photographs of post-war Liverpool was taken, not by the docks or in the city centre, but instead at its municipal airport. The airport, built in 1930, was a symbol of the city's expansionist suburban modernism. It was built as part of the comprehensively planned new satellite town of Speke, on the grounds of a Tudor rural estate that was once owned by the Watt family of merchants and slave trade profiteers. The photograph, taken at half past five in the evening on 10 July 1964, featured four men in suits descending from a recently landed jet. It was one of only a few times that the Beatles had arrived back in the city since their explosive, vertiginous rise to global fame and they were being greeted by more than 3,000 fans who crammed onto the airport's elegant art deco balconies overlooking the runway. The band had arrived from London for a reception at the Town Hall and to premiere their new film, *A Hard Day's Night*.

The Beatles were returning to a changed city. In Liverpool, the 1960s was a fleeting moment of stability and prosperity between two long phases of economic catastrophe. It was a time of frenetic optimism and wild cultural exuberance – when Liverpool FC and Everton vied for league titles and local bands bestrode the world. It was almost possible to believe, as the beat poet Allen Ginsberg quipped in 1965, that Liverpool was 'the centre of the consciousness of the human universe'.[1] Never had the passage of time felt so

The Beatles arrive at Liverpool Airport in Speke on 10 July 1964.

exhilarating and the direction of travel so certain. There was, during these years, a clear sense of which structures, neighbourhoods, industries and types of people were obsolete and which sparkled with the sheen of modernity.

The automobile became the symbol of this brief spell of historical certainty and modernist zeal. In the 1960s, the production and use of cars came to dominate Merseyside's economy and built environment, from the new car factories that opened in Liverpool's satellite towns, to the ambitious new system of roads and tunnels that cleft the city to the tankers that sloshed oil into the refineries and pipelines of the Wirral peninsula. It was during this short period of relative prosperity that the Lord Mayor proclaimed Liverpool to be the 'Detroit of Great Britain'.[2] For a few years, it was possible to imagine driving through the new Kingsway Tunnel under the Mersey in a Ford Escort made in the Halewood plant on the outskirts of Liverpool, powered with petrol that had been transported on a tanker made in Birkenhead and delivered to the network of terminals, pipelines and refineries that stretched along the coast of the Wirral.

Merseyside's dizzying 1960s modernity, however, left victims in its wake. Progress came at the expense of tramcars and overhead railways, of women and children trying to preserve their streets for outdoor play, of clandestine gay pubs and of small Welsh-speaking villages that were drowned to secure the city's water supply.

For the Beatles, their return to Liverpool must have been an uncomfortable experience in which the familiar had been made suddenly strange. In the days before arriving, Ringo Starr had told a *Liverpool Echo* journalist that 'all those other places in Australia and New Zealand where we went to civic receptions, they were… people we didn't know, like. But this is different.'[3] Looking back in 1967, John Lennon said, 'We couldn't say it, but we really didn't like going back to Liverpool… Being local heroes made us nervous.'[4] This chapter will begin by following the Beatles' movements during their brief visit, glimpsing, as we do so, the optimistic future planned for Liverpool in the 1960s as well as those this vision left behind.

Despite the disruptive cultural modernity that these four men embodied, the Beatles had many ties to Liverpool's old economy.[5] Both John Lennon and George Harrison's fathers had worked as seamen for merchant and passenger ships either side of the war. Paul McCartney's father had worked in a cotton warehouse and Ringo Starr's father had worked for a spell on the docks. Pete Best, the band's original drummer, lived an imperial childhood, born in Madras to a father in the military. Proximity to Britain's second biggest port influenced the band's music and the young men's social networks. In the days before mass trans-Atlantic air travel, Liverpool was an important site of face-to-face cultural exchange with the United States. The staff of the passenger liners that circulated between the city and American ports, known as the 'Cunard Yanks', brought with them new records by artists like Buddy Holly, Hank Williams and Elvis Presley.[6] These exchanges helped spark the Merseybeat sound of the 1960s of which the

Beatles were part, influencing artists such as the Hurricanes, the Searchers and Gerry and the Pacemakers. In their early years, performing as the Quarrymen, the group identified as a skiffle band, a specifically British genre that mixed white American folk music with African American blues music featuring a washboard used as percussion.

Except for Ringo Starr, who grew up in the Dingle, walking distance from the docks, all of the Beatles had been moulded from a young age by the satellite communities that were developed to diversify the city's economy and depopulate its urban core. Paul McCartney and George Harrison both spent parts of their childhood in council housing in Speke. John Lennon lived for most of his childhood in a two-storey semi-detached house built in 1933 in Woolton, a neighbourhood in the city's southern fringes. The three band members grew up in clean, modern suburban environments that were far removed from the outdoor bathrooms and tightly packed terraces that each of their parents had at some point lived in and in which George Harrison was born and Ringo Starr spent his childhood. Like so many of their generation, the musicians came from families that tried and failed to live up to the ideal of the two-parent male-breadwinner household for which Liverpool's municipal suburbs were built. After being abandoned by his father, Lennon was raised by his aunt, Mimi Smith, who worked as a nurse and private secretary, and her husband George Smith, who died when Lennon was a teenager, leaving Mimi in sole charge of the household. Paul McCartney's mother, Mary McCartney, worked as a midwife to supplement her husband's income at the Cotton Exchange, before she died of breast cancer when McCartney was 14. George Harrison's mother worked as a shop assistant to supplement her husband's earnings as a bus conductor.[7]

After their rapturous reception at the airport, the Beatles paraded in a police convoy from Speke to Liverpool Town Hall, where an estimated 100,000 people lined the streets, some of whom had been waiting for more than nine hours. In scenes that had become familiar from the Beatles' recent tours of the United States and the Commonwealth, the visit triggered a delirious outpouring of emotion from many of the assembled fans. Four hundred fainting cases were reported and forty-seven people were injured, requiring a local tailor shop to be commandeered by the police to use as a makeshift medical centre. According to one report, lines of screaming girls were treated with cold sponges like injured footballers.[8] Unsure how to place the significance of this event, the *Liverpool Post* likened it to the night that Everton last won the FA Cup in 1933.[9]

The Beatles' journey from the tree-lined cul-de-sacs and symmetrically planned industrial developments of Liverpool's southern suburbs north into the city's urban core was a journey backwards in time. While Merseyside's periphery had been frantically developed to absorb Liverpool's surplus population, the city centre was, to quote the urban planner Graeme Shankland, 'in all its essentials, very little different' from 'the Liverpool [of] 1865'.[10] The slow pace of Liverpool's urban redevelopment was even more surprising given the city was arguably one of the birthplaces of the modern science of town planning in Britain. In 1909, Liverpool University's Department of Civic Design was founded under the patronage of William Lever, the infamous philanthropist and soap manufacturer, with money he raised from a successful libel case following allegations of running a soap-making cartel. Lever, who would later be implicated in horrific forced labour practices in the Belgian Congo, had designed a paternalist model village for his workers on the Wirral peninsula called Port Sunlight. The new university department became one of the most significant town planning schools in the country, and, at one point, had been the workplace of Patrick Abercrombie, the famous planner who would re-make London after the war.[11]

Since the turn of the century, Liverpool's central core had been a mix of private affluence and public squalor. The city centre had seen a handful of spectacular new developments in the early half of the twentieth century, such as the Adelphi Hotel (1914), the India Buildings (1924–32), as well as the Royal Liver Building, the Cunard Building and the Port of Liverpool Building known collectively as the 'Three Graces' (1907–17). These were complemented by lavish department stores such as Lewis's, Bon Marché and George Henry Lee, and the multiple stylish blocks of flats designed by Lancelot Keay. This opulence was, however, also haphazardly dotted with ruined slums and transient hostels for Black and Chinese seafarers.[12]

Despite more than thirty years of aggressive slum clearance programmes, Liverpool recorded an extraordinary 88,000 houses that were unfit for human habitation in a 1960 survey of national housing conditions. Almost all these structures were obsolete dwellings in the city centre that were built before 1914 during the city's rapid nineteenth-century expansion.[13] Of the 36,500 people that lived by Liverpool's docks in 1951, 16 per cent still shared their toilet with other families and 23 per cent were without their own cooking stoves or sinks.[14] The docks, along with the city centre and the tracts of housing that connected them, were also the area of the city most affected by German bombing during the war, with more than 50,000 houses and 700 businesses damaged by the 100,000 bombs that fell between the summer of 1940 and the end of 1941.[15] In the 1960s, the rubble had been cleared but many bomb sites remained empty. In 1963, a journalist described the inner core of Liverpool as being riven with 'great bald patches' and looking 'like the belly of some mangy stuffed animal in a Victorian museum'.[16]

In the 1950s and early 1960s, writers and academics turned their gaze onto these remaining working-class residents, fascinated by what they imagined was an old way of life rapidly passing out of existence. Studies by John Barron Mays (1954), Madeleine Kerr (1958) and Charles Vereker (1961) oscillated in tone between nostalgia and anxiety for the racially diverse residents of Liverpool's remaining slums, which dotted the immediate hinterland of Liverpool's docks. For Mays, this dilapidated urban environment acted like a criminal force field upon its residents, claiming that 'many of the minor delinquencies of otherwise ordinary boys might be eliminated by environmental changes of a broad social character'.[17]

Meanwhile, in a study of the area around Crown Street immediately to the east of the city centre, Vereker uncovered a tight-knit working-class world in which more than a quarter of residents had been born within just a quarter of a mile of where they were currently living, and many lived within walking distance of their parents and their siblings. Despite the fact that more than half of Vereker's interviewees expressed a reluctance to move to new estates like Kirkby or Speke, it was a foregone conclusion for Vereker that affluence and urban regeneration would dissolve these communal ties and this world would soon pass away.[18] He called for the rate of change to be slowed in order to manage the extremity of the transition facing these inner-city communities in nineteenth-century terraced homes.[19]

Accounts such as Vereker's followed a script that was becoming familiar by the early 1960s. This genre, in which academics rediscovered the slums that had been left behind by the modernising thrusts of mid-century urban redevelopment, was pioneered by Michael Young and Peter Willmott's extremely influential 1957 book, *Family and Kinship in East London*. The book was a study of London's Bethnal Green, which, like Vereker's Crown Street, was found to be a tight-knit, family-focused community that was radically distinct from the clean and quiet suburbs that these residents were being uprooted to.[20] At a time of widespread faith in modernisation theory – the idea that economic development had the same causes and effects everywhere it occurred and could be replicated, regardless of scale or culture, from Britain to Brazil – it was easy to collapse time and space when thinking about these neighbourhoods. An extreme approach to this unified theory of modernisation was taken by the Social Psychologist Madeline Kerr, whose 1958 book, *The People of Ship Street*, was an exploration of the psychology of sixty-one families living in a Liverpool slum. Kerr had previously lived and worked in colonial Jamaica, studying the psychology of children in transitional rural communities. She carried out a series of personality tests on the children in her Liverpool sample and found that 'So many of them produced patterns so like the Jamaican and so unlike the English groups of the same chronological age on which the test was standardised.'[21] In this 1960s theory of linear development, inner-city Liverpool was to Kirkby what Bethnal Green was to Basildon and rural

Jamaica was to late industrial Britain as a whole. All were imagined to be different stages in the same journey towards a similar-looking future.

As they wound their way towards the Town Hall, the Beatles moved in and out of these different futures and pasts. When they finally arrived, they addressed crowds of fans from the building's Georgian balconies. Perhaps to relieve the tension, or perhaps as an ill-judged commentary on the newfound power the band was wielding over its fans, John Lennon performed an ironic Nazi salute, a gesture for which he later expressed regret. The Beatles were then played a tape recording of a 'welcome home song' sung by the shipbuilders working at Cammell Laird in Birkenhead. Afterwards they were presented with a cake featuring a map of the world and the words 'The City of Liverpool Welcomes the Beatles'.[22]

Apart from perhaps a small handful of councillors and civil servants, the 700 guests at the exclusive reception would have been unaware of the fact that the ballroom in which the event was held lay between two zones that had been earmarked for future redevelopment by Liverpool's radical architect planner Graeme Shankland. Shankland had been hired by the local government in 1962 to produce a plan for the comprehensive redevelopment of central Liverpool, a plan that was nearing completion when the Beatles arrived in 1964. Like the Beatles or Bill Shankly's extraordinarily successful Liverpool FC, Shankland was an ambassador for the affluence and modernist zeal of 1960s Liverpool. He was an intellectual and a figure of the New Left, a member of the Communist Party Historians Group along with figures such as Eric Hobsbawm and E. P. Thompson.[23] Shankland's plan for Liverpool, published in 1965, had a clear sense of where the future lay. He argued that the city's built environment was obsolete and unsuited to a coming age of affluence, leisure and mass car ownership:

> What goes on in Liverpool today, and therefore the bone and gristle of the city, the pattern of its roads and footways, were decided in the days of the horse and the cart, the steamship

> and during the heyday of cotton and coal… Liverpool must now, therefore, concentrate into a few decades the task of transforming a nineteenth century fabric into a modern urban area that will suit the second half of the twentieth century and look forward to the twenty-first… Obsolete buildings and transport arrangements must go. Fine individual buildings and groups of buildings must be cared for… The developing city must be clear, powerful and memorable in its overall form.[24]

Shankland imagined that Liverpool's new city centre would become a regional focal point for culture and entertainment, a hub of cinemas, restaurants and galleries that would cater to visitors as well as residents who were increasingly affluent and had time to spare. He hoped that such attractions would help repopulate the city with a middle class that rarely ventured into the city for leisure. Shankland cited the Beatles as a magnet, whose 'mystique' attracted visitors to the city.[25] The vision amounted to a prefiguring of the kinds of 'cultural industries'-led regeneration strategies that would shape Liverpool's future later in the century.

Shankland's most ambitious proposal was for Moorfields, the area immediately north of the Town Hall, which he intended to demolish and replace with a monumental twenty-acre mixed-use structure that would contain a bus station, a shopping centre, restaurants, a cinema, a car park and a pedestrianised plaza on its roof. The same development would support a spine of twenty-storey tower blocks that would house thousands.[26] While the Moorfields' plan went unbuilt, Shankland had more success with the area around Queen's Square by Lime Street train station. There, he oversaw the construction of St John's Shopping Centre, a fully enclosed, climate-controlled shopping centre, complete with its iconic 138-metre-tall Radio City Tower topped with a revolving restaurant.[27] St John's was built partly on top of what was once Liverpool's unofficial and clandestine gay quarter, a handful of pubs such as the Magic Clock, which were cleared to make way for the new development. Jo Stanley, who worked at the Magic Clock as a teenager, remembered the pub as a welcoming space for gay and trans clientele in the 1960s:

> It felt like a safe space… My favourite customer was Daisy/Geoffrey, a Bebington hairdresser who slightly cross-dressed. The other customer who stood out was a lunchtime guy called Johnny or Denny. He was an Irish building worker who flaunted his muscles, his gorgeous blue eyes alert for action. The clusters of businessmen ogled him. Whether men went into the ladies or gents was their business. I got used to sharing mascara and hesitating about whether to say she or he.[28]

In the mid-1960s, radical redevelopment schemes on the scale that Shankland envisioned still felt possible, as the city and the country rode a wave of economic growth and social mobility. Shankland's plan, most of which was never implemented, was predicated not just on increasing affluence and leisure time, but also on an increase in population. He predicted that Merseyside's population would rise by 20 per cent by 1981, when in fact the population of the region fell continuously from the time Shankland was writing until the early 2000s.[29] His vision of the future was one that would be annulled by the rapid unravelling of Liverpool's economy in the 1970s and 1980s.

There was no way for the Beatles to know this, however, as they were feted by dignitaries in the Town Hall. Amidst the commotion of their reception, another, less famous photograph was taken of the band that tells a different story to their glamorous arrival at the airport. It shows the band gathered in an ornate function room. In the foreground, complete with a cigar and a livery collar, is the Lord Mayor Louis Caplan and, seated in a plush wooden chair, Fanny Bodeker, his wife, the Mayoress. Liverpool's Labour MP, Bessie Braddock, a machine politician who dominated local politics for twenty-five years, is standing on the right. In this awkward, patrician image, the Beatles appear provincialised, held hostage by their own history.

Later that afternoon: the Beatles in Liverpool Town Hall with Labour MP Bessie Braddock (right), the Lord Mayor and his wife (centre) and local band The Chants.

Also present in the photograph were five Black singers, Edie Amoo, Nat Smeda, Joey and Edmund Ankrah and Alan Harding, who sang together as a harmony group called The Chants. Like the Beatles, The Chants had been influenced by the American rock and roll music that was arriving in the city from the docks and had mixed these influences with music that had circulated through Liverpool's Black community from African American servicemen stationed at nearby Burtonwood air base, where Black Liverpool-based musicians were often invited to perform.[30] Two of the band's members, Joey and Edmund Ankrah, were taught how to sing by their father, who played the organ at Pastor Daniels Ekarte's African Churches Mission.[31] While the Beatles were children of the suburbs, The Chants had grown up in Liverpool's inner city. Edie Amoo, who, along with his brother Chris would find success in the 1970s with a new band, The Real Thing, grew up in Myrtle Gardens, the block of council flats designed by Lancelot Keay in 1937, where they were the first Black family.[32] Edie and Chris' father Robert Amoo had travelled to London as a stowaway from Ghana in the 1930s, where he had performed as a guitarist and a tap dancer in Black-owned clubs and bars before moving to Liverpool, where he lived for a spell in a seaman's hostel. The Chants had begun their career performing in Stanley House, a community youth club on Upper Parliament Street.[33] They and the Beatles had performed together at the Cavern Club in 1962 and had briefly shared the same manager, Brian Epstein. Since then, however, their careers had taken radically different paths as the Beatles were elevated into circuits of unimaginable wealth and fame while The Chants were left behind.

After the reception, the Beatles left in a limousine for the Odeon Cinema and the premiere of a *Hard Day's Night*. Before the film started, perhaps to the men's polite bafflement, they were greeted by a performance of the Liverpool City Police Band, who played covers of their songs as well as, reportedly, the theme of the hit Merseyside-based police television drama Z Cars. In the end the Beatles did not even stay the night. After the premiere, they set off back south to the suburbs, to Speke, to the airport and onto a plane to London.

For a brief moment in the mid-1950s, it seemed as if Liverpool's transportation system was about to be revolutionised, not by cars, trams, buses or ferries, but instead by helicopters. As strange as it may seem, Liverpool was at the forefront of a flurry of interest from planners and politicians who imagined that an age of mass helicopter transit was just around the corner. With their vertical lift, small size and ability to land on the roofs of buildings, helicopters seemed ideal for short trips between and even within cities. From 1953, Liverpool's City Engineer, Henry Hough, began to draw up plans for a network of heliports that would connect seamlessly with buses and form the basis of an integrated ground and sky transit system. Hough organised for a test helicopter to land on a temporary car park in the city centre, travelled to New York to land helicopters on the roof of the Port Authority headquarters and gave a high-profile lecture to the

Royal Aeronautical Society about the ways that helicopter flight would change the look and feel of cities. After flirting with the idea of using floating pontoons in the Mersey to land helicopters, he settled on plans for a new integrated bus and helicopter station on a patch of bombed ground between Paradise Street and Canning Place.

Hough had some precedent to work with. Liverpool had played host to what was touted as being the first public helicopter service in the world. In 1950, for just £5, you could buy a ticket on one of two daily flights from the airport at Speke to Cardiff (with an optional stop-off at Wrexham), a journey that took one hour and forty minutes and carried three passengers. The flights were run by British European Airways as a pilot scheme to explore the feasibility of scheduled helicopter services that would be like 'buses in the skies'. The venture was unsuccessful and ended after less than a year, having only transported 819 passengers. Hough's plans too were a bust. According to Liverpool's Planning Officer, enthusiasm for the scheme dwindled 'due to the obsolescent character of parts of the Merseyside economy'. Like so many of the ambitious proposals for Liverpool's urban fabric during the post-war decades, the helicopter scheme was quietly abandoned.[34]

Ten years later, when Graeme Shankland drew up his proposals for re-making Liverpool's city centre, there was no mention of helicopters. By that time, fantastical visions of new types of public transportation had been bluntly foreclosed by mass car ownership. In 1951, only one in every fifty residents of Liverpool owned a car. By 1971, this figure had risen to one in eight. During the same two decades, the total number of cars in the six boroughs of Merseyside increased more than fourfold.[35] Instead of capitalising on the miles of silent empty sky hanging over Merseyside, tens of thousands of new cars required a monotonous proliferation of roads and tunnels on and beneath the ground, 'dead public space' in the words of the urbanists Peter Freund and George Martin.[36] In the 1960s, Liverpool's economy and its built environment became tethered to the car, with dramatic social and environmental consequences. As car ownership expanded, the alternative forms of public transport that had dominated the city's urban landscape in the first half of the twentieth century were declared obsolete, and progressively dismantled.

First to go was Liverpool's extensive municipal tram network, parts of which had existed since the 1860s. Electric trams had radiated outwards from the docks, connecting the newly built municipal suburbs with the city centre, and running through the central reservations of roads, bordered by strips of grass.[37] When the first generation of city residents to move to the city's new municipal housing developments were interviewed, the majority said that they commuted to work or to the shops on the tram.[38] By the late 1940s, however, these trams were clashing with the city's increasingly crowded roads, intensifying traffic problems by occupying precious road space and becoming dangerous for passengers who had to cross crowded streets to board. For this reason, Liverpool's 750 tramcars were phased out of use between 1948 and 1957.[39]

The next part of Liverpool's public transport system to be dismantled was the city's distinctive overhead railway. The railway was a single five-mile track with seventeen stations running from the Dingle in the south to Seaforth in the north, forming a steel band that acted as a barrier between the docks and the city centre. The line, which opened in 1893, was Britain's only overhead railway, a counterpart to the soaring gilded age urbanism of Chicago's 'El' and parts of New York's metro system. When it was built during Liverpool's late nineteenth-century heyday, it was a fitting monument for a city whose wealth and prestige emanated from its docks. The railway's frame provided shelter for the outdoor calls used to recruit dock labour in the years before the war, giving it the nickname 'the dockers' umbrella' (or, less charitably because of its exposed platforms, 'the pneumonia express'). During its war-time peak, it was used by fourteen million passengers a year, with 20,000 workers using it to commute to or within the docks each day, and in the mid-1950s the system was still recording nine million annual passengers.[40] By 1956, the railway was in desperate need of repair, an investment that the operating company could no longer afford.

As a result, services were suspended. National and local politicians from Liverpool spent a year trying and failing to secure funding for repairs from the government and even toyed half-heartedly with the idea of transforming the line into a monorail following a successful exhibition in the city of a proposed monorail between London and Heathrow.[41] The iconic structure was eventually demolished in 1957 and quietly replaced with a new bus service, permanently changing the skyline of Liverpool's waterfront, a symbolic development for a city whose future now lay inland.

Meanwhile, more conventional forms of mass public transit also withered in the face of a surge in private car ownership. Use of Liverpool's municipal bus network plummeted, from over 400 million passengers a year in 1960 to a little over 100 million by 1980.[42] Falling passenger numbers led to service cuts, which were a blow to the many thousands in Liverpool who were unwilling or unable to purchase a car. A 1971 survey of poorer neighbourhoods in inner-city Liverpool found that in those areas 52 per cent of all trips to work were still made by bus, compared with just 18 per cent by car.[43] Those in Merseyside's new satellite communities who were still dependent on travelling to central Liverpool to work and shop were also heavily affected. Of the 69 per cent of households in the peripheral Cantril Farm Estate who didn't own a car, 78 per cent said that they were dissatisfied with the bus service and 95 per cent said they were in a worse position now than before.[44]

Meanwhile, beginning in 1965, local politicians planned for an ambitious new underground railway that would mitigate the city's increasingly congested road network. The project, which forms the basis for the present Merseyrail train network, was only partially completed and was based on expectations that Liverpool's population would increase in the subsequent decades, predictions that, as we have seen, turned out to be dramatically wrong.[45] At the same time, many of the local trains that connected Merseyside's towns outside of the new network were heavily reduced. Between 1948 and 1960, five major suburban lines on Merseyside were closed. The 1963 Beeching Report, which led to the dismantling of great swathes of Britain's nationalised railway network to save costs, tore further holes in the region's railway infrastructure. The 1960s and early 1970s saw the closure of Liverpool's Riverside station and parts of Liverpool's Central station as well as Birkenhead's Woodside station.[46]

All the while, Merseyside's road network was expanding. In 1965, in a fit of optimism that would be cruelly exposed over the next twenty years, Merseyside's planners predicted a 15 per cent increase in job opportunities in the region by the early 1990s, including a 14 per cent increase in manufacturing jobs. During the same period, they expected that real-term household incomes would more than double and that the region's population would increase from 1.4 to 1.9 million.[47] All of these forecasts pointed to more cars and more roads. In the early 1970s, four motorways were built through Merseyside connecting different parts of the region to North Wales, Yorkshire and the M6, which bisected Lancashire and was built in phases through the 1960s.[48]

Probably the city's most dramatic road-building project, however, was underground. The Queensway Tunnel connecting Liverpool with Birkenhead on the other side of the Mersey was completed in 1934. Within twenty years it was overwhelmed with traffic. In 1946, 2.6 million vehicles drove through the tunnel each year, a figure that, by 1968, had risen to almost 19 million, triggering catastrophic gridlock.[49] The solution was a second tunnel under the Mersey, the Kingsway Tunnel, built in stages between 1968 and 1974 with a five-lane approach, described breathlessly in the local press as a 'jet age worm'.[50] The new tunnel was an ambitious, high-modern undertaking in a city that was nearing the end of a rare decade of relative prosperity. It was built using a 45-foot-long laser-guided drill, known locally as 'the mole', which had previously been used to construct Pakistan's Mangala Dam.[51] The technological feat required to dig the mile-and-a-half-long tunnel between Liverpool and Wallasey became a kind of performance, with the slow progress of the mole excitedly narrated by boosters and politicians. The digging began on both sides of the river and, when the two tunnels finally met underground after more than a year of work, representatives from both local governments met to shake hands through a small hole in the bedrock.[52]

The Kingsway Tunnel marked something of a limit case for Liverpool's precocious 1960s modernity. The project was set back, first by unexpected cracks in the Mersey's bedrock and then by the tunnel's spiralling costs, prompting a protracted battle between the local and the national government as to who would pay for the shortfall.[53] The new tunnel also required the demolition of homes on both sides of the river to make way for new approach roads. While many of the destroyed houses were dilapidated Victorian terraces, the Liverpool end of the tunnel also saw the demolition of fifty-one council flats in Scotland Road that were only seven years old.[54] Curiously, many of the displaced residents were willing to concede that the sacrificing of homes to build the tunnel was a sad but necessary fact of life. One Wallasey resident told a journalist, 'we know that progress is inevitable but we think the authorities could have selected another site'. Another said, 'I know we cannot stand in the way of progress, but I think the people responsible could have been more discriminating.'[55] Others, however, were less willing to recite this Faustian script. In 1968, a group of women living on Fontenoy Street near the new approach road on the Liverpool side of the tunnel threatened to barricade the road in protest at the construction lorries that thundered down their street each night.[56]

The grassroots activism of the women of Fontenoy Street in the face of massive new road-building projects was not unusual in post-war Liverpool. Beginning in 1948, the city introduced 'play streets', streets where cars were banned, allowing children to play outdoors. Play streets were a reluctant concession to a highly organised network of women living in central Liverpool who had gathered a petition the previous year. In 1956, a spectacular battle unfolded between the women of Hardwick Street, a now demolished street of terraced houses that acted as a shortcut between two busy roads, Prescott Street and Pembroke Place, and what the women saw as anonymous wealthy drivers that sped past their homes. The 'Battle of Hardwick Street' has been recounted by the historian Krista

Cowman. It began when Jennifer Jones, a two-year-old child, was hit by a car on the street, injuring her foot. The event precipitated a week of protest in which the women living in the street, almost none of whom owned cars themselves, created their own insurgent 'play street', preventing motorists from passing through. The local press described 300 women with babies and prams forming a 'Maginot Line' against the police and motorists, and repeatedly erecting barricades made of dustbins and chalking the words 'make Hardwick Street a play street' along its length. The result was an uneasy detente. Traffic through the street was briefly suspended and it was eventually redesignated as one-way.[57] The battle marked an precocious attempt by working-class women to re-imagine the nature and purpose of the city in which they lived. For a short period of time, they were able to invert Liverpool's singular vision of progress.

The explosion of car ownership after the Second World War not only re-made Liverpool's built environment, but also transformed the city's economy. As the number of cars in service in Britain rose from 3 million in 1950 to 12.6 million in 1970, an ocean of imported oil became necessary to keep this new infrastructure afloat.[58] Between 1950 and 1970, the amount of oil consumed in England and Wales increased sixfold.[59] Car ownership had a significant role to play in this rise. Between 1960 and 1970 alone, the amount of energy consumed by road transport more than doubled, while the amount of energy consumed by rail halved.[60] Before the development of North Sea oilfields in the 1970s, this oil was imported, and much of it arrived in Merseyside.

Merseyside's oil economy was born during the Second World War, when the closure of eastern ports meant that, for the first time, vital supplies of oil were re-routed via Bromborough on Merseyside and Avonmouth on the Severn Estuary. In 1941, a 130-mile underground pipeline was constructed along the Welsh border connecting these two ports.[61] In 1960, the region's status as one of Britain's most significant oil importers was confirmed by the construction of the Tranmere Oil Terminal on the Wirral side of the Mersey. The terminal was a joint venture between the

Merseyside Dock and Harbour Board and Shell. It replaced the Eastham Oil Terminal, which had opened in 1954 but was already obsolete, unable to cater to the new breed of deep-water oil tankers. After arriving at Tranmere, imported oil was funnelled to Stanlow Oil Refinery in Ellesmere Port on the southern end of the Wirral, ten miles to the south, where it was processed and then fed into Britain's pipeline network. At a time when import and export traffic through the port was in continuous decline, oil imports boomed. In 1962, six million tonnes of oil passed through the region. By weight, this was 40 per cent of all the imported material that passed through Merseyside's docks that year.[62] In 1968, Merseyside's oil economy almost triggered an environmental catastrophe when a tanker smashed into the terminal's south jetty, causing more than a million pounds' worth of damage to the structure while its tank, miraculously, remained intact.[63] As well as the Tranmere Oil Terminal and the Stanlow Oil Refinery, a third node of the region's oil economy was the Cammell Laird shipyard in Birkenhead. After the Second World War, the shipyard became the country's third biggest centre for the construction of specialist oil tankers. Between 1945 and 1965, Cammell Laird built eighteen tankers for Shell and nine for BP.[64]

While Merseyside's port and its shipyards were briefly rejuvenated by the glut of oil that flooded into Britain to sustain its new automobile economy, other parts of the region became more directly involved in car-making. As we saw in the last chapter, in 1949 Merseyside was given special status as a 'development area' and had thus been the beneficiary of policies that aimed to channel manufacturing jobs into the region to reduce unemployment. In the late 1950s, there was a revival of interest in industrial policy, and the Board of Trade looked to car-making as a portable growth industry that could be easily rolled out in places like Merseyside. In 1960, it was announced that three of the 'big five' car-makers who operated in Britain would open new factories in Merseyside: Standard Triumph in Speke, Ford, a few miles further south in Halewood, and Vauxhall in Ellesmere Port in the south of the Wirral. This was a massive coup for the region's economy. In total, the three factories were responsible for 30,000 new jobs, a net gain of 21,000 between 1960 and 1966.[65] These were jobs targeted at the region's surplus of unskilled men. This was the biggest and, for a brief period, the most successful of all the attempts to solve Merseyside's unemployment crisis, a problem that had haunted the region almost continuously since the First World War. So successful was this injection of jobs and money that, by 1968, officials toyed with removing Merseyside from the government's list of 'development areas' in need of extra support.[66]

The factories arrived during an era when car-making was enormously profitable. The three biggest companies on earth in 1970 were General Motors, Standard Oil and Ford. In 1970, 200,000 British workers made a tenth of all the world's cars.[67] Workers in British car plants had developed a radical workplace politics from scratch, earning a nationwide reputation for militancy despite having almost no history of activism before the 1940s. Amidst the assembly lines of Longbridge, Cowley and Dagenham, workers formed highly localised networks of shop stewards, union activists who would mould the workforce into an oppositional collective.[68] Shop stewards, by arranging shifts and organising walk-outs, allowed workers a degree of autonomy and control over their labour.

Managers at the new Ford Halewood plant on Merseyside, mostly recruited from Ford's massive complex in Dagenham, were determined to halt this practice from the outset, giving exclusive negotiating rights to two of the more conservative unions, the AEF and the NUGMW. A directive was issued to supervisors in the new plant encouraging them to closely surveil their workers: 'It is essential to record the time that employees leave their place of business other than on personal break... Only strict control from the outset will prevent the abuses current in other company locations.'[69] Ford attempted to recruit men who, managers hoped, would be easy to discipline, avoiding former dock workers, seafarers and those with backgrounds in unions, believing them unsuited for factory work. Despite these efforts, however, Ford were still forced into recruiting many men who had previous experience in Liverpool's old port economy and were reluctant to sacrifice the autonomy and independence that had characterised their prior working lives. From the outset, Merseyside's car workers developed a distinctive and radical working-class culture.[70]

The lives and experiences of the workers in Ford's Halewood plant, almost entirely young men, were documented by the industrial sociologist Huw Beynon.[71] Their work was governed by a constantly moving assembly line that stretched over two floors, each floor almost half a kilometre long. Fraught battles were fought over the pace of the assembly line that passed through the plant and dictated the rate of work. Deafeningly loud and physically taxing, the performance of rote manual tasks at a tempo outside of workers' control was tedious and took a terrible mental toll. Workers said that the pace of the line made it almost impossible to talk while working without losing concentration. One worker told Beynon, 'When you're on the line it's on top of you all the time, you may feel ill, not one hundred per cent but that line will be one hundred per cent.' Another agreed, 'It's the most boring job in the world. It's the same thing over and over again… it wears you out. It makes you awful tired. There's no need to think… You just carry on.' Another activist put it more simply: 'I hate Ford's. I'd give up a wage increase to have Henry Ford on this section and give him a good kick up the arse.'[72]

Managers found it difficult to subject workers who had grown up with the autonomous, seasonal patterns of the port economy to the mind-numbing routines of assembly-line work. At Ford, walk-outs, wildcat strikes and absenteeism were common as well as other forms of resistance that went well beyond the usual pattern of collective bargaining. In one story told to Beynon, a group of newly hired young men took revenge on their foreman by stealing one of his oranges, carefully peeling it and using the peel to cover a small mound of bostic, a highly explosive chemical used in the production process, then secretly returning the orange to the foreman's bag.[73] Meanwhile, the old dock workers' practice of 'the welt', where half a gang would work while the other half rested, was imported into the plant by those working night shifts at Ford. Workers would take turns working while their colleagues would catch up on sleep, play cards or, in one instance, watch a pornographic film in a clandestine cinema set up in the plant.[74] By the end of the 1960s, Ford and other car companies' hopes that Merseyside's surplus labour could be moulded and broken by discipline, surveillance and monotony were coming undone. In 1969, a strike that began in Halewood over the issue of withdrawing pay for unofficial workplace actions spread to Ford plants across Britain and made national news.

In the 1960s, the automobile briefly propped up both ends of Merseyside's economy – the old economy of shipping and trade and the new economy of suburban manufacturing. Merseyside's road network and the hollowing out of alternative systems of public transport would long outlive the region's car-making economy and the fantasies of prosperity and development that guided its planners and politicians in the 1960s, leaving in its wake a privatised and carbon-intensive urban landscape. In 1973, the French journalist and philosopher André Gorz wrote that the car was dissolving the collective nature of urban life and revealing an aggressive, zero-sum individualism, 'the illusion that each individual can seek his or her own benefit at the expense of everyone else'.[75] This was something that the women of Hardwick Street, battling to stop the anonymous commuters who careened down their narrow road encased in glass and steel frames, already knew. There was an irony, however, that while cars rendered the experience of urban public life lonely and atomised, their production, in Merseyside at least, entailed new and vibrant forms of workplace collective action and solidarity.

Cities are like cosmic bodies whose gravitational pull is felt far beyond their physical core. For much of its modern existence, Liverpool has commanded a vast and uneven hinterland through which flows of food, commodities, people, energy and capital have circulated. The city has absorbed migrants from rural Lancashire,

Wales, Ireland, West Africa and East Asia and then seen these residents scatter in turn like dandelion seeds to the new satellite towns of Runcorn or Skelmersdale, to London or even to join the millions who emigrated to the British settler societies of Australia and New Zealand. As the moon's gravity gradually alters the tides, traces of the pull of Liverpool's 1960s economy could be felt with varying degrees of intensity in Lancashire farms, Yorkshire coal mines, Nigerian forests or the oil wells of the Iraqi desert.

Today, those driving along the remote winding road that passes north of the Lyn Celyn reservoir in Gwynedd in the far north-western corner of Wales would be forgiven if they failed to notice that they were in Liverpool's hinterland. Below the still waters of the reservoir, visible from the road through the gaps in the thick bracken and rows of ash trees, lie the ruins of a village, existing for sixty years in silent darkness beneath a hundred feet of water. The flooding of the ancient Welsh-speaking village of Capel Celyn in 1965 by Liverpool's municipal water company to create a new reservoir was an event that pitted the city's vision of its future development against a host of alternative notions of community, nation and tradition. It was an event that triggered an extraordinary wave of protest across Wales and Liverpool that culminated in a brief-lived and now mostly forgotten terrorist insurgency against the British state.[76]

From the late nineteenth century, Birmingham and Liverpool had both looked to Wales to source water for their expanding industrial populations, generating simmering tensions between rural Welsh communities and these great urban centres over the border to their east. Liverpool had already overseen the flooding of Llanwyddyn, a small village in Montgomeryshire in North Wales in the 1880s, and in 1906 Joseph Chamberlain's expansive municipal socialist administration in Birmingham built the enormous Elan Valley Dam, which produced a network of reservoirs through Powys in Mid-Wales.[77]

In early 1955, a delegation of surveyors from the Liverpool Water Corporation descended on the Tryweryn Valley to scope out locations for a future dam. Rumours that Liverpool was searching for land prompted an immediate response, with Plaid Cymru, the Welsh nationalist political party, issuing a statement condemning 'Liverpool aggression wherever it occurred'.[78] By the end of the year, it was clear that the proposed dam would mean the flooding of the village of Capel Celyn, which was home to forty-eight people and consisted of twelve houses, a school, a post office, a nineteenth-century chapel, a cemetery and ten farms. The village was entirely Welsh-speaking and some of the tenant farmers worked for an estate whose owners had held the land since the sixteenth century.[79] As the plans took shape, Liverpool found itself the target of a massive wave of opposition from across Wales. One hundred and twenty-five local authorities voted to condemn the scheme and twenty-seven of thirty-six Welsh MPs voted against it in Parliament. In 1956, protestors marched through Liverpool with banners reading, 'Your homes are safe, save ours. Do not drown our homes.'[80] One letter written in the defence of the community compared the construction of the dam to an English invasion, comparable to 'the Soviet bloodbath in Hungary'.[81]

The protests invoked the ancient history of the village and its deep connections with its surrounding landscape. The inhabitants of the village sent a petition to the queen that read: 'Most of us have lived here quietly all our lives and our families for generations before us, and we have followed the good customs of our fathers on the land and in our social life.'[82] For many, Capel Celyn symbolised a set of religious, linguistic and cultural traditions that were seen as being under threat from urbanisation and the encroachment of English power.[83] The 1968 poem 'Reservoirs' by the poet and vicar R. S. Thomas is indicative of the ways that, for some nationalists, the fate of Wales itself was tethered to the drowned village:

> There are places in Wales I don't go:
> Reservoirs that are subconscious
> Of a people troubled far down
> With gravestones, chapels, villages even...[84]

Schoolchildren protesting the flooding of the Welsh village of Capel Celyn to create a new reservoir for Liverpool in 1956.

In 1956, Liverpool's Council voted in favour of the dam by ninety-five votes to one and the plans went to Parliament for approval. There, arguments were made in favour of the dam that were utilitarian and technocratic. Bessie Braddock argued, 'everyone deplores the fact that in the interests of progress, sometimes people must suffer, but that is progress'. John Tilney, the Conservative MP for Liverpool Wavertree, went further, paraphrasing the utilitarian philosopher Jeremy Bentham: 'It is the question of the greatest good for the greatest number, there can be no doubt about that.' Later, at the opening of the reservoir in 1965, one Liverpool Alderman repeated this line almost verbatim: 'it is not the case of Welsh people and the Merseysiders, but one people with the object of the greatest good for the greatest number'.[85] By both its proponents and its detractors, the different actors in the Capel Celyn dispute were arranged into a neat temporal order related to their presumed stage of development. The future lay with Liverpool and its water-hungry suburbs and factories, while the past cohered in the thick-walled stone cottages of Capel Celyn, encircled by farmland. This narrative was dramatised by a documentary, filmed in 1965, which captured the last months of the village, as its residents packed up and left. In its final scenes, shots of the new reservoir were juxtaposed with images of gleaming water-intensive council estates with washing machines and indoor bathrooms, busy shopping streets and the enormous frame of Ford's Halewood plant, while a voiceover commented, 'The hustle and bustle in the city centre of Liverpool would grind to a halt but for the pipelines that bring in water from afar and we would do well to remember that progress for many can still mean heartache for the few.'[86]

By the early 1960s, opposition to the reservoir was entering a new and more dramatic phase. In the dead of a snowy night on 10 February 1962, a five-pound bomb was detonated beneath an electrical transformer on the dam's construction site. The bomb was the work of the radical Welsh paramilitary group Mudiad Amddiffyn Cymru (MAC), meaning Movement for the Defence of Wales, which had been formed in response to the proposed dam. It followed two other acts of sabotage on the construction site the previous year, the flooding of an electrical installation with oil and a small fire started in a wooden shed.[87] Three young men, Emyr Llewelyn, Owain Williams and John Albert, were arrested after the attack. In an interview conducted with a local newspaper later in his life, Williams recounted how he visited the site for weeks in advance of the bombing undercover in a hard hat and wellingtons, timing precisely the movements of the security patrols with dogs.[88] In the end, Williams and Llewelyn were given a year's prison sentence. MAC arguably foreshadowed many of the European anti-colonial, radical left or separatist groups of the 1970s such as the revived IRA, Germany's Baader-Meinhof Gang, Italy's Red Brigade or militant Basque separatism in France and Spain. It is a marker of the perceived absence of threats to domestic British public order in the 1960s that the MAC members received such lenient sentences, which in some instances were a fraction of what would be meted out to some Black protestors in Toxteth twenty years later.[89]

The aftermath of Capel Celyn inaugurated what would turn out to be a decade of Welsh separatist terrorism. After Llewelyn, Williams and Albert were apprehended and MAC, under its new leader John Barnard Jenkins, began a wave of bombings across the country, targeting a tax office, English-owned businesses and, in 1967, successfully blowing up a pipeline carrying water from Lake Vyrnwy reservoir to Liverpool. Most famously, MAC attempted to disrupt Prince Charles' investiture as Prince of Wales in 1969 with three different bombs, one of which, intended for a local government office, detonated prematurely killing two MAC members while another was uncovered and accidentally triggered by a ten-year-old child, who was severely injured.

For Jenkins and the MAC, the fraught politics of English water extraction led them to a distinctive brand of radical nationalism, a politics that was closer in tone and ambition to groups like the Weather Underground than it was to Welsh rural conservatism. Jenkins, who was born to English parents in Cardiff, travelled the world as a British army officer in the 1950s and served in Cyprus, where he reportedly took inspiration from anti-colonial separatist movements. While serving a ten-year prison sentence in 1971, he wrote, 'the fight was not to stop water, but to create a state of mind'.[90]

Despite the protests, work on the dam continued and, in 1963, the residents of Capel Celyn were evicted. A small ceremony was held at the late nineteenth-century schoolhouse where prizes were handed out by one of its first graduates, and a final service was held at the chapel. The stone cottages, some hundreds of years old, were subjected to controlled fires that left nothing standing but their bare walls.[91] Shortly before the waters came, the bodies in the chapel's cemetery were exhumed. Some were later interred in a remembrance garden in a new memorial chapel built in 1971, a hastily assembled society of the dead that overlooks the new reservoir.

*

In August 2018, the Tryweryn Valley along with the rest of Britain was entering a third consecutive month of record-breaking temperatures. Later, the Met Office would declare that the summer of 2018 was the joint hottest ever recorded in Britain, along with that of 1976, 2003 and 2006, and that anthropogenic climate change was almost certainly to blame, making the heatwave thirty times more likely to occur.[92] In June, July and August 2018, England alone recorded 863 excess deaths due to the heat.[93] Porthmadog, twenty miles west of Tryweryn, registered 33 degrees Celsius, the hottest temperature recorded in Wales that summer. As a result of weeks of hot weather and drought, the Llyn Celyn reservoir began to slowly recede. By the middle of August, for the first time in more than fifty years, the ghostly remains of Capel Celyn reappeared. Visitors could see the damp stumps of hedgerows, rusted doorknobs, cracked paving stones and, in one instance, an eerie wooden sign reading 'Garnedd Lwyd', the name of a farm that had once existed in the valley.[94]

It was as if time was flowing backwards. The linear march of progress heralded by Graeme Shankland, Madeline Kerr, Charles Vereker and Bessie Braddock, and bitterly resisted by the women of Hardwick Street, the residents of Wallasey displaced by road-building and the farmers of Capel Celyn, turned out to be short-lived. Climate change distorts the way we usually think about historical time. The effects of the carbon released by previous generations amplifies and recurs, bearing down relentlessly on the present and on the future. The immediate, fleeting human past may haunt the unimaginably distant geological future. In the words of the critical theorist and climate activist Andreas Malm, 'the thermometer can be legitimately suspected as a barometer of the rolling invasion of the past into the present'.[95] The shocking re-emergence of the distorted ruins of Capel Celyn, like a repressed memory intruding into a pleasant dream, was proof that by the early twenty-first century what was the future and what was the past was not as clear as many had thought in the 1960s.

In 2005, on the fortieth anniversary of the opening of the dam, Liverpool City Council issued a formal, if somewhat indirect, apology. The statement highlighted the significant numbers of Welsh people who had lived in Liverpool for contributing to the city's development. It apologised for 'any insensitivity by our predecessor council at that time'.[96] The utilitarian technocratic future that had justified the dam, stitched together by council estates and car factories, was, by then, a past that lay in ruins. The terminus of Liverpool's mid-century decades of growth and urban development, of the miles of meandering suburbs, of the cars that poured out of Halewood and onto the city's new roads, of the oil that cascaded through the terminals, refineries and pipelines of the Wirral, was, unbeknownst to those who lived through it, a warming world that will threaten to undo the fantasies of progress that called it into being.

4

The Music of the World

In the end, Liverpool's brief economic recovery proved fragile and combustible. The relative prosperity of the 1960s was like a delicate but flawed sculpture that appears permanent, but that crumbles into dust when touched. Within ten years the city was facing an almost existential crisis. Dock work, which had been in gradual decline since the First World War, was suddenly decimated. Between 1971 and 1983, the number of registered dock workers in Liverpool dropped from 10,500 to just over 2,000, a blow that rippled through the associated industries and trades that depended on the waterfront.[1] At the same time, the new manufacturing jobs, painstakingly enticed to the region to compensate for the slow erosion of dock work, were battered by the economic climate of the 1970s.

For almost twenty years, unemployment rates in Liverpool were more than twice that of Britain as a whole, rising from 10 per cent in 1971 to 20 per cent ten years later, where they stayed for much of the 1980s, numbers not seen since the Depression. In the city's central wards, unemployment rose above 40 per cent. Among the city's Black population it was even higher. One observer estimated that the youth unemployment rate for Black people in Liverpool was more than 60 per cent.[2] Meanwhile, the steady flow of people leaving Liverpool for Merseyside's suburbs and satellite towns or further afield became a deluge. The decline of the city's population, underway since the 1930s, accelerated rapidly between 1960 and 1980, decades that saw more than a third of Liverpool's inhabitants flee the city.[3]

The disaster unfolding in Liverpool baffled observers and alarmed politicians, producing a lurid paper trail of national and local government reports, newspaper articles and documentaries. One report referred to the city as 'the Bermuda triangle of British capital'.[4] The writer Tony Lane likened the city's devastation to a 'peace time blitz'. Lane was apocalyptic about the immediate future, predicting nothing less than a generalised social breakdown followed by urban guerrilla warfare:

> The most realistic predictions are these. Unemployment will continue to rise and housing conditions in the public sector will worsen... violence will be projected inward with block set against block, tenement against tenement... A discrete cordon of police will surround the middle class and the city centre. Working class areas in the inner city and the perimeter estates will become 'no-go' areas subjected to sporadic raids by heavily protected task forces.[5]

At the heart of this story is the sudden and dramatic unmaking of Liverpool's docks. The docks were the primary justification for Liverpool's existence, the reason that a city of hundreds of thousands developed over centuries at the terminus of the River Mersey. In the 1960s, they still dominated Liverpool's landscape and economy, providing secure and prestigious work for tens of thousands who unloaded, handled and stored commodities from every corner of the planet, filling the air, in the words of the philosopher Walter Benjamin, with 'the music of the world'.[6] By the 1980s, however, the music had stopped. By then, dock work on Merseyside had been confined to a row of container terminals in Seaforth on the northern outskirts of the city, manned by a few hundred workers. Many of these workers found themselves, once again, on casual contracts. They oversaw a seamless flow of hundreds of thousands of identical steel shipping containers, containers that could be slotted onto trains or trucks and unpacked hundreds of miles from the ports in which they arrived.

The evacuation of dock work out of urban centres and into peripheral, mechanised enclaves such as Felixstowe in Suffolk, Elizabeth in New Jersey, Dammam in Saudi Arabia or Ningbo-Zhoushan in China has, since the 1970s, re-made the landscape of global trade. Shipping costs have fallen and supply lines have been stretched, enabling the cheap commodities and the offshoring of industrial production that have become characteristic of contemporary life across the world.[7] Liverpool's version of this story is one of the central dramas of the city's post-war history, a tragedy that tore through workforces on multiple continents and left a trail of dereliction and environmental carnage through the city's central core.

On 1 May 1956, a battered-looking ex-Second World War oil tanker arrived into port at Houston, Texas. Unlike the other cargo ships that came to Houston's port that day, the *Ideal X* had sealed its wares inside fifty-eight metal containers lashed together on the ship's deck. A large crowd gathered to watch as cranes removed these containers and placed them onto the beds of fifty-eight waiting trucks, which then set off back to New Jersey, where the ship had departed. The containers were full of cardboard boxes housing coal briquettes, judged to be the average weight and density of long-distance cargo. The purpose of this journey was not to move briquettes, but instead to test this experimental method of transferring goods. The experiment worked. The interior of each box, bone dry and still neatly stacked, were photographed as proof for the US Coast Guard, who had been anxiously monitoring the voyage, sceptical about its success.[8]

This trial journey was the brainchild of Malcom McLean, an enigmatic businessman from rural North Carolina who, six years earlier, had founded a trucking empire on the East Coast. The idea of moving goods in shipping containers originally stemmed from McLean's desire to avoid congested highways between New

York and the US South by driving fully loaded trucks directly onto surplus military ships that would sail up and down the eastern seaboard. McClean quickly realised, however, that the wheels and beds of the trucks would take up valuable space and that, instead, the trucks' containers alone could be detached at one end of the voyage and reattached at the other.

An early cost estimate for this new scheme was drawn up by Ballantine Beer, whose product McLean's trucking company transported from New Jersey to Miami. Ballantine calculated the cost of a traditional shipment, a process that involved a truck picking up beer from the company's brewery in New Jersey, driving it to port, unloading the beer into a shed, wrapping it in netting, hauling it onto a ship, then repeating the process in reverse when the cargo reached Miami. They then compared this to the cost of loading the beer into a ship-worthy metal container at the brewery and sending it all the way to Miami via truck and ship without any stops for opening or repacking. The results were quietly earth-shattering. According to Ballantine's calculations, containerisation was an astonishing 94 per cent cheaper than traditional shipping. These numbers would have profound implications for global trade. McLean's big invention was not the shipping container per se. Indeed, containers for moving goods were used extensively by the US military during the Second World War. His contribution, rather, was a conceptual shift, the idea that logistics could be *intermodal*, an integrated network of land and sea operations through which goods could circulate without obstruction. In other words, the revolutionary potential of McLean's maiden voyage lay not with the battered former oil tanker on which the containers were lashed, but with the trucks onto which they were gingerly lowered.[9]

At the same time as the *Ideal X* was sailing from New Jersey to Houston, Alec Grant was working as a cooper at Liverpool's Albert Dock. Coopers were trained artisans who specialised in making casks and barrels. Grant's job was to sort through the barrels of alcohol that arrived in port – rum from the West Indies, wine from France, sherry from Spain, Guinness from Dublin – gauging the goods, taking samples that were stored for more than six months, and sometimes repacking their contents. Each day he would line up hundreds of barrels and pierce a hole in their sides with a 'bung starter', a specialist tool made of oak attached to a long bamboo cane, allowing customs officers to inspect them. He would often start the day by drinking a draft of purloined rum given to him in a thermos by one of his fellow coopers. For Grant, working on the docks was a family trade. His father had been a foreman overseeing the importing of tobacco, a senior role that, as a rare non-smoker, he was given preference for. According to Grant, coopers would often allow dock workers into their shed at the end of the day to lap up the rum that had spilled onto the floor during the sampling process. He had memories of carrying comatose dock workers to the overhead railway at the end of his shift.[10]

Some of the barrels that passed through the hands of coopers would have ended up with Billy Cliff, who worked as a carter from 1950. Carters were responsible for moving goods over short distances mostly within the confines of the docks. Even as late as the early 1960s, many of these carts were still pulled by horses, and Cliff's job was closer to an animal trainer than an unskilled labourer. As well as barrels of Guinness from Dublin, Cliff and his horses transported frozen meat, bales of wool and butter. He had taken a job as a carter because he fell in love with horses at a young age. He remembered being mesmerised by the horses that the city employed to cart away the rubble left behind by digging up roads for electric lighting cables. He also remembered his father beating him for not learning a skilled trade. The horses were sourced from the Shrewsbury sales, where Cliff's boss used to go each month, returning to central Liverpool late at night with eight to ten new horses from the countryside who had 'never seen a tramcar'. Cliff's job was to break the new horses into the rhythm of life on the dock, helping them adjust to a diet of straw rather than grass and fitting them with new shoes at a local blacksmith. He remembers the horses as an intelligent, lively presence, they 'knew when they were going home on a night, they'd be full of life, they'd dance all the way home'. Cliff claimed his horses were so well trained that he could set them off slowly walking with a cart full of goods, slip into a pub, 'and you could ask for a pint, and you could go out the other door having had your pint, and the horses would keep on walking'.[11]

When Billy Cliff's horses needed new shoes, it is possible he would have called on the service of Jack Chester, a blacksmith who worked by the docks for almost twenty years either side of the war. Chester's workshop was a hive of blazing heat and complex machinery, with five industrial fires. Much of Chester's work came from ships that arrived in port in need of urgent, temporary repair, with job orders collated *en route* by seamen and handed to superintendents who were waiting on the docks. His workshop had its own culture, one shaped by masculinity and the relative autonomy of the work. The blacksmith's foreman, Ned Williams, known as 'the Spaniard', for his dark complexion, was famous for demonstrating his strength by pounding his stomach with seven-pound hammers.[12]

In the 1950s and 1960s, Liverpool's waterfront hosted a variety of different specialist trades, many of which were mutually dependent and operated together in a harmonious eco-system. Coopers, carters and blacksmiths jostled with sugar men ('sankeys'), customs officers, ballast men, ships, cleaners and stevedores. One seaman remembered, 'walking down onto the Queen's Dock... thinking how many people there were; you'd be passing loads of people: gangs coming off work, people provisioning the ships, crews returning, it was busy'.[13] It was a place where new technologies accumulated incoherently alongside equipment and working practices that were hundreds of years old. Electric cranes, lorries and, after 1962, a room-sized computer costing £100,000 housed in the port's main office existed together with horses, coal furnaces and ancient tools for breaking open wooden casks.[14] Not all of those in this eco-system were registered dock workers, but those who were continued to benefit from the job security guaranteed by the post-war NDLB. In 1962, the average dock worker's salary was a handsome £16 14s a week.[15] While dock workers were still entitled to a minimum weekly guarantee if they turned up for work each day and work wasn't forthcoming, this was an increasingly rare occurrence. In 1955, of a total of 58,000 registered dock workers across the country, an average of only 335 workers each week had their wages made up this way.[16]

As wages rose and registers gradually tightened, dock work became increasingly sought after. In 1962, a writer for *The Times* speculated that 'getting a job as a docker is a process as cumbersome and complicated, though not of course as expensive, as getting one's son into Eton and it depends much more… on the old boy network and the fact that father was also there…'[17] Dock workers had succeeded in protecting their security and autonomy in the first twenty years of the scheme through extraordinary feats of solidarity. In 1949, an attempt by the NDLB to purge thirty-three men from the London register, including an 82-year-old who had only worked six shifts in the last year and a 70-year-old who was barely able to walk, resulted in a mass walk-out, with calls for 'doctors not dismissals'.[18] Since then, dock workers had successfully resisted almost all subsequent attempts at compulsory redundancy. Most dock workers also spent the 1950s and 1960s jealously guarding their independence. Many in the NDLB had hoped that the scheme would eventually lead to permanent employment contracts between dock workers and specific companies, eliminating the need for call stands and floating pools of labour. Most dock workers were deeply sceptical of 'taking the perm', however, with many fearing being trapped in low-wage jobs and others having already benefitted from long-standing informal relationships with employers. In Liverpool just 11 per cent of dock workers had taken permanent contracts by 1964.[19]

By the late 1960s, this issue, rather than the looming threat of shipping containers, was the biggest source of upheaval and conflict on Britain's docks. Following two tempestuous parliamentary inquiries into dock work, prompted by anxieties about the increasing number of days lost to strikes, compulsory decasualisation was forced through in September 1967. The implementation of permanent employment contracts immediately triggered a wave of strikes at a number of ports, including Liverpool, which held out for almost six weeks, demanding higher rates of pay to compensate for the loss of autonomy.[20] When interviewed in the 1980s, the cooper Alec Grant fondly remembered his foreman, an Irishman nicknamed 'Paddy Crackers', a formidable presence, well known for his oft-repeated boast: 'Liverpool belongs to me until someone can take it off me.'[21] For the first two decades after the war at least, these words from a powerful dock foreman would have rung true.

All the while, off-stage, containerisation was gathering momentum. For now, shipping containers and Liverpool dock workers were like two characters in a novel that were yet to meet but whose destiny was entwined. Malcolm McLean continued to scale up his operations. By the late 1960s he had renamed his operation 'Sea-Land' to emphasise the seamless nature of the relationship between his ships and his trucks and was running services every few days from New York to Houston. Containerisation in the 1950s and 1960s was honed through trade between the US mainland and its imperial periphery, with McLean expanding his operation to include Puerto Rico, while another company, Matson Navigation, whose board was dominated by sugar and pineapple interests, pioneered a container line between San Francisco and Hawaii.[22] An important milestone was reached in September 1965, when the International Organisation for Standardisation (ISO) met in The Hague to approve the exact weight and dimensions of a shipping container for global use. Founded in 1947, the ISO exists, in the words of the architectural theorist Keller Easterling, to 'dictate the world's critical dimensions', making sure the outputs of an increasingly global economy are mobile, and that lamps made in Hong Kong can be plugged into sockets in Paris without exploding, or that credit cards from German banks can slot seamlessly into ATM machines in Argentina.[23] The new ISO-approved container would theoretically be able to fit onto lorries, trains and ships and pass beneath bridges and through tunnels across much of the world.

By now, the magnitude of the disruption posed by shipping containers was beginning to dawn on British port operators. In 1967, the British Transport Docks Board, a nationalised industry that managed a handful of smaller ports in Britain, commissioned a report about the implications of containerisation. It predicted that shipping containers would radically re-make British ports, reducing shipping costs, in some instances, by more than half, while seamlessly integrating global and national supply lines. It argued that Britain, as an island nation, had a 'unique opportunity' to take advantage of the coming upheavals in trade, while warning darkly that 'the desire to protect individual segments of [the industry] may impede' this vision.[24] Three years later, another report produced by a different government body predicted that, by 1975, half of all shipping in the North Atlantic would be containerised.[25] The writing was on the wall. By this time, the Mersey Dock and Harbour Board (MDHB), the public body created in 1858 to manage Merseyside's docks by levying tolls on incoming ships, was scrambling to install container berths to capture some of this trade. In 1967, the MDHB announced that three berths in Seaforth, its planned new development to the north of Liverpool at the mouth of the Mersey estuary, would be reserved for containers. In the meantime, a berth in the Gladstone Dock, a complex that was built in the 1920s, was hastily retrofitted to service containerships.[26]

When the NDLB was created in 1947, the question of what was and what wasn't dock work had seemed obvious to most. Registered dock workers were employed to handle cargo as a service and prohibited from handling goods directly on behalf of manufacturers and retailers. In practice, this meant that dock workers were confined by imaginary rings around each British port, beyond which they lost their special privileges.[27] Shipping containers, however, raised immediate, intractable questions about this definition. If a container of butter imported from New Zealand was shipped to Liverpool and then placed on a truck and driven to a warehouse in Nottingham, would the person who unpacked it at its destination be a dock worker? These questions were hashed out at a series of industrial tribunals in the late 1960s. The tribunals opted for a narrow definition of dock work, as being confined to the areas around ports and to work 'ordinarily done' by registered dock workers, meaning that new types of work generated by technological change were theoretically exempt. The precedent set by these rulings allowed new east coast terminals in places like Tilbury or Felixstowe to use unregistered labour.[28]

This was a catastrophic blow for dock workers, who, faced with the grave threat of containerisation, turned to collective action. In London, a wave of strikes in 1969 prompted the Labour government to form a committee of employer and union representatives to work out a new definition of dock work. The committee's report called for all cargo handling within five miles of any port to be redefined as dock work, a definition that was unworkably expansive, threatening to eat into numerous other trades. In London it effectively meant a five-mile exclusion zone running in a corridor through the heart of the city in which dock workers would monopolise the moving or unpacking of any kind of cargo. The draft agreement provoked an immediate backlash from haulage unions and from employers and was quickly abandoned.[29]

In Liverpool, the phoney war preceding the arrival of containerisation also erupted into outright conflict in 1969. The battle lines were drawn over a depot two miles inland in Aintree, one of the city's new suburban industrial estates built in the inter-war period. The company who owned the depot eschewed registered dock labour, even though they were only two miles inland and the depot was processing containers that were arriving directly from the port. When news broke of this decision, 8,000 Merseyside dock workers went out on strike, initiating a protracted definitional argument that dragged on for more than a year and had to be mediated by Jack Jones, the General Secretary of the Transport and General Workers' Union. It was eventually agreed that work at the depot would be conducted by dock workers, though employers were unwilling to concede the all-important semantic point that what was taking place at Aintree amounted to 'dock work'. In 1972, Liverpool dock workers went on the offensive again, demanding that all containers with partial loads be unpacked and repacked on the dock premises. While they were able to win back fragments of warehousing and hauling work that had migrated inland, the demand marked a tacit acceptance that they would never be able to work full container loads travelling directly to or from manufacturers.[30]

By then the battle was lost. McLean's humble steel boxes, by uncoupling the international movement of cargo from its packing and unpacking, posed an existential threat to dock work as an identifiable career distinct from any other in the service industry. What was dawning was an era in which industrial production, distribution and assembly would become part of the same process, with vast 'just-in-time' supply lines spanning multiple continents.[31] By 1970, it was becoming unclear whose jobs in this circulatory system would be protected and whose would be discarded. Sensing the coming change, one government official that year asked whether it made sense 'to preserve a kind of closed shop for the sons of mechanical conveyor operators, for truck drivers, button pushers, systems analysts and container controllers, merely because their ancestors were registered dockers? Why not registration for railway men, coal miners, steel workers, post office employees and countless others?'[32] The rationale underpinning the NDLB was becoming harder to justify and the brief window of job security for dock workers was coming to an end. Liverpool's docks were about to be transformed.

When seeing shipping containers for the first time on television, a man named Mr Sherman who had spent his career working ships was shocked by their efficiency, and deeply worried about the future of his trade: 'to unload cargo before [took] five days, but with containers today it takes thirty minutes… I saw a ship [that] only needed three people, captain, officer and chief engineer. Everybody in the gangway [was] not needed.'[33] Mr Sherman was watching these scenes not in Liverpool but in Liberia. The re-making of dock work in the global north in the 1970s and 1980s, whether in Liverpool, London, Marseille, or Baltimore, is usually narrated as a tragic fall from grace of a once proud and powerful working class, coded often implicitly but sometimes explicitly as white and male.[34] Liverpool's docks, as well as sustaining the livelihoods of thousands of dock workers who lived onshore in the city, also supported a more transient, more precarious network of seamen who divided their lives between Liverpool and their home ports. This was particularly true for the Kru, an ethnic group originally from Liberia to whom Mr Sherman belonged.

By the time Mr Sherman was watching containerships on Liberian television, the fate of the Kru had been tied to British trade for almost two centuries. From the 1790s, Kru workers had been hired by the British empire for military and construction projects along the coast of present-day Sierra Leone and Liberia, parts of West Africa that would be partially reserved for the repatriation of formerly enslaved people from the Atlantic world.[35] From its founding in 1868, Liverpool-based shipping company Elder Dempster hired Kru, both as seamen and as shore workers, in West African ports. Working as 'firemen' in sweltering engine rooms below deck or as cooks or stewards, 'kroomen' or 'krooboys' became central to the heavily trafficked trade routes between Liverpool and West Africa from the late nineteenth century onwards. Their labour was sourced and disciplined by a network of well-paid 'headmen' who were in turn contracted by companies such as Elder Dempster. In the words of Diane Frost, a leading historian of the Kru diaspora, the term 'kru', like many social classifications used by the British empire, was 'an ethnic category that became associated with an occupational one'.[36]

Although they originated in eastern Liberia, beginning in the early nineteenth century many Kru had migrated to ports along the coast of West Africa where they established communities that were used by British companies and officials as pools of labour. One of the largest Kru settlements was in Sierra Leone, where Kru settlers formed a recognisable neighbourhood along Kroo Town Road near the docks in Freetown, the nation's capital. It was in Freetown where most Kru were hired for seafaring work on North Atlantic routes. During the peak decades of trade between Liverpool and West Africa from the 1860s to the 1960s, thousands of Kru moved back and forth between Kroo Town Road and the seamen's hostels and lodging houses that made up Liverpool's Black enclaves near the docks. Their work was casual and often precarious, and, unlike the white workers in Liverpool at the other end of the same supply chain, there was no back-up pay to mitigate this insecurity save from a meagre system of insurance that was used for burial relief and to fund churches and schoolteachers along Kroo Town Road.[37]

Despite the lack of job security and even though Kru workers hired in Freetown were paid significantly less than white sailors hired to do the same job in Liverpool, Kru seamen were comparatively well off in the first half of the twentieth century. Many prided themselves that their wives didn't also have to work and that they were able to replicate the households of 1950s and 1960s Britain, with a man at work and a woman bearing the sole responsibility for domestic labour. These families were, however, cleft in two by the North Atlantic, with wives remaining in Sierra Leone, Nigeria or Liberia while men moved back and forth from Liverpool. Clifford Sullivan, a white sailor who worked for Elder Dempster in the middle of the twentieth century, was struck by the bifurcated lives of the Kru seamen, remembering: 'We would pick up anything between 60 and 80 "Krooboys"... they would come aboard with their [mothers] and their girlfriends seeing them off and they'd all be drunk. As soon as we'd go away the [women] would go ashore, and off we'd go and the next day they'd be sober and work like the devil.'[38]

By the 1950s, Elder Dempster was operating in a part of the world that was beginning to decolonise, a development that threatened to undermine the Liverpool/West Africa trade that the company had dominated for almost a century. In 1954, sensing an impending change in the political climate, the company scrambled to break up its onshore and offshore operations into different companies, making it more difficult for parts of the company to be expropriated by future post-colonial governments.[39] Elder Dempster also underwent measures to 'Africanise' its management by recruiting Black staff to oversee some of its operations on the ground.[40] In 1957, Ghana became the first of Britain's West African colonies to win independence, led by the pan-Africanist Kwame Nkrumah. Elder Dempster's fears were realised when Nkrumah's new government launched its own rival shipping line, the Black Star Line, named in honour of the shipping line created by the pan-Africanist Marcus Garvey in 1919 to facilitate the migration of Black Americans to Africa.[41]

Among British ports, Liverpool's success had been uniquely tied to empire. In 1960, 49 per cent of Liverpool's imports (by volume) came from the Sterling Area, the currency bloc comprising colonial and post-colonial states, while 62 per cent of its exports went the other way. The comparable figures for the UK as a whole that year were 41 per cent and 45 per cent.[42] As late as 1966, the city still saw eleven ships a month depart for Singapore, nine to Hong Kong and four to mainland China.[43] When Britain's empire began to collapse in the 1950s and 1960s, Liverpool's port economy was dealt a serious blow. Liverpool-based shipping companies began to lose their pre-eminence, cut adrift by a new global order where the European shipping conglomerates of the nineteenth and early twentieth centuries, like the empires that housed them, were beginning to disintegrate.[44]

At the same time as Elder Dempster were grappling with the new geopolitical contours of post-colonial West Africa, the Blue Funnell Line, which operated ships from Liverpool to the Far East, were running into similar problems.[45] Like other post-colonial nations, Malaysia and Singapore had founded their own shipping companies as part of a broader project of uncoupling their economies from the influence of former imperial powers, creating new competition for the Liverpool-based line. In China, meanwhile, which was then in the throes of the Cultural Revolution – an intense, decade-long burst of revolutionary nationalism – the company's ships were repeatedly harassed by Chinese officials. In one dramatic instance in 1970, a Blue Funnell ship that had departed from Liverpool was boarded by Chinese military police *en route* to Shanghai. After the crew were interrogated, the ship's captain was briefly kidnapped and accused of being a British spy. The Chinese officials ignored protests that this was a merchant rather than a military vessel, responding that 'sometimes the agents of the Imperialists use... seamen as a cloak to spy on the Chinese people'.[46] Confounded by the new contours of this post-colonial world, Blue Funnell began to divest from the East Asian trade and in 1980 moved its headquarters from Liverpool to London.[47]

In 1972, as decolonisation and the Cold War were reordering Liverpool's place in the world economy, Britain's entry into the European Economic Community saw the centre of gravity shift to the country's eastern ports. As trade with mainland Europe became an ever more crucial part of the economy, Liverpool began to fall behind ports like Felixstowe, Tilbury and Dover, which had easy access to the English Channel, places that in the mid-twentieth century were barely on the radar of British shipping. In 1966, Dover and Felixstowe were handling just a ninth of Liverpool's trade *between them*, but by the mid-1980s they were each alone handling 10 per cent more than the city. During the same critical twenty years, Liverpool's share of total British trade fell from 10 per cent to just 2 per cent.[48] By the end of the twentieth century, Liverpool was in the wrong part of the country, undone by a conspiracy of geography.

Meanwhile, the Kru workers who had serviced Elder Dempster ships fell between the cracks of this new global order. As we saw in Chapter 1, the rights of Black seafarers to spend time in Liverpool were repeatedly curtailed throughout the first half of the twentieth century, by government directives such as the 1925 Coloured Alien Seamen Order, by white mobs in 1919 and 1948 and by employers themselves, as when shipping companies tried to purge 'surplus' Black labour from its registers in 1950. Immigration restrictions introduced in 1962, 1971 and 1981 restricted the rights of former colonial subjects to live and work in Britain. Despite the hostile environment created for African workers in Liverpool itself, Elder Dempster still employed almost 2,000 African workers by the end of the 1950s, even as the era of labour-intensive steamshipping was also coming to an end.[49]

As work began to dry up in the 1960s and 1970s, Kru workers, unlike their white counterparts onshore, had no voluntary severance programmes or weekly wage guarantees to fall back on, aside from a basic insurance system of 'ship money' pooled between workers.

One British woman, interviewed by the historian Diane Frost, who married a Kru seafarer described the difficulty of getting by on the salary from his intermittent shifts, many of which were weeks or months apart: 'he'd be home for three weeks and maybe he wouldn't be working, so there'd be no money coming in, money had finished once he'd been paid off. And in those days there was such a lot of Africans, it was nothing to have fifty men waiting for your husband to come home from sea.' Her husband was eventually made redundant in 1970.[50] In Sierra Leone as well as in Liverpool, the era of relative social mobility and affluence conferred on Kru by imperial ship work was coming to an end, and by the 1970s many Kru women were having to take up supplementary work such as market trading to support their husbands, who were struggling to find shifts. Without citizenship rights in Britain, permanent migration out of Sierra Leone was effectively foreclosed. With work drying up, many Kru left Freetown to move back to Liberia, although some of these migrants would return again to Sierra Leone as refugees after the outbreak of the First Liberian Civil War in 1989.[51]

There are, therefore, two stories about the unmaking of Liverpool's imperial maritime economy. One is a familiar story about technological change, a story in which identical steel shipping containers reduced the number of workers required to load and unload ships, while laying waste to the principle of guaranteed job security for dock workers. As well as becoming more efficient and less labour intensive, however, Liverpool's share of national trade also sharply declined, as the city's colonial links began to fray and Europe became increasingly central to trade. As a result, Kru workers, like their white counterparts, were forced to reinvent their livelihoods after generations of relatively well-paid employment disappeared for good. Over the course of a hundred years the Kru in Sierra Leone had been proletarianised by the Liverpool trade, forming a low-paid workforce that had helped support the wealth and power of the city's docks.[52] By the 1980s, they were deemed obsolete, facing unemployment, displacement and warfare.

★

In September 1972, the MDHB took the extraordinary and irreversible decision to close the miles of dockland that ran through the heart of Liverpool, redirecting almost all its trade to terminals on the northern fringes of the city. The shipping offices, jetties and cavernous warehouses of the south docks were mostly more than a hundred years old, with parts of the docks dating to the mid-nineteenth century, when this thin strip of land commanded 40 per cent of global trade. In an era when goods travelled through the world in a torrent of steel shipping containers, these docks, with their shallow bays, their warehouses built so close to berths that dock workers could cart wares by hand from passing ships, their loading sheds built to shelter exposed goods from the rain and their messy hinterland of narrow streets and crowded houses, had outlived their purpose. The Mersey estuary itself, narrow and expensive to dredge, was too shallow for the new breed of containerships that increasingly made up the world's fleet. While a skeleton customs crew patrolled the shore, monitoring for the occasional small boat that was able to navigate the accumulating mud and silt that piled up by the dock walls and jetties, the complex remained largely empty for more than a decade, existing as a solemn and eerie presence a short walk from the city's centre.[53] In the words of one journalist, these vast deserted buildings looked like 'coffins left landlocked by a vanished race of seagoing giants'.[54]

Twelve years after the Albert Dock closed, a managing director of Granada Television, searching for real estate, described what it was like to tour the dock's office, a once grand building fronted by elegant columns completed in 1848:

> The rain was coming across from the Mersey horizontally, carried on a gale force wind... we walked around the derelict forlorn site and saw this shell of a building. The roof had gone, the gallery had collapsed, there was a pile of rubble in the middle of the hall and there were pigeons resting in the beams... The basement was like the wreck of the Marie

> Celeste. Each room still had a fireplace and a grate and there were high Dickensian desks with ledgers strewn all around almost as though the people had just got up and walked away.[55]

By then, the office was surrounded by long tufts of grass and weeds that had sprouted along the once heavily trafficked footways between silent and empty warehouses.

Liverpool was in the grip of an environmental crisis. By 1980, the Mersey was the most polluted river system in Britain, with one report finding that almost a third of its length was incapable of sustaining fish life.[56] According to one estimate, 360 million litres of sewage a day, the equivalent of a quarter of all of the untreated sewage in England and Wales, sailed past Liverpool's waterfront heading for the Mersey estuary mixing with runoffs from upstream chemical plants and the oil refineries.[57] Worse, the inundation of faeces and industrial waste was painfully slow moving. Sewage entering the estuary at Warrington at the river's

The Albert Dock, ruined and clogged with silt in 1980.

tidal limit could take as long as a month to find its way to the sea.[58] It was not uncommon for lumps of raw sewage or congealed masses of oil and fat to be seen floating on the river's surface or washed up onshore. When these slow-moving toxic pellets finally made their way into the ocean, they mingled with the radiation of five nuclear power plants, two to the south along the Welsh coast and three to the north, whose waste was also channelled into the Irish Sea basin.[59]

Some of the worst effects of this pollution had been kept at bay by the infrastructure of the docks. A latticework of gates built to maintain parts of the river at a constant level, regardless of tides, had held back accumulations of polluted material. The southern stretches of the Mersey had also been repeatedly dredged to prevent ships from running aground. With the gates left open and dredging operations radically reduced, however, conditions deteriorated. By the beginning of the 1980s, the docks sat next to an undulating underwater massif of silt, shot through with human faeces, in places rising thirty-five feet above the riverbed.[60]

The docks were only the most dramatic example of the proliferation of ruined and unused land that scarred stretches of the inner areas of Liverpool. In 1972, the same year the south docks closed, it was estimated that as much as 11 per cent of land in some inner-city neighbourhoods was either empty or derelict.[61] Much of this ruined land was left behind by aggressive slum clearance programmes initiated by the local government during a period of relative optimism in the 1960s. With no subsequent investment, however, these demolitions had left a pointillist scattering of empty, overgrown lots throughout Liverpool's inner areas. For a group of architects and planners commissioned by Ted Heath's government to investigate inner-city areas across the country, Liverpool's accelerating dilapidation had fused with the city's employment crisis to produce an interlocking aesthetic, economic and social crisis that had engulfed the city:

> For those who have to live with the day-to-day reality of large, rubble-strewn sites the impact is immediate, unsavoury

> and depressing. Packs of half wild dogs scavenge among bags of abandoned household refuse. Pools of water collect where badly filled cellars have subsided. Children build fires with cardboard cartons and the abandoned timber from demolished houses and play among the piles of brick, rubble and broken glass. Half bricks provide a ready and almost endless supply of ammunition for the frequent destruction of the windows and of surrounding houses. Mattresses, furniture, gas cookers, prams and even carts that have outlived their usefulness are dumped. There is a pervading smell of old town gas from the partly buried gas pipes of demolished houses and the stopped off gas mains.[62]

As for the abandoned docks, they were, for now, still the property of the MDHB. In 1970, with costs for the new container terminal in Seaforth spiralling, and Liverpool's share of world trade continuing to fall, the MDHB became insolvent for the first time in its hundred-year history. The following year the body was bailed out by the government and restructured as a private company that could borrow money. Now named the Mersey Dock and Harbour Company (MDHC), the rebranded organisation was tasked with stripping its obsolete assets in the form of land and workers. This, however, was not an easy task. Under the terms of the decasualisation agreements of the late 1960s, registered dock workers who were unable to find permanent employers or who had been made unemployed became the responsibility of the MDHC, who were compelled to continue paying their salary. The MDHC's only option was to tempt dock workers with a generous nationwide voluntary severance scheme, one that was worked out between employers and unions in 1969 and offered willing workers a one-time payment of £1,800, which amounted to more than two years' pay at the average wage.[63] Initially a scheme to induce older dock workers to retire from the register, this severance package became the mechanism by which thousands of workers in Liverpool and across the country would leave the register. The package was aggressively advertised in letters sent to every registered dock worker.[64] However, despite repeatedly upping the payments, in 1980 the company was still paying £3.4 million a year in fallback pay to hundreds of registered dock workers who were surplus to the needs of employers.[65]

Meanwhile, the MDHC, heavily in debt, spent more than a decade trying to sell its surplus land to service its loans. While, as later chapters will show, large swathes of the abandoned dockland would eventually be reinvented as a complex of museums and set-piece tourist attractions in the 1980s and 1990s, in the early 1970s these plans would have felt remote and fantastical. While marketing the dock's world historical significance, as well as preserving its distinctive Victorian architecture, would form the centrepiece of later dockland regeneration strategies, this preservation was also far from anyone's radar. Instead, somewhat optimistically, the city's Planning Officer recommended turning the south docks into a large industrial estate to stem the outflow of jobs from the city, a scheme that he acknowledged would take a long time to implement.[66] By the mid-1970s, the MDHC's most promising plans for its surplus land were relatively small-scale public-sector contracts, including a plan to sell the Albert Dock to the City Council to use as the grounds for Liverpool's Polytechnic University, and to sell the Canning Dock for use as offices by the central government. By 1976, however, both sales had fallen through, and the Company was back to square one.[67]

During these turbulent years, the MDHC was chaired by John Page. Page arrived in 1972 from Syria, where he had worked as chief representative of the Iraqi Petroleum Company, a body which had been founded by western oil interests to monopolise Iraqi oil production before its nationalisation by the Iraqi government. This was part of a twenty-year career working for private oil interests in the Middle East, which saw Page move between London, Haifa, Abu Dhabi, Iraq and Syria. Page ran the MDHC for twelve years between 1972 and 1984, overseeing rounds of austerity imposed on the Company by the government and by private creditors as a condition for continued loans.[68] Under his leadership the Company eventually succeeded in shedding thousands of registered dock workers and, following an extensive and bitter dispute over its price, selling much of the MDHC's remaining surplus land to the Merseyside Development Corporation, the body created by Michael Heseltine in 1981 tasked with urban regeneration.

During these years of restructuring, the MDHC also found other, more unusual sources of income. Beginning in 1978, the Company opened a consultancy service to advise developers and train labour forces in new ports in the global south. Over the following fifteen years, the MDHC's consultancy wing advised on construction, training and accountancy in ports that largely, though not exclusively, were in the former British empire, including projects in Saudi Arabia, Nigeria, Kenya, Sudan, China and the Gambia.[69] In 1990, the Company secured a contract to help rebuild Kuwait's docks following the First Gulf War.[70] As shipping containers standardised the logistics of trade across the world, advice on construction and management also became modular and replicable from port to port.

Meanwhile, in 1976, the MDHC created its own private police force, initially to crack down on new kinds of organised crime associated with containerisation. By 1979, however, the Company began offering its services further afield as a private security operation. Eventually trading as Neptune Security Services, this side-business was, in the words of Page, making a 'modest but useful' profit, and had become 'a somewhat unlikely source of financial relief'.[71] By 1981, Neptune too were doing consultancy work in overseas ports. Finally, by the middle of the 1980s, at last able to capitalise on some of its surplus land, the MDHC was also indulging in property development. This took the form of private housing complexes on both sides of the Mersey, including the redevelopment of derelict animal pens in Birkenhead into a 'village' of high-end homes and the transformation of a large warehouse in Liverpool's Waterloo Dock into expensive waterfront apartments.[72] These various initiatives were extraordinarily successful, transforming the fortunes of the once beleaguered port. By 1993, the MDHC was the wealthiest port company in Britain and was aggressively expanding. That year, the Company purchased Medway Ports, a peripheral stretch of container terminals in Kent whose biggest trade was importing and exporting vehicles. Medway Ports had recently sacked 300 of its workers for refusing to accept new contracts, forcing them to sell their shares in the company for £2.50 shortly before the MDHC bought them for £37.25 each.[73]

By the 1980s, then, some of the biggest problems that were facing Liverpool's port ten years earlier had been magically transformed into sources of profit. The port's strained links with under-developed and post-colonial economies had become a lucrative opportunity for paternalistic forms of consultancy and training. The port's high crime rate, likely driven by its location in one of the poorest cities in Britain at the time, had led to a wealth of private security contracts. Most of the port's surplus land, once a massive financial burden, had been sold, with what remained transformed into luxury flats. Having once resembled a failed state, a bankrupt patrician body indelibly linked to an economy and a global political order that was passing out of existence, the MDHC had become a securitised, financialised and entrepreneurial private company, fit for the neoliberal age. Meanwhile, the port had one last trick up its sleeve, perhaps the weirdest yet.

From the late 1950s, visitors to County Clare, a rural south-western corner of Ireland, may have stumbled across a hastily built fence running through a patch of drained bog a few miles inland from the sea. The fence marked the boundary between two wildly different economic regimes. On the eastern side of the fence was the economy of the rest of Ireland, an emerging post-colonial nation whose recent decades had been characterised by protectionism and relative isolation from the rest of the world. On the western side of the fence, towards the Atlantic, was the Shannon Airport Free Zone, an alternative economic realm where import and export duties and corporate tax rates were partly suspended.

Shannon in the 1950s shared many of the same problems faced by Liverpool in the 1970s and 1980s. Shannon airport, located on one of the most westerly points of the European continent, had once played an important role in the early decades of trans-Atlantic flight, where flights from the United States and Canada had to stop and refuel before moving on. By the late 1940s, the airport had effectively become a trans-Atlantic waiting room, open all night, where passengers were stranded for hours or sometimes days in the event of bad weather. The airport's hospitality operation, tasked with entertaining these captive travellers, was overseen by Brendan O'Regan, a government appointee who was a former hotel manager. In 1947, following an inter-governmental aviation meeting in Canada, O'Regan was given permission to set up a small duty-free shop in the airport's passenger lounge, the first of its kind anywhere in the world (previously, duty-free had only been available on ships). Over the next ten years, what was at first a small cupboard developed into a massive enterprise, thriving on a captive market of passengers waiting for their planes to be refuelled.[74]

By the 1950s, however, improvements in aviation were making stops at Shannon less and less necessary for trans-Atlantic flights. This small community in rural Ireland had developed with a single purpose, but it now risked becoming obsolete. In 1959, O'Regan presented the Irish government with a radical proposal to save his airport, one that was a natural extension of his duty-free empire. His plan was for a 'free trade zone' within the perimeter of the airport, where warehouses could store goods and light industry could manufacture products for export, all beyond the reach of Ireland's tax and regulatory regime.[75] O'Regan was given permission for his zone, and, within a few years, enveloped by the smell and sound of landing jets, a strange industrial community began to form, bunched at the foot of Shannon's runway.

While there are debates about whether Shannon was the world's first 'free trade zone', there is no doubt that within twenty years it would be a relatively familiar type of space. In developing economies that wanted to preserve a degree of protectionism and regulation while controlling their exposure to the world economy, places like Ireland but also Puerto Rico, Panama, Korea and, perhaps most famously, mainland China, free trade zones, special economic zones and export processing zones multiplied in the 1960s, 1970s and 1980s.[76] These zones represented a kind of political economy à la carte, where social democratic welfare states and in some instances communist economies sat streets apart from libertarian dreamworlds in which tax, customs and regulatory regimes were partially or fully suspended.

These experimental laboratories for free-market economics eventually migrated from the developing world to the former imperial heartlands, championed by right-wing governments enthusiastic about the possibility of creating mini free-market utopias in the heart of towns and cities.[77] In the 1980s, under Margaret Thatcher's government, Britain was an early adopter of these kinds of policies, two of which, 'enterprise zones' and 'freeports', were each seized upon as means of mitigating Liverpool's obsolescence. While Liverpool's enterprise zone is a story for a later chapter, the freeport, which opened in November 1984, was the final step in the transformation of Liverpool's docks. It was by far the largest and most ambitious of six freeports introduced across the country at both airports and traditional ports, the others located in Birmingham, Belfast, Southampton, Prestwick and Cardiff.[78]

While right-wing boosters tried to claim that freeports had a lineage dating back to the medieval Hanseatic League, the policy's origins bore a closer resemblance to the spiderweb of competing deregulatory zones and tax havens that had spread across the face of the Earth's surface since the 1950s.[79] Goods that entered, left or were stored within the boundaries of Liverpool's new freeport were exempt from most customs duties, VAT and EEC levies. The zone encompassed a 600-acre area that included most of Liverpool's working docks in Seaforth. As in Shannon, the zone was carefully delimited by three kilometres of steel palisade fencing.[80] Eleven acres of the new zone was reserved for a business park and for light industry, meaning that companies could rent office space, build factories, open warehouses, hire workers, import material and export products all within the boundary of this strange new nowhere-space erected between the cracks of the global economy.

By 1987, the freeport hosted an assortment of specialist industries including a Hong Kong-based clothing factory, a company that made specialist bed linen and a factory on a moored ship that processed cement imported from Greece.[81]

The purpose of Liverpool's freeport closely resembled Brendan O'Regan's stated aims for Shannon Airport. While O'Regan claimed that he wanted the zone to 'pull the airplanes out of the sky', the MDHC were hoping that Liverpool's freeport would pluck ships out of the North Atlantic.[82] On this count it was a success. By the end of the decade, the freeport had handled almost half a billion pounds' worth of goods, much of which was stored and then re-exported, with the benefits accruing to the port and by various local warehousing companies.[83] While the MDHC had turned its obsolete land and connections into lucrative consulting contracts, property development and private security operations, the core work of loading and unloading ships, at one time the city's *raison d'être*, mostly now occurred on the northern fringes of the city in a jurisdictional black hole sealed away behind miles of jagged metal fencing. The freeport echoed the observation made by the film-maker Patrick Keiller in 1996 that, while industrial dereliction abounded, Britain's new sources of wealth and production 'tended to be invisible', confined to intensive nodes of activity that appear eerily empty from the outside.[84] Liverpool's primary economic activity, once land- and labour-intensive, had narrowed to a single point, surrounded on all sides by under-employment and dereliction. It is through places like Seaforth, off-scene and half empty, that the imported goods of Britain's globalised economy now arrive.

During a 1989 visit to Liverpool, Margaret Thatcher presided over the opening of a new business park built entirely within the grounds of the freeport. Less than a month later, with little warning, Thatcher's government announced that the NDLB, then renamed the National Dock Labour Scheme (or simply 'the Scheme'), would be abolished. Almost overnight, the hard-won gains of a century of labour struggle were undone, and the remaining dock workers who had survived the extraordinary changes of the 1970s and 1980s were plunged back into insecurity. For the first time, dock workers could be chosen for compulsory redundancy. When Ernest Bevin was appointed to the war-time cabinet in 1940, he quipped that, just as Gladstone was famously said to have been Treasury Secretary from 1860 to 1930, 'I'm going to be Minister of Labour from 1940 to 1990.'[85] In the end, Bevin fell short by about six months. The MDHC was jubilant, delighted that it was no longer obliged to pay the salaries of registered dock workers who could not be assigned permanent employers.[86]

By 1989, just over 1,000 dock workers remained on the register and close to 300 of them would lose their job over the next year.[87] Abolition prompted a massive strike in Liverpool, although without the support of non-scheme ports across the country it quickly proved futile. After the strike ended, those who kept their jobs returned to the docks, marching in formation from the town centre led by a bagpipe band. When they arrived, they found their working conditions noticeably degraded. One worker, interviewed by the historian Brian Marren, remembered that, on their first day back, the company they worked for made them sweep the quay rather than go home after finishing their work, which was seen as unnecessary and punishing 'busy work'.[88] The new labour regime was characterised by myriad petty humiliations such as these. Another dock worker remembered how, on his first day back at work after the strike:

> They told us there would no longer be any demarcation between jobs. We would be expected to do any job necessary regardless of title… and they called us all POWs, short for Port Operations Workers, or as we called it, 'Prisoners of Work'. I'm sure this title was purposely abbreviated this way just to send us a message as to who was now going to be in charge… most of us were handed brooms and told to sweep the quay. Dockers never did that before, that was a cleaner's job… This boss turned to [a] stevedore… and he said 'I have a special job for you, I want you to go… and clean out the toilets…' The foreman then shouted so everyone could hear

> him, 'From now on since the Scheme is gone you will do what you're told, or go fuck off back to where you came from!' So the old fellow took the cleaning materials and walked towards the toilets... He turned to me and said 'I can't do this.'... With that he walked back to the office and told the foreman, 'I can't do this. I want to leave...' I could see this poor old fellow was a broken man.[89]

Meanwhile, another indignity came a few years later when a dock worker fell and was killed in the hold of a ship. His employer refused to allow his workers to take a 24-hour break as a mark of respect, an ancient customary tradition.[90]

Along with this loss of status came the return of precarity. After 1989, the MDHC hired independent companies to recruit workers on insecure contracts to supplement the labour once performed by registered dock workers. In 1993, in line with these more flexible working arrangements, shift patterns at the Seaforth container terminal were changed to a twelve-hour schedule based on 117 hours over three weeks with flexible start times and labour permanently 'on call'. This entailed waiting by the phone to be summoned into the docks to work shifts at unpredictable times. The MDHC would often hand-deliver messages to their houses or their neighbours if they couldn't be contacted on the phone. Workers who weren't home when needed would be quizzed on their whereabouts at the beginning of their next shift.[91] A dock worker's wife described the terrible toll this took on family lives:

> He'd go to work in the morning, come home in the evening. Work would then call at say 9 o'clock at night. They'd say report back to work at 4 o'clock in the morning... the phone would ring again, and they'd say disregard the last message. A half-hour later the phone would ring yet one more time and they'd tell him... they need him back on the docks at 2 o'clock in the morning. This would go on day and night. I can't begin to tell you what a terrible intrusion this was into our lives. I mean you couldn't realistically go out for

> a drink or plan anything… It was beginning to affect our home life. I mean my husband used to be the life of the party… but around this time he just became withdrawn and depressed.[92]

This is where, by the end of the twentieth century, the long historical arc of Liverpool dock work had finally touched down. Instead of the fraught call stands of the early twentieth century, dock workers were being summoned from their homes by repeated telephone calls with mixed messages sometimes late into the night.

In 1971, the historian Gareth Stedman Jones published *Outcast London*, one of the most influential works of British social history.[93] Like many histories written during that era, the book was an account of the formation of Britain's working class in the nineteenth century. However, unlike similar narratives that tended to dwell on waged labour in the industrial heartlands of the north, Stedman Jones focused instead on the fleeting, casual, transient and unorganised workforce in London. The book told the story of how dock workers, builders and other seasonal labourers, once denigrated as outsiders to Britain's social order and deemed a threat to liberal orthodoxies, were eventually incorporated into Britain's national community through war, permanent work and extraordinary instances of solidarity.

Unbeknownst to Stedman Jones, he was writing this account during the same decade that many of these victories would be undone. Reading *Outcast London* in the ruins of the world it describes, from a place where the working class are composed of Deliveroo workers, Uber drivers, outsourced office cleaners and university lecturers on fixed-term contracts making less than minimum wage, it is tempting to indulge in nostalgia. However, as we have already seen in this book, and as future chapters will show, even at its mid-century heyday working-class affluence and job security was limited and conditional in Britain. African seafarers who loaded and serviced many of the ships that arrived in Liverpool continued to battle against insecurity and low rates of pay, and as victims of the decline of the docks they are largely forgotten, banished from sight by restrictive immigration policies. Likewise, as we saw in Chapter 2, the women who worked as typists, canteen servers and ships' cleaners tended to be excluded from the unions that had rescued their male counterparts from precarity. Indeed, it is telling that the most shocking indignity described by Liverpool's male dock workers on their return to work after the 1989 strike was having to clean the quay and the toilets. It seemed that the best way for employers to reveal to dock workers their new, fallen status was to give them work that had historically been performed by women. The conditions of the sections of the labour force that remained precarious throughout the twentieth century turned out to be contagious. Like a small wildfire left unattended, these working conditions were allowed to spread once again through the rest of the workforce.

In September 1995, Liverpool's dock workers were dismissed *en masse* by the MDHC after they refused to cross a picket line in solidarity with workers who had been made redundant by Torside, a contractor who had been hiring low-paid supplemental labour. The event triggered a strike that was something akin to a last stand for the small number of dock workers who remained employed. As much as anything else, this was an act of inter-generational solidarity. Many Torside workers were the children of former registered dock workers who could only follow their father's footsteps by taking outsourced insecure jobs.[94] The strike of 1995–8 was one of the longest in the city's history, and garnered support from celebrities such as Noel Gallagher and Robbie Fowler (who was fined for displaying a shirt advertising the dock workers' cause while playing for Liverpool in a European Cup Winners' Cup game in 1997). As with the Miners' Strike ten years earlier, the strike also provided a limited opportunity for women's involvement in a forum that had previously been dominated by men. A group called the Women of the Waterfront, largely made up of wives and mothers of dock workers, supported pickets, raised awareness of the strike and sung Jimmy Nail's dirge about the collapse of industry on the Tyne, 'Big River', outside the homes of scabs and managers.[95]

Most importantly, however, the strike struck a chord with a nascent community of dock workers across the world whose working conditions had also been eroded by technological change and neoliberal labour reforms over the previous two decades. The strikers were early adopters of the Internet as a tool for publicity and horizontal organisation. They used a website called LabourNet, run by an activist from Cambridge and a freelance journalist from Liverpool, to gather stories and pictures and forge global networks.[96] In January 1997, the movement succeeded in organising 24-hour simultaneous shutdowns of more than a hundred ports across twenty-seven countries including the United States, Sweden, New Zealand, Australia, South Africa and Japan. While the action succeeded in closing the western seaboard of the United States, dock workers in Los Angeles and Oakland, each an overwhelmingly Black workforce, limited their strike to just eight hours, suspicious of why, in a diverse post-colonial city such as Liverpool, every dock worker was white. These concerns were partially diffused by dock workers in Durban, South Africa, who highlighted the unqualified support shown by Liverpool's dock workers for the anti-apartheid struggle.[97] Later that year, this hastily assembled global community drew a symbolic picket line around a single ship, the *Neptune Jade*, which had been serviced by scab labour at the MDHC's newly purchased Medway terminal. The movement of the ship was tracked online and, after failed landings in Oakland, Vancouver, Yokohama and Kobe, the ship had to be sold.[98]

If we are very optimistic, we can see in the events of 1995–8 a blueprint for the future. Among these various actions, co-ordinated across the planet, there is hope, perhaps, that the limited solidarities that won job security for segments of the working class in the twentieth century, albeit temporarily, may be expanded, and vested with new imagination, in the twenty-first.

5

Made Surplus

At the beginning of the 1980s, during Margaret Thatcher's first term as Prime Minister and a period of profound economic crisis, millions of Britons watched a television show featuring a fictional gang of unemployed tarmac-layers from Liverpool. From the perspective of our current time, an era when few people could say how tarmac is laid or by whom, this is hard to imagine. *The Boys from the Blackstuff* was a brief and wildly acclaimed series based on a 1978 play by the left-leaning social realist Alan Bleasdale. Like the millions of other unemployed people across Britain, the show's characters spent their time on screen piecing together odd-jobs and struggling to survive in a world without work, all in the labyrinthine ruins of Liverpool's inner city. In the first episode, the characters, perpetually on the run from a hapless pair of 'sniffers' – welfare officers tasked with proving that the men were breaking the terms of their unemployment benefits – take an under-the-table construction job to supplement their income from the dole. At the end of the episode, it's revealed that the structure the men had been hired to build was a brand-new unemployment office. There is perhaps no better image of the circuitous nihilism of Liverpool's late twentieth-century labour market than this: a group of men engaged in informal, criminalised work to build the infrastructure that sustained their own obsolescence.

It was never meant to be this way. Since the 1930s, local and national governments had been fashioning a life raft for

Liverpool's economy. As we saw in Chapter 2, this took the form of hundreds of new factories compelled by incentives and nudges into setting up their operations in new industrial estates in Liverpool's expanding suburbs. While few predicted that dock work would collapse so quickly in the 1970s and 1980s, the squat, low-rise factories, tethered to mile after mile of suburban cul-de-sacs hastily built over Lancashire farmland, were supposed to be shock absorbers, compensating for the volatility of Liverpool's port economy. However, at the same time that decolonisation and containerisation displaced thousands from secure work on the waterfront, the new jobs inland were decimated by the recessions of the 1970s and early 1980s.

Open any issue of the *Liverpool Echo* during these years and you will find article after article about plant closures and layoffs big and small. In a brief recessionary window between 1979 and 1982, Merseyside saw 384 factories close for good, taking with them more than 25,000 jobs.[1] These included older firms that had been associated with the region's port economy such as Tate & Lyle, which employed 1,500 and closed in 1981, as well as the newer fruits of government industrial policy such as the Dunlop factory in Speke that employed 8,000 and closed in 1979. Many factories, such as the Huntley and Palmers biscuit bakery, which was founded in 1822 and moved to Huyton Industrial Estate in 1955, quietly vanished in Liverpool's economic twilight. Others, such as the 4,600 workers at Standard-Triumph's subsidiary assembly plant, also in Speke, fought bitterly and with small degrees of success against the demise of their work. In the 1970s, the plant was facing closure thanks in part to overseas competition and the rising cost of oil. Its workers launched a dramatic seventeen-week strike to try and save their jobs, a battle they eventually lost in 1978.[2]

By the end of the 1970s, Liverpool was no longer able to outrun its own obsolescence. In 1969, officials had confidently predicted that Merseyside would attract 37,400 new manufacturing jobs by 1991.[3] Instead, during roughly the same period, the region lost a staggering 92,000. At a time of high unemployment and economic turbulence across the country, the region fared worse than almost anywhere else in Britain, losing 61 per cent of its manufacturing jobs and 25 per cent of all jobs of any kind between 1981 and 1996. By 1986, close to 15 per cent of the city's population had been unemployed for more than five years.[4] The economic base of one of the largest urban areas in the country had collapsed. The region's tightly packed grids of terraced homes, its verdant, hastily built suburbs, its soaring council flats and its grand, shabbily converted Victorian mansions were stacked with people whose lives were indefinitely suspended.

Before delving into the drama of Liverpool's 1980s history, it is worth pausing on what this meant in two very different parts of the city: the mostly white working-class new town of Kirkby and Toxteth, the inner-city neighbourhood with the highest rates of post-war Black settlement. It was in these two places that obsolescence was felt most strongly in the 1970s. It was also in these places that the collapse of the city's economy ushered in a period of vivid political imagination and experimentation. As the promises of an embattled welfare state to provide secure work for white men were turning to ash on the streets of Merseyside, feminist and Black activists in Kirkby and in Toxteth began to construct radical alternatives. We know, of course, where this story would eventually lead. The activist state constructed after the war to guarantee male employment as well as healthcare, housing and education eventually gave way to a new brand of authoritarian, free-market Conservative politics heralded by Margaret Thatcher and her successors. But, among the poor of post-industrial and post-colonial Liverpool, workless and intensively policed, the future was still up for grabs. For a brief moment, new ways of being in the world and new types of solidarities flashed thrillingly into being.

For the first families that moved to Kirkby, history seemed to be moving very fast. In the space of thirty years, the new town, six miles from the centre of Liverpool, had grown from a handful of farms into a bustling, relatively prosperous industrial neighbourhood, only to become obsolete, almost before the paint on the houses and tower blocks had fully dried. We last encountered Kirkby in Chapter 2, as an example of Liverpool's ambitious post-war plans to relocate its slum dwellers and diversify its economy. Liverpool's local government acquired Kirkby in 1947, back when it was a village of 3,000 abutting a Second World War ordinance factory, and set about building an industrial estate and homes for 60,000 people. Between the two census dates of 1951 and 1961, Kirkby was the fastest-growing conurbation in Britain. Its population, 99 per cent of whom were white, were almost all decanted from neighbourhoods in Liverpool's inner city that had been slated for slum clearance.[5] With unemployment rates below 5 per cent for much of the 1960s, Kirkby's origins seemed promising. The town's newcomers were mostly young families. In 1961, almost half of Kirkby's population was under sixteen, and the new town had acquired the nickname 'bunnytown'.[6]

Bunnytown: prams outside Woolworths in Kirkby in 1964. In 1961, almost half of Kirkby's population was under 16.

In its early years, Kirkby had few shops, pubs or restaurants to support the residents of its sprawling estates. Indeed, one early settler compared Kirkby to Siberia.[7] This was a comparison made more apt by the fact that, according to one survey, a third of the town's new residents had been housed there against their will.[8] From the outset, this population was precariously dependent on a handful of employers on the town's industrial estate. Non-industrial work was almost non-existent, comprising mainly of a few clerical jobs in the back-room offices of factories. Most of Kirkby's biggest employers were branch divisions of companies that were headquartered elsewhere, a fact they had in common with many of the large manufacturers that had been attracted to Merseyside's outer estates during the post-war decades. As manufacturing contracted during the multiple economic crises of the 1970s, the newer factories of established companies with headquarters elsewhere were some of the first to close.[9] Between 1971 and 1984, Kirkby lost 13,000 manufacturing jobs. In just four years between 1978 and 1982, the town's industrial estate saw the closure of eight plants and major redundancies announced at another thirteen, all of which were owned by companies headquartered elsewhere.[10]

By the late 1970s, the once promising futures of the tens of thousands of former slum dwellers who had been uprooted to Kirkby had been effectively cancelled. Life for many in Kirkby had become a kind of incarceration. In most cases, residents were wards of the local authority, forced to depend on punitive unemployment benefits, much of which were in turn recycled into council housing rents. A survey of Kirkby residents in the winter of 1981 found that half were receiving some form of supplementary benefit. More than two-thirds said they had no money left after paying their bills and half admitted to going without necessities in the form of food and clothing.[11] The thousands of children who were born and raised in 'bunnytown' in the 1960s aged into this crisis in the 1970s and 1980s. When the remaining manufacturing firms hired new workers, they tended to call on their in-house registers of redundant former employees rather than advertising for new hires, meaning that the labour market for young school-leavers was effectively non-existent.[12] As one Kirkby resident put it: 'If they send the career officer [to schools] then they should send the dole officer [too].'[13] By 1987, just 7 per cent of school-leavers in Kirkby found jobs.[14]

Kirkby's residents were scrutinised and pathologised by journalists and politicians, some of whom drew analogies from the post-colonial world to make sense of what was happening. In a series of lurid articles in 1975, illustrated with pictures of graffiti and littered with references to 'no-go' areas, the *Daily Mail* boldly declared that Kirkby had 'joined the third world'.[15] These claims were echoed by the *New Statesman*, which claimed that Liverpool had been allowed to 'regress to a third world economy'.[16] In his memoirs, the Liverpool Labour politician Peter Kilfoyle would describe how the city's outer estates such as Kirkby had become 'bantustans', a reference to the fabricated political communities of Black South Africans created under the apartheid regime.[17] As time was passing, the relative spoils of whiteness that had conferred state-backed housing and secure work on former inner-city slum dwellers in Liverpool was becoming meaningless. The great rescue missions undertaken between the 1930s and 1960s to save parts of the city's working class from obsolescence were coming undone.

The collapse of manufacturing in Kirkby, as well as deteriorating housing conditions, was felt acutely by the town's women. Planners were initially insistent that Merseyside's mid-twentieth-century industrial estates prioritise male employment to compensate for the erosion of dock work.[18] However, as was the case with many factories across Britain that utilised repetitious, assembly line-driven labour, the firms that set up shop in places like Kirkby employed large numbers of women.[19] These jobs did not automatically entail social or economic security. The work was back-breaking and intensively regulated, and women often still shouldered the sole responsibility for childcare and housework. One woman who gutted chickens in a vast open-plan food processing plant in Kirkby along with hundreds of others described her routine:

> I work from six to two and two to ten… up at half four… I leave the house at five. It's very tiring. You come in at half two… but you have to catch up on all the housework that you've missed out through the day.… You have to have everything done by five o clock, [for] the husband coming in, and then you have to start cooking… You have to try and be in bed by 9 or 10 at the most so it doesn't take it out of you too much.[20]

Unlike the collapse of dock work, the unravelling of Liverpool's suburban manufacturing economy in the 1970s resulted in mass redundancies for women as well as men. As the economy contracted, women in Kirkby were often the first to lose their jobs or the first to opt for redundancy packages when offered. Between 1971 and 1984, women's employment in industry fell in Kirkby by a staggering 62 per cent, compared with 53 per cent for men.[21]

It was in this moment of transition, as the ability of the post-war welfare state to guarantee jobs for men in places like Kirkby or on the docks began to fall apart, that Liverpool witnessed an explosion of feminist critiques of women's oppression in the workplace and the household. Beginning in the early 1970s, feminists sought to expand the definition of 'work' to include the unpaid labour usually performed by women in the home, whether this was the daily grind of cooking and cleaning or the less tangible but often equally draining emotional labour of caring for children and men. Beginning in 1972, a loosely affiliated network of activists, primarily in Italy, the United States and Britain, began to call for 'Wages for Housework', a demand that women be paid by the state for this work.[22] The idea was originally proposed by Selma James, an American feminist and wife of the Trinidadian anti-colonial historian and activist C. L. R. James. James argued that reconceiving of housework as work like any other would shatter the social isolation of housewives and allow women to 'begin to come together with other women not only as neighbours and friends but as workmates and anti-workmates'.[23]

The demand for Wages for Housework was productively ambiguous and triggered more than a decade of argument in feminist circles. For its advocates, it was less a concrete policy proposal and more a way of drawing attention to the contradictions of the mid-twentieth-century household, specifically the necessary yet unpaid labour required to reproduce society.[24] In the words of the Italian feminist Silvia Federici, one of the more prominent theorists of Wages for Housework, 'When hundreds and thousands of women are in the streets saying that endless cleaning, being always emotionally available, fucking at command for fear of losing our jobs is hard, hated work which wastes our lives, then they will be scared and feel undermined as men.'[25]

One of the most prominent radical groups in Britain to advocate for Wages for Housework was Big Flame, an organisation founded in Liverpool in 1970 and named after a Ken Loach radio play about a fictional strike on Liverpool's docks.[26] Big Flame drew on an Italian 'autonomist' tradition of Marxism in which workers themselves were organised independently of any formal political party. In its early years, Big Flame were particularly successful in recruiting in Merseyside's peripheral towns and suburbs. In these places, where both women and men's formal employment was collapsing in the 1970s, the group was insistent on viewing the region's economic crisis through a feminist lens. Activists in Big Flame encouraged women to re-imagine housework as comparable to the assembly line-driven industrial labour of the town's factories. As one publication put it, 'Husbands often act as foreman without realising it. And women accept their work as a labour of love and think it's a personal "problem" if they can't cope with it. But... it's no more their "fault" than it's a worker's fault who can't cope with the monotony and pace of the assembly line.'[27]

Meanwhile, as debates about housework circulated among feminist activists in Britain and elsewhere, the residents of Kirkby's council estates, workless and trapped on the remote fringes of Liverpool, were looking for strategies to contest their newfound obsolescence. Nowhere was this isolation and poverty more acute than on the Tower Hill Estate. Tower Hill was one of the last housing estates to be built in Kirkby, a huge, hastily planned sprawl of tower blocks and maisonettes strung together by featureless courtyards and ringed by a moat of busy roads. From the outset, the estate was plagued by mould, leaks and ruptured gas lines that, in one instance, prompted a minor explosion.[28] As one tenant lamented, 'I wonder if they built these flats deliberately to hurt us?'[29] Parents frequently complained about the lack of amenities for children, who were forced to play in stairwells or in dangerous, overgrown courtyards. With no nearby school and no designated school bus system, the older children had to cram onto unreliable commuter buses each morning.[30] Within a few years of its construction, the estate had an unemployment rate four times higher than the nation as a whole.[31] In this miserable climate, many residents, particularly women, were prescribed 'nerve pills' to get by. Speaking to a documentary film-maker in 1973, one Tower Hill resident described her feeling of abandonment and despair:

> I just dread for another day you know because there is nothing to look forward to… I go to the doctor's… and he gives me some tablets… You go down for stronger ones, you just start all over again. Same routine over and over, you just keep going for the bottle. You get that way that you empty them all on your hand to take them. It's the children that stop you. The first twelve months I was living here… I had to go to the doctor's and get my stomach pumped.[32]

Big Flame opened a base of operations in Tower Hill in 1972, and began working with the estate's women, creating a group for childcare and mutual support.[33] While Tower Hill's men contested their obsolescence on the factory floor, the estate's women battled with the local authority over the provision of services to make their lives bearable. Big Flame helped set up blockades to improve the safety of the roads that ringed its outskirts and campaigned to secure more reliable school bus services, recognising, in language typical of advocates of Wages for Housework, that the added labour required in getting children to school was akin to working 'unpaid overtime' from their shifts on the industrial estate or their work as housewives.[34]

Within a few months of Big Flame's arrival on the estate, 3,000 residents of Tower Hill began a rent strike, a decision triggered by the Housing Finance Act passed by Ted Heath's government, which raised council rents to levels that were almost intolerable. The strike lasted sixteen months, during which time a committee of residents, with the help of Big Flame, squared off with the local authority and developed complex systems for securing the estate from police raids to arrest those who were in arrears. A series of spies and signals alerted residents to any intruders. Rent collectors brave enough to enter the estate were followed and obstructed, a practice that led to the accidental kidnapping of a Granada Television reporter, with activists then 'using the opportunity to educate him'.[35] The arrest of two strikers, Brian Owen and Larry Doyle, triggered air raid sirens across the estate summoning tenants to march together to the industrial estate where workers at multiple different plants staged walk-outs.[36]

As in many political battles over rent and housing, women played a central role in the Tower Hill strike.[37] As the primary household consumers, Tower Hill's women were at the sharp end of the rent rise and most bore an unequal responsibility for the impossible task of raising young children on the estate. The rent rise added to a feeling of indefinite incarceration. One woman described the financial burden of the new rents for those who were unemployed and unable to find any other kind of housing: 'Why should we struggle to try and clothe and feed our kids as best we can on the same wage each week while the government… get fatter and fatter on our hard-earned money? … What do we do? Starve?'[38]

Despite the hardship involved, for many of the women in these campaigns, this was an enormously politicising and fulfilling experience. Although the strike eventually ended in defeat, one housewife, May Stone, described how her participation in the movement had changed her outlook on the world:

> Before the rent strike it was looking after the house, seeing to the kids, getting them off to school, what I was going to do for tea, having a talk with the women you know about

> babies and the problems you have with them... I still talk about things like that but there's a lot more to it, you know, it goes a lot more deeper... when you're talking about babies and you're talking about the clinics they go to, you're no longer discussing the baby's teething problems, you start talking about the clinics that's there for you... and when you start talking about what you're going to do for the meal... you start talking about prices... which is something that I've never, never ever done before... I knew that there was problems there but I didn't think... they had anything to do with me.[39]

In the agonising furnace of Kirkby's economic crisis, a new kind of political consciousness was forming.

The overnight ferry from Dublin arrives in Liverpool at 6.30am. Its passengers disperse from Pier Head each morning into a city that is still half asleep. In the late 1970s, depending on the day and the time of year, these passengers would have been a mix of workers, tourists and visitors travelling to see family and friends. Sometimes, however, there would also have been at least one pregnant woman who was travelling to Liverpool for an abortion. These women would often journey alone and in secret. After arriving, they would have to wait until 10.00am for the councillor's office to open. From there, they would be referred for an appointment the following morning, usually at the British Pregnancy Advisory Service, a clinic in an imposing Victorian mansion in Parkfield Road in Aigburth, a suburb in the south of the city. After the procedure, they would be kept overnight at the clinic before being discharged at 8am, when they would have to wait until nightfall for the boat back to Ireland.[40]

Between the legalisation of abortion in Britain in 1968 and its long overdue legalisation in the Republic of Ireland in 2018, and Northern Ireland in 2019, the Irish Sea separated two places in which reproductive rights were entirely different.[41] The bans in both the north and the Republic were made even more punitive by the social and financial disgrace faced by women who had children out of wedlock in conservative Catholic or evangelical Protestant families.[42] Between 1980 and 2016, 170,000 women travelled to Britain from Ireland, sometimes by plane to London but often by boat to Liverpool, to have an abortion.[43]

In the late 1970s and early 1980s, many of those who were forced into making this journey were met at the ferry by a group of women called the Liverpool Abortion Support Service (LASS). LASS was an early example of a grassroots abortion network, a type of organisation that became common in Britain before Irish legalisation in 2018, as well as in the United States, particularly after the criminalisation of abortion in more than a dozen states following the overturning of *Roe v. Wade* in 2022.[44] The group was comprised of more than thirty volunteers who used a rota system to collect women from the ferry and feed, house and care for them as best they could during their two-day stay in the city.[45] The group hosted women from both the north and the south of Ireland during some of the most intense years of warfare in Northern Ireland. For many women, these meetings with Irish strangers required a face-to-face confrontation with the conflict, something the group quickly realised, with one volunteer noting obliquely, 'we'd had insufficient political discussion of the context in which the network would be functioning'.[46] Despite these difficult conversations, the members of LASS were performing an act of unconditional internationalist solidarity.[47]

At the same time as working-class women living precarious lives in Kirkby were forging a new kind of political consciousness, the Women's Liberation Movement arrived in Liverpool, further upending the city's social order. Women's Liberation referred to a global movement that began in the late 1960s, emerging out of the great civil rights and anti-colonial struggles of that decade.[48] It was at the forefront of what became known as a 'second wave' of feminist activism, one that coalesced around economic, sexual and social rights to complement the partial political victory of suffrage won by 'first wave' feminists earlier in the century.

On Merseyside the movement began in 1969 with a handful of informal meetings in the living rooms of activists and in pubs. Early participants included Sheila Abdullah, a health activist who worked as a GP in Toxteth, social worker Pat Wilson and Catherine Meredith, an architect and town planner who worked for the local council.[49] Women's Liberation and groups such as Big Flame or the Wages for Housework movement had much in common. They all sought to expand the battlefield of politics to include the gendered inequalities of everyday life. Despite these shared aims there can be no doubt that the Women's Liberation Movement on Merseyside was more diffuse, more middle class and less willing to view women's freedom using the terms of the traditional labour movement.

From their earliest meetings, this new federation of women established two clear strategies: the discussion and sharing of ideas and experiences with one another and the launching of formal political campaigns to address a variety of problems that had been identified locally. In 1970, they collectively ratified eight demands that had been popularised by Women's Liberation groups across the country:

1) Equal pay for equal work
2) Equal job opportunities and training facilities
3) Equal educational opportunities
4) Equal legal and social status and responsibilities
5) State nurseries and nursery schools available for every child
6) Sex education in schools
7) Free contraception under the N.H.S.
8) Implementation of the Abortion Act within the N.H.S.[50]

These demands were intended to fight on multiple fronts – to support the status of women in paid employment, to insist on parity within the welfare state and to establish greater autonomy and wellbeing within the family. The group wrote that the demands would entail the 'creation of a new woman' that would 'of necessity, mean the creation of a new man'.[51]

Throughout the 1970s, the Merseyside Women's Liberation waged a series of battles on this terrain. As well as social gatherings where women shared experiences and heard talks from activists and intellectuals from across the country, they produced pamphlets for nurses and doctors about abortion and contraception, and opened a rape crisis centre.[52] The movement also created a network for queer women to meet each other and organise politically.[53] In 1978, activists from the Women's Liberation Movement opened a Women's Centre in the Rialto Community Centre on Upper Parliament Street. For 50p a year, women had access to a space where they could play pool, use a communal payphone and attend regular workshops on practical household skills that had been traditionally seen as male, such as plumbing and electronics, and evening classes on women's history, poetry and mental health.[54] The movement's archive offers partial glimpses of the thrilling feeling of newfound autonomy felt by many women who joined. Reflecting on her participation in an education workshop, one woman who worked in a factory wrote: 'I left school at the age of 15… my mother used to say girls don't need to both[er] about an education because all they do is get married and have children. I remember standing at the end of my conveyor belt thinking there must be more to life than this.'[55] Another woman kept detailed notes on a lecture about Sigmund Freud and the myth of the superiority of vaginal rather than clitoral orgasms on letterheaded paper from her husband, a senior academic at the university.[56]

Across Britain as well as in Liverpool, Women's Liberation forged an alternative social and political infrastructure for women, a vantage-point from which activists could challenge the patriarchal forms of the workplace or the family. Along with the Women's Centre on Upper Parliament Street, News From Nowhere, a bookshop that opened in 1974 and occupied various premises in the city centre, became an important place for assembling Liverpool's feminist subculture. Named after an 1890 utopian novel by William Morris, News From Nowhere was opened by two student activists: Maggie Wellings, a descendant of Liverpool's Chinese community, and Bob Dent. Although not formally aligned with any political tendency, the bookshop specialised in anarchist and feminist literature that departed from the city's longer-standing traditions of male-dominated trade union militancy.[57]

In 1984, when Dent left to become a journalist, the bookshop became a women's-only collective. During these years, visitors would find copies of books by feminist intellectuals such as Germain Greer and Shulamith Firestone as well as Soviet dissidents and Irish Republicans. At any given time, one might have come across an exhibition of photographs about Palestine, a meeting of a writer's workshop, a talk by the feminist intellectual Andrea Dworkin or the Labour politician Tony Benn, or the underwear of an old anarchist who used to wash his clothes in the backroom and hang them up to dry. During the early 1980s, the bookshop was repeatedly attacked by far-right groups who, as one worker remembered, would knock over shelves, break windows and put up stickers on an almost weekly basis. During these years, the bookshop suffered more than six night-time arson attacks.[58]

In the 1970s and 1980s, both News From Nowhere and the Merseyside Women's Liberation Movement struggled to forge meaningful links with the city's Black community. In the 1990s, the News From Nowhere co-operative made a commitment to hire only Black workers until half their staff were Black. However, due to a low rate of staff turnover and insufficient links with Liverpool's Black community, this proved to be an unsuccessful gesture.[59] Meanwhile, despite its origins meeting in private homes and rooms in Toxteth, the Merseyside Women's Liberation Movement was also a largely white organisation. The group was most successful in participating in international rather than local forms of anti-racist and anti-imperial struggle, including the campaign to free the US Black activist Angela Davis from prison or protests against the apartheid regime in South Africa.[60] Many feminist activists in Liverpool from the 1970s and 1980s remembered that relationships between Black and white feminists in the city were more strained than in other parts of the country. In a recent interview with the historian Natalie Thomlinson, one white feminist who worked at News From Nowhere remembered an incident where Liberty Hall, a left-wing social club, allowed a performance from a white woman who had been accused of saying something racially insensitive in the days before. This decision 'riled a number of Black women about all sorts of subtle things that had gone on for a long time… that people hadn't recognised'.[61] Another white woman who also worked at News From Nowhere recounted that it 'always seemed… very separate… I don't think it was a good relationship at all, really'.[62]

Instead, Black women in Liverpool went their own way. From the 1970s, an alternative domain of Black feminist politics emerged in the city that was mostly distinct from either the Merseyside Women's Liberation Movement or radical groups like Big Flame, who operated in the city's overwhelmingly white peripheral towns. Across Britain, Black feminists were fighting what the theorist Hazel V. Carby termed the 'triple oppression' of Black women, referring to their unequal place within hierarchies of class, gender and race.[63] The vocabularies of white feminism, labourist trade unionism or male-dominated Black radical politics were insufficient for articulating this emerging politics. In Liverpool, the fraught tensions between white and Black women's organising reached a crisis point in late 1981, when a Black woman called the Liverpool Rape Crisis Centre only to be told 'Well, what do you expect?' after confiding that her attacker had been a Black man. The event prompted a group of Black women to stage an occupation of the Centre and take control of the phonelines themselves.[64]

The most significant and longest-lasting Black feminist organisation in the city was the Liverpool Black Sisters, a group that emerged out of the Liverpool Black Women's Group, which itself evolved out of a more informal network of women who had been organising together since the early 1970s. These included Liz Drysdale, who would become the city's first Black female councillor in 1987, and the documentary film-maker Bea Freeman.[65] The Sisters were both a protest group and a provider of care. Black women in Liverpool and across Britain had to fight to secure their place within a hostile state where doctors, teachers and social workers were associated more with punishment than welfare. In doing so, they were often forced to establish a shadow infrastructure of medical provision, childcare and mutual support. As we will see in Chapter 10, women of colour were at the forefront of political movements to improve access to healthcare for the Black community. By the 1980s, the Black Sisters had two full-time and two part-time workers and were organising drop-in centres for Black women victims of domestic violence as well as an after-school creche for children whose parents were working. The group also organised demonstrations against the deportation of migrants, offered advice for foster parents of Black children and worked closely with legal aid groups helping victims of police harassment.[66] As the Sisters became more and more dependent on external funding for survival, they became increasingly institutionalised, eventually becoming a registered charity in 1989 and founding the Kuumba Imani Millennium community centre on Princes Road in 2004.

One of the great hopes of feminist politics in the 1970s and 1980s was a belief that activism could dissolve the barriers between strangers from different worlds, whether it was the working-class council tenants of Kirkby, the middle-class professionals at the forefront of Women's Liberation, the Irish women passing through the city in need of an abortion or the Black women battling for recognition within a hostile welfare state. In the end, gender, like class or race, was always too fragile a vessel to contain these diverse experiences. While all the different manifestations of second wave feminism in Liverpool succeeded in opening up a new terrain of political struggle and action, its battles were fought in relative isolation.

While Toxteth would soon become one of the most infamous urban neighbourhoods in Britain, few in Liverpool in the early 1970s would have been able to say with confidence exactly where it was. Although the neighbourhood has no formal boundaries and its exact borders are a source of dispute, most would agree that it encompasses a rectangular stripe of parks, boulevards, terraces and large subdivided homes that radiate outwards from the south of the city centre, roughly parallel to the Mersey.[67] Toxteth was a place made by history rather than cartography. In the words of the great philosopher of urban life Michel de Certeau, those who truly know a city 'make use of spaces that cannot be seen; their knowledge is as blind as that of lovers in each other's arms'.[68] Toxteth was given its modern meaning by the poverty and the political resistance of its significant Black population during the last third of the twentieth century.

For a hundred years from the mid-nineteenth century, the smooth operation of Liverpool's maritime economy had been dependent on the cheap labour of Black and Chinese workers recruited in West Africa and East Asia. By the last third of the twentieth century, these communities had become the vestigial remains of an economic regime that was passing out of existence. Although Liverpool's Black population were still mostly confined to the lowest rungs of manual labour, insecure jobs that the Black theorist Darcus Howe called 'shitwork', the predominant experience was increasingly one of unemployment and abandonment rather than exploitation.[69] They had been largely excluded from the housing and industrial policies that had attempted to save Liverpool's white working-class population from precarity and unemployment in the mid-twentieth century. While the residents of Kirkby and those of Toxteth may have known little about each other, both places were made and unmade by the collapse of Liverpool's imperial economy and the social order left in its wake.

At the beginning of the twentieth century, most of Liverpool's Black population lived not in Toxteth, but a few blocks inland from the south docks, close to what is now the gentrified food courts around the Baltic Market. This was where many of the boarding houses for African and Chinese seafarers run by shipping companies were located. It's also near where Pastor Daniels Ekarte opened his African Churches Mission on Hill Street in 1931. Sometimes known as 'sailortown', this thin strip of land, with its transient populations of seafarers, its shops selling foreign wares, its travel agents and its dormitories for migrant workers, was arguably one of the most cosmopolitan places in Britain. A journalist who visited sailortown in 1906 described seeing:

> A motley population of British, Chinese, negroes and Scandinavians, coming and going on their own mysterious affairs, lounging and conversing on public house steps and in their own restaurants. The street has been successively 'Little Africa,' the temporary home of natives of Manila… and finally, with portions of Pitt Street, the lodging place of Chinese cooks, stewards, deck-hands, firemen etc. who have been coming to Liverpool in increasing numbers.[70]

Much of sailortown was levelled by slum clearance, a process finished off by German bombs. Between 1930 and 1950, Liverpool's Black population moved inland. In the decades after the war, the imperial shipping routes that had sustained Liverpool's frenetic cosmopolitanism disintegrated, along with much of the empire itself, while many Black and Chinese sailors were either deported or purged from shipping registers. As the city was increasingly cut off from the rest of the world, Liverpool's Black population regrouped a mile to the east, mostly settling in the Granby ward of Toxteth.[71]

It is difficult to know for certain how big Liverpool's Black community was for much of the twentieth century. Estimates of its size in the 1970s and 1980s vary wildly, ranging from 20,000 to 40,000.[72] Until 1991, British census records did not include questions about ethnicity, meaning that Black Britons who were not born overseas were difficult to tally. In the 1970s, this was the majority of Liverpool's Black population. Unlike other British cities of a comparable size, Liverpool did not register the same influx of migrants from colonial and post-colonial territories in the decades after the war. While some of the early ships of the 'Windrush' era – the window between 1948 and 1962 when colonial subjects could claim British citizenship – arrived in Liverpool's port, few of their passengers stayed. In 1954, for example, Liverpool's Colonial

Welfare Committee noted that of the more than 1,000 colonial migrants that their office had registered as arriving in the city, only thirty-six remained.[73] Liverpool, once one of the most diverse cities in the country, was becoming comparatively whiter than the rest of Britain. The frenetic and sometimes fractious cosmopolitanism of sailortown had passed away leaving one of the most segregated cities in the country.

In Toxteth, people were living amidst the ruins of an obsolete Victorian housing stock. Anyone who has walked through Princes Drive will have been struck by the neighbourhood's distinctive Victorian mansions, with their tall ceilings and grand entranceways. These houses had once belonged to prosperous merchant families and the upper echelons of professors or deans who worked at the city's university. As the wealthier residents of Toxteth moved to the suburbs, these houses were bought by enterprising slum landlords and disassembled into multiple apartments. By the 1950s, they were riven with thin, hastily built partition walls. Communal kitchens consisting of gas rings were installed in the landings between two or three apartments.[74] Although the tightly packed terraced homes further north of Princes Road were sometimes in better condition, many had been reduced to patches of rubble by ad hoc slum clearance programmes and others were empty and shuttered. It was common for contractors to trap wild dogs in abandoned homes to deter copper thieves – dogs that would often escape and run loose through the neighbourhood.[75] By the early 1970s, over half of the houses in the Granby ward of Toxteth still had no hot water and two-thirds had no bathtub. Ten per cent were overcrowded compared with a national rate of 1.6 per cent.[76] In 1971, one in five of the ward's residents were unemployed, compared with one in ten in Liverpool as a whole. Over the following decade, Granby's unemployment doubled, reaching almost 40 per cent for men and 34 per cent overall by 1981. A 1982 survey found that in some areas of Toxteth the unemployment rate was as high as 73 per cent.[77]

A combination of police violence, day-to-day acts of white racism, council housing allocation and employment discrimination had effectively trapped Liverpool's Black residents in this small area of the city. As in many cities across Britain, the hopes of Black or mixed-race people for secure housing, and the social mobility that it entailed, were foreclosed in part by racism within the local housing department.[78] In the 1980s, two damning reports authored by the Commission for Racial Equality found evidence of systematic racism in the ways that council housing had been allocated in Liverpool, with people of colour, if they were lucky enough to get on housing lists, being shunted into older, shabbier homes concentrated in inner-city neighbourhoods.[79] Of 311 Black occupants of council housing interviewed in Liverpool, 24 per cent said they had been discriminated against on the grounds of race. One resident said, 'they make sure racial minorities are kept together, suburbs are kept for whites only'. A Black woman in Toxteth interviewed by the report said, 'Black people get housed in this area and they don't get given a chance to move out, they're just dumped here. I think the council has been racist for years.'[80]

A case heard by the Race Relations Board in 1974 is revealing of the difficulties faced by Black people in Liverpool who attempted to move even further afield by purchasing suburban homes on the private property market. A young, non-white married couple whose families had lived in Britain for four generations attempted to purchase a house in Liverpool's northern suburbs. After securing a mortgage, paying a deposit and signing their part of the contract, they were declined by the developer, who had concerns that he would be unable to sell the house next door 'because of fears that having coloured neighbours would adversely affect the market'.[81] While their complaint was upheld, it is likely to have been the tip of an iceberg of minor racist infractions such as the withholding of certain addresses by estate agents to Black families, the deduction of points by housing officers, the outright violence of white neighbours or the denial of mortgages that flew below the radar of the legal system.[82]

In 1972, the allocation of council housing became the subject of an explosive five-day burst of violence.[83] The unrest centred around the Falkner Estate, a comprehensively planned warren of five-storey blocks of flats built just east of the city centre and just north of Toxteth. It had been unofficially earmarked by the Council for residents of the neighbourhood. This rare decision to provide new, high-quality council housing for the city's Black residents prompted a backlash from the white residents of the older, more run-down estates that encircled Falkner. Shortly after the estate opened and while it was still half-finished, it was attacked by a white mob who mostly came from the nearby Windsor Gardens Estate. The mob, armed with sticks and bottles, paraded around the estate, smashing windows and, according to an interview with one resident, chanted 'n****rs all out, get back to your tents'. Over the following night, not trusting the police to help, the Black tenants organised a defence of the estate, recruiting dozens of young men to erect barricades and repulse subsequent attacks from skinhead gangs.[84] For Black tenants, establishing themselves in new housing estates outside of traditionally Black neighbourhoods was a dangerous and protracted exercise, requiring something akin to urban warfare.

For the small number who were able to escape, a passage to a different neighbourhood in Liverpool was not an automatic route to stability and safety. While racism within the housing department was often structural, institutional and insidiously difficult to prove, the grassroots racism of white people across the city was starker and more violent. The Merseyside Community Relations Council admitted that in the late 1970s and early 1980s they had received reports of racist abuse 'from almost every part of the county ranging from Southport to Halewood and the Wirral to St Helens'. Everywhere, that is, except Toxteth, where Black people were less isolated and vulnerable.[85] One local organisation in Toxteth reported that some Black families who secured council housing in Huyton had asked the Council to be moved back because they felt frightened and isolated and were concerned at the scale of racial abuse suffered by their children. Meanwhile, a Black woman who moved to a white neighbourhood not far from Toxteth reported that, during the time she had lived there, every single window in her home had been smashed, dog excrement had been put through her letterbox and her house had been pelted with eggs and bags of flour. Of twenty-nine families that were moved to a housing trust in North Liverpool, all but one had left within three years following sustained campaigns of racist harassment.[86]

For the white residents of Merseyside who didn't live in Toxteth, Liverpool's Black population – estimated to be between 4 and 8 per cent of the city's population in 1981 – was all but invisible. Residential segregation was compounded by the concentration of Black residents of Liverpool in low-skilled industrial jobs. An investigation in 1968 found that less than 1 per cent of all of those who worked in shops in the city centre were Black, and of those who worked front-of-house, greeting customers, this figure was less than 0.1 per cent. Some managers expressed concerns about Black people cooking and serving food.[87] Liverpool's whitewashed city centre was a telling contrast to London's Oxford Street during the same period, where the word 'coloured' was banned and 32 per cent of workers were from non-European backgrounds.[88] At the same time, the City Council, one of Liverpool's biggest employers, had an equally bad record. In 1982, out of more than 29,000 people employed by the Council, just 272 (or 0.9 per cent) were Black.[89] Locals claimed that the free council newspaper, *The Liverpool Star*, which advertised council jobs was deliberately not delivered to houses in Toxteth, a fact that one official blamed on high rates of crime in the area.[90]

Meanwhile, the city's two football teams, each conspicuous vehicles of social mobility for working-class men in an age of diminishing manual work, remained almost entirely white for much of their immediate post-war history. Liverpool FC's first Black player was Howard Gayle, a Toxteth-born winger whose first appearance was as a substitute in 1980 against Manchester City, after which he made three more appearances before being loaned to Fulham. While he arguably paved the way for Black Liverpool players in the later 1980s and 1990s such as John Barnes, Gayle remembered suffering repeated racial abuse from his own teammates, including legendary defender Tommy Smith, who confided in him that he wouldn't live next door to a Black family or let his daughter date a Black man.[91] Everton were a little faster in signing Black players. Although a Cornish mixed-race winger, Michael Trebilcock, made several appearances for the club in the mid-1960s, the club's first Black player is commonly remembered as being the Liverpool-born Cliff Marshall, who made his first appearance in 1975 and played six more times over the next year.

By the late 1970s, the toxic alchemy of council housing allocations, workplace discrimination and violence had created an invisible blockade that encircled Toxteth, trapping Liverpool's Black residents within a few square miles. Rather than the aggressive, expansionist racism of Liverpool's previous imperial maritime economy, this racism was shaped by unemployment, environmental ruin and obsolescence. It was a kind of racism that the theorist Stuart Hall identified as 'indigenous… the racism, not of a dominant, but a declining social formation'.[92] The deterioration of race relations in Liverpool and the scale of hostility that faced the city's Black population also exploded the myth, widespread in the 1950s and 1960s, that the city's long Black history meant it was a model of integration and racial harmony that other cities should emulate. Liverpool's racism, reproduced over generations, was a blow to colourblind liberal hopes of seamless assimilation elsewhere. When it was created in 1965, the Race Relations Board saw no need to base an officer in Liverpool because of its 'long tradition of accepting strangers'.[93] By the 1980s, particularly after the 1981 Toxteth uprising, the subject of the next chapter, the city's unequal racial order was no longer possible to hide. In the infamous, chilling words of the Gifford Report, written as a response to the 1981 uprising, racism in Liverpool was 'uniquely horrific… nowhere else in Britain are Black people so exposed to threats, taunts, abuse and violence if they go outside a confined area of the city; nowhere else is there such a devastating lack of mobility'.[94]

Faced with this hostility, Liverpool's Black residents organised. Black and Chinese settlers staked their place in a city in which they were increasingly unwanted. By the 1980s, Liverpool's Black population, now multiple generations old, had assembled its own distinctive culture of opposition, one that was stitched together by music, sport and childcare as much as it was by formal political organisations. While this community faced many of the same challenges that marked the lives of people of colour elsewhere in Britain, Liverpool's Black residents had a history that, in most cases, significantly predated the era of post-war mass migration from the decolonising parts of Britain's empire. For this reason, many in the community have felt unrepresented in national histories of Britain.[95]

The community of African seafarers and their descendants that moved from sailortown to Toxteth in the 1930s and 1940s had already formed a constellation of different Black social and political organisations that they brought with them as they moved east to Toxteth. When studying at Liverpool University in 1952, Douglas Manley, the older brother of Michael Manley, the future socialist Prime Minister of Jamaica, counted thirteen such groups.[96] Some, such as the Yoruba Association or the Nigerian Association, were ethnic or national groups set up by those who moved frequently back and forth between Liverpool and West Africa. Others, such as the African Social and Technical Society, were open to all Black people in the city.[97] The most radical of these organisations in the 1950s was the communist-aligned Colonial People's Defence Association (CPDA). As we have seen, the CPDA was formed to oppose the purging of African seafarers from shipping registers after the war and fought with the Transport and General Workers' Union over their hostility to the employment of Black workers by the City Council.[98] Other groups had explicit links with anti-colonial struggles in their homeland, such as the Liverpool branch of the Ghanaian Convention People's Party, the nationalist party led by the country's first post-colonial leader Kwame Nkrumah, who himself visited Liverpool in 1947.[99] These early years in Toxteth were also characterised by a more ad hoc and less institutionalised social world. During his study of the area, Manley recorded visiting multiple informal shebeens in private homes and apartments that opened after the pubs closed. This nightlife was made possible by an unofficial all-night taxi service run by Black residents.[100]

While Liverpool would eventually develop its own distinctive forms of Black feminist activism, these early groups were dominated by men, reflecting the overwhelmingly male proportion of the city's Black population in the middle of the twentieth century. While no white men were admitted to these organisations, many admitted white women who were married to Black residents of the city. Some of these women took on leading, albeit traditionally gendered, roles. Women members of the CPDA, for example, were often called on for childcare, organising a trip for 300 Black children from Liverpool to visit Chester Zoo in 1951 and hosting a children's Christmas party later the same the year.[101] Likewise, the white women who were admitted to the African Social and Technical Society were tasked with hosting the group's social get-togethers, a decision that prompted a minor scandal after one of the women 'began a flirtation with male committee members', resulting in her expulsion.[102]

One of the most successful and long-lasting Black organisations in Liverpool was Stanley House, a youth club that opened in 1946 on Upper Parliament Street in Toxteth. Originally proposed by the Colonial Office as a paternalistic solution to the 'problem' of Black youth delinquency in mid-century Liverpool, Stanley House, named after the Colonial Secretary, Tory politician and minor aristocrat Oliver Stanley, did not have a promising beginning.[103] After bankruptcy and a brief closure, however, the club was re-opened with an all-Black board and became one of the most significant cultural institutions of Black Liverpool in the post-war decades. Stanley House was a mix between a nightclub, a gymnasium and a hostel. Behind its Victorian façade, adorned with a logo of a Black hand clasping a white hand, visitors may have encountered Merseybeat bands such as The Chants playing to a packed dancefloor, white working-class teenagers killing time or the makeshift bedrooms of Nigerian seamen who had deserted in protest of their rates of pay. Its meeting rooms were where many of the early Black organisations described by Manley would regularly meet, including the CPDA and the West Indian Federation.

As well as music and politics, sport played an important role in shaping a distinctive Black identity in Toxteth. In the 1950s, the gym in Stanley House was where Hogan Bassey and Dick Tiger, two world champion boxers who emigrated from Nigeria to Britain, trained. Both men would become some of the most successful athletes to be associated with post-war Liverpool. Bassey became the first Nigerian-born world champion in 1957, and Tiger became a middleweight champion in the 1960s, before moving to the United States and dying in relative poverty working as a security guard at the Metropolitan Museum of Art in New York.[104] Furthermore, the subsequent decade saw the emergence in Toxteth of one of the first predominantly Black basketball teams in Britain. Named 'Atac', the team developed a distinctively American style of play and fashion. In an interview with the historian Michael Romyn, one former player, Paul Ambrosius, remembered: 'We all had these big mad 'fros… [opponents] saw the 'fros, they saw the attitude, and we had a kick-arse uniform as well… we were the first junior team to have an American kit.' Prohibited from playing in schools, Black basketball players in Toxteth in the 1960s and 1970s, like the boxers of the previous generation, trained in Stanley House, where a hoop 'requisitioned' from a nearby girls' school was fixed onto the fire escape in the backyard.[105]

Meanwhile, twenty minutes' walk north of Stanley House, ensconced on Mount Pleasant in the shadow of Liverpool University, were the headquarters of the Merseyside Community Relations Council (MCRC), a more staid and bureaucratic body formed in 1970. The MCRC was one of hundreds of 'community relations' organisations that emerged out of the 1968 Race Relations Act as a means of grappling with the consequences of post-colonial migration to British cities.[106] While these councils were useful tools for airing grievances and helping assimilate newly arriving immigrants, their bureaucratic structure and enthusiasm for co-operation with local and national government led more radical

Black activists to treat them with suspicion.[107] The MCRC, whose leadership included both the Lord Mayor and the communist, pan-Africanist activist Dorothea Kuya, embodied these contradictions. On the one hand, the Council worked with police and authorities to harass sex workers and channel allegations of police brutality into official complaints procedures that were ineffective and circuitous. On the other hand, the Council provided funding for cultural activities and played an important role in reaching out to otherwise isolated immigrant communities in the city.[108]

The MCRC also forged a vital link with what remained of the city's Chinese community. After the deportations of the 1940s, Liverpool's Chinese community had gradually recovered, reaching an estimated 7,000 by 1977, more than 90 per cent of whom worked in family-run labour-intensive Chinese restaurants or fish and chip shops.[109] As with the city's Black population, this segregation of employment diminished the Chinese population's visibility within the city. Although the city's Chinese community were more dispersed across Liverpool than the city's Black population, language barriers had produced high levels of isolation among many small family units. The community tended to live in deteriorating housing conditions. A 1979 survey of 141 Chinese families across six postcodes found high levels of overcrowding, with an average of 1.4 people per room and only 60 per cent having sole use of a cooker and 50 per cent sole use of a bath.[110] This significant yet insulated population were struggling to navigate a hostile welfare state, with many too afraid to see an NHS doctor and others struggling with council housing applications.[111] After failing to make links with the Chinese community beyond a handful of English speakers, the MCRC hired a Chinese-speaking worker in 1977 and within a few years were building bridges with local organisations.[112] Indeed, some of what we know about the early years of Chinese settlement is based on oral histories gathered by S. Craggs and Irene Loh Lynn, funded by the MCRC.[113]

Meanwhile, Liverpool's Black community experimented with their own autonomous methods of education. In 1974, the Charles Wootton Centre for Further Education was founded on Upper

Parliament Street, a college that primarily served Toxteth's Black community. The college, named after a Bermudian sailor who was murdered by a white mob in Liverpool in 1919, specialised in teaching a Black Studies curriculum, advertised as posing 'a threat to the fundamental assumptions of the British education system'.[114] This was Liverpool's contribution to a wider turn towards 'Black Studies' in Black communities across Britain in the 1970s.[115] Often operating outside formal institutions of education, Black Studies enabled people of colour to learn and help construct alternative histories and artistic traditions that had been denied by an education system that remained overwhelmingly white, utilitarian and nationalist in orientation. The Charles Wootton Centre coupled this project of self-recognition with an attempt to mitigate Black unemployment through various training programmes. In 1983, hoping to anticipate the city's future post-industrial employment base, the college opened a 'tech centre' that taught programming and word processing to young, primarily Black students.[116]

In the early and mid-twentieth century, Black activist groups in Liverpool had organised primarily as colonial migrants. Despite some extraordinary incidences of solidarity, such as the anti-colonial activism of Daniels Ekarte and the CPDA, the city's Black politics in the 1930s, 1940s and 1950s tended to be siloed into distinct and comparatively small groups organised by occupation, place of origin or even ethnic group. As the century wore on, however, their descendants formed a distinct and increasingly united Black community, one that was moulded by shared hopes and shared experiences of inequality and oppression.

What we can see in Liverpool by the 1970s was the emergence of what many theorists and activists have termed 'political blackness', a category that included the multiple diverse migrants from the Black Atlantic and even beyond.[117] At its most expansive, political Blackness was shared by West African sailors and their descendants, the city's significant mixed-race community, more recent South Asian migrants escaping post-colonial violence in East Africa and the subcontinent, Somali seamen, the city's Chinese population and perhaps even some of the white wives of Black settlers who played such a key social and political role in Black Liverpool. Despite their enormous differences, these communities in Liverpool had all been shaped by the British empire and its aftermath. Many were now finding themselves unemployed and abandoned by imperial networks that no longer existed. As the 1970s ended and a new decade began, the city's Black community would be about to face its greatest test.

Despite its critical acclaim, *The Boys from the Blackstuff* was only the second most successful television show to be made on Merseyside. Set in a fictional northern city, but filmed mostly in Kirkby, the gritty police procedural *Z Cars* would often attract ten million viewers or more during its marathon 801-episode run between 1962 and 1978. *Z Cars* focused on a troubled group of policemen, grappling with social problems and day-to-day crimes while managing their own tempestuous private lives. It depicted a new era of modern, technologically sophisticated policing, choosing to focus on fleets of 'panda' cars communicating through radio networks and responding to centralised commands rather than foot patrols. The decision to film in Kirkby was no coincidence. The Lancashire Constabulary were one of the first forces in Britain to experiment with special patrol cars beginning in 1958, partly as a response to the growth of new towns on Merseyside, as the force realised that its levels of staff and on-the-ground knowledge could not keep up with their rapid expansion.[118]

Policing was another way in which the fortunes of Kirkby and the fortunes of Toxteth were subtly bound together. For while these new technologies of police surveillance, communication and control were perfected in the Lancashire suburbs, it was in Liverpool's inner cities that their effects were felt most strongly. More so than the deteriorating housing conditions, the workplace discrimination or the crumbling schools, it was the police that made life intolerable for Liverpool's Black citizens in the post-war era. While their solutions varied wildly, every Black organisation identified police brutality as one of the biggest, if not *the* biggest, problem in Toxteth. An explosive conflict between the police and Black residents was about to change Liverpool's history forever, dramatising the city's obsolescence to the world.

6

The Uprising

It began with an unknown motorcyclist speeding through Toxteth in the mid-summer twilight. The young Black man was driving down Selborne Street, pursued by an unmarked police car. It was 9.30pm on 3 July 1981. As he reached the corner with Granby Street, perhaps because of the rain earlier that day, he skidded, losing control of his bike and bringing the chase to an end. The driver was fortunate, however, to have crashed at a meeting spot where a handful of locals had gathered to take in the mild evening. A confrontation immediately ensued, as the group prevented the police from making an arrest. Outnumbered, the police doubled down, radioing for eight more cars, which arrived minutes later. It remains unclear why the police were interested in the motorcyclist. Perhaps they assumed the bike was stolen. No justification was offered to the crowd, however, and the small army of police that were assembling at the intersection felt like an absurdly disproportionate response. The confrontation soon evolved from shouts and threats to batons and thrown stones.[1]

In the crowd was Leroy Cooper, a 20-year-old whose family had been repeatedly harassed by the police. His father, Lester Cooper, who had migrated to Liverpool from Jamaica eighteen years earlier, worked at the Ford assembly plant in Halewood. That summer, Lester was suing the Merseyside Police for damages following the repeated persecution of his other son, Paul, Leroy's brother. Paul, who was seventeen and unemployed, had been arrested fourteen times in the previous two years and required to participate in twelve police identity parades. He was charged on only three of these incidents. In fact, just the day before, Paul had been acquitted of an assault charge after it was discovered that the authorities had improperly altered a witness statement, although not before Paul had spent three months awaiting trial in a cell in Risley detention centre. With these memories fresh in his mind, it is no surprise that Leroy was one of the more enthusiastic participants in the increasingly tense showdown with the police. At some point during the melee, he was arrested for assaulting an officer and taken into custody as the police retreated from the scene.[2]

Even in Toxteth, where stories of police harassment were widespread, the treatment of the Cooper family was well known. As night fell, word about his arrest spread and anger intensified. Four groups of young men, each about a dozen people in size, patrolled the neighbourhood, stoning any police car they saw and breaking the windows of at least six. The next morning the city awoke to an uneasy peace, as both the police and many of the residents of Toxteth began to prepare for a full-scale war. In all the commotion the motorcyclist, his identity still a mystery, disappeared back into the Liverpool evening. Perhaps he lives in the city to this day, occasionally thinking of extraordinary events that his journey precipitated.

The stage had been set for a major confrontation between the police and the residents of Toxteth years before Leroy Cooper's arrest. Ever since its formation as the epicentre of Black settlement in the city, the neighbourhood had been under siege. The neglect of Liverpool's Black population in the post-war era by employers and local politicians was underwritten by police violence. In a city that was being made obsolete by the changing world economy, the police were called on to maintain an unequal and unworkable social order on streets that were hopeless and desperately poor. There was an important difference between this type of policing and the disciplinary measures – workplace tribunals, factory assembly lines, covenants to regulate the behaviour of council tenants – which shaped the lives of many of the city's white beneficiaries of state-backed jobs and housing in the immediate post-war decades. While the former measures were intended to mould their targets into productive and respectable subjects, the policing of Toxteth went hand in hand with the organised abandonment of the neighbourhood. In the words of one local councillor, Liverpool's police existed only to 'keep the lid on the dustbin of discontent'.[3]

With just four Black police officers in a force of almost 5,000, the police in Toxteth were like an occupying army.[4] Since its opening more than ten years before the uprising, the MCRC had been flooded with complaints about the police, ranging from muttered slurs to acts of unprovoked violence and deliberate wrongful arrests. Particularly damaging were 'sus' laws, powers granted by the 1824 Vagrancy Act that criminalised the transient homeless population that emerged in the economic crisis after the Napoleonic Wars. This archaic legislation allowed police to 'stop and search' anyone deemed to be suspicious. Across Britain, these powers were wielded disproportionately against people of colour and had been intensifying throughout the 1970s, a decade that saw a spike in anxieties about urban crime. Three-quarters of all sus charges in 1978 occurred in just three police jurisdictions, London, Manchester and Merseyside.[5] In the first seven months of 1981 alone, the four police subdivisions that overlapped with Toxteth recorded a staggering 3,482 instances of 'stop and search'. Black people on Merseyside were 7.5 times more likely than white people to be subject to these searches.[6]

Often these interventions were targeted, and police had ways of producing what they wanted to find. As early as 1971, there were reports that the police were freely using the term 'agriculture' to describe the planting of drugs on people they wanted to arrest.[7] Speaking under oath in Liverpool Crown Court in 1988, David Scott, who had served as a community police officer in Toxteth for twelve years, confessed to the scale of prejudice within the force. As well as detailing the day-to-day use of racial slurs, Scott noted that he himself had been targeted by his colleagues for having a mixed-race wife. In one instance, his colleagues scratched 'Yankee n****r lover' into his helmet and on his locker wrote 'don't speak to him, he's married a n****r'.[8]

At the apex of this structure was Merseyside's Chief Constable, Kenneth Oxford. Sallow, bald and ruthlessly uncompromising, Oxford had served in the Air Force before rising through the ranks of the Metropolitan Police in London and taking command of Liverpool's police force in 1974. With a cruel yet hapless verbiage reminiscent of a colonial governor, Oxford was notoriously unable to understand or empathise with the city's Black community. Despite being urged not to do so, he frequently referred to the city's mixed-race residents as 'half-castes' in public statements.[9] Betraying an astonishing naivety about the history of the city's generations-old Black community, Oxford was reported to have said, 'why can't these people come to our country and learn to fit in with our ways?'[10] In 1978, a BBC journalist who spent a month embedded with Liverpool's police described the Black community in terms that were reminiscent of the eugenicist language of the 1930s, writing that 'half-castes' in the city were 'the products of liaisons between Black seamen and white prostitutes in Liverpool 8, the red light district… After doing the round of homes and institutions they gradually realise that they are nothing.'[11] The article sparked fury and widespread protests in the city. While many were angry at the journalist's choice of words, it was widely believed that the article reflected the prevailing opinions of the police force and, by implication, Oxford himself.[12]

The breakdown in relationship between the police and the Black community in Liverpool was perhaps the worst manifestation of a problem that was becoming general across Britain by the late 1970s. Migrants from Britain's disintegrating empire had produced established enclaves in multiple cities. Although these communities tended to be less isolated than in Liverpool and had shorter histories and different origins, they were similarly scarred by unemployment and by widespread housing discrimination from local authorities and private landlords. Places like Brixton and Southall in London, Chapeltown in Leeds, Handsworth in Birmingham and Moss Side in Manchester shared with Toxteth a feeling of wilful, deliberate abandonment. In each of these places, the police had aided in this containment, cultivating an ambience of day-to-day hostility.[13] While police violence was often subtle, insidious and hidden, sometimes, as in the case of David Oluwale, a homeless Nigerian migrant who was found drowned in the River Aire in Leeds in 1969 resulting in the arrest of two officers, it produced vivid, national scandals.[14]

In 1980, the summer before Leroy Cooper's arrest, the Black residents of St Pauls, a neighbourhood in Bristol, had staged their own uprising. Since the 1950s, St Pauls was where West Indian migrants to Bristol had settled, partly compelled by a now familiar pattern of discriminatory housing practices. The neighbourhood had a rich history of Black protest. It had been the epicentre of the 1963 Bristol Bus Boycott, inspired by the 1955 bus boycott in Montgomery, Alabama, led by Rosa Parks. The boycott in Bristol was triggered by the refusal of the city's municipal bus company to hire Black workers.

The 1980 uprising began when police launched a heavy-handed raid of the Black and White Café, which they claimed had been operating without a licence. The café was a popular local hangout for the Black community and the raid took place on a warm April afternoon, with many turning out to watch and heckle. Eventually, an altercation ensued that gradually escalated into a neighbourhood-wide battle between the police and hundreds of residents. The police were temporarily and humiliatingly beaten, forced to retreat to what was collectively agreed to be the border of St Pauls.[15]

Although the police regained control of the city within the span of a few hours, there was a sense that the events in Bristol were mobile and thrillingly contagious. Throughout the night of the uprising, rumours spread, sparked by anonymous tips, that coaches and cars full of guns were being delivered to Bristol, from London, Coventry and Birmingham, to reinforce the embattled protestors. Panicking, police responded by setting up roadblocks on the M5 in the dead of night to search every vehicle heading towards the city.[16] Although these fears proved unfounded, it wasn't long before graffiti in South London appeared reading, 'Bristol yesterday, Brixton today' and 'Bristol now, Brixton next?'[17]

These were prophetic words. Like Toxteth and like St Pauls, Brixton had its own bleak history of unemployment, obsolescence and police violence. As new towns and expanding suburbs had depopulated inner London in the decades immediately after the war, Commonwealth migrants tended to settle in the dilapidated terraces that were left behind in places like Brixton. In 1981, the unemployment rate for young Black men in Brixton was estimated to be 55 per cent.[18] The neighbourhood's Black population had been terrorised by the Metropolitan Police's 'Special Patrol Group', a tactical squad formed in 1961 to maintain public order, which conducted arbitrary raids and incessant stop and search exercises.[19] Meanwhile, in January 1981, thirteen young Black men were killed in a fire at a house party in New Cross in South London.[20] Infuriated by the sluggish and indifferent response of the police to this tragedy, Black activists across London launched the Black People's Day of Action, a protest that mobilised more than 20,000. An already tense situation was exacerbated at the beginning of April by Swamp 81, an intrusive police operation in Brixton that saw an escalated police presence and almost 1,000 stop and searches during its first few days.[21] Many in Brixton suspected that Swamp was a revenge exercise for the Black People's Day of Action. It was also widely believed that the operation was named after Margaret Thatcher's notorious comments in 1978 that white Britons risked being 'swamped by people of a different culture'.[22]

Brixton finally erupted on 11 April. The night before, there had been a confrontation after a police officer intercepted a young Black man who had been stabbed, with many believing, probably incorrectly, that the officer was to blame. Over the ensuing hours, the Metropolitan Police ramped up its presence in Brixton, pushing ahead with Swamp 81. The police were keen to avoid a repeat of what had been seen as a humiliating retreat the previous summer in Bristol. The following day, when a group of officers tried to search an innocent minicab driver's car for drugs on a crowded street, the situation rapidly deteriorated. During the course of that evening, known as 'bloody Saturday', thousands of protestors clashed with police from across London on the streets of Brixton, with dozens of stores burned and looted and hundreds injured.[23] The events were a portent for a coming summer of widespread civil unrest.

After Brixton and Bristol, it felt like Toxteth was living on borrowed time. Earlier in the year, the Liverpool Teachers' Association had published a pamphlet called 'Before the Fire', featuring an article called 'Can it Happen Here?' that drew comparisons between Bristol and Liverpool – both former slave ports with substantial, over-policed Black populations – and noted that 'both cities… [have] a very naïve and complacent perception of race relations… it can happen here because the pattern is similar'.[24] In an interview with a journalist, one participant in the uprising remembered how 'We talked about [Brixton] for weeks and weeks… All the circumstances that led to Brixton were exactly the same, mirrored ours… although there were youths arrested, there were also police officers injured – and it focused a lot of attention on that Black community.'[25]

In fact, many in Liverpool had been on high alert for over a decade. In 1971, Margaret Simey, the bombastic councilwoman from Granby and outspoken critic of the police, had predicted a 'civil war in the city' if officers continued on their current path. When that summer passed without a major disturbance, she confided that 'I never thought we would make it.'[26] After the 1981 uprising, Simey said that things had reached a point where 'I would regard people as apathetic if they didn't riot.'[27] The bigger question, perhaps, was why something didn't happen sooner.

According to any measurement, the Toxteth uprising was the biggest instance of civil disorder on mainland Britain in the post-war era. Between 3 and 6 July and during a second flare-up on 27–28 July, 462 arrests were made and 781 police officers were injured (with 258 requiring hospitalisation). Overall, 150 buildings were destroyed and 214 police vehicles were damaged. There were more arrests, more injured police, more destroyed police cars and more destruction of property in terms of value than the Brixton and St Pauls disorders combined.[28] The event is best known, of course, as the Toxteth Riot, a name that this book eschews in favour of the word 'uprising'. As the social historian Charles Tilly has pointed out, the term 'riot' implies 'a political judgement', with authorities labelling 'as riots the damage-doing gatherings of which they disapprove'.[29]

The uneasy peace that reigned for much of the day after Leroy Cooper's arrest was broken when an anonymous phone call reported a stolen car in Toxteth. When the police arrived, they were pelted with missiles and surrounded by 150 people on Upper Parliament Street. The evening of 4 July marked a new stage in the conflict, as police and protestors began to square off in a more organised fashion, fighting for territory, advancing and retreating until 7am that morning, hours after the sun had risen. That night the police suffered significant losses. The city's officers had one tactic, one that was familiar from the streets of Brixton and Bristol: the baton charge. This entailed a column of officers rushing at protestors with truncheons and Perspex riot shields. It was a dramatic and intimidating manoeuvre, particularly when accompanied by the deafening percussion of truncheons on shields. However, it was also predictable and had diminishing returns.[30]

The protestors, meanwhile, graduated from stones to bricks to petrol bombs and to cars with accelerator pedals tied to the floor aimed at the police lines. In a city-scape punctuated by half-ruined buildings and abandoned construction sites, missiles were easy to come by. More sophisticated tactics were also reported. Police later claimed that gangs of kids on motorbikes had lured them into the courtyards of new housing estates where they were exposed to attack and unable to escape.[31] Decades later, many still remember the thrill of those early victories on 4 July. One participant, interviewed in 2011, confessed, 'I'm trying to restrain the euphoria, even after all this time I can feel a rush… To see the power of people, a community united as one with one target. People actually standing together and drawing a line in the sand… and they won!

Can you imagine that, to see them running, to see officers actually getting up and running away?'[32]

It wouldn't be long, however, before the police were better prepared. The uprising reached an extraordinary crescendo on the night of Sunday 5 July, perhaps the most dramatic single night in Liverpool's post-war history. At 2am that morning, Colin Bedford, the rector of a church in Toxteth, remembered looking out of the skylight in the roof of his home and counting more than forty fires.[33] Each conflagration told a different story. One of the largest was the Rialto Ballroom on Upper Parliament Street. The grand venue, which had once hosted the Beatles, had become a used furniture store called Swainbanks, which many locals claimed fed parasitically off the unemployed residents of Toxteth who had been forced to sell their furniture to make ends meet. Its owner, John Swainbank, was a Tory councillor with deep roots in Toxteth who had been unable to hide his dislike of the new Black residents who had settled in the neighbourhood since the war. In an interview ten years earlier, Swainbank had said, 'I've tried to get on with the coloured people in the area – my God, I've tried... it just doesn't work. Especially with those half-caste kids... all I see around me are layabouts, whom I'm supporting.'[34] His store was an obvious target.

A few hundred feet up the road, the Liverpool Racquets Club was also ablaze. Founded in 1877, the Club was a symbol of Toxteth's old moneyed elite, most of whom had left the neighbourhood. For the Club's wealthy members, its lavish halls with expensive artworks and polished brass were their only experience of Toxteth. The Racquets Club was best known in the neighbourhood for being popular with the city's judges, a group of people whose main relationship with the residents of Toxteth was meting out fines and prison sentences. For this reason, the Club had become a hated institution, whose opulence stood in awkward dissonance with the surrounding poverty and devastation of the neighbourhood.[35]

There was a messy logic to these targets, an order to what was selected for destruction and what was spared. No residential buildings or community centres were burned, a pattern familiar from the uprisings in Bristol and Brixton.[36] The Sefton Park Conservative Club, a significant distance away from the front lines, was hit by a petrol bomb, and protestors smashed the windows of Thatcher's Tea and Coffee House, a café run by the local Conservative Association.[37] When the fire from the Racquets Club spread to the Princes Park Geriatric Hospital next door, however, the protestors made way for the emergency services, and some aided in the evacuation of the ward's ninety-eight patients. The exception to this pattern was the widespread looting of Lodge Lane. Lodge Lane was the main commercial artery that ran through Toxteth, a street with dozens of shops and other locally owned businesses. Over the course of Sunday night, many of these shops, half a mile behind the main front line on Upper Parliament Street, were heavily looted, and some were set on fire. Most locals claimed that this was a rear-guard action carried out by outsiders to the neighbourhood, most of whom were white and tacitly enabled by the retreating police.[38]

The night was full of subplots, strange solidarities and minor happenings, stories that have been lost in the chaos and smoke. The boundaries between spectator and participant blurred. One Toxteth resident remembered the eerie sight of streams of locals pouring out of their homes and heading down Princes Road towards Upper Parliament Street, some to participate, others just to watch.[39] A journalist remembered being asked for a light by a child no older than twelve. Thinking she was too young to smoke, he was about to hand her his matches nonetheless when he discovered that her intent was to light a petrol bomb.[40] This sight was made even stranger by the fact that most of the belligerents in the uprising, both police and protestors, were male. Protestors looted javelins from a school sports office to throw at police lines. Milk floats were seized and turned into weapons. A fire engine hose was commandeered and turned on the police.[41] A police officer remembered being ordered to charge with batons at a group of people who had assembled on Upper Parliament Street. When the crowd dispersed, he ended up chasing a single person across a patch of derelict ground, at which point 'he turned around and confronted me, and I looked around and there was no one anywhere near me… and he's got this big long stick and I've just thought "Oh dear, this is it"… and my response was "I'll see you again" and I just retreated.'[42]

Sometime on Sunday night, Derek Worlock and David Sheppard, the city's Catholic and Church of England bishops, ventured out together into the chaos. They had been asked by Wally Brown, chair of the MCRC, to secure megaphones so he could urge protestors to go home. The two bishops from different denominations would have cut a strange sight amidst the chaos. They were able to secure a handful of megaphones from a police station. Not thinking it wise for Brown to be associated with either of them, they passed the megaphones on to a group of young children who wove through the crowd bringing them to him on the front line.[43]

At the same time, in a backroom in Stanley House, the Liverpool 8 Defence Committee was meeting for the first time. The Defence Committee, an ad hoc group of local Black leaders, was one of a number of Black organisations formed across the country in cities that were in the midst of uprisings. Although unwilling to deal with Oxford, the group established an emergency line of communication with his deputy, Peter Wright, so that they could keep track of arrests. In the coming days, they moved their headquarters to the basement of the Charles Wootton Centre. The Defence Committee would do much to shape the narrative of the uprising, calling for the resignation of Oxford and organising boycotts of any community meeting in which he was involved, as well as raising bail money for those arrested and condemning the looting of Lodge Lane by white outsiders.[44] Crucially, as we will soon see, the organisation also collected dozens of sworn witness statements detailing instances of police racism during and in the weeks after the uprising.

Meanwhile, the first four hours of the conflict on Sunday night were not going well for the police. Over the previous two days, officers from around the country had been pouring into the city on coaches to reinforce Liverpool's shattered and overwhelmed police force. Equipment as well as manpower was flooding in from elsewhere. Fleets of armoured Land Rovers similar to those used in Northern Ireland were arriving along with 400 new helmets from the Ministry of Defence and hundreds of military camp beds for the improvised army of police to sleep on.[45] Toxteth was playing host to one of the biggest co-ordinated police operations in modern British history. Toney Rooney, a sergeant in the Cumbrian police force, was watering his plants on his day off when a phone call ordered him to collect his toothbrush and a spare set of clothes and head off on a five-hour coach journey to Liverpool. In an interview with a journalist Rooney said, 'I'm a native of Belfast but seeing the troubles here is a different kettle of fish. We've never been involved in anything like this as police officers.'[46]

By the early hours of Monday morning, the fighting had narrowed to a 200-foot stretch of Upper Parliament Street. This was the north-western extremity of what could reasonably be described as Toxteth. Any further, and the road began its downward slope past the Anglican Cathedral and into the city centre. While the police had been in an almost continual retreat, protestors had been reluctant to advance further than the burning Rialto, and there were suggestions that the conflict, having reached a stalemate, was beginning to subside for the evening. Whether or not Kenneth Oxford knew this was unclear. Later, in a report to the city's Police Committee, when the Chief Constable was in serious risk of losing his job, he would claim that the police were facing an 'attack of the scale and ferocity, which, I believe, was unprecedented' and suggest that, unless urgent measures were taken, protestors would proceed down the hill and lay waste to the centre of the city.[47]

Oxford intended to launch a final, decisive show of force. At approximately 1.45am on the morning of 6 July, he made a phone call.

Two hundred miles south of Liverpool, the Home Secretary, Willie Whitelaw, was fast asleep in his home in London.

Whitelaw was a viscount from a long line of Scottish landed gentry. He had been shuffled in and out of various Tory cabinets since his election in 1955 as the MP for Penrith and the Border, a rural constituency in Cumbria. Since Margaret Thatcher's election two years earlier, Whitelaw, now in his sixties, had been a relatively moderate and unassuming presence in her fractious and radical new cabinet. At about 2am the minister was woken up by his private secretary, who told him that Kenneth Oxford had requested permission to use CS gas on protestors in Liverpool. It was an extraordinary request. CS gas, also known as tear gas, had never been used before on mainland Britain. Still bleary-eyed, Whitelaw made a snap decision to defer to Oxford's instincts and said that the final call should be the Chief Constable's to make. 'Amazing as it seems now,' Whitelaw wrote in his memoirs almost a decade later, 'I turned over and went to sleep.'[48]

Since 1965, British police forces had held reserves of CS gas for emergency use. Rather than being an instrument for controlling protest, however, Home Office guidelines had stipulated that the weapon should only be used in sieges or other instances where individuals were secreted inside buildings, potentially with hostages, and needed to be flushed out.[49] The gas canisters stockpiled by police forces had been manufactured solely for this purpose and were never intended to be used against crowds. The pressurised gas was stored inside cartridges that were designed to fracture and explode like miniature bombs on impact. Liverpool's reserves had been made by AAI, a US-based company headquartered near Washington DC, which profited from military contracts. When a journalist from the *New Statesman* called one of AAI's US-based technicians in the days after the uprising and told him what had happened, he responded, 'It's distressing. It's a lethal cartridge. The purpose is to fire through a window or door, not at people.'[50] At 2.15am, two battalions of marksmen in bulletproof jackets assembled on Upper Parliament Street with pump-action shotguns. They loaded their guns with canisters whose packaging was adorned with the words 'specifically designed for barricade penetration only… do not fire at any person or crowd' and proceeded to do exactly that.[51]

It is worth pausing, exactly as the first round of missiles were unleased at 740 miles per hour, to reflect on the longer history of this weapon. While chemical weapons had never been used on mainland Britain, they had been used extensively in Britain's empire. Colonial police forces from the Caribbean to South Asia were equipped with tear gas from 1933. It was used for the first time in Burma in 1939, and, within a few years, tear gas had been used against crowds to quell unrest in India, Kenya, Jamaica and Trinidad. At the same time, the weapon had been deemed unfit for use in Britain itself. Even while truncheons, guns and tanks had been used against massive labour uprisings during the inter-war years, tear gas had remained taboo.[52]

In 1969, CS gas came to Northern Ireland. The weapon was first used during the Battle of the Bogside in Derry, during which parts of the Catholic community launched a two-day insurgency against the police in one of the earliest and most dramatic instances of the Troubles. It was used again in Republican parts of Belfast in 1970 and in 1972. Indeed, the spectre of the conflict in Northern Ireland hung over the uprisings in Bristol, Brixton and Toxteth. After the police retreat in Bristol, Whitelaw had been afraid that civil disobedience might create 'no-go' areas in mainland Britain, similar to the neighbourhoods of Belfast and Derry that had effectively expelled the police.[53] Kenneth Oxford, meanwhile, claimed that participants in the uprising had learned street fighting tactics from watching footage of the Troubles on television.[54] On 14 July, when the uprisings across the country were subsiding, a delegation of senior British police travelled to Northern Ireland to be taught riot control techniques by the Royal Ulster Constabulary.[55]

The moral distance that had opened between Liverpool's police and the city's Black community had enabled forms of violence that had hitherto been unimaginable. After Toxteth it seemed that the destabilising, late colonial violence seen in places like Malaya, Kenya and Northern Ireland was coming home. As the Tory MP John Biggs-Davidson prophesied in 1973, 'if we lose in Belfast we may have to fight in Brixton or Birmingham'.[56] Many have described the 1981 uprisings as being heirs to a rich tradition of British unrest that stretched back to the uprisings of the eighteenth and early nineteenth century and beyond – incidents that were characterised by Eric Hobsbawm as 'collective bargaining by riot'.[57] A better precedent, however, might be the frequent suspensions of law and order in the face of emergencies in the colonial world.[58]

In the end, the police fired twenty-five to thirty canisters into the crowd. Phil Robbins, a young Black footballer for Southport FC, was hit in the chest with a canister while helping protestors escape the gas by climbing over a railing. Witnesses saw him fall to the ground clutching his chest, blood squirting through his fingers. A journalist on the scene overheard a policeman turn to a colleague, moments after Robbins was hit, and, 'with an air of grim triumph', say, 'they've just suffered their first casualty'. Robbins was rushed to hospital for an emergency operation that saved his life. Kenneth Anderson, who was walking home through the crowd from the Sierra Leone club, was hit in the groin while trying to run away from the shooting, an impact that ruptured an artery in his leg. Anderson was rushed to the operating theatre at the same hospital as Robbins. Afterwards, he was told by doctors that he was lucky to be alive. At the same time, the Coleman family were driving home with their three-year-old child after visiting friends. They had taken a circuitous route, hoping to avoid the front lines of the riot, but had miscalculated, and approached the police line sideways on. The police fired three canisters directly at their car, smashing the windshield and tearing into one of the doors, forcing the family to cower with their toddler on the backseat.[59]

The extraordinary night of 5 July marked the end of the first and most dramatic phase of the Toxteth uprising. As the fires cooled and the losses were counted, disorder continued to spread across the country. While Toxteth burned, Southall, on the fringes of South-West London, witnessed a pitched battle between Asian youths and white skinhead gangs who had travelled to the neighbourhood for a punk concert.

The period from 7 to 11 July saw similar scenes in Moss Side in Manchester. Moss Side, abandoned by capital, over-policed and with a large Black population, had much in common with Toxteth. The uprising in Liverpool strained the already fraught relationship between police and residents of the neighbourhood. Following repeated provocation from the Manchester Police, protestors stormed Moss Side police station, forcing police into a humiliating retreat and leading to multiple nights of conflict. Instead of repeating the mistakes of Toxteth, where stationary lines of police stood haplessly behind shields where they were vulnerable to projectiles, James Anderton, Manchester's Chief of Police, instead deployed roaming 'snatch squads' of Land Rovers to charge at small groups of protestors. As further evidence that the line between military and civilian counter-insurgency methods was fraying, this was a tactic that had been imported wholesale from Northern Ireland.[60]

As the summer progressed, uprisings spread across Britain like mushrooms after a rainstorm, finding fertile ground in cities and towns marked by poverty and police violence. By the end of the summer, as well as in Brixton, Toxteth, Southall and Moss Side, there had been significant civil unrest in Birmingham, Blackburn, Derby, Leeds, Nottingham, Portsmouth, Sheffield, Southampton and Wolverhampton, as well as in a handful of smaller towns like High Wycombe, Cirencester, Reading and Halifax. Nowhere, however, had seen the same scale and intensity as the battle for Toxteth on 3–6 July. The police and politicians, having regained control with a terrifying show of force, were about to unleash a tide of reaction across Liverpool and the rest of Britain.

Even as an uneasy calm began to settle over Liverpool, the shadow of further violence hung over the city. Senior politicians made it clear that the uprisings had created an emergency situation in which precedent was indefinitely suspended, and in which no show of force would be off the table. David Alton, the Liberal MP for Liverpool's Edge Hill constituency, demanded that the government put the army on standby.[61] In Parliament, the morning

Police tackle blazes during the Toxteth uprising.

after the gassing of protestors in Toxteth, Whitelaw was asked by a Tory backbencher if he would consider reintroducing the Riot Act, the draconian eighteenth-century law that gave authorities the power to arrest any group of more than twelve people. Whitelaw confirmed this was something the government was considering.[62] During a lightning five-hour visit to Liverpool on 13 July, Margaret Thatcher confirmed in a press conference that the police would have permission to use whatever means necessary to quell disorder, from CS gas to water cannons and even rubber bullets. She also noted that the government was considering a new Riot Act.[63] Meanwhile, during the uprising and in the weeks afterwards, so many people were arrested in Liverpool that prisons and temporary detention centres overflowed, a problem exacerbated by industrial action from prison guards. A small number of detainees had to be remanded in Rolleston, a former military camp in Salisbury five-hours' drive south of Liverpool, which later housed military prisoners during the Gulf War.[64]

This extraordinary reaction was given its intellectual justification by repeated claims that the 'riots' were merely the product of criminal opportunism – the logical extension of a perceived

Margaret Thatcher during her five-hour visit to Liverpool the week after the uprising.

urban 'crime wave' that had been identified during the 1970s, and which fuelled media-driven anxieties about muggings, burglaries and randomised instances of street violence.[65] Proponents of this pseudo-Hobbesian analysis were quick to deny any context or justification for what had occurred. Instead, civil unrest was deemed to be a symptom of a moral rot that was untethered from the context in which it played out.

Margaret Thatcher herself set the tone during Prime Minister's Questions on 9 July by insisting that the violence could not be explained by poverty, saying: 'There are many poor societies that are scrupulously honourable in everything they do and would not sink to some of the things that we have seen in Merseyside in recent days.'[66] Thatcher had been under considerable political pressure to downplay any material causes for the uprisings, which risked implicating her government's economic policies, particularly her brief and disastrous dalliance with monetarism, a highly experimental tactic of restricting the amount of money in circulation, accelerating the loss of industrial jobs in places like Liverpool. In a televised broadcast to the nation that aired on 8 July, Thatcher spent much of her speech defending this policy, reserving only a few sentences for the disorders that were then spreading from Liverpool to Manchester and were dominating the country's news cycle.[67]

Meanwhile, Enoch Powell, the far-right MP whose 'Rivers of Blood' speech calling for the forced repatriation of colonial migrants in 1968 had become a rallying cry for white nationalists, was also quick to downplay any social or material context that might explain what had occurred. In an interview on Radio 4, Powell castigated what he termed a 'deprivation' thesis that ascribed material causes to the disorders, instead blaming what he claimed was the inherent immorality of Britain's Black community. Revealing a breath-taking ignorance of modern British history, Powell claimed that 'we have had deprivation, unemployment and all the rest for generations and people have not turned out to... attack the police'.[68] These comments went down particularly well among Liverpool's own Tory elite. In the wake of his interview, the city's Conservative Association passed a resolution calling on Margaret Thatcher to replace Whitelaw with Powell as Home Secretary.[69] Even Michael Heseltine, often remembered as a moderate, dissenting voice within Thatcher's cabinet, wrote in his memoirs of the uprising, 'if there was a moment when Enoch Powell's dread forecast in his "rivers of blood" speech might have assumed a hideous reality, this surely was it'.[70]

Similarly, much of the nation's print media covered the uprising as if the protestors were in the grip of an irrational, premodern evil. The journalists who wound their way through the streets of Toxteth during the disturbances covered what they saw with a mixture of horror and dark fascination. Under the headline, 'Don't Their Parents Care?' the *Daily Mail* wrote, 'At midnight, by the red light of the fires they have lit, the young of Liverpool look truly scary. Like stunted demons they emerge from the shadows with throwing arms raised.'[71] In an editorial, the *Liverpool Daily Post* similarly portrayed the residents of Toxteth as gripped by an animalistic social degeneration, writing, 'it is useless screaming for money, jobs, and better housing while there remains in the community a mass of people who are destructive either by design or through disregard of responsibilities'.[72] The search for theories of causation that were moral rather than material or historical required some creative sociological book-keeping. In a different editorial published just two days after the most destructive night of the conflict, the *Liverpool Daily Post* blamed the tennis player John McEnroe's refusal to obey the umpire during Wimbledon that same summer for contributing to the 'weakening of authority' that had produced the uprising.[73]

While rarely made explicit, some of Britain's press echoed Enoch Powell's claim that the moral failings of Liverpool's Black community were to blame. The *Daily Mail* referred to protestors in a headline as a 'pack of hyenas'.[74] Although the paper's journalists acknowledged the presence of white protestors in Toxteth, it was implied that they were being given instructions by Black leaders on motorbikes.[75] The *Daily Express*, meanwhile, had no qualms writing that 'a chanting mob of 1,000 Black youths' invoked 'scenes reminiscent of the film "Zulu"'.[76] Tabloid photographers were accused of staging scenes of Black criminality. Early in the evening of 5 July, a group of housewives interrupted a photographer who had encouraged a group of local youths to assemble a pile of car tyres in the road and pose gleefully with stones and missiles.[77]

These same notes of moral degeneracy and inherent Black criminality were also hit by Kenneth Oxford. Speaking to the press on the night of 5 July, Oxford said the uprising was 'not a racial issue' and was caused 'exclusively' by 'a crowd of Black hooligans intent on making life unbearable and indulging in criminal activity'.[78] In the days after the uprising, Oxford found himself battling for his job, facing widespread calls for his resignation from the city's Black community and intense scrutiny from the County Council's Police Committee. Oxford was able to hold on to his job for another eight years, in part thanks to a massive groundswell of support from Merseyside's white, wealthy suburbs. Five thousand signatures were collected by the Young Conservatives in peripheral shopping centres in support of the Police Chief.[79]

Meanwhile, as the journalists and politicians departed Liverpool for Manchester, the city's police were preparing their own quiet retaliation. In early August, the Liverpool 8 Defence Committee began to collect depositions about instances of police racism and brutality in the immediate aftermath of the uprising. These accounts, which have only recently re-emerged, are evidence of a chilling counter-insurgency against the city's Black population. Heavy-handed raids of the homes of suspected participants were common. One witness, herself the daughter of a policeman, reported seeing police rushing into the block of flats in which she lived, several weeks after the uprising, rapping their batons against the walls and dragging two men out of one flat whom they proceeded to beat in the hallway, while groups of officers outside drummed their batons against their shields. When two Black women tried to intervene, one was arrested and the other was also beaten on the spot by three officers. A camera crew from ITN news arrived on the scene and were told by the police not to film the beatings. The witness alleged that the police then staged an arrest of a white person in the alleyway by the block of flats 'and told the cameramen to make it look good'. In her statement the woman said, 'I have never seen violence like that in my life.'[80]

In late July, one woman, unable to sleep, was looking out of the window of her home in Toxteth when she saw four young men walking down the street and a police Land Rover slowly approaching them. Her account of what happened next is worth reproducing in full:

> They appeared to look as if they were going past the youths then suddenly they drove onto the pavement, pinning 2 of the youths to the wall. They were screaming for help. There was no one in sight... The other 2 youths, I presumed they would arrest them, but about 10 policeman loaded out of the

> van, one of the youths was lying on the floor, 4 policeman dragged him up by his right arm and all the police kicked him. I shouted out the window 'There's no need for that, you murderers.' Everyone booted the kids in the face. I felt really ill and my kids did... My daughter had to smack me in the face to shut me up. I shouted from the window 'I witnessed that,' because before that my sympathies were on both sides, but they are not now. They just acted like animals... I woke up at 10.00am today and there was a big blue police van outside my Close, watching my house, staring up at the windows for three hours.[81]

The archive is full of accounts such as these, many of which were reported by Black women who played a key role in assembling evidence to protect the community from these kinds of attacks. One woman with two young children described seeing a young Black man run along the landing past the door to her flat. The next moment the police 'forced their way in and asked for Black n****rs and whores, and asked for a youth who had run in. I said nobody had come into the house... Eight policemen ran upstairs... They tipped the cot over and bruised the baby on the left eye... They woke up the little boy, 2 years old, and as he was going down the stairs the police hit the baby with a truncheon.'[82] Another woman described police descending on her council estate in Land Rovers shouting 'black bastards go back on the banana boat' and hammering on doors. They dragged a half-dressed man out of his flat, 'calling him names "n****r" etc. We all started shouting to leave him alone because he was innocent... The police were shouting abuse and said [possibly referencing Enoch Powell's speech] "there will be blood flowing here tomorrow night."'[83] Another woman described standing at the front door of her house when they were rushed by a passing group of policemen who shouted 'get the wogs'. The family barricaded themselves inside their home as the police unsuccessfully tried to smash down the door with truncheons and a brick.[84]

Some of the witness statements reflected the surreal chaos in

Toxteth in the aftermath of the uprising. One Toxteth resident had invited two policemen from the street into his home on 7 July for a cup of tea as a gesture of goodwill. Just as tea was being poured a heavy knock on the door announced the presence of twenty riot police, who stormed into the witness' home and dismissed the two baffled officers who were already inside. In the witness' words, they then 'pushed me onto the settee. They put my arms up my back and one tried to strangle me. I was gasping for breath. They were beating me with their fists.' The witness was then taken to a police station where he was charged with breaching the peace and where 'there was a plain clothed officer with a Polaroid camera. PC 706 asked him to take a picture of us both so he could show his wife and tell her he had arrested "a black bastard".'[85] Other witness statements capture a quiet, quotidian menace. One man who lived in Toxteth reported walking through central Liverpool in the middle of the afternoon three weeks after the uprising when he was approached by two officers, one of whom stamped a foot down on his and said quietly, 'you're scared now, aren't you? There's only one of you and there's two of us.' When the man asked if he was under arrest the officer simply said, 'its against the law to arrest people for no reason... Get on your way.'[86]

The frenzied police reaction that swept across Liverpool in the weeks after the uprising reached a climax in the early hours of the morning of 28 July. It came after two further nights of clashes between police and protestors. During this second phase of the uprising, the police jettisoned their failed strategy from earlier in the month of forming discrete lines behind shields and charging with batons. Instead, roaming cars and vans were deployed to quickly descend on and disrupt assembled groups. These were tactics that had been borrowed from Moss Side and that in turn had been influenced by the Royal Ulster Constabulary in Northern Ireland. One Black youth, Paul Conroy, had his back broken after a police vehicle mounted a pavement and crushed him against a brick pillar. As he was dragged to a police van, one officer was heard shouting 'make way for the nignog, boys'.[87] At 10.30pm that evening, an even more serious incident occurred when a police van slowly approached a group of protestors, revving its engines as a warning that it was about to accelerate into the group. While most of the crowd were able to scatter, David Moore, a white 23-year-old who had been partially disabled from a childhood accident, was unable to run fast enough. The accelerating car hit Moore in the back, sending him under its wheels and killing him. While two officers were charged with manslaughter, they were each quietly acquitted the following year after a short trial.

From the earliest days of the uprising, a handful of liberal and left writers and activists, mostly white, have attempted to put forward a colourblind explanation of what took place, arguing that unemployment rather than racism and police violence lay at the root of the conflict. This was the official response of the Labour Party to the uprisings, with senior Labour MP Roy Hattersley saying, 'I do not believe that the principal cause of last week's riots was the conduct of the police. It was the condition of deprivation and despair in the decaying areas of our old cities.'[88] It was also the line taken by Liverpool's Militant Trotskyist councillors who ran the city in the mid-1980s.[89] This framing of events was the tacit conclusion of the Scarman Report, the official government inquiry into the 1981 disturbances, which focused mainly on Brixton and emphasised that police brutality was a background condition rather than an immediate cause of the conflict.[90] On 15 July, ITN polled its viewers on what they thought had caused the riots. While the most popular explanation, at 36 per cent, was 'unemployment', the least popular, at 1 per cent, was 'police methods'.[91] This, it turned out, was an overwhelmingly white interpretation. A later poll would find that among Black people aged 13–24, 52 per cent blamed the uprisings on police harassment.[92]

While Toxteth was a neighbourhood profoundly shaped by precarity – a precarity that had a longer and more extreme history for the neighbourhood's Black residents – the witness statements collected by the Liverpool 8 Defence Committee show this explanation to be necessary yet not sufficient. The Committee had no doubt about the causes of the uprising, putting the blame squarely at the feet of Kenneth Oxford. Likewise, Margaret

Simey, a local councillor representing part of Toxteth, described the uprising as 'one massive complaint' to the police.[93] The police officers on the ground, with their documented history of racist violence, would themselves likely have been baffled by depictions of the uprising that focused solely on jobs and housing.

It was indeed the case that a significant number of white people participated in the uprising, not least David Moore who lost his life. While hundreds of young white men were arrested on the streets, there were reports that some middle-aged white women helped make petrol bombs to be thrown at the police.[94] For the Black critical theorist Stuart Hall, the most striking fact of the Toxteth uprising was that elements of the city's white working class found common cause with 'a whole community being silently consigned to the scrapheap', with the result that 'something of a black-white common front began to emerge'.[95] There can be no doubt, however, that Black resistance to police racism was the master-narrative that overlaid these events. In fact, we might even go as far as arguing that these temporary, emergency alliances with the city's poor white residents marked the extreme limit of 'political blackness' in the face of a shared experience of obsolescence and abandonment. This was the argument of one Black observer of the St Paul's uprising in Bristol, who claimed that while people from various backgrounds participated, 'politically they were all black'.[96] In other words, the history of the Toxteth uprising ran not only through the rise and fall of Britain's domestic welfare state and the fluctuations of its labour market, but also through Liverpool's imperial maritime past, which had shaped the city's society. In the hundreds, possibly thousands of young people who turned out to confront lines of police in Liverpool, we can see a tantalising glimpse, however incoherent, of the kinds of post-imperial, multi-racial solidarities that Britain's post-war welfare state was rarely able to forge.

On 11 August 1981, one month after the uprising, the Chancellor of the Exchequer Geoffrey Howe typed up his secret memo to

Margaret Thatcher calling for the effective abandonment of Liverpool. Howe and Thatcher had recently met with Michael Heseltine, the Environment Secretary, who had returned from an extended visit to the city with a set of proposals for its regeneration. While Howe confessed there was much to like about some of Heseltine's proposals, he also warned the Prime Minister 'not to over-commit scarce resources to Liverpool' and that Heseltine's ideas might be better suited elsewhere, in 'more promising areas such as the West Midlands or even the North East'. Howe concluded on a chilling note, 'I cannot help thinking that the option of managed decline… is one which we should not forget altogether. We must not expend all our resources in trying to make water flow uphill.'[97]

Howe's notorious memo was more descriptive than it was prophetic. Since the unravelling of the city's suburban employment policies in the late 1960s, what had been occurring in Liverpool if not 'managed decline'? The warehousing of unemployed workers in Kirkby's council estates, the intensive policing of the descendants of Black seafarers now forced into crumbling houses in Toxteth, the accumulation of raw sewage and ruined warehouses along the banks of the Mersey were all signs of a city that was being quietly abandoned. The events of 3–6 July signalled a dramatic refusal by the city's young multi-racial population to submit quietly to obsolescence and a hopeless future.

In 1983, two years after the uprising, as radical experiments with urban regeneration were sweeping through the city, an anonymous writer for a Liverpool-based Black magazine called *Black Linx* looked back on the events of 1981. Referring to Michael Heseltine, whose role in transforming Liverpool will be documented in the next chapter, the writer made an important point: 'The issue you politicians out there forget is that you got a Minister for Merseyside *because* of the disturbances… The disturbances were fought by the Black community [who] fought to be heard… a question that Maggie, local politicians, government Ministers, senior probation officers and the like refuse to acknowledge.'[98] The contribution of the participants in the 1981 uprising to Liverpool's re-making must be acknowledged with at least as much gratitude as that which has been bestowed on leaders like Michael Heseltine. If the redevelopment of Liverpool in the 1980s and 1990s can be seen as a positive step in the city's history, then the agency of Black and white protestors who channelled their anger into a co-ordinated uprising against the city's police force must be recognised.

7

Disneypool

In his 2009 novel, *The City and the City*, the science fiction writer China Miéville describes an alternative world in which two different cities occupy the same geographical space.[1] Residents of these cities live next door to each other or walk past each other on the street, all the time being careful to avoid recognising each other's existence. While many have interpreted Miéville's novel as a comment on life in partitioned cities, places like Belfast, Jerusalem or El Paso, it could also be read as an account of Liverpool in the 1980s. Margaret Thatcher's government oversaw a frenetic redevelopment of Liverpool, which saw the city fragment into multiple different economic and governmental jurisdictions that awkwardly and unevenly tessellated, like sheets of shattered glass. As we saw in Chapter 3, the 1960s had generated a shared vision of the future that was accepted by both its advocates and its critics. During these brief, relatively prosperous years, Liverpool seemed to be on an undeniable path towards suburban affluence and government-subsidised industrial jobs. This future, however, had been cancelled by the almost total collapse of the city's economy in the ensuing years. By the early 1980s, there was no longer any agreement about what the future had in store. Being a pedestrian on Merseyside in the 1980s, whether walking through the ruins of Speke or crossing the dock road at the busy intersection by James Street station, meant moving between radically different visions of Britain's future. It meant inhabiting multiple cities, all running on different timelines.

During the 1980s, the principles that had underpinned almost half a century of British urban policy began to give way. Once, local governments had been expected to raise money through taxes to fund infrastructure, housing and, to a lesser extent, jobs. By the end of that decade, however, cities were increasingly forced to compete against each other on a global playing field to attract private capital, which would, theoretically, achieve the same ends. In this environment, cities were expected to become entrepreneurial monads, slashing taxes, bending regulations and acting as clearing houses for private-sector contracts. The targeted industrial policies created in the 1930s, 1940s and 1950s to revive obsolete areas of the country were uncannily inverted. Development areas, where factories were compelled to move by local and national governments, were replaced with 'enterprise zones', libertarian power vacuums with low taxes and little regulation. The development corporations that had been founded to lay the infrastructure for new towns in the 1950s and 1960s were re-purposed as instruments for tearing down crumbling docks and factories and courting property developers to build luxury flats and gated office parks. The city of the early twenty-first century began to take on a recognisable form, as politicians, planners and consultants starting rebranding declining urban areas to attract investors, tourists and desirable middle-class knowledge workers.

In the early years of the 1980s, this new type of supply-side urbanism was tested and showcased in Liverpool. During these years, despite or perhaps *because* of its radical Black politics and its highly organised workforce, Liverpool found itself in the surprising position of being at the avant-garde of Thatcher's revolutionary national project. Merseyside was subjected to a rash of highly experimental policies – an enterprise zone in Speke, the freeport that enveloped the remaining docks in Seaforth, an urban development corporation that overrode the city's democratically elected Council and a gigantic competitive gardening show staged to reclaim derelict land – all in the service of transforming an obsolete landscape into a vast advert for a deregulated economy. While each of these new spaces marked a profound rupture with the urban policy of the mid-twentieth century, they each had fixed jurisdictions and invisible borders that passed through Merseyside, sometimes unnoticed. They existed side by side with streets that, for much of this period, were under the jurisdiction of a radical Labour Council, one that was preparing to mount a final battle to defend an earlier vision of municipal socialism.

For Thatcher and her government, it was hoped that Liverpool would set out the future that was in store for the rest of Britain. In this sense, enterprise zones, freeports, urban development corporations and garden festivals in Liverpool would create demonstrative spaces – spaces where time seemed to be moving faster and where people were invited to look forward to a right-wing future of property speculation and homeownership. To borrow a phrase from the Russian film director Andrei Tarkovsky, Thatcher and her ministers were attempting to sculpt with time, and Liverpool would be their clay.[2]

Michael Heseltine arrived in Liverpool on 20 July 1981, two weeks after the climax of the Toxteth uprising. For the next two-and-a-half weeks, his wide, square forehead and unkempt mane of greying hair was a ubiquitous presence in the city, towering over local politicians and greeting residents with a sonorous, halting voice. Heseltine was a property speculator and wealthy businessman who had risen quickly through the ranks of the Conservative Party. Since 1979 he had held the post of Minister of the Environment, his first cabinet position, a job that had already seen him squabble behind the scenes with more orthodox Thatcherites such as the Chancellor Geoffrey Howe and the Secretary of State for Industry Keith Joseph.[3] The Prime Minister and the Home Secretary had both paid fleeting visits to Liverpool in the days after the uprising, but it was Heseltine who would become the face of a sustained attempt to re-make the city. His role as the self-proclaimed 'Minister for Merseyside' would be a defining moment in the career of this still relatively young politician who had prime ministerial ambitions.

Michael Heseltine is mobbed by children during his two-week stay in Liverpool.

Upon his arrival, Heseltine set up a base of operations in the Atlantic Tower Hotel, an austere modern building that fronted the Mersey. His first attempt to reach out to Liverpool's Black community was a minor fiasco. Within hours of his arrival, Heseltine met with community leaders and journalists at a YMCA in Toxteth. After a few minutes in which Heseltine tried to explain his intentions, the Black delegation stormed out of the meeting, leaving the minister in a mostly empty room. Heseltine, who had moved seamlessly from boarding school to Oxford to the elite professional world of publishing and Tory politics, and who had recently purchased a vast eighteenth-century country home with rolling grounds in Northamptonshire, was a long way from his comfort zone.[4]

This became even clearer a few days later when Heseltine succeeded in scheduling a meeting with the Liverpool 8 Defence Committee at their headquarters in the basement of the Charles Wootton Centre. Twenty years later, Heseltine would describe this as 'the most demanding meeting that I have ever chaired'. The minister and two civil servants were escorted to the Centre on Upper Parliament Street by armed policemen who were made to stand outside for the duration. In a sign of the absurd degree of terror felt by officials towards the city's Black community, a member of the Special Branch quietly slipped Heseltine's private secretary a revolver in a brown paper bag to take with him into the meeting. The nervous politicians feared that, in the words of Heseltine, 'the wrong gesture, the wrong remark and the whole thing could have exploded'. Inside, the delegates, many of whom still bore wounds from the battles of the previous two weeks, blocked off Heseltine's exit from the room and attempted to impress on him the scale of alienation, harassment and precarity faced by the city's Black community.[5] Throughout, Heseltine remained sceptical of the 'political' Blackness on display from what he saw as a fragmented group of Toxteth residents from different backgrounds. In his memoirs, Heseltine argued that, in the context of the 1980s Toxteth, the term 'Black' had 'served only to widen the community of protest' and was associated with 'African-originated American protest groups', which he implied were alien to Britain.[6]

During his two weeks in the city, Heseltine subjected himself to a breathless slate of meetings with residents, politicians and police officers, punctuated by frequent press conferences. He brought with him a nostalgic and relatively uncomplicated view of Liverpool's past, claiming that each evening, from his hotel window, with a glass of wine in his hand, he would stare in wonder and sadness at the Mersey and the city's skyline, marvelling at the accumulated accoutrements left behind by the city's imperial maritime economy and despairing at their obsolescence.[7] As Heseltine shuttled frantically around Merseyside, provisional solutions to this obsolescence began to develop in the back of his mind. They came together in a hastily written 21-page memo titled 'It Took a Riot', authored by Heseltine within a few days of his return to London, which was circulated widely in government and leaked to the press. In the memo, the minister began with a compelling, although now familiar, account of Liverpool's economic collapse, followed by a warning about the radical politics that were emerging among the city's poor. His solution was Janus-faced. On the one hand, he called on power to be centralised, with Westminster superseding and pairing down local governments that were seen as too left-wing, too divided and too subject to rapid changes in leadership. On the other hand, he called for the burden of urban regeneration itself to be left to the private sector, which, he argued, could be induced to flood Liverpool with new jobs and homes. Heseltine was clear, however, that the private sector would need help with this task. To unleash the power of the free market, the state had to clear away Liverpool's ruins and create a vacuum of deregulation into which capital would be drawn.[8]

The early years of Thatcher's premiership saw a torrent of new and clumsily named urban policies that were showered on cities: 'Right to Buy' (1980), urban development corporations (1981), urban development grants (1981), enterprise zones (1981), derelict land grants (1983), national garden festivals (1984) and freeports (1984).[9] These were all issued by a central government intent on building a free market from the bottom up. By encouraging council tenants to buy their housing from underneath them, or by creating unaccountable new bodies that had the final say over urban regeneration, these policies each had the effect of reducing the authority of elected Labour councils in deindustrialising cities. The policies were examples of how a 'free economy' and a 'strong state' were no longer mutually exclusive – they went hand in hand. Liverpool was to be the proving ground where these experiments in neoliberal top-down urban planning would be tested.

In his final few days in Liverpool, Heseltine choreographed a surreal stunt to dramatise this faith in the ability of the private sector to re-make obsolete urban landscapes. The minister ordered his private secretary to telephone the chairs of some of Britain's biggest companies and encourage them to come on a tour of Merseyside. After a week of hesitation and brow-beating, the minister succeeded in assembling twenty-six no doubt baffled senior business leaders who, along with Heseltine, his wife and a gaggle of civil servants, were packed onto a bus. The bus, with its unlikely cargo of wealthy, besuited tourists, then set out on a bleak tour of some of the more spectacular areas of dereliction in the city. As well as passing through Toxteth and stretches of ruined dockland either side of the Mersey, the tour visited the ailing Kirkby Industrial Estate and the 'Piggeries', an enormous council estate in Everton that had been effectively abandoned. Crucially, rather than trade or manufacturing, the invitees came from the world of finance and banking, an early sign that Heseltine wanted to break with Liverpool's previous sources of wealth.[10]

The first, and arguably for Liverpool most consequential, step in this new direction was the formation of urban development corporations. These were Heseltine's idea from the outset. While they were already in the works when the uprisings began in the summer of 1981, the civil unrest drew attention and added urgency to these strange new bodies. Their bland name masked an astonishing transfer of power from local authorities to the central government and property speculators. Urban development corporations were modelled on the development corporations that had been formed in the 1940s, 1950s and 1960s to plan new towns such as Runcorn and Milton Keynes, whose personnel were directly appointed by the government and were given exceptional powers to buy, sell and redevelop land.[11] However, unlike the new town development corporations that were granted rural land in places like Lancashire or Buckinghamshire, urban development corporations were trusted with large areas of existing towns and cities. Instead of assembling the landscape of council estates, modernist shopping precincts and ready-made factories that were distinctive of mid-century new towns, they were tasked with disassembling ruined docks and factories and reclaiming polluted land for property speculators to do with what they wished.

In 1981, Heseltine succeeded in winning permission for his scheme from the more reluctant members of Thatcher's cabinet, and in March that year two urban development corporations were formed – one in the London Docklands and the other in Liverpool.[12] The Merseyside Development Corporation (MDC) and its more than forty full-time staff were headquartered in the Liver Building, the soaring turn-of-the-century landmark that overlooked the Mersey. Its first Chief Executive, Basil Bean, had previously worked on the planning team for the new town of Skelmersdale, which had been built in the 1960s to absorb Merseyside's surplus population. Bean, in his early fifties, with slicked-back hair and thick-framed glasses, bragged of his long working hours and his domestic incompetence. Each Monday he commuted into Liverpool from Northampton with five labelled meals to eat during the week cooked by his wife.[13]

During its seventeen-year existence the MDC accumulated thousands of acres of land on both sides of the river, much of which was ceded at fire-sale prices, mostly from local authorities, British Rail and the beleaguered Merseyside Dock and Harbour Company. Most of this land was in ruins – crenellated with disused warehouses, empty silos and abandoned offices and sat atop a subterranean labyrinth of rusted pipes and tangled, disused electrical cables. Using generations of topographical surveys archived by the local government, the MDC took stock of these complex new assets.[14] With the help of the Manpower Services Commission, a government-run employment programme founded in the early 1970s, the MDC employed hundreds of workers to begin the work of cleaning and demolition. Meanwhile, within months of its formation, the leadership team of the MDC set out on a tour of port cities in North America that had been similarly decimated by containerisation such as Baltimore, New York, Philadelphia, Boston, Toronto and Montreal. Some of these places, most notably Baltimore, had already re-purposed their former docks as pedestrianised entertainment complexes. While the team were impressed by what they saw, they also noted that, in most of these cities, the patches of ruined dockland paled in size when compared with the dereliction in Merseyside.[15]

Despite its extraordinary powers, the body had few clear long-term plans for the overall look and feel of the land it acquired, and was happy to outsource much of its work, mostly to private developers. The MDC relentlessly reiterated that its sole mission was to prime the pump for private capital.[16] While the core staff of the MDC remained small and the body employed very few workers on permanent contracts, they established relations with more than 130 different consultants in its first two years.[17] Branding was an early part of this strategy. Four public relations firms were invited to give presentations to the board, after which a company called 'Creative Business' was hired to promote the Development Corporation across Britain and overseas.[18]

The MDC's most famous and most conspicuous project was the re-making of Liverpool's immediate riverfront, and, in particular, the grand Victorian complex of docks and warehouses that made up the Albert Dock, just a short walk from the city centre. The redevelopment of the Albert Dock was outsourced to a private property developer named Arrowcroft, who were given a 150-year lease of the land and the buildings in 1983. Built in the 1840s, the Albert Dock's ornate, fireproof warehouses had been used to store cotton, much of which had been grown by enslaved people in the US South, which was then channelled inland to fuel Lancashire's textile mills. Its warehouses and offices were listed buildings and widely regarded as architectural wonders.[19] Although its dock had been rarely used since the Second World War, its many warehouses and offices still teemed with life until the redirection of shipping to Seaforth in the early 1970s. By then, the Albert Dock had outlived its function. The dock had been abandoned for more than a decade by the time the MDC acquired it. Plans to turn the site into a government-sponsored industrial estate or a new polytechnic university had stalled. These earlier visions had belonged to a prior regime of state-directed planning.[20] Instead, the MDC proposed something radically different: to turn the Albert Dock into a gigantic entertainment and leisure complex to attract tourists.

Over the space of half a decade, the dock's loading bays and jetties were re-made into a warren of bridges and walkways, offering visitors views of Liverpool's skyline as well as of Birkenhead across the Mersey. Cafés, restaurants and shops were opened in the sides of the dock's internal quadrangles. The old Piermaster's House and an adjoining warehouse were converted into a new Maritime Museum, which opened in 1984. We will see in a later chapter how this waterfront development formed the basis of a new 'heritage'-based economy for Liverpool in which the city's imperial maritime history would be put to work in a quest to attract tourists and money.

At the same time, in a decision that would have baffled urban planners of an earlier generation, art was called on to accelerate the alchemic process of urban regeneration. In 1985, it was announced that Tate Liverpool, a new art gallery funded jointly by the MDC and the central government, would be retrofitted into the grounds of a former Albert Dock warehouse, scheduled to open in 1988. This was to be one of the major centrepieces of Liverpool's regeneration – a statement that the future economy of the city would depend on the deployment of culture to attract visitors. From the outset, the announcement was framed in the local press as a boon for tourism and finance rather than art. Even the gallery's first director, Alan Bowness, was dismissive of one of its first sculptures, an arrangement of fireproof bricks by US artist Carl Andre. Bowness made light of the sculpture, joking that 'of course there are many piles of bricks around Liverpool'. He was quick, however, to point out the real purpose of the gallery: 'if an American crosses the globe to see [the sculpture], he will have to go to Liverpool for the experience'.[21]

At first, the gallery provoked a cynical response from art critics, local residents and Labour councillors. The *Guardian*'s art critic Waldemar Januszczak dismissed it as a 'tourist trap' and noted that 'art has been annexed by the Liverpool entertainment industry'. The critic was sceptical that the purpose-built Victorian warehouse could be so easily converted into a gallery, noting its low ceilings, multiple windows and 'thick, petrified forest' of cast-iron columns.[22] Meanwhile, letters condemning the development were frequently published in the local press. One local said the gallery was like 'giving a video to a starving man', while another predicted that it would become 'a white elephant' and yet another worried that the gallery was merely a space to 'unload unwanted modern rubbish… a direct insult to the City which is in need of almost everything else'.[23] More pertinently, Tate's bold claim of providing fifty new jobs was mercilessly mocked by Labour councillors, one of whom pointed out the irony of the fact that the Tate & Lyle sugar refinery, from which the Tate was philanthropically descended in the 1930s, closed in 1981 costing the city hundreds of jobs, far more than would be employed in the gallery.[24]

Another important milestone in the regeneration of the Albert Dock was the conversion of the dock's main office into the headquarters of Granada Television's flagship news operation in 1985. Inspired by CNN, Granada's outfit was a radical venture for British broadcasting and pioneered the now familiar tactic of having presenters broadcast in front of a live pool of working journalists rather than in a separate walled-off studio.[25] The cavernous, open-plan dock office was ideal for this new spatial arrangement. This project was typical of the supply-side ethos of Liverpool's new urban regime. A grand, shabbily maintained building inherited from a previous era, cleaned, prepped and marketed across the country, had become the home of a new breed of middle-class knowledge work. The money it brought was expected to migrate, through a mysterious process of osmosis, into a city of unemployed former dock workers and assembly-line factory workers.

It is only a thirty-minute walk from the northern boundary of Toxteth to the revived Albert Dock. To many in the Black community who lived in the neighbourhood, however, it might have felt impossibly distant. The attention that was directed from the government towards Liverpool in the 1980s was, arguably, this community's doing. Indeed, the title of one of the foundational documents of 1980 British urban planning, Heseltine's memo 'It Took a Riot', was a clear statement about the role of radical protest in forcing the hands of reluctant policy-makers. Despite the circumstances of Heseltine's frantic visit to the city and the promises he made, however, Toxteth was all but forgotten by the practitioners of this new type of urban regeneration. Speaking to an American political scientist ten years after the Albert Dock redevelopment, one Toxteth resident noted that while 'institutions like MDC actually came about because of the riots here in Toxteth… Going down on the site of the Albert Dock there was not one Black working on… it. There were no Black contractors.'

The same interviewee referred to the admission fees that controlled entrance to the MDC's new museums as well as the garden festival as being akin to an 'informal immigration' check.[26] Indeed, in a 1986 report written for the House of Commons Employment Committee, representatives of Liverpool's Black community noted that 'by and large the Black community have been excluded from access' to the MDC.[27]

There is a story, often repeated within Toxteth's Black community, that the only thing that Heseltine ever brought to the neighbourhood was the planting of trees along Princes Avenue, the wide boulevard that stretches through the heart of the neighbourhood. True to the style of urban regeneration that Heseltine and his government pioneered, these trees were planted by contract workers bused in from elsewhere.[28]

In 1967, while drinking together in a London pub, some friends devised a thought experiment that, unknown to them at the time, would set out to change the look and feel of many British cities such as Liverpool. Peter Hall, Reyner Banham, Cedric Price and Paul Barker were all writers for *New Society*, a witty and irreverent weekly magazine with a small, educated readership, which published articles about sociology, urban planning and modern art. In line with the magazine's ethos, all four of the men occupied a grey area between the technocratic intelligentsia of Britain's post-war planning state and the counter-culture of the 1960s. Peter Hall was an urban planner who had worked as a consultant for Harold Wilson's Labour government. Reyner Banham was the magazine's art critic, an exuberant aesthete whose weekly columns extemporised on topics such as the design of the Mini Cooper and the merits of different styles of sunglasses. Cedric Price was a disgruntled and self-described socialist architect, whose iconoclastic designs (which included a 'pop-up' House of Commons) were often exhibited but rarely built. Paul Barker was *New Society*'s editor in chief, a former intelligence officer who had briefly worked as a philosophy lecturer in Paris.[29]

Over drinks the friends discussed what would happen if all planning controls were abolished in a handful of carefully chosen areas of Britain. In the weeks and months that followed their initial discussion, this odd quartet wrote up their thought experiment in a series of articles under the headline 'Non-Plan: An Experiment in Freedom'. The group sketched out the fantastical and hallucinatory future society that they expected would form in a handful of county-sized deregulated 'non-plan zones' in different parts of the country. They imagined, for example, that an imaginary zone covering Southampton, Portsmouth and the Isle of Wight would be populated by mobile villages of caravans connected by treetop chair-rides. In this fantasy, the Solent would be filled with houseboats, serviced by 'sail-in movies and row-in bars' as well as floating grandstands with public address systems. In Essex, meanwhile, a mini-Las Vegas strip of casinos and motels would carve a path through the countryside. They imagined nudist colonies and geodesic domes, 24-hour pubs and 'pot shops instead of all of those declining tobacconists'. The writers argued that the zones would be an experiment in democracy. Without the guidance of Britain's town planning apparatus, which had gradually accreted over the course of the previous century, non-plan regions would be sites where the true inner desires of residents (rather than planners) could finally be ascertained.[30] The world described by the non-planners was a pop-art fantasy, kitsch, colourful and disposable. The articles prompted a minor sensation within *New Society*'s relatively niche world of urban planners, intellectuals and artists, resulting in weeks of letters and debate. They were lauded by figures across the political spectrum, from the anarchist Colin Ward to the liberal sociologist Michael Young and the right-wing journalist Alfred Sherman, before being largely forgotten.[31]

Few ideas in twentieth-century British history have had such strange and unexpected afterlives. While the writers went their separate ways in the 1970s, Peter Hall was unable to let their 'experiment in freedom' lapse from his memory. Shortly after the articles were published, Hall moved to the San Francisco Bay

Area. From his post as a professor at the University of California Berkeley's City and Regional Planning Department, Hall observed the embers of the student protests that had engulfed the university in 1969 and been savagely repressed by the California National Guard. He also made frequent trips as a consultant planner to Hong Kong, still a British colony in the 1970s, where he marvelled at the city's extraordinary economic boom propelled by low-wage sweatshop work. Through these experiences, Hall honed his passion for non-planning, coming to associate the individual freedom of Berkeley's counter-culture with the laissez-faire economics of Hong Kong, and delighting in both.

Hall returned to Britain in the late 1970s, as structural unemployment and environmental ruin were engulfing cities such as Liverpool. Amidst an ambience of urban crisis, he gave the keynote speech at the Royal Town Planning Institute's annual address in 1977, where he exhumed this old idea, one that had lingered in his mind for almost a decade. He advocated for blighted inner-city areas to be freed from all regulation, taxation and customs, calling for places like Liverpool as well as the former docklands of London and the declining coalfields of South Wales to secede from the rest of the country, becoming mini libertarian power vacuums for the unimpeded play of free-market forces. Like Hong Kong, these areas would be designated 'Crown Colonies', exempt from the customs regime of the nascent European Union. In this fantasy, passport controls would be erected around the crumbling docks of Liverpool and London, beyond which would lie a lawless, planless paradise.[32] These new zones were more radical versions of the freeports and special economic zones that, as we saw in Chapter 4, were already operating in places like Shannon on the West Coast of Ireland and which would find their way to Liverpool's remaining docks in 1984. While freeports were formed to lubricate the international movement of goods and money into airports and docks, Hall's proposed zones were intended to redesign the legal structure of entire cities of hundreds of thousands, possibly millions of residents. This idea was the *New Society* 'non-plan' manifesto resurrected for a time of deindustrialisation and mass unemployment, refracted through the lens of California and colonial Hong Kong.

Hall's idea was swiftly seized on by Geoffrey Howe, then the Shadow Chancellor of the Exchequer under Margaret Thatcher's leadership.[33] In a 1978 speech delivered in the ruins of the East London docks to a right-wing think tank, Howe used Hall's speech as the basis for an idea he would eventually call the 'enterprise zone'.[34] While Howe publicly emphasised the role that enterprise zones would play in regenerating depressed areas in cities such as Liverpool, behind the scenes Howe's vision was both more radical and more insidious. In a series of secret memos exchanged between Thatcher, Howe and chief Tory strategist Keith Joseph while still in opposition, Howe and Joseph argued that enterprise zones would be laboratories for experimenting with radical forms of economic deregulation, which would then be rolled out on a national scale. The idea, wrote Joseph, would be 'to move administratively more quickly than we could legislate and to pave the way for legislative change later'. He wrote that the zones would be 'demonstration areas… where conditions more encouraging to enterprise might be established – to show what would then result'.[35] Elsewhere the zones were described as 'a test bed of Conservative philosophy'.[36]

While urban development corperations were products of the Department of the Environment under Michael Heseltine and were tempered by his distinctive one-nation paternalism, enterprise zones were a product of Geoffrey Howe's Treasury, the intellectual powerhouse of Thatcherism. They were an intervention that arrived glistening with the radical sheen of true belief. When we think about utopias, we tend not to think of the political right. The creation of bounded worlds where new ways of living and working could be perfected and demonstrated have tended to be the monopoly of socialist planners, religious sects or free-thinking counter-cultures. This way of thinking about the relationship between space and society calls to mind Thomas More's mythical island where all property was shared, the nineteenth-century co-operative mill towns built by philanthropists, anarchist enclaves in the California desert or protest movements like Occupy Wall Street. Nonetheless, there was something utopian about the enterprise zone, even in the diminished and watered-down form that it eventually took in policy.

In 1981, the government created eleven enterprise zones, each a few hundred acres in size, in post-industrial towns and cities across the country. Although these zones were less ambitious than either the non-plan areas or Hall's proposal for autonomous Crown Colonies, they were still substantial deviations from the norms of economic management. While there were no passport controls set up through Toxteth, Moss Side and the Isle of Dogs, businesses in enterprise zones could still expect full capital allowances for industrial or commercial buildings, a streamlined planning process, an exemption from the Development Land Tax that was introduced under a Labour government to curb property speculation, exemptions from industrial training boards and almost complete freedom from the requirement to supply the government with statistical information. The removal of all fire and building regulations, bus and taxi licensing, and the suspension of laws forbidding gender and racial workplace discrimination were seriously discussed but never implemented.[37] Needless to say, the fantasy that had most captivated the non-planners, that these areas would be spaces for social as well as economic liberty, populated by nudists and weed dispensaries, was never under consideration by the Conservative government. The heady freedom and dreamy experimentation that had characterised the enterprise zone's speculative ancestors had been stripped away. The scope of political imagination had been narrowed to a fine point.

Merseyside's enterprise zone was established not in Toxteth or along the ruined former docks but instead in Speke. As we saw in Chapter 2, the new satellite town of Speke had been an early attempt by Liverpool's leaders to diversify its economy in the inter-war decades. What had once been the beatific ancestral grounds of a wealthy merchant family had been paved over by coils of semi-detached homes whose fortunes were tethered to an industrial estate that was initially planned and owned by the local government. The new housing and manufacturing jobs in the town were designed to compensate for the long-term decline of the city's docks and the dilapidation of its Victorian slums.[38] In the 1960s, Speke, like many other parts of Merseyside, had further benefitted from the new car-manufacturing plants that had been compelled to move into the area by government industrial policy. In 1959, the Triumph Motor Company opened an assembly plant in the town, which was absorbed into British Leyland in 1968.

In the late 1970s, however, Speke suffered a series of economic disasters. In 1978, the Dunlop rubber factory, which had started life as an aircraft factory adjacent to Speke's small municipal airport during the Second World War, closed, taking with it 8,000 jobs. Meanwhile, the British Leyland plant was beset by crises through the 1970s, caused by intensifying international competition and the rising price of oil. None of this was helped by the spectacular commercial failure of the plant's flagship product, the Triumph TR7, which had its disastrous debut in 1974 and is widely remembered as being one of the worst cars ever made. In 1978, the factory closed, costing the town another 4,000 jobs.[39] At the same time, in a pattern now familiar across Merseyside, Speke's planned industrial estates had been decimated by the economic turbulence of the 1970s, which had seen companies with headquarters elsewhere shut up shop.[40] By 1980, the town was undergoing a crisis of obsolescence comparable with Merseyside's other peripheral towns such as Kirkby. Speke had been created purely to serve local and national industrial policies that were no longer functioning, leaving behind tens of thousands of residents who were suddenly superfluous, condemned to an indefinite, workless future.

Despite Howe's ambition that enterprise zones would be crystal balls, neighbourhoods where Britons could witness the dynamic potential of free-market capitalism, the reality of Speke's enterprise zone was muted. The zone's designation order, with its pages of restrictions and caveats, marked a quiet admission that some forms of planning control were necessary. The proximity of the zone to Liverpool's airport meant a prohibition on any business that worked with lasers in case they interfered with low-flying aircraft. For the same reason, strict height restrictions were imposed on all buildings. The use or storage of nuclear material was also strictly banned.[41] The zone was split into two discrete areas, one covering the husk of the former British Leyland factory and another less than half a mile south covering the former Dunlop plant and two small industrial estates on the outskirts of Liverpool Airport. By an accident of geography, the southern zone also included Speke Hall, which had once been the seat of the Watt family's country estate. This small fragment of Merseyside had become a palimpsest of centuries of British history, having been a rural estate acquired by landed Tudor gentry, the home of a wealthy family of merchant slave-traders, the site of an ambitious municipal jobs-creation programme and a radical thought experiment in right-wing economics.

The enterprise zone was slow to develop. Despite its generous tax breaks, no one was willing to purchase the abandoned 1.2 million square foot grounds of the former British Leyland plant. The factory was left to decay for more than a year before it was purchased by a property developer who began re-engineering its grounds into an 'enterprise trading park' for companies who wanted to take advantage of the zone's benefits.[42] By 1985, dozens of new firms had opened in the former Leyland plant as well as in the small industrial estates in the southern part of the zone. Its overall effect was, however, fairy marginal. A study that year reported that the areas covered by the zone had seen just 525 net new jobs, a small number given that Speke had lost another 4,000 manufacturing jobs in the same five years.[43] The jobs in the zone accounted for just 3 per cent of all jobs in Speke and less than 0.5 per cent of all jobs in Liverpool.[44] Three years after the opening of the zones, a national team of consultants discovered that many of the first round of enterprise zones had done little more than reshuffle the locations of already existing firms. Subsequently, they had become ringed by halos of dereliction, as existing small businesses simply moved a few streets down to take advantage of tax breaks inside the zone.[45] In Speke, for example, many of the 'new' firms that set up shop in the enterprise zone such as Tudorgrade and J. Rose Tyres had moved from elsewhere in Liverpool while others, such as

Metal Box and Vestric, were subsidiary branches of already existing Liverpool-based companies.[46]

The failure of Geoffrey Howe's great experiment in free-market urban planning did not stop the Chancellor from returning to the London Docklands in 1988, by that point a thicket of skyscrapers containing banks and luxury flats, to proclaim that the policy was now redundant, as his government had turned the whole of Britain into 'one big enterprise zone'.[47] He may have had a point. Towards the end of its ten-year lifespan, after the further erosion of the city's industrial base, the defeat of the city's radical Labour council in the mid-1980s and the continued march of the MDC up and down the banks of the Mersey, the clear boundary between Merseyside's enterprise zone and the surrounding region would have felt increasingly hazy, more like the memory of a dream than a tangible border in the here and now. Within a few years of its opening, an even stranger and more consequential experiment in urban planning was taking shape a few miles to its north.

In 1983, hundreds of unemployed men and women were temporarily hired to tear down the skeletal remains of the Herculaneum Dock. It is possible that, for at least some of these workers, the dock was their former place of work. Less glamorous than the ornate Albert Dock a mile to its north, its structure dated back to 1866 and for much of its life specialised in storing and processing oil. Like its northern cousin, it had also been closed since 1972. The workers were clearing space for what would end up being one of the largest and certainly one of the strangest engineering projects in the city's long history. The docks, along with a garbage tip that had been owned by the City Council since the 1950s, were being dismantled in order to be transformed into a gigantic, temporary garden show.

Moments of extraordinary transformation in Britain's modern history tend to have been reflected in enormous set-piece national events. The country announced its global industrial supremacy, backed by a regime of free trade, with the 1851 Great Exhibition, a gargantuan six-month-long showcase of the fruits of Britain's 'workshop of the world'. The exhibition centred on Joseph Paxton's extraordinary Crystal Palace, erected in Hyde Park, which featured extravagant displays of wares from across Britain's empire and was attended by more than six million, a third of England's population at the time.[48] A hundred years later, in 1951, the post-war Labour government hosted the Festival of Britain, an event intended to usher in a new age of social democracy and state-directed technocracy. This festival saw the South Bank of the Thames transformed into a gleaming modernist Jerusalem, with pleasure gardens, art exhibitions and demonstrations of scientific and industrial progress.[49] These two events were didactic and pedagogical affairs, drenched with meaning, whose aim was to announce a rupture with the past and herald a new kind of political regime. They were spaces where visitors were encouraged to glimpse the future. Although the Liverpool Garden Festival of 1984 is less well remembered, possibly because it was held outside of London, it was arguably an event of similar significance, occurring during an equally profound historical rupture.

The festival, which was open for four months in the summer of 1984, was one of the most spectacular, ambitious and well-attended occasions of the 1980s.[50] The event was a mix between a gardening competition, an international expo and a theme park. Its grounds hosted themed gardens, model pavilions, mock steam trains and sail ships, live music shows and temporary pubs. It was visited by almost three and a half million people in the summer that it was open, roughly seven times the entire population of Liverpool.[51] The aim of this event was twofold. First, it would accelerate the reclamation of a stretch of derelict and toxic land, land that would be levelled, scrubbed clean and eventually made available to property developers after the festival had concluded. Second, it aimed to revive the image of Liverpool after the unrest of 1981, rebranding the city as a globalised hub for tourism and entertainment rather than a racially divided, former industrial port trapped in a spiral of decline. Liverpool's festival would become a blueprint for managing obsolete urban environments across

An aerial view of Liverpool's International Garden Festival.

Britain, with subsequent garden festivals held throughout the 1980s and early 1990s in Stoke-on-Trent, Glasgow, Gateshead and Ebbw Vale. By the last festival in 1992, at least one in every ten people in Britain had attended one of these events.[52]

If enterprise zones were the product of California and imperial Hong Kong, garden festivals had their origins in West Germany. Since 1951, West Germany had held *Bundesgartenschau*, federal garden shows, every other year, initially to accelerate the redevelopment of areas of German cities that had been damaged during the war.[53] During the 1970s and early 1980s, support for similar events in Britain had circulated among fringe groups such as the Joint Council for Landscape Industries, who had repeatedly lobbied Thatcher's government on the issue and been fobbed off by a brief in-house report on the German festivals. This report ended up on Michael Heseltine's desk in August 1981, just after the minister had completed his whirlwind trip around Liverpool. Heseltine was immediately enthused with the idea, not because it promised to stimulate the gardening industry, but because it offered the possibility of a year zero for cities such as Liverpool that had been deemed obsolete.[54] Here was a chance to showcase the values of the new Conservative government in an enormous public spectacle that would also speed up the preparation of hundreds of acres of soiled land to be sold to the highest bidder. In other words, when Heseltine announced on 5 September 1981 that Liverpool would host Britain's first garden festival, he was thinking as a former property speculator rather than a keen gardener.

The land was prepared at a breakneck pace by the MDC. While German *Bundesgartenschau* were usually designated eight years in advance of their opening, preparations for the Liverpool festival took just nineteenth months. The dismantling of the Herculaneum Dock was followed by the reclaiming of hundreds of acres of land from the Mersey, a task that involved the removal of 700,000 tons of the accumulated polluted silt that had congealed on the river's bank and its replacement with an equal amount of fresh sand dredged from elsewhere.[55] The work became a kind of performance, part of the self-made mythology of the festival. Some of the original material of the derelict site was recycled for use in the event. Wooden jetties from the former dockland site, made of timber imported from the Caribbean, were turned into benches, while the methane drained from the landfill site would be recycled to heat the festival hall for several years.[56]

Throughout the festival, gardening was used as a powerful metaphor for renewal and growth. Like the free market itself, flowers, trees and grass would grow and spread in ways that could be loosely cultivated (rather than deliberately prescribed) by planners and politicians. At a speech at the opening of the festival, the queen made a point of noting that while 'plants wither and die… with the coming of Spring growth begins again… garden exhibitions blooming on this site are symbolic of what we all wish for Liverpool'.[57] The festival's blooming gardens and grassy plains were to be compared, favourably, with the dilapidated industrial skyline of the rest of the city. As if this comparison wasn't clear enough for visitors, a small patch of the industrial land that had once occupied the festival's grounds was left in place for visitors to contrast with the immaculate festival site.[58]

This environmental critique belied the micro-managed artificiality of the festival. Almost all of the plants were grown off-site and transferred to the festival grounds shortly before it opened. The interiors of many of the dock's old warehouses were sealed and refrigerated to simulate winter and extend the planting season.[59] While the gently undulating landscape of the festival grounds appeared natural to its visitors, this was also carefully constructed. A range of small hills were manufactured along the riverbank from the rubble and garbage that once occupied the site to protect the grounds from the gale force winds that often blew in from the Mersey. A model replica of this landscape was tested in a wind tunnel off-site.[60] At the same time that the healing powers of 'nature' were invoked, the natural environment was also being presented as something to be re-engineered and then hastily disposed of.

The word 'environment' was everywhere in the festival's publicity. Indeed, the event had been commissioned by the Department of the Environment, a ministry created in 1970 with a mixed brief consisting of housing, urban and rural conservation. Despite its ubiquity, those involved with the festival were coy about what exactly this meant. While the event put forward a critique of the human imprint on the natural world, this was mostly aesthetic, bound up with the banishment of unpleasant sights and smells and the ruins of a messy, defunct regime for the movement of global commodities. It was a critique, in other words, that posed no challenge to property speculation, mass long-distance travel and limitless economic growth. The existential challenge of climate change, which was just beginning to be understood in the 1980s, remained off-scene and had no place in the festival's vision of free-market-led environmentalism.[61]

Meanwhile, the festival embodied the new kind of competitive and entrepreneurial urban planning that the government had championed after the uprising. To this end, everything was outsourced. The large number of gardens that made up most of the festival grounds were not planned by the festival organisers. Instead, they were delegated to various public and private bodies including banks, charities, local councils, horticultural organisations and overseas national organisations. Many of the elements of the Liverpool festival were decided on by open competitions advertised to members of the public. Amateurs were encouraged by the organisers to submit entries for their own garden plots, the results of which were judged by juries of experts. A garden was ceded to the children's television programme *Blue Peter*, which held a competition among their young viewers to design the site with almost 20,000 entrants. A competition was even held among schoolchildren to name the festival's pub, 'The Britannia', while a local fabric company won a contract to manufacture 'Oliver', the soft toy representation of the festival's official logo.[62]

More significantly, perhaps, the festival was a dizzying riot of corporate sponsorship. The Liverpool festival's steam train was sponsored by NatWest Bank, an ominous portent of the privatisation of Britain's railway system, still eight years into the future. The site also featured a 'photographic trail' created and sponsored by Kodak, in which visitors would be loaned branded cameras for a tour of a small patch of manufactured parkland with twelve marked spots to take photographs.[63] The children's playground, meanwhile, featured a large slide in the shape of a Pepsi can. Perhaps the most significant instance of advertising on the festival's grounds, however, was the Home and Garden Feature exhibition hosted by the private house-builders Wimpey and Barratt. Festival attendees were invited to tour six model homes, each of which was detached and low-rise, examples of the kinds of private suburban homeownership Thatcher's government had been seeking to popularise following the 1980 Housing Act, which had heavily incentivised council tenants to purchase their homes from the state. When the festival came to an end, the six houses were sold to festival-goers who had made bids during their visits and formed the basis of a suburb of over a thousand homes that was built on part of the site when the festival closed.[64]

Although much of the festival's content was gleefully delegated, forms of explicit political dissent were forbidden. A controversy briefly ignited over a garden plot that was outsourced to a radical landscaping group called The Diggers, a name derived from a proto-communist seventeenth-century sect. The group originally planned to build a fibreglass pond, from which a hand would emerge holding a UB40 form (the notorious piece of paperwork that all of those claiming unemployment benefit had to complete). They intended for the exhibit to protest the high levels of unemployment in Liverpool in the early 1980s and thus be an implicit critique of Thatcher's government. This design was, however, vetoed by the festival's organisers. Instead, The Diggers were made to produce an interactive 'Quiz' garden about local trivia, which was deemed to be a safer, less confrontational option.[65] Meanwhile, an application by the Campaign for Nuclear Disarmament for a garden plot at Liverpool's festival was denied by the Department of the Environment as it was deemed 'improper' for the festival to 'include a political element'.[66]

The festival, like so much of Liverpool's regeneration, was an implicit response to the 1981 uprising. But, when the festival opened three years later, it was an affluent and largely white affair. Surveys of attendees found the average visitors to be wealthier-than-average families with young children.[67] While official surveys kept records of the class, gender, age and hometown of visitors, it is telling that no information about race or ethnicity was recorded. While it is hard to comment on an absence, it seems clear that, despite the festival's origins, its target-audience was not the unemployed multi-racial residents of Toxteth. Robert Parry, the Labour MP for Liverpool Riverside, the constituency in which the festival was taking place, argued in Parliament that the unemployed should be offered discount tickets, a suggestion that was considered by the MDC only to be rejected.[68] At the same time, non-white faces were strikingly absent from both the festival's promotional material and the sculptures of 'typical' Liverpudlians that dotted the festival's riverside walk. Indeed, Liverpool's historic Black community did not feature at all in the various ways the city was represented throughout the course of the festival – with a focus mostly on local icons such as the Beatles, or the liver bird. Meanwhile, the Merseyside County Council's Jam Garden featured a golliwog, a notorious branding image used by Robertson's Jam, which prompted letters of complaint from Liverpool's Black community.[69]

The festival was, however, far from parochial. Instead, it invoked the entire world. Planned by the MDC and commissioned by the government, it was also overseen by an international agency called the Bureau International des Expositions (BIE). The BIE was founded in Paris in 1923 to bring order to the increasing number of industrial trades expositions being held across the industrialised world. It assessed bids from different national governments to host officially recognised national expositions, meaning that, by the mid-twentieth century, national exhibitions had become globally standardised affairs. Liverpool's festival was officially approved as an 'A1' event, BIE's most prestigious category.[70] With the backing of the BIE, the Liverpool festival called into being a peculiar global community on the banks of the Mersey, with plots of land and exhibition status awarded to more than thirty different nations from across the world. Participant nations included Japan, India, the United States, West Germany, Portugal, Sri Lanka, Australia, Denmark, Thailand and Israel. China, then still relatively closed to the world, also participated, a fact touted as a major diplomatic breakthrough.[71] Behind the scenes, however, the Chinese Embassy in London was reportedly critical of the 'slipshod' nature of China's exhibit, which, some officials claimed, was not as impressive as the neighbouring Japanese garden.[72]

Each participating country was obliged to provide activities to fill hundreds of hours of scheduled events. The result was an absurdist internationalist bricolage, featuring Chinese lion dancing, totem-pole carving, mock American pop concerts and a 'Japanese kimono laser spectacular'.[73] Many of the overseas delegates were patronised in the print material produced by the festival and treated as strange curiosities. The Chinese presence at the festival, for example, became an object of derision in a children's book used to publicise the festival (narrated by two cartoon birds): '[The Chinese workers] even brought their own cook with them, but they didn't leave much for us, did they?', 'To be honest, my friend, I can't say I'm sorry; I don't fancy the idea of eating bird's nest soup!'[74] Liverpool's significant and established Chinese community, which, as we have seen, were subjected to intensive forms of policing and aggressive deportation drives not more than a generation earlier, were, along with Liverpool's Black history, quietly erased from the festival.

Although the festival was designed to capture the essence of the city's population and its history, the event was planned and organised by the Westminster appointed MDC with little input from the elected city and county councils. While it was originally intended that the City Council would have joint authority over the site, the Council pulled out of the project late in 1982 citing spiralling costs and expressing scepticism at the economic benefits of the event. One Labour councillor referred to the festival as 'the most expensive jobs creation programme since the space race'.[75] As with the MDC's other riverside redevelopment schemes, then, the festival would be an exclusion zone, another beachhead in which the elected local authority had no power.

We are arguably all still living in the country that the Liverpool Garden Festival was built to showcase. Like many across the global north, Britons are used to living in cities that weaponise nature in the service of economic development, whose governments have been reduced to marketplaces for the distribution of private-sector contracts and that promote a cosmopolitanism that leaves older inequalities of empire untroubled. To many of us alive today, the 1984 Liverpool Garden Festival may feel like a very familiar space, far more familiar than the docklands that it replaced.

On the morning of 23 June 1984, readers opening the *Liverpool Post* would have been confronted with the headline 'Disneypool'. The paper had obtained the details of an urban regeneration plan that was even more fantastical than the glittering enclaves already taking shape along the banks of the Mersey. According to the article, politicians from Liverpool were in advanced, secret negotiations with The Walt Disney Company and it was hoped that the city would host the first Disneyland theme park in Europe. More specifically, the park was to be built in Speke, inside the boundary of Merseyside's enterprise zone on the disused Northern Airfield of Liverpool Airport.[76]

'Disneypool' would have been a massive undertaking – bigger in size than Disney's flagship park in Southern California. While Disney were scoping sites in Frankfurt, Paris and Alicante, it was reported that an English-speaking location such as Liverpool would be favoured. According to one rumour, the park was to be accompanied by a new monorail along the banks of the Mersey connecting the development with the Albert Dock and Liverpool's central waterfront, an eerie Disneyfied homage to the overhead railway once used by commuting dock workers. The tone of the article was one of unchecked, boosterish excitement. Even Derek Hatton, the enigmatic Trotskyist and one of the leaders of the Militant faction in Liverpool's City Council, admitted that the proposal would be seriously considered.[77] Disneypool turned out to be a fantasy. A few months later, it became clear that the city's local politicians had been quietly fobbed off by Disney's executives, who informed Liverpool's disappointed MPs that the company had narrowed down its search to either France or Germany.[78] The boosters had been getting ahead of themselves. At the end of 1985, to the despair of political leaders in Liverpool, Frankfurt and Alicante, plans for Disneyland Paris were announced.

At the end of the same decade, the eminent geographer David Harvey tried to summarise the way that urban governance had been upended since the 1970s. He argued that cities had been forced to become 'entrepreneurial'. Instead of managing infrastructure and providing services to their residents, cities were instead compelled to find ever more creative ways of attracting private capital from elsewhere, jostling with rivals across the world to improve their position within globally segmented chains of production and consumption. Necessitated by the collapse of industrial manufacturing and the destruction of organised labour, and lubricated by the increasingly seamless movement of money through the world economy, these were changes that were happening across the global north.[79] Harvey did not use the battle between Liverpool, Frankfurt and Paris for a new Disneyland to illustrate his argument, but he may as well have.

During these years, Liverpool was leading rather than following this transformation. There was perhaps nowhere else in Britain where this profound shift in the overall purpose of urban government was more evident. The city led the way in a distinctive style, via a patchwork of experimental interventions dictated by Westminster. The urban development corporation, the enterprise zone and the garden festival, as well as the freeport described in Chapter 4, were small incisions, perforating Liverpool's once coherent economic cartography. The post-war strategies to mitigate the city's growing obsolescence were in the early stages of a dramatic inversion. While Merseyside's economy had once been a dying star, with thousands of small manufacturers producing goods for a domestic market that beamed outwards from the region, it was now becoming something more akin to a black hole, a vacuum into which tourists and finance would be sucked. However, despite Margaret Thatcher's oft-repeated claim that there was 'no alternative' to the free-market restructuring of places like Liverpool, her government's plans were far from the only show in town. By the mid-1980s, a very different strategy for Liverpool's future was being drafted by the City Council. Liverpool was about to play host to one of the most dramatic financial and political battles in this period of British history.

8

Structural Adjustment

Although the city was not mentioned by name, the most famous passage in what is possibly the most well-known Labour Party conference speech ever delivered was about Liverpool. It happened on 1 October 1985, when Neil Kinnock, a reformist moderate two years into his nine-year spell as leader of the party in opposition, addressed a packed auditorium in Bournemouth. Midway through the speech, with his sonorous Welsh accent competing against undulating waves of cheers and boos, he unleashed the following invective:

> I'll tell you what happens with impossible promises. You start with far-fetched resolutions. They are then pickled into a rigid dogma, a code, and you go through the years sticking to that, outdated, misplaced, irrelevant to the real needs, and you end up in the grotesque chaos of a Labour council hiring taxis to scuttle round a city handing out redundancy notices to its own workers. I am telling you, no matter how entertaining, how fulfilling to short-term egos, you can't play politics with people's jobs and with people's services or with their homes... The people will not, cannot, abide posturing. They cannot respect the gesture-generals or the tendency-tacticians.[1]

A few days earlier, Liverpool City Council had hired a fleet of black taxis to deliver notices to 30,000 council employees informing them that they had been made redundant. This was the latest move in the city's dramatic attempt to expand its provision of jobs and housing in the face of funding cuts imposed by the Conservative government. Without a legal budget, the city was facing bankruptcy. The event marked the beginning of the end of a three-year period in which Liverpool was run by Militant Tendency, a Trotskyist organisation that had taken control of the city's Labour Party. Kinnock's speech castigating Militant foreshadowed the group's imminent expulsion from the Labour Party, condemning their confrontational brand of municipal socialism to the margins of British politics.

Ask any British person of a certain age what they know about Liverpool's modern history and they will likely say three things: the Beatles, the Hillsborough disaster and Militant Tendency. At a time when local politics is mostly a muted, bi-partisan and technocratic affair, this may seem strange. Indeed, there are perhaps millions of Britons who know more about the politics of Liverpool forty years ago than they do about the local governments they presently live under. Along with the uprisings of 1981, the Miners' Strike and the poll tax protests, Liverpool Council's decision to take the city to the brink of bankruptcy by refusing to implement cuts to public services was one of the most high-profile acts of resistance against Margaret Thatcher's premiership. The events of 1983–6 have become part of the mythology of contemporary British politics. The era's cast of characters, principally the slippery, combustible Derek Hatton, who can be heard shouting 'you lie!' from the audience of Kinnock's speech, but also the grave and cerebral Tony Byrne, have become cyphers for the repressed fears and fantasies of more than a generation of subsequent public figures. The corpses of their lost causes are exhumed almost annually by politicians and journalists as lessons about the limits of what is politically possible. The termination of Militant's government in mass redundancies and expulsion from the Labour Party is frequently invoked as a morality tale about a surfeit of ideological zeal in the face of hardened economic facts.[2] For many local politicians and boosters in Liverpool today, the defeat of Militant marked the end of what was seen as a pathological deviation from the politics of the rest of the country, and the beginning of a long process of normalisation.[3]

It is a story, therefore, that has a powerful legitimising role in modern British life. However, it is also one that is only partially told and frequently misunderstood. Unlike most accounts of Militant, and despite how this chapter opens, what follows will not be another reflection on the internal politics of Britain's Labour Party. Militant's time in power saw an alternative vision for mitigating Liverpool's obsolescence. While Michael Heseltine's urban development corporation created beachheads of free-market enterprise along the banks of the Mersey, Militant attempted to resolve the city's twin housing and jobs crisis by employing thousands to build new homes. For all their confrontational rhetoric, however, theirs was a relatively modest programme of Keynesian deficit spending and job creation, albeit one that the city was prohibited from financing. In office, the dreams of an explicitly revolutionary left-wing movement amounted to little more than the construction of thousands of low-rise, semi-detached homes with parked cars out front concealing within a nuclear family with secure union-backed jobs. They were at times unable and more often unwilling to incorporate the radical Black and feminist political movements that had transformed the city's recent history. The legacy of the administration is tarnished, not by its belligerent tactics, but rather because Militant had little interest in the ways that Liverpool's society had been shaped by the city's imperial history.

Those with even a passing knowledge of contemporary Liverpool, where Labour votes are weighed instead of counted, might be surprised to discover that the city has a long and largely forgotten history of Tory political supremacy.[4] Before we arrive at Militant's tempestuous spell in power, it is important that we take stock of Liverpool's distinctive political eco-system – an eco-system which laid the groundwork for Militant's political victory. Unlike almost all other large cities in Britain, Liverpool was a latecomer to Labour politics. Indeed, it wasn't until the 1950s that the city first elected a Labour council.[5] Like so much else in the city's history, this curious fact had everything to do with the city's imperial maritime economy.

For much of the late nineteenth and early twentieth centuries, politics in Liverpool was a proxy for battles taking place on the other side of the Irish Sea. Throughout the nineteenth century, five million people emigrated from Ireland, a considerable number of whom passed through Liverpool. Tens of thousands of these migrants remained in the city, putting down roots for generations.[6] As a result, Liverpool's political fabric unspooled along sectarian lines, with an anti-colonial Irish nationalist minority squaring off against a nativist Protestant majority mobilised by the Conservative Party. While many Irish settlers would have participated in mass strikes, such as those in 1911, 1919 and 1926, labourist politics were expressed at work rather than at the ballot box, where they tended to vote along anti-colonial rather than exclusively class-based lines.

From 1885, Liverpool Scotland, a Parliamentary constituency that included the heavily Irish neighbourhood of Scotland Road, became the only place in mainland Britain to return an Irish Nationalist MP, the journalist T. P. O'Connor, who represented the neighbourhood for more than forty years. Meanwhile, the Orange Order, a secretive Protestant fraternal club, forged their own distinctive political culture in the city. The Order organised massive marches through the city each year on 12 July to celebrate the 1690 Battle of the Boyne, when King William II defeated forces loyal to his Catholic rival James II in Ireland. As late as 1974, there were still 177 branches of the Orange Order in Liverpool, and these marches could still attract upwards of 10,000 participants.[7] In other words, rather than being, as one social historian put it, 'good rioters but bad socialists', Liverpool's working class had other battles to fight.[8] For some, this entailed a struggle with empire rather than with capital. For others, however, local politics was about defending Protestant hegemony.

From the 1930s, however, these sectarian conflicts were cooling, and the contours of Liverpool's politics were beginning to change. Class rather than faith would eventually determine voting patterns and the anti-colonial energies of Liverpool's Irish diaspora were reorientated towards domestic concerns.[9] Many of Liverpool's old neighbourhoods were dispersed by slum clearance programmes that saw both Catholics and Protestants scattered into mixed suburban neighbourhoods on the city's periphery. Scotland Road's tightly packed tenements, for example, had been cleared within a few years of the end of the war, and replaced with high-rise council flats that housed people from across the city.[10] By the 1950s, the descendants of the electorate that had voted for T. P. O'Connor were now mostly living in Kirkby, Huyton and Halewood. It was in this context that the Labour Party became a significant presence in Liverpool, many decades later than in most other British cities of a comparable size.

In 1955, Labour finally broke through to form a majority on the City Council for the first time. Although the new Council leader, Jack Braddock, was an avowed atheist, the party inherited the patronage networks of the city's Catholic Irish diaspora. Jack effectively shared power with his wife, Bessie Braddock, who sat as MP for the Liverpool Exchange constituency. She was last seen in these pages posing with the Beatles in 1964 and making the Parliamentary case for flooding Capel Celyn. Together the Braddocks ran a tightly controlled political machine referred to by the political journalist Anthony Howard as Cook County UK, referencing the corrupt Democratic Party patronage network that controlled the politics of Chicago for multiple generations. Jack Braddock seemed to relish in these comparisons, wearing a gigantic Stetson hat and referring to any dissenting political voice as a 'young cowboy'.[11]

Decision-making power during these years was the reserve of a small handful, shielded from scrutiny by an opaque and unwelcoming local party structure. Party membership was among the lowest in the country. Peter Kilfoyle, who served as the Labour MP for Walton between 1991 and 2010, remembers trying to join his local branch of the party in the 1960s only to be told the ward was 'full up' and that there was 'an extended process' for admitting new members. He argued that the mantra of Labour in Liverpool during these years may as well have been 'Keep it closed. Keep it tight. Keep new blood out.'[12] In the Liverpool Exchange constituency, meanwhile, Labour was dominated by a single family, the Parrys. When Bessie Braddock stood down from the constituency in 1970, her seat was awarded to Bob Parry. Of the twenty-four people who voted for him, nine of them shared his last name. After he won the selection, twenty-four votes to five, John Hamilton, who ran against Parry, alleged that Parry immediately 'wanted to know who the five were who had ratted on him'.[13] Meanwhile, Arthur Irvine, who had represented Edge Hill since 1947, treated the constituency like an absentee feudal lord, returning to Liverpool only once a month from his law practice in London to hold surgery and stay overnight in a hotel. Irvine was twice de-selected by his increasingly exasperated local party only to use his legal knowledge and connections to have the decision overruled on a technicality.[14]

Despite the city's proud history of working-class activism on the shop floor, the Labour Party and its predecessors had carefully isolated itself from being over-exposed to the whims of the population it governed. However, as slum clearance further dismantled the sectarian and familial networks that had supported both Labour and Conservative administrations in the city, the Liberal Party unexpectedly emerged as a force in local politics. This was a radical departure in Liverpool's political history. The fact that Liverpool's wealth stemmed from trade rather than industry meant that, unlike Manchester or Birmingham, Liverpool had lacked a social base for Liberal politics. Its wealthy families in the late nineteenth and early twentieth centuries were merchants, shipping magnates and financiers rather than industrialists, and the city had little in the way of a skilled and upwardly mobile working class.[15] In 1973, however, the Liberals took city leaders by surprise by weaponising the growing alienation and disaffection many felt towards Labour's impenetrable political machine. Mobilising an ad hoc coalition of white-collar workers, anxious and mortgaged homeowners and parts of the city's increasingly isolated Tory base, the Liberals, in coalition with the Conservatives, were in and out of power for a decade. At a time when the Labour and Tory political machines showed little interest in innovative campaigning strategies, Liberal canvassers drove through the city with megaphones blaring music onto the streets. There was even a rumour, probably apocryphal, that Liberal activists would carry dead rats and soiled mattresses with them on the campaign trail to theatrically reveal to voters and journalists to make a point about the poor state of street cleaning in the city.[16] Ultimately, Militant's success must be seen within the context of the failure of Liberal administrations to live up to the populist energy they unleashed. The Liberal Party broke apart the established political machines that had run Liverpool for the best part of the twentieth century but had no solution for the city's deepening economic and environmental crises.

Meanwhile, Liverpool's imperial maritime history had produced a rich, although transient and fleeting, history of socialist politics that left little electoral trace. Many of the dozen or so anti-colonial groups active in Liverpool's Black community that were documented by observers such as Douglas Manley and St Clair Drake in the 1940s and 1950s were on the radical left, not least the communist-aligned CPDA. The Liverpool Chinese Seamen's Union, which organised a successful strike among Chinese sailors during the war, was affiliated with the Communist Party. As we have already seen, new left groups with broadly emancipatory and often explicitly socialist politics ranging from Big Flame to the Liverpool Black Sisters were active in Liverpool in the 1960s and 1970s.

When compared with many of Liverpool's earlier political movements, the origins of Militant Tendency were somewhat more parochial, a product of the way in which decolonisation and the collapse of the city's docks had isolated its politics from more internationally orientated networks. Like many radical left political groups operating outside of the communist world in the post-war era, Militant were self-declared followers of Leon Trotsky, the Russian revolutionary leader whose exile by Joseph Stalin led to a split within international communism. In exile, Trotsky had called on his various supporters across the world to join established centre-left parties such as the Labour Party or the German Social Democratic Party to shape their agenda from the inside. In Britain, the result was a constellation of small groups, usually affiliated to short-lived newspapers, which hovered around the fringes of the Labour Party.

Militant was originally the name of a newspaper founded by Ted Grant, a South African Trotskyist émigré whose parents had fled Russia under Tsarism and who was on familiar terms with Trotsky's son. By the time Militant was founded, Grant had already been active in different British Trotskyist groups for thirty years, including in Liverpool where, in 1955, he had stood unsuccessfully for Parliament in Walton. Militant emerged from the ashes of a tiny group called the Revolutionary Socialist League, led by Grant, with branches in both Liverpool and London. Unlike the many dozens of Trotskyist groups with double digit membership lists that came and went, Militant would have staying power. At first, this was mostly due to its awkward but effective coalition of young working-class activists in Liverpool, middle-class students at the University of Sussex and an older guard, based in London and represented by Grant, whose politics could be traced back to the 1930s and to Trotsky himself.[17]

Over the next fifteen years, the group slowly but successfully infiltrated the Labour Party Young Socialists (LPYS), a broad network with branches across the country in each electoral constituency. Militant took a calculated approach to winning control of these branches one by one. In each branch, one or two Militant supporters would start attending LPYS meetings, selling newspapers and inviting other Militant members to give talks as self-proclaimed experts on topics such as Chile or Spain. If there was no Militant activist already in the constituency, a supporter would be encouraged to uproot their lives and move in from elsewhere, becoming, in the language of the day, a 'bedsit Trot'. Activists would then reorganise branch meetings to be longer and more frequent, alienating those with more active social or family lives from decision-making processes. Through this process of attrition, Militant gradually shored up power within the LPYS, becoming a national force with a significant presence existing just below the surface of the Labour Party.[18] By the early 1980s, the Militant newspaper had an estimated circulation of 20,000 (Militant themselves claimed it was as high as 40,000), making it the most popular left-wing newspaper in the country after the *New Statesman*. By this point, the organisation had over 300 full-time employees, more than worked for the Liberal Party.[19]

Militant called for a transitional political programme that would lay the groundwork for a more revolutionary transformation of the economy and society. The centrepiece of this transitional programme was the immediate nationalisation of the largest 200 companies and banks in Britain, which would be accomplished by a Militant-influenced Labour government granting itself emergency powers.[20] Militant had little time for addressing the feminist, Black, abolitionist or environmentalist politics that had mobilised a younger generation of activists since the 1960s, an omission that, as we will see, would have profound consequences in Liverpool. Their insistence on the absolute primacy of class as a starting point for all political action led to some eccentric choices in party policy. Militant refused to join the rest of the left in calling for the withdrawal of British troops from Northern Ireland, for example, instead arguing for the formation of a fantastical cross-denominational militia to secure peace in the region. The party called for the ongoing criminalisation of minor drug offences on the grounds that drugs would only 'disorientate and weaken' the working class. Meanwhile, even as the AIDS crisis was gathering pace in Britain, gay rights were dismissed by the group as a 'petty bourgeois diversion'.[21]

To this end, Militant activists were encouraged to live austere and disciplined lives, avoiding drugs, alcohol and sex, and going to bed early. It wasn't unheard of for Militant activists to be expelled from the group for smoking weed.[22] It was this almost monastic commitment among many members that allowed activists to devote the necessary hours to frequent, interminable committee meetings, which would wear away the patience of local branch members. As well as the money raised by selling newspapers, Militant was funded through donations from its activists, a demand that often took a toll on the finances of its working-class supporters. Shakedowns for 'fighting funds' were common at meetings. One former activist remembered 'people who used to hide their last 30p so they could get home on the bus'.[23]

On Merseyside, as Labour's post-war political machine unravelled, it created a power vacuum that Militant were able to fill. Activists were entering a local party that had been radicalised by the city's economic collapse. In 1978 and 1979, a cohort of seven Militant activists were elected to the City Council. This group formed alliances with the Council's growing and increasingly well-organised left flank. Unlike many of the machine politicians in Labour's recent past, Militant had deep connections with the city and with its labour movement. The tendency had a strong base of support among the powerful unions that represented public-sector workers. While Merseyside's Militants may have been 'entryists', they were far from outsiders. When the Labour Party won control of the City Council in 1983, a moment widely seen as the beginning of Militant's rule of the city, the organisation was officially supported by just sixteen out of fifty-one Labour councillors. Much of their disproportionate influence was due to the skilled leadership and outsize personalities of this group, not least Derek Hatton, who became deputy leader of the Council after 1983.

Handsome, devilishly charismatic, immaculately dressed and with a mane of quaffed black hair, Hatton grew up in a council house in Childwall Valley in Liverpool's eastern suburbs and had attended the same school as Paul McCartney and George Harrison, although he was a few years behind in age. Affectionately known as 'Degsy', Hatton left school at fifteen as an aspiring actor. He would later compare the thrill of running for office to playing Gratiano in a production of the *Merchant of Venice*.[24] He spent the 1960s and 1970s moving between professions, first as a high-end tailor, then as an office assistant working in the Liver Building and later as a firefighter, where he became interested in union organising. After a brief spell in London studying for a degree in community organising at Goldsmiths, Hatton returned to Liverpool, where he became involved with the Labour Party and, eventually, with Militant.

Militant transformed Hatton's life, launching his career as one of the most famous local politicians in Britain's post-war history. His charisma and extravagant social life stood out among the group's more earnest and prudish rank-and-file members. From a young age, Hatton's appeal was his ability to occupy two contradictory ways of being in the world. On the one hand, he was somehow an obstinate fanatic, prone to flares of temper and extremes of feeling. He was, for example, banned from his amateur football league for punching a referee after disagreeing with his decision.[25] On the other hand, however, he was enigmatic, inscrutable and opportunistic. He struck many observers as an unreal, even cynical, operator. One of his colleagues in the Council even predicted that he would eventually end up as a Tory peer in the House of Lords.[26] The screenwriter Jimmy McGovern, born and raised in Liverpool, described Hatton as 'your typical bolshie scouser, good-looking, very uppity… overpassionate, handsome… My God! Britain's worst nightmare! A scouser like that with power.'[27]

Hatton was introduced to Militant by the older less charismatic but more committed activist Tony Mulhearn. Mulhearn had grown up in a Catholic family in Everton and had worked in both Liverpool's old and new economies, as a ship's printer for Canadian Pacific and a worker at the Ford plant in Halewood. As the eventual head of the Militant-controlled district Labour Party, Mulhearn had a powerful role in the movement. One can tell the difference in temperament between Hatton on the one hand and Mulhearn on the other by reading the books they each wrote on leaving office. While Mulhearn co-wrote an earnest social history of Liverpool and the Trotskyist movement, Hatton wrote a lurid autobiography, *Inside Left*, in which he repeatedly referred to himself in the third person.[28] Meanwhile, another important player in the years to come was Tony Byrne. Byrne was a dogmatic municipal socialist with an intense eye for detail who effectively commandeered the Council's housing and urban planning unit during Militant's years in power. Balding, with a greasy, uneven beard and always dressed in tracksuits, Byrne cut a strange figure when pictured next to the clean-shaven and expensively dressed Hatton. A final key figure in Militant's impending regime was John Hamilton, the official leader of the Council during their spell in power. Although he was never a member of Militant, Hamilton was on the left of the party. As a kindly and well-liked Quaker, who often had soup stains on his shirt, Hamilton's key role in supporting Militant's brinksmanship with the government is often forgotten.[29] Together, this unlikely group was about to open one of the most dramatic chapters in Liverpool's already tempestuous modern history.

Derek Hatton addresses 50,000 supporters outside Liverpool Town Hall on the day of the 1984 city budget.

*

When Derek Hatton knew for sure that Labour had won control of the City Council with Militant at its helm, he was driving over the Churchill Way flyover, a clumsy strip of elevated highway, now demolished, that towered over central Liverpool. It was election night, and he was *en route* to a television studio for a round of interviews while votes were still being counted. The news broke on the car radio that Labour had won Warbreck ward, the safe Tory seat that had been held by the leader of the Council's Conservative group. With the city at his feet, struck by the magnitude of the victory, Hatton whooped, almost losing control of his car. Across the country, the local elections on 5 May 1983 had been a catastrophe for the Labour Party. Despite a turbulent first term in office, Margaret Thatcher's Conservative Party made huge gains, laying the groundwork for her decisive re-election the following month. Liverpool, however, had bucked the national trend, seeing a 2.4 per cent swing towards Labour, who won fifty-one out of ninety-nine seats on the Council, an outright majority. After talking to the media, Hatton and Tony Byrne made their way slowly back to Hatton's home ward of Netherley, stopping for drinks at every Labour club on the way, eventually arriving in the small hours of the morning. According to Hatton, it was then, in the dead of night and after countless pints, that Byrne turned to him and said, 'What the hell are we going to do?'[30]

Militant entered office with no illusions about the enormous difficulty they faced in building a socialist government amidst Liverpool's ruins. The economic fire that had consumed the city's economy in the 1970s had also burned massive holes in its finances. During this period, local governments had two sources of income. First, they raised money from their residents with local taxes known as rates as well as with the rents collected from council homes and other assorted service charges. Second, they were issued direct grants from the government. By the beginning of the 1980s, the first of these income streams was running dry. The simultaneous disintegration of shipping, dock work and light industry, coupled with the departure of hundreds of thousands of residents to neighbouring towns and suburbs or to other parts of the country, meant that the city had few resources to draw on. Between 1971 and 1980, the total number of taxable industrial and commercial properties in the city fell by 17 per cent and 27 per cent respectively.[31] The Council was servicing an infrastructure that had once supported close to a million people with a tax base of just a few hundred thousand, significant numbers of whom were unemployed. The situation was made even worse by a decade of Liberal and Conservative coalition governments, which had sought to keep taxes low as a means of buying off middle-class supporters. Between 1974 and 1979, the amount of money collected in rates by the Council fell by 25 per cent. This left the city precariously dependent on government grants, which, by the beginning of the 1980s, made up over 60 per cent of the city's budget.[32]

As Liverpool's economy eroded, the public sector, and in particular the Council, was fast becoming one of the biggest employers in the city – an ad hoc solution to the collapse of all other kinds of work. At the end of the 1970s, close to 35 per cent of workers in the city worked in the public sector and by the mid-1980s close to 40 per cent of these were employed by the Council.[33] These 30,000 council employees included teachers, street cleaners, construction workers, typists and civil servants. Three of the most powerful unions in the city, the National and Local Government Officers' Association (NALGO), the National Union of Public Employees (NUPE) and General Municipal Boilermakers and Allied Trade Union (GMBATU), represented white- and blue-collar public-sector workers respectively and, initially at least, were supportive of Militant.

More than most other British cities, therefore, Liverpool's employment base was tied to the health of its government finances. This meant that Margaret Thatcher's Conservative government, which was hellbent on reducing grants to local authorities, posed a critical threat to the city. By 1983, due to government cuts in grants, Westminster's contribution to Liverpool had plummeted from over 60 per cent to 44 per cent of its total budget. The city's finances faced an uncertain future.[34] Liverpool's brand-new Labour administration had a solution to this problem that was powerfully simple, summed up by the slogan: 'no cuts in jobs and services'. The idea was to refuse to comply with Westminster's impossible fiscal demands and instead set a budget that would be 'illegal' – in the sense that it would spend more than the city could raise – taking the city into bankruptcy if necessary.[35] It was argued that the responsibility for Liverpool's crisis lay with the government, and it should be left to them to pick up the tab.

These kinds of budgetary conflicts were becoming frequent across the deindustrialising world. As post-industrial cities haemorrhaged people and jobs, their tax bases collapsing in the process, it became common for cities to be disciplined by national governments into slashing their finances.[36] If the new supply-side urban policies like enterprise zones and development corporations that were bestowed on Liverpool and other British cities were carrots, providing the incentives for cities to become entrepreneurial in their courtship of private capital, budgetary austerity was the stick. In the context of these localised forms of structural adjustment, as urban budgets became subjected to new kinds of auditing and technical oversight, they also became sites of political contest. Perhaps the earliest, most dramatic example of this was New York City's fiscal crisis of 1975–7, in which the city's generous municipal infrastructure, welfare and education systems were dismantled under the terms of a federal bailout.[37] In Britain, battles over the right of councils to control their finances raged from the early 1970s, culminating in the 'poll tax' protests of 1990. The first battle in this decades-long war occurred in the remote Derbyshire mining town of Clay Cross in 1972. There, councillors had refused to implement Ted Heath's Housing Finance Act, which raised rents on council housing, resulting in their expulsion from office and the drafting in of unelected government commissioners to run the small local authority.[38] For many in 1983, the fate of Clay Cross loomed large as a premonition for what the coming months and years might have in store for Liverpool.

The new Labour councillors took their seats just weeks after the final Liberal/Conservative budget in May 1983, which had promised to plug a six-million-pound shortfall with cutbacks made throughout the year.[39] For the 1984 budget, Labour planned a small rise in rates of 9 per cent, enough to cover inflation. Even without any increase in spending, the city would still have run out of money. However, under Byrne's direction, the Council also forged ahead with an ambitious programme of house-building and urban renewal, which attempted to solve, in one stroke, the city's jobs, housing and dereliction crises. It was a massive financial commitment – and thus a dramatic, precocious gamble that put the city on a collision course with the government. Unless the government agreed to make up the ever-expanding shortfall between income and expenditure, the city would go bankrupt, prompting mass redundancies and the suspension of services.

The Council prepared the ground for the coming fight by unleashing a gargantuan publicity campaign in Liverpool and across the country, orchestrated by a newly created and highly controversial 'Central Support Unit', effectively a propaganda wing for the new administration. Its first task was organising a massive demonstration by the waterfront called 'Merseyside in Crisis', attended by 20,000, which culminated in speeches from famous left-wing Labour politician Tony Benn and David Blunkett, then the leader of Sheffield City Council. The group printed 210,000 leaflets and 180,000 copies of a pop-up newspaper called *Not the Echo*.[40] Between April and June 1984, more than forty public meetings were held with a combined total of 5,000 attendees.[41] When Liverpool played Everton at Wembley in the 1984 League Cup final, activists handed out red and blue stickers to the respective groups of fans who travelled to London.[42] On the day of the budget itself, 25,000 turned out to march through the city.[43]

During these months, Liverpool was radicalised. Many more than just the small cadre of Militant supporters and activists were swept along. One non-Militant Labour supporter remembered, 'The streets were absolutely packed. You couldn't see the end. I remember on one demonstration going "How far back does this go?" You had that sense, people were with you. The city was politicized.'[44] An activist who would later become a Labour councillor and a fierce critic of Militant conceded, 'I'm not going to pretend for a moment it didn't have enormous support in the city... Lots of people saw this as the only game in town.'[45] Opinion polls in the spring of 1984 reflected the mix of hostility and excitement. One poll of Labour voters in Liverpool showed that 55 per cent supported a general strike as the next phase of escalation and an astonishing 68 per cent supported an occupation of the Council offices in the event of redundancies.[46]

The popular hunger in Liverpool for a confrontation with the government in 1984 belies a simplistic story, often told, about a city in thrall to a small handful of egomaniacal 'tendency tacticians', artificially grafted onto a hostile citizenry.[47] Militant's biggest success was in politicising the city's budget, something that both the national government and Militant's local political rivals had insisted was technical and beyond dispute. It had the effect of recasting the narrative around Liverpool's crisis and decline. Widespread feelings of abandonment and alienation could now be linked directly to the annual process of setting a budget, giving the city's population someone to blame for its obsolescence. Just as Thatcher and Heseltine had sought to turn Liverpool into a laboratory for a new brand of right-wing free-market urbanism, Militant wanted to use their time in power to show how obsolete, post-industrial cities could put unemployed residents and derelict land to work in municipally directed urban regeneration projects. This was, therefore, more than just a conflict over how best to manage Liverpool's finances.

On 29 March 1984, with tens of thousands of protestors in the streets outside, their voices audible in the Council Chamber, Labour proposed a budget of £267 million, £55 million above the government limit.[48] During an eight-hour sitting, the budget was fiercely debated before being narrowly defeated after six Labour councillors, branded afterwards as either the 'scabby six' or the 'sensible six', depending on your allegiances, sided with the Conservative and Liberal minority. Attempts to secure an alternative, legal budget were also defeated, despite Westminster's last-minute promise of additional Manpower Services Commission funds if the city complied.[49] With no budget, Liverpool was financially adrift. All eyes then turned to the local elections in May to break the impasse. The government hoped that Labour would be defeated, or at least lose its majority, ending the city's fiscal insurrection. Labour, however, with the help of the Central Support Unit, pulled off another stunning victory, winning 46 per cent of the vote and increasing its majority by six, removing the influence of the rebels.

The government figure responsible for dealing with this crisis was Patrick Jenkin, who had replaced Michael Heseltine as Environment Secretary in 1983. Unlike his predecessor, Jenkin was an unassuming, hapless and now largely forgotten figure, mocked by Hatton for being 'out of his depth'.[50] Jenkin had the option of sending in a team of unelected commissioners, backed by force if necessary, to restructure the city's finances. This option had last been used in 1979, when commissioners had been sent in to run the Lambeth, Lewisham and Southwark health authority in South London after it refused to implement spending cuts. There was no precedent, however, for the implementation of commissioner rule in a large city such as Liverpool. Such a move would have been perceived as a right-wing *coup d'état*. Jenkin privately feared that direct action would sabotage any attempt to take control of the city by force. He reportedly confided to an advisor that 'the caretakers have to unlock the doors, the computer has to be set up. There are twenty-five things that have to happen before you can sit in your grand office and pretend to run the city.' There were even concerns that commissioners would be stopped from entering the city by barricades along its entry roads.[51] Instead, shortly after the election, Jenkin agreed to the formation of a task force to negotiate a settlement with Liverpool. A few weeks later, Jenkin came to visit Liverpool, a tactical blunder that would shift momentum to Labour. The minister was given a tour of some of the worst housing in the city, after which he appeared visibly stunned by the scenes of dereliction and poverty, saying to reporters, 'I have seen families living in conditions the like I have never seen before.'[52] This was an admission of the city's desperate need for funding that played directly into the Council's hands.

The negotiations, with Hatton, Mulhearn, Hamilton and Byrne on one side of the table and Jenkin and his advisors on the other, took place in Jenkin's office in London in early July, with Hatton claiming that the four men from Liverpool 'ran rings around' the minister.[53] Jenkin eventually conceded a package worth twenty million pounds. Much of this money was to be distributed through a series of aid schemes for environmental improvements and urban regeneration. He also promised that 'positive progress' would be made towards next year's budget, a statement that Byrne would fatefully misinterpret to mean a promise of more money down the line.[54] The failed 1984 budget was restructured with creative accounting measures making up most of the remaining shortfall. Housing repairs, for example, were capitalised rather than expensed, meaning that they would be paid for over multiple years into the future, a one-time-only accounting trick that temporarily restored millions to the budget.[55] Meanwhile, a handful of Labour's spending commitments were quietly dropped. Within hours of arriving back in Liverpool on the train, the four councillors presented their hard-fought compromise as a major victory for the city. Hatton's statement was typically incendiary: 'There is no way even Thatcher can take on the might of the working class of this city. And this is just the start… next year we will start to see the kicking out of Thatcher herself.'[56] While it captured neither the spirit nor the fine details of the agreement, the declaration of victory was an effective propaganda exercise and a humiliating blow for Jenkin, who had been under the assumption the agreement would be kept under wraps for the time being.

Another, arguably more significant victory was achieved a few months later in February 1985. It came shortly after Jenkin had announced a 20 per cent cut in the housing budget for councils such as Liverpool whose housing stock did not include enough co-operative or housing association tenancies, an announcement that many saw as a mortal blow for the city's already imperilled finances. In return, however, Byrne stunned both the government and the press by revealing that he had secured an independent deal with the French bank Banque Paribas, recently nationalised by François Mitterand, who had agreed to buy the mortgage payments from 7,000 council houses that the city had recently sold. Byrne claimed this as a victory for municipal autonomy, an example of how other councils could expand their housing programmes in the face of government cuts. Jenkin was forced to concede the deal's legality, though he immediately promised to ban such deals in the future. Liverpool was also given an added boost when dozens of other Labour councils across the country agreed to join what became known as the 'rate capping rebellion', an agreement to stand together in refusing to pass a budget that year in protest against new limits on how much they could raise their local tax rate.[57] These victories and alliances bought the city some time, but they did little more than that. Both Jenkin's initial compromise and the financial deal with Banque Paribas fell far short of what Liverpool needed to resolve its fiscal crisis.

The government, meanwhile, were regrouping. In the summer of 1984, Thatcher was in the midst of fighting the Miners' Strike, arguably the biggest set-piece showdown between the government and unions in the post-war era. Her government had little energy for a fight with Liverpool. The following year, however, with the miners defeated, Liverpool was firmly in the government's crosshairs.[58] By the end of 1984, relations between the government and Liverpool were deteriorating. When Thatcher visited in the autumn, it was a frosty, unproductive meeting at which Hatton and Byrne refused to stand to shake her hand, forcing her, they later claimed, to lean awkwardly over the large negotiating table.[59] Jenkin, meanwhile, was preparing for war. He likened Militant's provocative declaration of victory following the previous round of discussions to the councillors 'dancing' on his 'political grave'.[60] Early in 1985, the Audit Commission, a new, typically Thatcherite agency created in 1983 to monitor the accounts of public-sector bodies, appointed a new auditor named Timothy McMahon to deal with Liverpool. McMahon arrived with a reputation for toughness. Mulhearn described him as 'Thatcher's hired gun'.[61] The auditor immediately tore into Liverpool's finances, giving the city until 1 June 1985 to set a working budget. Meanwhile, ominously for Liverpool, the fiscal rebellions led by other councils were petering out or had reached individual settlements, leaving the city isolated. The Militant administration was running out of road.

Militant had always been torn between two opposing desires. On the one hand, they wanted to run a successful socialist city that would demonstrate a meaningful alternative for managing obsolete urban economies. On the other hand, they wanted to wage war on Margaret Thatcher's government, a war that would discredit her national policy of neoliberal restructuring. By the summer of 1985, the latter was the only course of action that remained. Further government cuts, accumulated debts from the last budget and an inability to call on some of the creative accounting measures that had bailed the city out the previous year had resulted in a massive discrepancy between income and expenditure. According to one estimate, the city would need a 220 per cent local tax rise to cover the losses.[62] By this time Byrne, seeing which way the wind was blowing, was hoping that his urban regeneration scheme, complete with thousands of new council houses, was close enough to completion that even bankruptcy couldn't stop it.[63] On 13 June, at a sombre meeting lacking the exhilarating, fractious atmosphere of the previous year, the Council passed a rate rise of just 9 per cent, leaving the city with a massive deficit of £117 million. Liverpool was once again in uncharted fiscal territory. The forty-nine councillors who voted for the budget exposed themselves to a raft of legal consequences ranging from prison sentences to personal financial liability for lost incomes.

With financial Armageddon on the horizon, things fell apart quickly. McMahon made it clear that the city had three options: either raise taxes, make cuts to services or draw up redundancy notices for its 30,000 employees. By the end of the summer, the Council were leaning towards the third option. The plan, extraordinary as it seems, was to make the entire council workforce redundant, and then re-hire everyone once the dispute was solved. The 30,000 workers would be able to live on redundancy payments until the end of the year while the city continued to negotiate with the government.

The unions, many of whom had initially supported Militant, were realising, with horror, that the Council might be willing to gamble away their jobs. White-collar public-sector unions feared that redundancy would lead to long-term unemployment with no strategic benefit for the city. GMBATU, however, with its blue-collar membership base for whom redundancy payments, combined with unemployment benefits, would increase their income, announced their support for the policy. There followed a week of bitter fighting between and within these unions about the way forward, during which the City Hall was occupied by anti-Militant union activists. Nevertheless, the administration pushed ahead with redundancies. In a theatrical gesture, one that would, a few days later, be immortalised by Neil Kinnock's famous speech, the Council hired fleets of black taxis to fan out through the city delivering notices to thousands of council workers informing them that they had lost their jobs.

The redundancies marked the beginning of the end of Liverpool's fiscal insurrection. In the following weeks the Labour Party, including representatives from other Labour councils, took an active role in trying to resolve the crisis, presenting the city with a handful of options, all of which included some mix of cuts and tax rises and all of which the Council rejected. On 22 November, with Neil Kinnock threatening to support the sending in of unelected commissioners to take control of the city, Byrne revealed another extraordinary *deus ex machina*, a sixty-million-pound loan from a Swiss bank. Along with yet more creative accounting measures, the loan allowed the city to pass a legal budget, removing the immediate threat of bankruptcy. Many activists felt manipulated and blindsided by the sudden announcement of a deal that Byrne had been secretly negotiating since August, arguing that they had been treated like pawns. Three days after the budget, Liverpool's Council leadership – along with anyone associated with Militant – was expelled from the Labour Party. While the Militant Council won re-election the following year, it was a pyrrhic victory. At the beginning of 1987, the councillors who had refused to set a budget, including Hatton, Byrne, Mulhearn and Hamilton, were fined £2,500 and permanently barred from office. Liverpool's alternative model for municipal finance – in the end little more than a modest programme of Keynesian demand-side investment – had been ruled out indefinitely. The city's structural adjustment was complete.

The vast tobacco warehouse at Stanley Dock still stands – a building that once claimed to have more floor space than any other on earth. Built in 1901, the warehouse, two miles north of the city, spans fifteen storeys encompassing 1.6 million square feet. Like so much of Merseyside's waterfront, it is now being hastily transformed into luxury flats. For more than forty years, however, after the strategic abandonment of much of the docks, it stood empty, an eerie holdout against the rampant redevelopment unfolding on all sides. At sunset, its hundreds of bare windows would unleash clouds of bats that diffused across the waterfront like a fine dark mist.

If you were to set out from the warehouse, with your back to the Mersey, and walk just a few minutes inland, crossing beneath a railway track, you would find yourself in a radically altered world: a quiet suburban cul-de-sac, lined on all sides by redbrick three-bedroom semi-detached houses, each with their own small driveway. While this neighbourhood was once part of Scotland Road, one of Liverpool's late nineteenth- and early twentieth-century zones of Irish settlement and anti-colonial politics, almost no trace of this history remains. Instead, other than the sound of seagulls, the occasional smell of salt or the odd, surreal glimpse of the imposing warehouse in the distance, you could be standing on any other street in Britain.

These houses were among the 5,000 built by Militant's Urban Regeneration Scheme.[64] During its short spell in power, the

Militant administration oversaw one of the largest and one of the least remembered urban redevelopment projects of the 1980s, the funding of which was a primary source of the city's financial difficulties. In total, 40,000 people in seventeen designated 'priority areas' saw their neighbourhood transformed in just a few years.[65] Some of the city's most notorious council estates, built during the era of Labour machine politics, were demolished. These included the dilapidated fourteen-storey tower blocks that made up 'the Piggeries' in Everton, as well as the cluster of tower blocks that had replaced the tenements of Scotland Road and were only a few decades old.[66] Dozens of new sports centres and parks were built. Most importantly, given the dire state of the city's economy, this intensive burst of redevelopment created thousands of new jobs in the construction industry.[67] The Council claimed it was the largest public house-building programme anywhere in the country at that time.[68] While many Britons are familiar with the *Sturm und Drang* of Liverpool's budget showdowns in the mid-1980s, Militant's actual policies are less well known to those outside of the city.

Perhaps the single most surprising thing about Militant's time in power is how closely the Council's ideas about housing and urban design aligned with those of Margaret Thatcher. While Derek Hatton and Margaret Thatcher had little in common, they both read and admired the eccentric right-wing housing campaigner Alice Coleman, whose book *Utopia on Trial* argued that hostile architecture and advanced systems of surveillance could 'design out' crime from cities.[69] Coleman believed that human beings were biologically predisposed to live in nuclear families in small, fortified family homes and that high-density housing would lead to 'homosexuality and other deviations'.[70] Coleman was perhaps the only person in the world to be warmly received and showered with praise by both Hatton and Thatcher. In September 1985, at the peak of the budget crisis, Coleman visited Liverpool and enthusiastically complemented the Council's new housing, citing the city as a 'pioneer' for the kinds of developments she wanted to see built across the country.[71] Over the last two chapters, we have seen how both Michael Heseltine and Liverpool's Militants attempted to create duelling utopias on Merseyside – rival visions of what the future of British urban life should look like. It is a curious fact, then, that Militant's low-rise suburban housing schemes were almost identical in look and feel to the model housing development built as part of Heseltine's National Garden Festival. Indeed, many were even built by the same developer: Wimpey.

The new streets of houses built in Vauxhall, Everton, Toxteth, the Dingle and many other parts of the city were curiously traditional and almost prudish when compared with the outlandish radicalism of the Council. Militant were intensely critical of any kind of architectural experimentation, associating the modernist housing schemes of the mid-twentieth century with attempts to subdue and override the desires of working-class populations.[72] The result was a muted Trotskyist suburbia.[73] Houses were repetitive in style – semi-detached, fronted by small individual driveways, sealed off behind fences and laid out along meandering curvilinear streets. The Council's statement of intent for the Urban Regeneration Strategy was a remarkably paranoid and authoritarian document, castigating against vandalism and loitering, and arguing that public space needed to be minimised and closely surveilled.[74] The document is an extraordinary window into Militant's vision of an ideal society:

> Children play safely within their own gardens; neighbours gossip over fences, secure in their own territory; teenagers are less likely to lapse into anti-social behaviour or vandalism, burglary and mugging because there is significantly less opportunity and they would be seen. Residents do not feel like they are living under siege within their dwelling with a hostile and unsafe environment immediately outside their front door.[75]

Low-rise, car-centric, devoid of public space and riven with fences to enhance the psychological sense of security and enclosure, the most radical local government in the post-war era built housing that looked like anywhere else in 1980s Britain.

The prim conservatism of Militant's house-building programme is surprising until one considers how resolutely uninterested the group were in the social order of the city they governed. Class, as it was understood in the narrow, productivist context of late-industrial Britain, was the only lens through which they viewed the world. As Hatton himself put it in his autobiography, shortly before misattributing Rosa Luxemburg's famous line about the choice between socialism and barbarism to Karl Marx: 'when I talk about Marxism or Militant, I am talking about an exact political science'.[76] Liverpool's Militants were derisive of other 1980s left-wing Labour councils such as Ken Livingston's Greater London Council or David Blunkett's administration in Sheffield that had fought for a more socially expansive, yet less confrontational, politics inflected by the counter-cultural movements of the 1960s and 1970s.[77] The implication, never fully explained, was that the coalitions forged between feminists, gay rights campaigners and Black activists were related to these councils' unwillingness to go as far as Liverpool in their brinksmanship with the government. Hatton denounced these councils as 'the looney left…', more interested in 'black mayors and gay rights than… building new homes' and 'more concerned that we called the chairman a chairperson or a manhole cover a personhole cover, than they ever were about real issues'.[78]

The Militants delighted in an aggressive, masculine approach to politics. Hatton, in particular, relished confrontation. He surrounded himself with security guards clad in green uniforms who became known as 'Hatton's army' and who earned a reputation for physically intimidating journalists at press conferences.[79] He was often a clumsy, provocative presence in meetings. In a discussion with politicians from London about a national rally, he responded to requests that the platform had equal numbers of men and women by telling John Hamilton to go and put on a skirt. On a different occasion, Hatton was accused of sexism after telling Margaret Hodge, who was then leader of Islington Council, that if she couldn't stand the heat she should stay out of the kitchen.[80] According to one calculation, only 10 per cent of Militant's paid staff were women.[81] Militant's lack of social imagination, however, was felt most acutely by the city's Black community, with whom the Council had an explosive, catastrophic relationship.

For much of its history, Liverpool's Black radical tradition had left little footprint on the city's formal political structures. Although it would be another seven years before the city saw its first locally born Black councillor, Liz Drysdale, 1980 saw the formation of the Liverpool Black Caucus, an influential cross-party committee of councillors and representatives of Black groups dedicated to mitigating some of the diabolical inequalities of jobs and housing that had widened under the previous decade of Liberal and Conservative rule.[82] The Caucus became the official, professionalised vehicle for race relations management in the city and sat atop a less formal and more radical network. Its sixteen non-councillor members, who were elected through the MCRC, took an expansive, political definition of Blackness, which included Chinese and South Asian representatives. Its initial aim was to instigate a cross-party Equal Opportunities Policy that would monitor and seek to redress the spectacular degree to which Black people in the city had been marginalised by the Council. It was a policy that would eventually trigger a dramatic showdown with the Militant Labour administration.

The first sign of trouble came in 1981, when Hatton, recently elected and sitting on the opposition benches, spoke out against a vanilla and up until that point uncontroversial motion, put forward with the support of the Black Caucus, to 'examine ways' to increase the number of Black council employees. Hatton objected on the grounds that it would exacerbate racial tensions. In doing so, he won the support of a handful of other Labour councillors, prompting a ferocious debate in the Chamber that the Lord Mayor had to adjourn until tempers cooled.[83] If there had ever been a political consensus over the need to directly address the extreme racial disparities in council employment, it was already falling apart.

Militant subscribed to the view that racism was merely a symptom of a divided working class, a problem that would be automatically solved with a greater redistribution of wealth and power.[84] In power, Militant were ruthless about enforcing a dogmatic, colourblind approach to race relations. Byrne, for example, took the extraordinary decision to reject a plan for an elderly care home in Toxteth catered to the Black community. This was despite the fact that 75 per cent of the scheme's funding was footed by the national government, and the fact that Liverpool had one of the worst track records for Black elderly care in the country.[85] Militant were also fiercely critical of a proposal from the city's Social Services Department to create a special unit tailored to the needs of the city's beleaguered Chinese community.[86] It was largely because of this refusal to consider affirmative action that, during their years in power, Liverpool saw little improvement in the catastrophic under-representation of Black workers in council jobs. At the beginning of the 1980s, the Black Caucus had been campaigning for 5–8 per cent of council jobs to be held by Black workers, a figure that was still a little less than proportionate to the city's Black population. Instead, between 1982 and 1987, the percentage of Black council workers increased only infinitesimally from 0.9 per cent of the total (272 out of 29,908) to 1.6 per cent (490 out of 30,410).[87]

The implications of Militant's colourblind approach was perhaps most acute when it came to housing. Liverpool's new pop-up suburbs were effectively reserved for the city's white population. As we have already seen, throughout the post-war era Liverpool's Black population had been effectively excluded from the newer and better housing developments, both public and private, which had modernised the day-to-day lives of hundreds of thousands of white people in the city. In 1984, during Militant Labour's first full year in power, the Commission for Racial Equality (CRE) published an investigation that, for the first time, revealed the dramatic extent of these inequalities and urged the Council to take action.[88] The CRE wrote directly to the city's new Militant administration, warning them that without monitoring and other forms of affirmative action the Urban Regeneration Strategy risked reproducing these inequalities.[89] The 1984 report and the CRE's subsequent warnings were ignored by the Council. While almost all other large urban authorities in Britain were introducing policies that would mitigate, if not redress, the massive scale of housing discrimination in the post-war period, Liverpool remained an outlier.

In 1989, a follow-up investigation from the CRE focusing on the years of Militant rule found what many had already suspected: there had been widespread discrimination in the ways that its newly built homes had been distributed among Liverpool's citizens. The investigation concluded that the Council had 'discriminated both directly and indirectly' against Black residents in the city.[90] White people were between two and four times more likely than Black people to be allocated one of the city's newly built homes. The report found that a quarter of white applicants were allocated a house with their own garden compared with only 6 per cent of Black applicants. In a statistic that is deeply revealing about the continued under-development of the city's housing stock, the report found that a staggering 64 per cent of Black applicants were allocated homes that still had no central heating (compared with 37 per cent of white applicants).[91] All of this, the report argued, was a direct result of the Council's refusal to engage in any kind of affirmative action. The quiet new suburban cul-de-sacs, with their manicured driveways and fortified boundary fences, that underwrote an imagined, atomised social world where 'children play safely within their own gardens' and 'neighbours gossip over fences' were ultimately coded as white spaces for white residents. Given this fact, and the ways in which law and order in Liverpool had been racialised by a hostile police department, the Urban Regeneration Strategy's intense emphasis on crime and security seems especially sinister.

By the autumn of 1984, relations between the Council and the Liverpool Black Caucus were about to explode. The fuse was lit when the Militant administration reluctantly agreed to the creation of a Race Relations Unit to be headed by a new Race Relations Advisor. To the astonishment of much of the city's Black population, the Council hired a man named Sampson Bond, a completely unknown Black construction worker and Militant supporter from London who had no connection with Liverpool, little understanding of the distinctive history and challenges of its Black community and no experience of race relations work.[92] Worst of all, he was resolutely opposed to affirmative action. Hatton, in a rare admission that his hands were tied by structures beyond his control, admitted in a later interview that he had been put under intense pressure from Militant's London HQ to make the hire.[93] While the racism of the Council's housing policies was still invisible – or at least hidden behind as yet uncollected statistics – the 'Sam Bond Affair' became a bitter, at times violent, conflict between Militant and the Black Caucus that raged for over a year.

Bond's voluminous polemical writings, often expressed in the dozens of angry letters he would write to journalists and politicians who he believed had misrepresented his position, show a consistent disdain for the liberal anti-racist tradition associated with the institutionalised and state-backed 'race relations' industry.[94] At their most convincing, these writings were a clumsy attempt to align himself with thinkers such as Ambalavaner Sivanandan who were arguing for a more materialist approach to Black political organising in the 1980s, one that borrowed both from Marx and from the anti-colonial politics of the global south.[95] Bond's intellectual pretensions were, however, undermined by his fluency in Militant's rebarbative jargon and eagerness to take the side of the administration against much of the city's Black population. For these reasons, many Black activists in Liverpool saw in Bond little more than a Militant puppet, a figure whose purpose was to override the Black Caucus as an autonomous site of potential resistance to the Labour administration. In the words of one critic, 'Frantz Fanon… labelled people in Sam Bond's position as people with Black skins and White masks.'[96]

Things moved quickly. The day after Bond's hire, forty Black activists forced their way into the Council offices to confront Hatton about the appointment and instigate a sit-in that went on for five hours. Cornered in his office, Hatton agreed that Bond's offer would be withdrawn and the post would be re-advertised. The following day, however, the Militant-dominated local Labour branch agreed to uphold Bond's offer and claimed that Hatton only agreed to withdraw it because he was held hostage and threatened with physical violence.[97] The day after that, Black activists in the city announced that they would refuse to co-operate with Bond and boycott all posts within his unit, a move that was eventually ratified by the city's major public-sector unions and by the MCRC. From the very beginning of his tenure, Bond was an isolated figure, a paper tiger with little support and little to do, forced to travel everywhere with police protection.

Over the following months, the conflict over Bond's appointment became an all-out war, complete with an undertow of very real violence. In early 1985, it was alleged that one of Bond's bodyguards physically assaulted a group of Black students.[98] Meanwhile, Hatton claimed to have been punched in the face by a supporter of the Black Caucus before an event at which he spoke with a bleeding ear.[99] Subsequent allegations of violence, bribery and intimidation, most of which are difficult to substantiate, were made by both sides, threatening to destabilise the troubled social peace that had reigned in the city since 1981. The conflict's nadir occurred in the spring of 1985. When the new Race Relations Liaison Committee, which Bond had been appointed to head, met for the first time, the Black Caucus used their presence on the Committee to pass a motion condemning his appointment. To the horror of the Caucus, the administration announced that the Committee would be abolished. This meant that Liverpool, arguably the city with the worst race relations in Britain, was left with no effective political institutions to mitigate this bleak track record. A major showdown occurred when the Council met to ratify this decision. Two hundred Black protestors occupied the lobby of the Council and thirty were allowed into the Council Chamber as witnesses on the assumption they would be allowed to address the councillors. When they were refused permission to speak, they erupted in protest. In what was alleged to be a predetermined and stage-managed action, Hamilton summoned the police to forcibly remove the protestors, including many Black women, from the Chamber.

Militant's solution for Liverpool's obsolescence was to use the

City Council to make surplus workers build houses for surplus people, often on surplus land. It was a strategy that, following the mass exodus of private capital from the city, felt like the only alternative to managed decline. With council jobs and council housing becoming the last reliable source of economic stability and social mobility, it mattered even more that these things continued to be privileges mostly reserved for the city's white population. There were deep similarities to the 1940s and 1950s, when national and local governments attempted to rescue sections of Liverpool's white working class from obsolescence by building houses and attracting new industrial jobs. Then, as well as in the mid-1980s, these were life rafts that left Black residents behind.

On 1 October 1985, just after 5pm, as the autumnal evening darkness was settling over Liverpool, a group of Black protestors gathered outside the Hope Street police station in Toxteth. Earlier that day, four men had been tried at the Magistrate's Court in connection with the murder of a Londoner who had travelled up to a carnival in Toxteth the previous August. Despite protests outside the courtroom, the four men had been refused bail. At Hope Street, a window was smashed. The protestors then made their way down Princes Drive, destroying several vehicles including a post office van. Events moved with predictable speed, as if they had already been scripted and rehearsed. Over the course of the night, reviving the controversial tactics that had been perfected in the summer of 1981, the police responded with a massive show of force. Roaming 'snatch squads' of police vans accelerated into groups of protestors.[100] These were followed by the now familiar sight of lines of police officers drumming Perspex shields with truncheons, shouting, according to one witness' official deposition to the Liverpool 8 Law Centre, 'Come on you black bastards!'[101]

Order was restored the next day. Bleaker, shorter, less dramatic and arguably less hopeful than its counterpart in 1981, the 1985 uprising immediately became enmeshed in the ongoing row between Militant and representatives of the city's Black population. The day after the uprising, Sampson Bond's office accused the Liverpool Black Caucus of instigating the events. A subsequent, anonymous pro-Militant leaflet accused the Caucus of 'profiting' from the disturbances.[102] Within twenty-four hours, a statement authored by the MCRC and signed by eighteen Black organisations condemned the accusation as an 'act of gross irresponsibility'.[103] In the end, Militant's faith in political order was selective. The same organisation that would meet in each other's homes to discuss glorified histories of the mass working-class uprisings that preceded the Russian revolutions of 1917, that instigated sit-ins, walk-outs and wildcat strikes, had little interest in supporting the protests against racism and police violence that were also occurring on their doorstep.

Militant's administration and the uprisings of 1981 and 1985 were two disarticulated responses to the same crisis of obsolescence. They each drew on different radical traditions, mobilised different constituencies and had different visions of the future. They each, in their own distinct way, marked a refusal to submit to the austerity, superfluity and immiseration that was being imposed upon the city as a *fait accompli*. The tragic fact that a more unified political movement never emerged meant that grassroots Black activists and Trotskyist city councillors were left fighting over scraps. Contrary to almost everything that has been written about Militant in the decades since their extraordinary showdown with the government, we should remember the movement as having a dearth rather than an excess of political imagination. Militant's politics reverberate today, not in the eco-system of left political movements that challenge the myriad inequalities of early twenty-first-century capitalism, but rather in the authoritarian conservativism and suburban respectability of recent and present Labour governments.

Meanwhile, the official report on the 1985 uprising compiled by the county solicitor contains a crucial throwaway remark, easy to miss on first read. Many of the police tactics that were deployed, it noted, particularly the roving 'snatch squads' of police vehicles imported from Northern Ireland, had been taken from a classified document called the *Public Order Tactical Operations Manual*.[104] The manual had been drafted in the wake of the 1981 uprisings, and its existence had come to light the previous year, following the Battle of Orgreave, when the South Yorkshire Police deployed some of these tactics in its brutal suppression of a group of striking miners. There was a contagious quality to police violence in late twentieth-century Britain. Tactics such as CS gas and snatch squads that had been developed in anti-colonial wars in Northern Ireland or elsewhere had become means of policing multi-racial uprisings in inner cities. The use of these tactics in Orgreave showed how the same kind of violence, implicitly sanctioned by the assumed disposability of surplus peoples, was now being meted out to white as well as Black populations. The consequences for Liverpool of this shift were soon to be felt. Once again, the South Yorkshire Police would play a central role.

9

The Semi-Final

Liverpool's success at football in the post-war era defied economic gravity, blossoming in inverse proportion to the city's precipitous decline. In the twelve years between 1978 and 1990, there were only two seasons in which a team from Liverpool didn't win the league. While Everton had won in 1985 and 1987, most of this glory belonged to Liverpool FC. In a thirty-year period between 1960 and 1990, the club won twelve league titles, four FA Cups and four League Cups. With the possible exception of the Beatles, football, and particularly Liverpool FC, did more than anything else to shape the city's reputation in the post-war era. The weekly migrations of thousands of away fans to cities and towns across the country to watch Liverpool or Everton flaunted and exported the city's distinctive and frenetic youth subcultures, cemented by fanzines and flamboyant fashion.[1] Scouse accents broadcasted joyous terrace songs such as the old showtune 'You'll Never Walk Alone', made famous by the city's own Gerry and the Pacemakers in 1963. Liverpool won the European Cup in 1977, 1978, 1981 and 1984, and Liverpool players and fans were regular, often unwanted visitors to terraces in Milan, Madrid, Lisbon and Munich.

This extraordinary period of dominance had been fashioned by the explosive and charismatic Scottish manager Bill Shankly, who was in charge between 1959 and 1974. Shankly inherited a ruined and provincial club in the Second Division, whose now famous ground, Anfield, was a wreck. He was an obsessive tactician and a ruthless micro-manager. Shankly operated out of a small office nicknamed the 'Boot Room', with a tight-knit team of confidantes, many of whom, such as Bob Paisley and Joe Fagan, would go on to manage the club themselves. Shankly and his cohort of tacticians transformed Liverpool FC and, arguably, football itself, pioneering a well-drilled and technocratic style that emphasised collective rather than individual glory. It was a style rooted in an era of mass working-class solidarity and top-down state planning. But it was also enhanced by his magnetic charm and wit. Shankly styled himself as a working-class icon, wearing tracksuits rather than lounge-suits and preaching a vernacular socialism that was reflected in how he governed his teams. He refused, for example, to allow significant wage differences between his players.[2]

At the end of the 1980s, under the stewardship of former player Kenny Dalglish, Liverpool were at the crest of their generation-long spell of dominance. On 15 April 1989, Liverpool were hoping to reach their second consecutive FA Cup final, where they had the tantalising prospect of meeting their local rivals Everton. All that stood in the way was a semi-final against Nottingham Forest, a game which, as usual, would be played at a neutral ground to offset any home advantage. It was to be played at the Hillsborough Stadium in Sheffield.[3]

On the afternoon of the match, Liverpool city centre was full of shoppers taking advantage of a warm Saturday in spring. For anyone walking through the city that day, the build-up to the game would have had a quiet, almost spectral presence. It would have been audible in snatches of radio commentary heard in shops or from passing cars or visible on televisions glowing in the dark recesses of pubs or in the windows of electronics stores. The city centre might also have felt unusually quiet. Despite the warm weather, thousands in Liverpool and hundreds of thousands across Britain were at home, settling in to watch coverage of the game on *Grandstand* or listen to results and commentary on the radio. Many would be thinking, perhaps with envy, of their parents, children, partners or friends who, at that moment, were lucky enough to be eighty miles away, on the other side of the Pennines, converging on Hillsborough.

At 2pm, an hour before kick-off, Ed Doyle, his brother and a close friend were finishing a quick pint in a pub a short walk from the ground.[4] As seasoned match-goers they knew they had plenty of time. Their tickets, after all, said to arrive only fifteen minutes before kick-off.[5] Ten minutes later they found themselves in a long, stalled queue for the turnstiles. Carefully segregated from Nottingham Forest supporters, the 24,256 Liverpool fans in attendance had been allocated Hillsborough's northern and western stands. All of these fans had to arrive through Hillsborough's Leppings Lane entrance, which had just twenty-three turnstiles. This was less than half the number that serviced the Nottingham Forest fans.[6] As expected, most Liverpool fans were, like Doyle, arriving forty-five minutes to half an hour before the 3pm kick-off. Doyle and his companions found themselves caught in a bottleneck where, by 2.30pm, a considerable number of fans were packed into the funnelled approach.

Inside the ground, in a rickety control tower overlooking the Leppings Lane entrance, David Duckenfield, a Chief Superintendent in the South Yorkshire Police force, was in charge. He was not really supposed to be there. Duckenfield had been appointed just twenty-one days earlier after his predecessor, Brian Mole, had been quietly moved from Sheffield to Barnsley. The circumstances of this move remain murky, but it was likely the fallout of a vicious initiation prank. The previous year, some officers under Mole's command dressed in military fatigues and balaclavas and kidnapped a 24-year-old officer at gunpoint, handcuffed him, dragged him to a waste-ground, pulled down his trousers and made him believe he was about to die only to take a photograph of him instead.[7] Mole was an experienced matchday commander who knew Hillsborough inside out. He had overseen the previous year's FA Cup semi-final, a game that had also been played at Hillsborough and had also featured Nottingham Forest and Liverpool FC. Duckenfield, on the other hand, had not policed a football match for more than ten years.

Although this wouldn't become evident for another half an hour, several catastrophic errors had already been made. Warnings that the limited number of turnstiles at the Leppings Lane entrance in previous high-profile games had resulted in bottlenecks and crushes and that the terraces behind the goal had the potential to become dangerously overcrowded were either ignored or never crossed Duckenfield's desk. The Chief Superintendent had visited the ground twice in the previous month for two under-attended league games in which Wimbledon and Millwall played Sheffield Wednesday, events that bore little relation to the sold-out FA Cup semi-final.[8] Duckenfield was under the impression that the responsibility for the safety of the fans lay with club stewards rather than with his force. In all, 1,122 officers were called up to police the game, a deployment consisting of 38 per cent of the entire South Yorkshire Police force.[9] None were given instructions before the game for how to handle overcrowding either at the turnstiles outside the ground or on the terraces.

By 2.45pm the situation outside was becoming increasingly tense, and Duckenfield was out of his depth. Ed Doyle had jammed his arms by his sides to protect his ribs. In the distance he could see an unconscious ten-year-old boy being passed over the heads of the crowd to the front.[10] People all around him were remonstrating with a panicking police officer on horseback. Some fans began climbing the dividing fences, not because they didn't have tickets, but because they needed to escape the crush.[11] Meanwhile, the radio link that connected the officers in different parts of the ground with the control room was malfunctioning. With thousands of fans still outside, and minutes to go until kick-off, Duckenfield considered and then rejected the option of delaying the start of the game. An officer stationed in the melee outside had made numerous requests through the crackling and malfunctioning radio system to open one of the ground's exit gates to relieve the pressure, requests that were ignored at first by the overwhelmed Duckenfield.

The Chief Superintendent was concerned that opening one of the large gates that would normally remain shut until after the game was finished would allow fans without tickets into the ground. At

2.50pm, ten minutes before kick-off, the officer by the turnstiles sent another, more emphatic plea to open one of the gates, warning that unless action was taken now people would start to die in the crush. Duckenfield relented. However, instead of opening an exit gate that led onto the pitch, at 2.52pm Duckenfield decided to open Gate C, which led to the terraces behind the goal. Relieved to escape the crush by the turnstiles, 2,000 fans streamed through the gate. Oblivious and excited for the start of the game, many had no idea that they were walking towards their deaths.

Like many football grounds across Britain, Hillsborough was a relic from a late industrial age of ungoverned mass spectatorship. More than half of all the clubs in the top four tiers of English football played in grounds that were built between 1889 and 1910. Hillsborough was no exception. The stadium was built in 1899 on an elbow of the River Don on what was then the northern outskirts of Sheffield. Since its initial development, the ground had been repeatedly and awkwardly renovated. By the late 1980s, it had a kaleidoscopic mix of different features jarringly assembled from multiple eras of Britain's footballing past. The south stand, for example, was designed and built during the First World War by the Scottish architect Archibald Leitch. Leitch cut his teeth designing tea factories in imperial Ceylon, now known as Sri Lanka, before moving on to design various football stadiums including, by a twist of fate, both Liverpool FC's Anfield and Everton's Goodison Park. Some features of the ground were even older. Its clock dated from Sheffield Wednesday's first ground where the club had played in the 1880s and 1890s, parts of which had been dismantled and moved brick-by-brick to Hillsborough. The Leppings Lane end, where Liverpool supporters were allocated space, consisted of a primitive shelf of terraces punctuated by evenly spaced 'crush barriers' to mitigate surges among standing fans. The stand had been rebuilt in preparation for the 1966 World Cup, a renovation that had seen a second tier of seating added above the terraces. Access to the pitch from the stands was barred by an eight-foot-high metal fence with a fifteen-inch switchback at its summit making it almost impossible to climb.[12]

Throughout the 1980s, the Leppings Lane terraces underwent a round of subtle yet significant alterations. In late 1981, radial fences were constructed through the middle of the terrace, dividing it into three distinct pens. Each pen had a gate at its base that led to the pitch, which was sealed with a spring-loaded bolt during matches. The fences didn't extend all the way to the back of the terrace, making it theoretically possible, although not easy, for fans to move between the pens. In 1985, another fence was added, subdividing the central pen into two pens, numbered pens 3 and 4. The overall effect was bleak and carceral. Before the fences were added to the terrace its capacity was deemed to be 10,100. While the addition of the fences should have reduced this figure by at least 100, it remained unchanged.[13] Regardless, this number was effectively meaningless. Once fans passed through the external turnstiles there was no way of monitoring their movements within the ground, meaning there was no sure way of knowing how many were in each pen at any moment. The addition of internal turnstiles was discussed by the club in 1985 but was dismissed as too expensive.[14]

The Leppings Lane end had other problems, too. Visitors entering the ground were confronted with a steep tunnel above which was a sign marked 'standing'. To anyone unfamiliar with the ground, this seemed like the only route to the terraces. The tunnel in fact led directly to pens 3 and 4, and access to the pens either side was easily available, although poorly signposted, by turning left or right instead. What's more, every ticket for the Leppings Lane end had the letter B printed on it, which was also printed above the tunnel.[15] In the 1981 FA Cup semi-final, thirty-eight Spurs fans had been injured on the Leppings Lane terraces after its capacity had been exceeded by 400.[16] The police narrowly averted fatalities by blocking off the tunnel from incoming fans and releasing people from the terraces onto the pitch. At that time the terrace hadn't yet been divided into pens, meaning that many could move sideways to avoid the crush. What's more, just one year earlier, when Nottingham Forest had played Liverpool at Hillsborough in the previous FA Cup semi-final, overcrowding in the central pens had also led police to close the tunnel to avert disaster. In fact, the strategy of closing the tunnel even had its own name, the 'Freeman Tactic', named after a police officer John Freeman who had deployed it in 1987.[17] None of these prior incidents had been relayed to Duckenfield and neither had been incorporated into the official Operational Order, which had been distributed to all the police officers working that day. By opening Gate C, Duckenfield had unleashed thousands of fans into the ground with no plan for where they would go, little understanding of the layout of the stand and no means of closing the tunnel and mitigating their flow into pens 3 and 4 behind the goal.

Ed Doyle and his companions were some of the last people through the turnstiles before the gate opened. The men stumbled through, bruised and short of breath. Thinking their ordeal was over they headed down the tunnel into the pens behind the goal, following the signs and thinking it was the only way inside. In a vivid handwritten account compiled twenty years after the event, Doyle remembered emerging into a tight, roiling mass of fans behind the goal and being separated from his brother, each swept away by the crowd. After a while, the movement settled into something tighter and more rigid. In his words, he felt 'stuck like cement when it hardens'.[18] Also in the crowd was 19-year-old Adrian Tempany. Tempany had arrived early and had been taking in the atmosphere before the game. By 2.30pm, even before Gate C had been opened, things were getting, in his words, 'strangely uncomfortable'. The crowd had briefly carried him off his feet and, as kick-off approached, he found himself stuck near the imposing metal fences at the front of the terrace.[19] Photographs taken of the terrace shortly before the game showed that, while pens 3 and 4 were now dangerously overcrowded, the wing pens on either side were still half empty. Commentating on the game for the BBC, John Motson noted the curious emptiness of the wing pens where patches of bald concrete were visible and there were even fans sitting down reading newspapers.[20]

At 3pm, the match kicked off. Eight cameras were filming from different parts of the ground, with footage to be broadcast later on the BBC.[21] In the second minute of the game, Nottingham Forest won a corner at the Leppings Lane end. The Liverpool player John Barnes, who came up to defend, remembered how, 'standing there, defending the near post, you began to pick out familiar faces. I saw a couple of the girls we'd always see, cheering us on, and I thought, "That doesn't look good." They were squashed right up against the fence.'[22] Three minutes later, at the other end of the pitch, the Liverpool midfielder Peter Beardsley scuffed a shot from the box that hit the bar. According to one survivor, Beardsley's miss was a narrow escape. If he had scored, then dozens more may have been killed in the commotion.[23]

With Gate C open and thousands of fans pouring into the already overcrowded pens, things were becoming desperate. In pen 3, Tempany was now fighting for his life:

> Every minute or so, 50 or 60 people would wheel as one under the pressure from behind; as they moved, impaling someone's chest or ribs on metal or flesh or bone, a voice would cry out, then fall silent. The crowd would settle again, helpless and exhausted, trying to draw breath and scream… people… seemed to be falling, sinking beneath us.[24]

At one point, possibly after Beardsley's near miss, a crush barrier in pen 3 collapsed, unleashing a wave through the crowd to the front of the pens, where bodies were now piled. Tempany remembered seeing people all around turning blue, vomiting and some screaming or crying. Some were already dead. Later he would write:

> I was losing strength; I knew I couldn't survive much longer. My head was trapped in a channel, looking slightly to the left, to the North Stand, when into that channel walked a policeman. He stopped and looked into the terrace and straight into my eyes. I knew I had him, and I slowly, simply

mouthed the words: 'Help. Help me. Help.' The police officer narrowed his eyes, looked at me keenly and paused for a few seconds. Then he screwed up his mouth and smiled, uncertainly, and he walked off.[25]

A minute or two later, certain that he would die, Tempany started losing consciousness: 'I began to float away, taking in the end of my life. I looked up at that beautiful blue day, opened my mouth towards the sky and sucked what I could out of it. And then I closed my eyes.'[26]

Doyle and his friends were also in serious trouble. Only able to move his head, Doyle saw with relief his brother walking on top of the crowd 'as if he was on a staircase' and climbing a fence to safety. Soon he was drooping forward, losing consciousness, the sound of the crowd beginning to dim. It was an experience that he later described as peaceful and painless, a feeling of giving in. His friend saved him by yanking his head upward by the hair. The men had been deposited by the crowd in a tiny pocket of space against the radial fence dividing pen 3 from the still half-empty pen 2. Fans in the emptier pen were organising to help the escape of as many as they could from the other side. Doyle was pulled to safety over the eight-foot fence by a ladder of fans in pen 2, his body raked painfully over the spikes at its summit.[27]

As the match began, the police patrolling the perimeter of the pitch should have realised the scale of the disaster unfolding in pens 3 and 4. Twice, the gate connecting pen 3 and the pitch exploded open from the pressure of fans and twice it was slammed shut again by police who feared a pitch invasion. One officer radioed the control tower to ask if the gates could be opened to relieve the pressure and received no reply.[28] They were opened nevertheless, and fans began stumbling onto the pitch. Duckenfield, meanwhile, was relieved that the decision to open Gate C had dispersed the crush outside the ground and enabled the game to go ahead on time. Despite having a perfect view of the terraces from his control tower, a view supplemented by numerous CCTV feeds, he failed to register what was happening.

When fans began scaling the fences and tumbling out of the pitch-side gates, Duckenfield radioed for all his officers to converge on the Leppings Lane terrace to avert what he thought was a pitch invasion.[29] When police arrived, they found fans that were unconscious, blue, covered in vomit. Some were hideously contorted against the wire fence. One officer realised with horror that 'the first three or four rows within my view were dead'.[30] At 3.06pm, the Superintendent in charge of the operation inside the ground radioed to the control tower asking for the game to be suspended. Hearing no answer, he ran onto the pitch and alerted the referee himself, bringing the game to a halt.

Meanwhile, moments after his escape, Doyle joined in the rescue attempt, trying to get his friend over the fence. By now, however, the vice had tightened further and his friend couldn't be freed from the ossified mass of bodies. Instead, Doyle ran to the now open gates of pens 3 and 4, hoping to relieve the pressure further back. With the help of other fans, he began rescuing people from the compressed tangle of dead and dying bodies. These included two unconscious young girls who had been protected by the people around them. Many of the bodies that Doyle retrieved were passed backwards to the desperate and ad hoc CPR operations happening on the touchline performed by fans and police.[31]

The only official medical assistance was provided by the St John's Ambulance volunteers, who had thirty paramedics stationed by the ground. While hundreds of stretchers were needed at the mouths of the slowly emptying pens, only six were available on the ground, plus three more entombed in a single ambulance that belatedly drove onto the pitch, mobbed by supporters who were desperately trying to draw the driver's attention to dying family and friends.[32] With the Leppings Lane tunnel still congested, the only way to get the injured out of the stadium was at the other end of the ground, through the East stand. Fans began tearing down advertising boards to use as makeshift stretchers to carry the injured and the dead the length of the field. It took twenty minutes for more ambulances to arrive. When they did so, many were barred by police from driving onto the pitch. One ambulance driver who arrived at 3.35pm, almost half an hour after the game had been suspended, remembered being told by a confused police officer that he couldn't access the pitch because, in his words, 'they're still fighting'.[33] Later inquests would determine that, were it not for the unbearably slow medical response to the disaster, many lives might have been saved.[34]

Back in the pens, the escape of fans through the now open gates had released some of the pressure. Ed Doyle's brother and his friend survived. So too did Adrian Tempany, who regained consciousness when the pressure eased. Tempany would go on to become a journalist and write one of the authoritative accounts of the disaster. Doyle and his companions, meanwhile, had managed to reunite by the halfway line, where, less than an hour earlier, one of the most anticipated games of the season had kicked off. They marvelled at how, in a matter of minutes, the football ground had been transformed into something resembling a military field hospital. After some time had passed, the men asked a police officer how they could escape the ground and to their astonishment they were told to exit out of the Leppings Lane end, walking through the same narrow tunnel through which they had entered. They picked their way through the now ghostly terraces noting the 'twisted metal' of the collapsed crush barrier and 'the stench of urine'. On the other side, walking through the hinterland of tightly packed terraced houses, locals who had heard the news were coming out of their homes to offer water and use of their telephones to Doyle and other survivors.

After driving home in silence, the men, along with thousands of others, spent the following few days numb with shock, processing what they had seen. Doyle was haunted by flashbacks and nightmares. The night after the disaster he was heard screaming in his sleep. He took solace in the pub, drinking heavily each day, and phoning in sick to work. Five days later his brother hanged himself. His life was saved at the last minute after being discovered by his partner.[35]

*

Pens 3 and 4 of the Leppings Lane stand, photographed the day after the Hillsborough disaster.

What had unfolded was the worst event in Liverpool's modern history. It remains the biggest loss of life to ever occur at a European football match and the third largest football disaster in the global history of the sport.[36] Ninety-four people died on the day and three more succumbed to their injuries in later weeks and years. At 3.15pm, Graham Kelly, the Chief Executive of the Football Association, and Graham Mackrell, the Club Secretary of Sheffield Wednesday, had burst into the police control tower to ask Duckenfield what had happened. As fans were still dying on the pitch, Duckenfield replied with a lie. He said that drunken, ticketless Liverpool fans had forced open the exit gate and stormed into the ground.[37] As recent legal hearings after decades of tireless campaigning by survivors and relatives have established, the Hillsborough disaster was emphatically the fault of the South Yorkshire Police.[38] It is worth pausing here, then, with Duckenfield's lie – the first of many that would be told by police in the days, weeks and years after the disaster – to attempt an explanation of how social murder on this scale was possible.

Hillsborough was the grim culmination of a chain of deadly stadium disasters that stretched back to the early 1970s. In 1971, sixty-six fans were crushed to death in a stairwell at Ibrox Park in Glasgow at a game between Rangers and Celtic. A legal ruling later found Rangers FC responsible for not heeding repeated warnings about the dangerously narrow exit. In 1976, during a league match between Liverpool FC and Wolverhampton Wanderers at Wolves' Molineux Stadium, a wooden exit gate spectacularly collapsed under the weight of supporters in a dangerous crush outside the ground. After fans flooded the terraces, hundreds were forced to escape onto the pitch by climbing over advertising boards, leaving many injured.[39] Then, in 1985, during a Third Division game between Bradford City and Lincoln City at the Valley Parade ground in Bradford, a small fire ignited a discarded pile of litter that had fallen through the cracks of the terraces. Within just four minutes a minor blaze became a terrifying inferno that consumed the entire main stand, killing fifty-six, many of whom were trapped behind locked exit doors. A later inquest found that the club and West Yorkshire County Council were at fault for poor maintenance of the ground and inadequate preparation.[40]

Just two weeks after the Bradford fire, Liverpool fans were implicated in a major disaster at a European Cup tie with the Italian club Juventus, held at the Heysel Stadium in Brussels. The match followed several years of conflict between Liverpool fans and fans of various Italian clubs. The previous year, forty Liverpool fans had been injured in knife attacks by A. S. Roma supporters in the build-up to the European Cup final in Rome.[41] In Heysel, running battles on the terraces between Liverpool and Juventus supporters resulted in a deadly crush against a stadium wall that collapsed, killing thirty-nine people, mostly Juventus fans. Liverpool fans' involvement in the tragedy led to a ban on all English clubs from European football competitions. The Heysel Stadium was a ruined hulk in desperate need of repair and clearly unfit to hold a game of such importance. The police officer in charge had never supervised a football game before and many of the Belgian officers in the ground had no batteries in their walkie-talkies. Preposterously, as the dead were still being identified, the game went ahead as planned, watched by millions. The next day, the leading French football paper *L'Equipe* famously declared, 'if this is football, then let it die'.[42]

That football stadiums were becoming killing fields across Britain and Europe had everything to do with the ways in which the game's supporters were being pathologised as deviant and troublesome – a suspect group in need of policing. In the eyes of many politicians, journalists and police officers, football had become, in the notorious words of a *Sunday Times* editorial, 'a slum game played in slum stadiums watched by slum people'.[43] Like the emptying factories that orbited them, football grounds were crumbling, unreconstructed holdouts from a prior developmental age of working-class prosperity. It was not a coincidence that the run of football disasters between 1971 and 1989 was coterminous with the unravelling of a brief period of economic security for many British workers.

In the 1970s and 1980s, football had entered a period of decline. In the English First Division, average attendances fell by more than a third between 1972 and 1984, plummeting from 31,829 to 18,856.[44] In the vacuum created by diminishing crowds, football fans were becoming younger, more organised and more intense in their support. Clashes inside and outside grounds – sometimes planned, sometimes random – between what came to be known as 'hooligans' were luridly reported by the press. Football supporters came to be seen as mysterious and unknowable, objects for sociologists, criminologists and investigative journalists to study from a distance. For many academics and at least one historian in the 1980s, the arrival of hooliganism heralded the decline of the stable and affluent working-class communities of the 1940s and 1950s.[45] Some, such as the celebrity anthropologist Desmond Morris, whose 1981 book *The Soccer Tribe* featured photos of football supporters juxtaposed with sub-Saharan African tribes, subjected fans to a kind of racialisation.[46] For Peter Marsh, one of the leading sociologists of 'hooliganism', fan behaviour could be derived from that of chimpanzees or from supposedly 'premodern' cultures such as 'Plains Indians' who 'decorate themselves in traditional symbols of warfare' and 'engage in set dances and issue prayers to spirits'.[47] An agricultural vocabulary emerged to describe the governance and containment of match attendees. The escorting of away fans from train stations and car parks by police was referred to as 'corralling'. The new subdivisions that appeared on terraces of grounds like Hillsborough were called 'pens' or 'enclosures'.[48]

As with the other threats to 'public order' that emerged in the 1970s and 1980s, from Black protestors to striking workers and Republican paramilitaries in Northern Ireland, 'hooligans' became subject to newly militarised forms of policing, justified by the social chasm that had opened between fans and the British establishment. In the 1970s and 1980s, stadiums were fitted with hostile architectural features designed to regulate and monitor the movement of fans and prevent clashes between supporters of different teams. Many of these alterations were mandated by the 1975 Safety of Sports Grounds Act, a piece of legislation that was passed partly as a response to the Ibrox disaster and which elided the issue of safety with the repression of unruly fans. Ringed by police, surveilled by control towers and riven with imposing spiked fences such as those that carved up the Leppings Lane terraces at Hillsborough, stadiums began to resemble high-security prisons. Both of Liverpool's football stadiums, Anfield and Goodison Park, were pioneers of these tactics. In 1975, Liverpool FC approved the construction of an imposing pair of parallel steel fences that flanked the Anfield Road approach to the ground, complete with three-foot gaps for police to extract fans. It was described at the time as Liverpool's 'Iron Curtain'. Two years later, perimeter fences sealing the terraces off from the pitch were constructed at both Liverpool grounds. Further interventions were an uncanny mix of the modern and the medieval. On the one hand, both Liverpool clubs became the first in the country to install colour CCTV cameras linked to screens in control rooms that had the ability to immediately print images of troublesome fans to be distributed among officers. On the other hand, both clubs had dungeon-like 'detention rooms' fitted with primitive steel shackles for restraining fans.[49]

The police's responsibility for the Hillsborough disaster and the subsequent cover-up of their complicity, abetted by a willing press, was enabled by the penological disposition towards football fans that emerged in the 1970s and 1980s. In the build-up to the match, Duckenfield's primary concern was with policing rather than protecting fans. The twelve-page Operational Order compiled before the match had no contingency plans for the likelihood of a build-up outside the insufficient Leppings Lane turnstiles, or instructions for how to close the access tunnel to prevent overcrowding in the central pens. It did, however, contain multiple references to the segregation of fans of the two clubs and the importance of minimising crowd unrest and pitch invasions. For example, in a passage that was written in capital letters and underlined, it stipulated that the fences connecting the pens to the pitch would 'remain bolted at all times' with 'no one… allowed access to the track from the terraces without the consent of a senior police officer'.[50] Fears of the uncontrolled movement of fans or the breach of the ground by those without tickets ultimately drove Duckenfield's decision to delay measures that would have relieved the crush outside the ground, and to open the gates to the pens to rescue the dying supporters. Even as late as 3.06pm, when police were radioed from the control tower to head towards the Leppings Lane terraces, officers were bracing themselves for conflict, expecting that they were about to contain a pitch invasion.[51]

In the hours and days after the disaster, the South Yorkshire Police did everything they could to downplay their own culpability by blaming Liverpool fans. By evening, Duckenfield had already been forced to go back on his instinctive lie about Liverpool fans breaking down the exit gate. This was not before Graham Kelly, the FA chairman, had repeated the lie he had been told to the waiting press, meaning that a false story about rampaging Liverpool fans framed the first media reports of the catastrophe. Within minutes, Alan Green, BBC Radio 2's sports journalist who was at Hillsborough, was reporting that Liverpool fans had torn down the exit gate and stormed onto the terraces, causing the crush.[52]

By evening, the media narrative was being directed by Peter Wright, the Chief Constable of the South Yorkshire Police who had been responsible for Duckenfield's appointment. This is not the first time that Wright has appeared in this book. During the 1981 uprising in Toxteth, Wright was serving as deputy to Kenneth Oxford, Merseyside's Chief Constable. At his first press conference, Wright incorrectly blamed the disaster on 'the late arrival… of three or four thousand Liverpool fans… just five minutes before kick-off'.[53] The implication, again untrue, was that Liverpool fans without tickets engineered the crush to force the police to open the exit gate, allowing them into the ground.

Establishing that fans had been drinking was an important part of the police's attempt to deflect blame. In the gymnasium adjacent to Hillsborough, which, by late afternoon, had become a makeshift morgue, officers were instructed to take blood samples from the corpses to check their alcohol levels. Samples were even taken from some of the eleven children who had died. A police photographer was dispatched to take photos of discarded cans of beer around the ground for evidence.[54] Grieving families who were beginning to arrive at the ground after making the terrible journey from Liverpool to identify their loved ones were asked intrusive, leading questions about how much the victims had drunk.[55] In April the following year, just three days after the first anniversary memorial, the blood alcohol levels of the dead were read out during a coroner's inquest to the horror of the mourning families in attendance. The truth was that many of the dead had drunk nothing at all, and only a small fraction were over the legal driving limit.[56]

These insinuations aerosolised, however, spreading to every corner of the establishment. While Margaret Thatcher visited Sheffield and met with grieving relatives, she was briefed behind the scenes by police that the disaster had been caused by 'drunken Liverpool fans'.[57] Joe Ashton, a Sheffield Labour MP, blamed supporters for being late to the ground and said that the disaster occurred when Liverpool fans 'all ran to the entrance behind the goal'.[58] Even more extreme was Jacques Georges, the then president of UEFA, who referred to Liverpool fans as 'beasts waiting to charge into the arena' and claimed that what happened was 'not far from hooliganism'.[59] The press enthusiastically bought into a narrative that was carefully and deliberately cultivated by the South Yorkshire Police and orchestrated by Wright's press conferences. The next day, the *Sunday Mirror* reported that 'Liverpool fans pushed seemingly uncontrolled into Hillsborough' and *BBC News at One* reported that the exit gate was opened 'to relieve a massive build-up of Liverpool fans' and that this was standard practice by police when 'there's a risk of serious trouble outside'.[60] That Sunday's *Observer* meanwhile saw an article claiming that 'in truth, no one should have been surprised when thousands of indignant and potentially disruptive fans arrived yesterday'.[61] In the ensuing weeks, journalists terrorised survivors and the families of the dead. During the disaster itself, photographers disrupted rescue efforts to photograph the dead and dying.[62] Tabloid journalists pretended to be priests to access the homes of grieving relatives. One *Sun* journalist demanded a picture of a family's dead son, threating to print a picture they had on file of his corpse being given CPR if they didn't relent. When the family reluctantly complied, the *Sun* printed the image of his corpse anyway.[63]

On 19 April, four days after the disaster, the *Sun* newspaper announced on the front page to its three and a half million readers that Liverpool fans had no one to blame but themselves.[64] Under the headline 'The Truth', the newspaper falsely claimed that fans had picked the pockets of the dead, urinated on police officers and attacked first responders. It was a lie that flew in the face of the heroic rescue attempts organised by survivors such as Ed Doyle that, given the inadequate and belated emergency service response, likely saved many lives. The source for some of these claims was the Tory MP Irvine Patnick, who had been drinking in the Niagra social club on the evening of the disaster, where he had been fed these stories by multiple officers of the South Yorkshire Police who happened to also be there. These officers, later legal inquiries showed, were well aware of the dangerous architecture of the stadium and of Duckenfield's unfitness to be in charge of the game.[65] Kelvin MacKenzie, the paper's editor, had toyed with the alternative headline: 'You Scum'.[66] The defamatory article prompted an immediate and well-organised response on Merseyside, where the *Sun* (sometimes referred to locally as the *Scum*) continues to be boycotted. Some political scientists have argued that this boycott has had a meaningful effect on the city's politics, mitigating the development of the authoritarian populism that has shaped the electoral landscape of many other post-industrial communities over the last thirty years.[67]

While the *Sun*'s response was, perhaps, the most famous and the most egregious example of the libelling of Liverpool fans in the wake of the disaster, other outlets ran stories that differed only in degree rather than in kind. Two days after the disaster, the columnist Peter McKay, writing in the *Evening Standard*, noted, 'this catastrophe was caused first and foremost by violent enthusiasm for soccer, in this case the tribal passions of Liverpool supporters. They literally killed themselves and others.'[68] The following month, in a review of a benefit concert for the tragedy, *The Observer*'s culture supplement ran an *ad hominum* broadside against Liverpool fans. The author, David Honigman, wrote that 'an honest representation of English football' would feature Liverpool fans 'smashing bottles and urinating... turning up to matches without a ticket... It would show lovable Liverpudlians killing Juventus fans at Heysel.'[69] Six days after the disaster, an editorial in the *Daily Express* launched an attack on the city of Liverpool as such. The paper wrote, 'the visitor's overwhelming impression is of defeat, not endurance, of slovenliness, not local pride, of disintegration, not community...

and the sacred tenet of the spirit of Liverpool is that it is all somebody else's fault'.[70]

Representing one of the poorest cities in Britain, a place that had become associated with Trotskyist politics and Black militancy, Liverpool supporters were particularly vulnerable to the pathologies and fantasies that were projected onto football fans across the country. Liverpool fans, and by implication the city's entire working class, were presented as unruly, superfluous and in need of authoritarian forms of policing. In the cultural response to the disaster, we can almost see a return to the language of the eugenicist sociologists of the inter-war period such as David Caradog Jones who had expressed concerns over what was imagined to be a dangerous and disorganised underclass in the city.[71] Liverpool's spectacular economic decline in the 1970s and 1980s led to the ejection of the city's poor from the national community into which many had briefly been incorporated by state-backed industrial jobs, secure employment and council housing. In this sense, then, the Hillsborough disaster and the police and press response can only be understood within the context of Liverpool's creeping obsolescence. It was a catastrophe made possible by the cheapening of the lives of people deemed to be surplus in a city that was derelict and abandoned. We might even say that Hillsborough was a moment when the same kinds of police violence, disbelief and institutional neglect that had tarnished the lives of Liverpool's Black community for much of the twentieth century were generalised across its working class.

The Hillsborough disaster marked the nadir of English football. It also heralded its reinvention. Within a few years, the cultural and economic space occupied by the sport had changed utterly. We can see this transformation by reading the volumes of annual reports and mission statements published by Michael Heseltine's MDC in the early to mid-1980s. These documents are the closest thing we have to a comprehensive vision for Liverpool's regeneration – a strategy for marketing the city on a global stage to court visitors and capital. Despite operating during the extraordinary zenith of both Everton and Liverpool FC's post-war success, football went unmentioned in the Development Corporation's plans. Associated during this period with poverty and a vague ambience of violence, both of the city's football clubs were kept at arm's length from the spectacular regeneration of the city's waterfront. Jump forward to the early 2020s, however, and the situation is profoundly different. The enormous, glittering new Everton Stadium is at the heart of the city's ambitious regeneration plans for the north docks. Replacing the 130-year-old Goodison Park, the new stadium cost half a billion pounds and juts into the Mersey on an infilled patch of former dock basin.[72]

Two days after the Hillsborough disaster, the government appointed Peter Taylor, a prestigious high court judge with a dazzling array of establishment credentials, to lead an official inquiry into what had taken place. A few months later, when Taylor published his findings, it caught the government and the police by surprise. The Taylor Report was a serious and unexpected blow to the narrative, carefully constructed by the police and dutifully reported by the press, that fans were to blame. Instead, it found that 'hooliganism' had no role to play in the disaster, that responsibility lay largely with 'the failure of police control' and specifically with the failure to close the Leppings Lane tunnel, which was described as a 'blunder of the first magnitude'.[73] Taylor was intensely critical of many of the police officers he interviewed whom he found uncooperative and evasive, with the quality of their evidence varying in 'inverse proportion' to their rank.[74] While Taylor's findings went some way towards establishing a true version of events, for survivors and families it remained insufficient – littered with omissions and inaccuracies. In particular, the Report had little to say about the disastrous response of the emergency services and the careless, punitive way in which the injured and the families of the dead were treated in the hours after the crush. In 1991, a coroner's inquest at which families and survivors were interrogated, belittled and had to pay for their own representation established a cause of 'accidental death', formally letting the police off the hook. Justice for the ninety-seven who died would have to wait much longer.

Taylor followed his initial account of the events with a second, arguably more consequential report about how football itself should be re-made. The Report castigated against the shabby and decrepit ambience of stadiums, where 'fans eat their hamburgers or chips standing outside in all weathers' and 'there is a prevailing stench of stewed onions'.[75] Unable to compete with television or with other leisure activities, which were more welcoming spaces for women and children, football attendance, he argued, was becoming a residualised experience. All of this was enhanced by the prison-like architecture of stadiums – 'the spectacle of these huge cage-like fences is inconsistent with a sports ground being for pleasure… Having to stand in a cage for your Saturday afternoon recreation inevitably causes resentment.'[76]

To be made safe and to be redeemed in the eyes of politicians, broadcasters and investors, football had to be gentrified. Taylor recommended the complete abolition of all standing terraces such as those at the Leppings Lane end of Hillsborough and their replacement with fixed tiers of seating, a recommendation implemented across the country by 1994. The Report also recommended early kick-offs and Sunday matches to stagger arrivals, reduce the time in which fans were able to drink before games, regulate traffic, maximise television viewers and generate a greater sense of occasion.[77] These alterations would be coupled with a massive expansion of more technologically sophisticated and less visually intrusive systems of surveillance, particularly CCTV.[78] The gentrification of football coincided with the sale of the game's television rights to Rupert Murdoch's satellite-only Sky Sports channel in 1992 and the creation of the Premier League the same year. These changes saw the gradual exclusion of Britain's poor from football grounds. Between 1989 and 1999, top-flight ticket prices increased by 312 per cent. Some grounds reported a 1,000 per cent increase between 1991 and 2011. By 2008, it was calculated that 75 per cent of Premier League attendees had middle-class incomes.[79]

High fencing is dismantled at Anfield, Liverpool FC's ground, shortly after the Hillsborough disaster.

It was partly because of the changes recommended in the Taylor Report that English football clubs have become wildly lucrative financial instruments, traded between distant owners across the world. By the end of the twentieth century, they had become safe and commensurable assets – predictable revenue streams with significant property portfolios. Neither Liverpool FC nor Everton were immune from these changes. In 2010, Liverpool FC was purchased by Fenway Sports Group, a US-based sports and property development empire headed by the Boston-based businessman John W. Henry, who had made his fortune trading soybean futures in the 1970s. Everton, meanwhile, were purchased in 2016 by Farhad Moshiri, an obscure Iranian businessman who owned a Russian mining company. Football, once an unwanted by-product of a prior industrial age, had, by the beginning of the twenty-first century, been put to work in the service of economic growth and property speculation. In the 1980s, football sat at an awkward tangent to mainstream cultural and political life in Britain. Financialised, globalised and increasingly unequal, by the end of the 1990s the sport was at the avant-garde of Britain's ongoing neoliberal revolution.

Meanwhile, the long fight for justice in the wake of the Hillsborough disaster has continued. That we now know the truth about that day is thanks to a gruelling 35-year campaign led by survivors and families. It is because of their resolve and investigative work that historical accounts such as this are possible to write. Organisations like the Hillsborough Justice Campaign and the Hillsborough Families Support Group were and continue to be a key part of the complex ecology of political resistance in late twentieth- and early twenty-first-century Liverpool. The struggle for justice after Hillsborough is another example of how Liverpool's residents refused to accept the terms of their presumed obsolescence. It is a struggle that has insisted on life's worth in the face of those that attempted to render it disposable.

In June 2016, after decades of twists and turns, a second coroner's inquest ruled that the victims of the Hillsborough disaster had been unlawfully killed as a result of gross negligence by the police and emergency services. Attempts to prosecute those involved, including Duckenfield, are still ongoing.

10

Redefining Care

In 2017, two Princeton economists, Anne Case and Angus Deaton, made a discovery that confounded the presumed trajectory of medical science. Breaking down mortality data from dozens of US states, the two scholars found that, in large parts of the country, death rates had been increasing. This was particularly true in rural and former industrial regions – places like West Virginia, Kentucky and Arkansas – where rising death rates had led to falling life expectancies. That life expectancy was supposed to gradually increase over time had become an iron law of public health. Throughout their long careers and in true Ivy League style, Case and Deaton had been optimistic about the future of capitalism, technological innovation and medical improvements, and imagined that the future would be characterised by abundance and longevity. Their findings shattered these assumptions.

Upon closer inspection, these deaths were the aggregate effect of a massive social crisis. Middle-aged white Americans – mostly men without college degrees and mostly without work or precariously employed – were dying from suicide and substance abuse. Case and Deaton coined the term 'deaths of despair' to describe what they were seeing. The wave of recessions, offshoring and automation that swept through American industry from the late 1960s had caused enormous damage to Black Americans, many of whom had only recently achieved legal and political equality. Now, however, the same processes of unemployment and obsolescence that had catastrophically unmade Black communities in American inner cities was having a similar effect on white Americans.[1]

Following the two economists' lead, subsequent research has discovered that, far from being limited to the interior of the United States, stagnating life expectancies caused by rising rates of addiction, suicide and crumbling infrastructures of care were endemic in other parts of the global north and had been for some time. Indeed, some post-industrial regions of Europe and the United States are experiencing a slower and less dramatic version of the surge in mortality rates seen in Russia after the Soviet collapse, where male life expectancy fell by almost six years between 1991 and 1994.[2] In 2020, a team of public health experts based at the University of Glasgow led by the epidemiologist David Walsh began gathering fifty years' worth of data on mortality rates in ten different towns and cities in order to see whether Case and Deaton's discoveries could also be found in Britain. It is perhaps no surprise that they found that, in England, Liverpool had seen the greatest incidences of 'deaths of despair' since 1981.[3]

These deaths took many forms. Walsh's model only included excess deaths from alcohol abuse, drug abuse and suicides, but we can also add the city's unusually high rates of heart disease and cancer. While Liverpool's crippling economic crisis had left its urban landscape scarred, hollow and polluted, it was also slowly destroying the bodies of many of its residents. In the 1980s and 1990s, poverty and ill-health, compounded by a range of spectacular new public health crises, ground away at an under-employed and abandoned population. Unlike the Hillsborough disaster, which unfolded on national television, these deaths were quiet and structural, occurring in the city's shadows. They were concentrated among those who dwelled in the city's social margins – gay men, heroin addicts, sex workers and people of colour from all backgrounds. In Liverpool, we can trace the longer history of what, according to the journalist Sarah O'Connor, doctors in declining towns and cities in Britain have recently started calling 'shit life syndrome'.[4]

In defiance of national and local governments that seemed willing to abandon them to an early death, however, these constituencies organised from below to establish new and radical networks of care. Groups such as the Liverpool Racial Minority Health Group, the Mersey Drugs Project and AIDS support networks such as the Merseyside AIDS Support Group and Mersey Body Positive fought both inside and outside the welfare state for a new kind of healthcare that would better serve Liverpool's heterogenous, unequal and post-colonial social order. New solidarities, quietly forged in hospital rooms, needle exchanges and elderly homes, marked a hopeful and determined refusal to be cut adrift.

For much of its modern history, healthcare in Liverpool had followed the rhythms of the city's imperial maritime economy. Liverpool was caught in the middle of a global epidemiological whirlpool, exposed to the viruses and other ailments that circulated among transient seafarers, migrants and animals dead or alive as they moved between ports on every continent on earth. The city's public health landscape was inseparable from its status as one of Britain's most trafficked borders.

As late as the 1940s and 1950s, the port's Chief Medical Officer was tasked with managing and containing the tropical diseases that washed up on the city's shores. In the first two years after the Second World War, Liverpool saw cases of diphtheria, typhoid fever, amoebic dysentery, bacillary dysentery and leprosy, all of which arrived through the port, carried by the crew or the passengers of inter-continental ships.[5] Smallpox stowed away on ships to wreak havoc in Liverpool, long after the disease had been effectively eliminated in Britain in the 1930s. In 1946, the city saw a minor epidemic of smallpox totalling thirty cases and eleven deaths.[6] Bessie Braddock, the MP for Liverpool Exchange, repeatedly called for more stringent quarantine measures and harsh punishments for those who had been exposed to the illness but refused vaccination.[7] Malaria, meanwhile, was a persistent problem, with 200–300 cases recorded and treated in Liverpool each year in the late 1940s.[8] Chinese sailors in Hong Kong signing on for work on Liverpool ships were subjected to rigorous health screenings, with tuberculosis and venereal disease of particular concern.[9] Diseases lived in goods as well as people. The processing of animal products meant that dock workers were sometimes exposed to anthrax – usually a few cases each year.[10] In the immediate post-war decades, the containment of these diseases prompted scenes that were a curious mix of the post-war modern and the Victorian gothic. Ill sailors laid low aboard ships from tropical outposts were collected at the port by ambulances and quarantined in NHS hospitals in the city's suburbs.

At the same time, port medical authorities feared even greater monsters. In 1947, a massive cholera outbreak in Egypt meant that all ships that had passed through Egyptian ports had to have their drinking water sterilised and their fresh produce destroyed on arrival in Liverpool.[11] Meanwhile, fear of psittacosis, an acute respiratory disease carried by tropical birds, meant that ships had to be inspected for parrots, which were destroyed if discovered.[12] More frightening still was the prospect of bubonic plague. The last case of bubonic plague in Liverpool was in 1926 when a watchman on the docks was stricken with the disease.[13] It was fear of plague, in particular, that motivated the port's elaborate battles with rats, both on arriving ships and on the docks. The Merseyside Dock and Harbour Board loaded and emptied 160 traps and 155 poison baits each day and, in the immediate post-war years, between 20,000 and 25,000 rats were killed each year by an army of professional rat catchers.[14]

The decline of Liverpool's maritime economy in the 1960s and 1970s led to a more parochial microbial environment for the city. The country's border shifted to inland airports. Goods enclosed in sterile metal containers were handled by fewer and fewer workers. The dramatic fall in the number of malaria patients recorded in the city – from 261 in 1948 to just three in 1973 – tells its own story about Liverpool's post-war de-globalisation.[15] The same motors of historical change that unmade the city's maritime economy – decolonisation, technological change, containerisation, recession and deindustrialisation – were, however, at the same time producing their own interrelated public health crises by the end of the twentieth century.[16]

According to almost any measure, 1980s Liverpool was less healthy than Britain as a whole. In 1981, the city's overall mortality rate was found to be 10 per cent higher than the rest of England and Wales.[17] Rates of respiratory cancer, blood disease, brain damage and pneumonia were 30 per cent higher in Liverpool than the average. Meanwhile, rates of heart disease were 20 per cent higher and rates of breast cancer 10 per cent higher.[18] As we have already seen, David Walsh's survey of six English cities including Manchester, Leeds and Sheffield found that, since 1981, Liverpool has had the highest prevalence of poisonings by drug-taking, one of the leading 'deaths of despair'.[19] In fact, other than congenital anomalies, the only mortality indicator in which Liverpool fared better than the rest of the country was the number of people dying in car accidents, a figure explained by the fact that the city's poverty had resulted in lower rates of car ownership.[20]

As early as 1980, the Black Report, an influential study commissioned by the Department of Health, found, to many people's surprise, that despite overall improvements in health during the twentieth century there existed massive and widening inequalities between people of different classes and regions of the country. The Report found that in some age cohorts unskilled workers were dying at more than twice the rate of the professional middle classes.[21] Liverpool, with its large number of poor, unskilled and precariously employed workers, was particularly vulnerable to this trend. In 1981, one Liverpool GP wrote to the *British Medical Journal* to draw attention to the ways that his patients had been profoundly affected by the loss of work. In middle-aged or older men, redundancy had resulted in more requests for sicknotes. At the same time, married women were suffering with increased rates of anxiety and depression as often 'it is the wife who is left to cope with financial problems'. Under these circumstances, doctors were left to pick up the pieces of a ruined economy. As the GP put it, 'in these instances the doctor has become the agency, par excellence, who is expected to cure the problems and alleviate the symptoms, and it is difficult to explain that a prescription for benzodiazepines will not make the unpaid electricity or gas bill miraculously disappear'.[22]

This was never supposed to have been the case. After all, for much of the twentieth century, the health of the population of Liverpool, like that of Britain as a whole, had been improving. This was true particularly in the years after the formation of the NHS in 1948. Between the 1930s and 1980s, for example, the percentage of children who died either in stillbirth or in the first year of infancy fell from 10 per cent to 2 per cent on Merseyside. According to one calculation, if this improvement had not occurred, there would be 200,000 fewer people living in the region, an extraordinary figure given the region's already significant collapse in population during the post-war era.[23] By the 1980s, Liverpool's ill-health was calling into question the expectation that the massive improvements of the twentieth century would continue into the twenty-first.

For people of colour in Liverpool, however, this came as less of a surprise. As with housing and employment, the city's Black population had long held a subordinate position within Britain's health service. The Black Report had found that people of colour of all class backgrounds had significantly higher mortality rates than white residents of England and Wales.[24] Many doctors were baffled and uninterested in diseases that were particularly prevalent among migrant populations, such as sickle cell disease.[25] Across Britain, migrants, particularly women of colour, had provided much of the labour that underpinned the early NHS, particularly its underpaid and overworked nurses.[26] In Liverpool, however, there were exceptionally few Black nurses working in the city's hospitals, an effect of the intense racial segregation of the city's labour market. In 1982, out of 170 student nurses in training, only two were Black. Of the city's ninety-two ward sisters, only two were Black, and there were no Black nurses in Liverpool working above the level of ward sister.[27]

Racial inequalities in healthcare systems were acutely felt by the city's elderly Black population, who were all but excluded from care homes and other support services in the post-war period.

In 1983, a major report from the city's social services department found that there were only seven Black elders in the city's 1,143 council-owned elderly care homes. What's more, of the 4,553 elderly people in the city using the free, council-run 'meals on wheels' food service, only nine were Black.[28] These inequalities were particularly consequential for the city's small but established Somali community. Most of Liverpool's Somali community had arrived in a single cohort during the 1950s as seamen to make up for labour shortages on British ships. By 1985, an investigation into this community found that its small population had high numbers of single, elderly and isolated men. As practising Muslims, most of the men had been unable to eat the food provided in the meals on wheels service and were dependent on various local charities for housing and social activities.[29]

Mental health, however, was perhaps the area where the dissonance between the needs of Black people and the provision of care was the greatest in post-war Liverpool. Black people tended to be subjected to more coercive and intrusive mental health interventions. One report published in 1987 found that, across Britain, Black people were twenty-five times more likely than white people to be referred to psychiatric institutions by a court order and that, on arrival, 59 per cent of Black patients were given major tranquillisers compared with just 38 per cent of white patients.[30] In the late 1980s, Black mental health activists in Liverpool gathered evidence of multiple instances in which Black people suffering a mental health crisis had been mistreated by a hostile overlapping bureaucracy that included healthcare professionals, social services and the police.

One of the stories gathered by these activists is worth recounting at length. It concerned Jane, a young Black woman from Toxteth who had been suffering from post-partum depression after the birth of her first child. After a fight with her partner, Jane checked herself into hospital late at night in a state of distress, wanting a bed and a sleeping tablet. The next morning, when visited by a registrar in the hospital, Jane insisted, in the words of a doctor who was interviewed later, on discussing 'major political issues, major social issues particularly issues relating to race'. Irritated by these comments, the registrar prescribed her a strong tranquilliser, which she refused to take, and during the following day she continued to talk to doctors and consultants about 'world problems'. At one point, Jane joined a consultant on their round of the hospital, engaging them in conversation, before returning to her bed after being confronted by a group of nurses, saying that she didn't want any violence. The following afternoon, she again engaged the same consultant during their rounds who, getting frustrated, 'sectioned' her under the Mental Health Act of 1983, meaning she could be detained for up to seventy-two hours and forced to take the major tranquillisers she had been prescribed. Another doctor, interviewed later, expressed concern about the consultant's decision, confessing that 'I think on that day he was a little angry' and noting there seemed little evidence that Jane posed a threat to herself or others.

After being detained and forced into taking tranquillisers against her will, the situation escalated. Jane told a doctor that she thought she might be a potential 'African queen'. The doctor classified this statement as a psychiatric delusion, justifying the decision by noting that while 'it is possible for Derek Hatton to believe, despite all his political problems, that he will be Prime Minister in the future… it is more unlikely for a Liverpool 8 housewife who is not involved in politics to become Prime Minister'. Later interviews with Jane, however, established that her father had been descended from West African royalty. Her claim, classified as a psychiatric delusion, was in fact far more believable than Hatton's prime ministerial hopes. Nevertheless, Jane was given a cocktail of intensive tranquillisers and sleeping pills over the following days. Three months after her stay in hospital, researchers found that Jane was 'really not well' and developed 'uncontrollable shaking' as a side effect of her ongoing medication.[31]

Jane's story shows how, for Black people in Liverpool, particularly women, mental health provision overlapped with forms of coercive state violence and policing. Her radical politics, a politics forged by the day-to-day experience of being a poor Black woman in Toxteth, was pathologised to the most extreme degree and used to justify a litany of unwanted, intrusive and unnecessary medical interventions. In another instance, recorded by mental health activists, a West Indian migrant in Liverpool was incarcerated in a mental asylum for expressing the hope, common among Rastafarians and pan-Africans, that he would 'get his people to their God in Africa'.[32] By the 1980s, the residues of the world-making political ambition of many of the city's mid-twentieth-century Black activists, from Pastor Daniels Ekarte recruiting schoolchildren in the 1940s to the internationalist protests organised by the CPDA in the 1950s, was being equated to madness.

Faced with this hostility, Liverpool's Black residents organised their own care, staking their place within a crumbling healthcare system. The way was forged by Black women. Across Britain, Black feminists had called attention to the racism and condescension of white, male, middle-class doctors working for the NHS, highlighting how Black women were often encouraged to accept intrusive forms of contraception based on false assumptions about their sexuality.[33] In Liverpool, groups like Priority, founded by two Black women in 1983, ran support groups to boost confidence in dealing with the NHS and articulating health problems to doctors.[34] This was also the aim of Mary Seacole House, named after a Black nurse who served in the Crimean War, which emerged out of a drop-in clinic run by the Liverpool Black Sisters in the late 1980s. The House was founded specifically to offer help to Black people suffering mental health problems. It offered emergency treatment but also help with navigating the often punitive and labyrinthine system of social care.[35]

The most radical and systematic critique of the city's healthcare establishment was made by the South African sociologist and healthcare activist Ntombenhle Protasia Khotie Torkington. In 1980, Torkington was one of the founders of the Liverpool Racial Minority Health Group. As well as gathering data on racial health inequalities and lobbying officials, the group performed their own DIY forms of care. Torkington and her colleagues set up a regular blood pressure screening service in the city's Caribbean Centre. The group worked with the isolated community of Somali women in the city to help build bridges between them and a healthcare service that had been hostile to some of their specific religious needs. They also helped set up a translating and interpreting service to work across the health authority, helping speakers of ten different languages. Finally, they founded a mental health drop-in centre in Toxteth, where Jane's account, recounted above, was identified and recorded.[36] Like many Black critics of Britain's care infrastructure, Torkington argued that the NHS should be viewed as an instrument for disciplining bodies and maximising productivity, treating people, in her words, as 'mere productive units' and focusing on individual rather than structural or environmental causes of illness.[37]

By the end of the twentieth century, Liverpool faced something close to a generalised public health crisis. While no longer so exposed to the diseases that arrived aboard ships from distant ports, the destruction of the city's economy created new health problems born out of poverty and hopelessness. Like those in the Appalachian mountains, where Case and Deaton did their fieldwork, Liverpool's deaths of despair were layered on top of an already deeply unequal and often carceral healthcare system that had mistreated people of colour from its inception. From the mid-1980s, with its population already ground down by disease and early death, Liverpool would also bear the brunt of two interrelated public health catastrophes that tore through the bodies of some of its most vulnerable residents: heroin and AIDS.

Merseyside's heroin crisis began not in Liverpool but on the Wirral peninsula – the thick strip of land to the west of the city sandwiched between the Mersey and the Irish Sea. The Wirral is often thought of as verdant and affluent, a place where retired footballers and minor gentry ride horses and go sailing. In the last third of the twentieth century, however, many of the peninsula's major population centres – places like Birkenhead and Moreton – were experiencing a profound social crisis. Like Liverpool itself, parts of the Wirral had seen their main sources of employment, such as dock work, shipbuilding and light manufacturing, wither and die. By 1985, parts of the peninsula had unemployment rates as high as 33 per cent.[38] The Wirral had become a patchwork of affluent suburbs and villages interspersed with workless council estates and ruined relics of a former industrial era.

Before the 1980s, heroin was extremely rare in Britain. In 1968, there were just 1,000 known users of the drug in the country and only 147 outside of London.[39] In the 1960s, the drug was mainly associated with artists and bohemians. It was taken in nightclubs or at parties rather than in darkened private rooms. In the 1970s, addicts were mostly an ageing cohort of refugees from the 1960s counter-culture, with new addicts under the age of 20 falling for much of the decade.[40] Heroin's reputation as a cheap, highly popular street drug with tens of thousands of long-term addicts in working-class former industrial communities was forged in a brief window between 1983 and 1985. During those years, Britain was engulfed by a tsunami of cheap brown heroin, most of which was grown in the mountainous borderlands between Myanmar and China and arrived in the country through a customs regime that had been perforated by under-staffing from Thatcher government cuts.[41] In 1983, the number of police seizures of heroin doubled from the previous year. By 1985, there were four times more people found guilty of heroin-related drug offences than there were in 1980 and five times more heroin addicts registered with local doctors – a tiny fraction of the whole number. The number of addicts receiving methadone treatment doubled between 1980 and 1984, then doubled again by 1987.[42]

Like most places in Britain, the Wirral had only a small number of known long-term drug users at the beginning of the 1980s. Within a few years, however, the peninsula had what was widely agreed to be one of the worst heroin problems in the country. Between 1980 and 1987, the number of known heroin users increased from fewer than 100 to 5,000.[43] By 1988, more than 8 per cent of all 16–24-year-olds living on the sprawling Ford housing estate on the western fringes of Birkenhead were known addicts.[44] The ensuing epidemic of addiction tore through the social fabric of the peninsula. In 1984, Birkenhead was famously described as

'Smack City' by *The Observer*. Newspapers printed lurid and almost certainly false stories about heroin being sold to children hidden in ice-cream cones outside school gates.[45]

Aghast at the scale of the crisis, a handful of investigative social workers attempted to piece together what had happened. They found that, from the late 1970s, Wirral GPs had been prescribing opioids to patients suffering from minor ailments such as headaches and backaches. These pills, such as Diconal and Palfium, were extremely addictive and were doled out in huge quantities. While some of the patients who received these prescriptions were genuine, others were found to have been exaggerating or fabricating illnesses to gain access to the drugs. As a result, small beachheads of addiction were emerging undetected, priming the peninsula for a full-scale invasion. The fuse was lit when, at some undetermined point in the early 1980s, a heroin dealer from Liverpool made enough money from his trade to buy a home and set up shop in one of the more affluent areas of the Wirral. Capitalising on the region's slow-burning prescription opioid crisis, this dealer began shifting larger and larger amounts of heroin to nearby housing estates. Soon he had enlisted a massive network of smaller dealers, most of whom were likely to have been addicts themselves, funding their habit in the absence of any other kind of work.[46]

Within a few years, the Wirral's heroin crisis had crossed the river to Liverpool. By the late 1980s, Liverpool had become well known as a heroin hotspot. One of the best-selling and most lurid accounts of heroin addiction written that decade was by Tam Stewart, a Liverpool addict whose book, *The Heroin Users*, published in 1987, helped cement the city's association with the drug. Her memoir glamorised what she called the Liverpool 'heroin scene', referring to the drug as a 'kind of inner-city homeopathy, the ultimate self-medication, the final antidote to stress, violence and ambition'. For her, the drug was a way of compensating not for unemployment but for the drudgery of a 'repetitive, disappointing, everyday grind'. Stewart talked readers through every aspect of addiction and recovery, from learning to use the gear, to where and how to score from drug dealers, to the effect of the drug on the user's sex life.[47]

Stewart, a middle-class university graduate with a steady job, was not, however, representative of most of the city's addicts. As in the Wirral, heroin in Liverpool thrived among populations that had been rendered surplus by economic collapse. By the late 1980s Toxteth had become one of the focal points of the city's heroin trade. In 1989, the Gifford Inquiry into the causes of the 1981 uprisings noted that in the intervening seven years Granby Street, a busy thoroughfare of shops that bisected the neighbourhood, had become an open-air market for the sale of heroin. Shopkeepers on the street complained that the drugs trade occluded all other kinds of commerce. One shopkeeper even claimed that dealers would use his scales to measure and cut quantities of the drug. A local who testified to the inquiry claimed that 90 per cent of the drug traffic was driven by outsiders to the neighbourhood, many of whom arrived in taxis to make purchases. In some instances, Black activists in Toxteth took it on themselves to drive drug dealers out of the neighbourhood.[48]

The heroin epidemic on Merseyside and in other parts of Britain had raised new questions about how the drug would be policed and regulated. As a major port, Liverpool had a long history with opium – heroin's unrefined predecessor – a drug that became associated with the city's Chinese community and had been an invitation for intensive policing and border controls. As early as 1906, for example, the *Sunday Chronicle*'s notorious and sensational accounts of Liverpool's Chinatown printed the false rumour that the city's Chinese's community were injecting opium into the sweets sold to white children in the neighbourhood's shops, an eerie prefiguring of the scare stories in 1980s Birkenhead about the selling of heroin to children in ice-cream cones.[49] As we saw at the beginning of this book, the assumed prevalence of opium smoking had been invoked by officials as a justification for the deportations of Chinese merchant seamen in 1945 and 1946.

However, outside the racialised moral panics in Liverpool and other port cities, opium and heroin had, for much of the twentieth century, been the preserve of the middle and upper classes. It was prescribed to addicts whose addiction was treated as an illness rather than a crime, many of whom were recovering from long-term illnesses and many of whom were themselves doctors.[50] Indeed, for the first two post-war decades, cannabis, a drug associated with Britain's Black migrant communities, was far more intensively policed than heroin or opium. In 1968, for example, there were 3,071 prosecutions for cannabis-related drug offences, compared with just seventy-three for opioids.[51] The discrepancy between the medicalised middle-class heroin user collecting their weekly dose from the GP and the criminalised Chinese or West Indian migrant selling and smoking opium or cannabis was striking. It bore a resemblance to contemporary US drug laws, where possession of crack cocaine, associated with the US Black community, has been punished far more intensively than possession of regular cocaine.[52] This bifurcated 'British system' of drug regulation lasted until 1971, when a new Misuse of Drugs Act ended the prescription loophole and introduced a blanket ban on the consumption of heroin in any context.

For the first decade after the passage of the Misuse of Drugs Act, Britain's small cohort of heroin addicts were dealt with by an ad hoc mixture of clinical treatment and police intervention. It was only in the early 1980s, when heroin became newly associated with Britain's workless underclass, that police enforcement of the Misuse of Drugs Act was radically stepped up.[53] Within just a few years, any alternative to outright suppression had become unimaginable. In Liverpool, this new consensus in favour of intensive policing was reaffirmed by a peculiar incident in 1988. That autumn, the neoliberal economist Patrick Minford publicly declared his support for the full legalisation of heroin. Minford, a professor at Liverpool University and a prominent advisor to Margaret Thatcher, was an unlikely advocate for decriminalisation. His fame came from a paper published in 1984 in which he outlined what became known as the 'Liverpool Model' of right-wing economics, an argument that a drastic reduction in taxation, a minimal state and high levels of unemployment would stimulate growth.[54] It was an argument that was stubbornly oblivious to the bleak realities of the city in which he lived and worked. In 2022, Minford's public profile had a mini resurgence when, during her brief premiership, Liz Truss prominently cited him as an influence.[55] Minford's public insistence that legalising heroin would lead the price of the drug to fall, disincentivising crime and saving money on policing, was a chapter of his career that is now almost entirely forgotten.

The economist's comments prompted a minor sensation in the city. His views were immediately disowned by a spokesperson for Thatcher. Bob Wareing, the Labour MP for Liverpool West Derby, announced that it was 'absolutely astonishing that a man like Professor Minford, who claims to be an intellectual, can put forward such ideas'.[56] One city councillor, Roger Lafferty, meanwhile, went even further, calling for Minford to be fired from his job at the university and declaring him a 'muckspreader' who was 'as bad as traders who sell T-shirts with drugs logos on them'.[57] At a combustible meeting of the Council's subcommittee on drugs, it was agreed that Minford should be hauled in to explain his views. In the end, Richard Stevenson, one of Minford's allies at the university and a fellow believer in decriminalisation, was given the unfortunate job of defending their views before the committee. There, he was rounded on by politicians and activist parents. When Stevenson argued that heroin should be as cheap as cigarettes, one mother from a neighbourhood family support group announced that 'I feel like screaming when I hear you say that', and stormed out of the meeting close to tears. A police officer, meanwhile, demanded that he spend the day with him on his rounds. The meeting ended with the committee's chair urging him to reconsider his views.[58]

Despite this deeply felt consensus among city leaders about the ongoing necessity of criminalisation, the realities of policing Liverpool's heroin crisis in the 1980s were more complex. Drug Squad officers in Liverpool likened attempts to police the drug to stepping on jelly: 'it splatters all over the place'.[59] In Toxteth, much to the frustration of many locals, officers seemed to oscillate between appeasement and spectacular arrests.[60] In an incendiary testimonial to the Gifford Inquiry, an ex-police officer named David Scott who had worked in Toxteth alleged that officers in the district focused on arrests of minor local dealers to the detriment of investigating organised crime further up the chain of command. The effect of this, Scott argued, was that drug dealers 'appeared to be making individual deals with individual police so that their own activities would not in fact be curtailed'. Even more seriously, Scott alleged that 'The force policy in general appeared to be that anything, since the 1981 riots, was better than a public order confrontation in Liverpool 8 and therefore... the community would be left to "dope itself up"... Meanwhile, local officers would be allowed to work increasing amounts of overtime.'[61] Instead of an open antagonism between police and drug dealers, what had emerged was a complex ecology, one in which all parties benefitted from the ongoing abandonment of the Black population of Toxteth.

Even though Toxteth was an important venue for the buying and selling of heroin, the drug was rare among Black communities in Liverpool and across Britain more broadly.[62] Instead, heroin was the drug of choice for the downwardly mobile – those who had once been able to expect satisfying and economically secure lives but who were now condemned to a workless future. A survey of heroin users on the Wirral found that addicts were primarily young, unemployed men whose futures had been cancelled by the ongoing erosion of secure work. It found that 81 per cent of users were unemployed, 56 per cent were aged between 18 and 22 and that there were 3.6 male users for every woman.[63] For the white and mostly male populations who had been rendered obsolete by the changing world economy, heroin had become an alternative way of killing time, sourcing pleasure and making and spending money.

In the autumn of 1982, *Gay News*, the leading newspaper for Britain's gay community at the time, ran an extended feature about gay life in Liverpool. What they found was a mixed picture. Liverpool's gay scene was lively yet disorganised. While they found little in the way of sustained political activism or consciousness, there existed a dynamic network of pubs and clubs. These included the long-standing Masquerade Club, affectionately known as 'the Mazzie', and the Lisbon, whose manager, Monica, ran a service for gay Liverpool seamen allowing them to 'ring in from all over the world to check their beloveds are toeing the line'. The journalists were pleasantly surprised by the city's well-developed trans scene, who they spent an evening with at the Link, a busy if somewhat run-down centre that served the gay community. The trans community had a weekly phoneline and an informal support service for the spouses of trans women, both of which had a claim to being the first of its kind in Britain.[64]

The epicentre of Liverpool's gay scene was Toxteth. Uprooted by German bombs, slum clearance and the closure of the docks, Liverpool's gay community had followed the city's Black community on an inland migration away from the docks and into the city's southern neighbourhoods. There, they had been contained by a housing policy that prioritised the needs of heterosexual couples. As Elvis – a DJ at the Masquerade Club who claimed that three-quarters of all the gay people he knew lived in the neighbourhood – told the journalists, 'a single person trying to find a flat in Liverpool will only ever get offered one in... Toxteth'. The relationship between the Black and gay communities in the neighbourhood, of which, the article noted, there was naturally some overlap was, by all accounts, mostly harmonious.[65]

The scene had inevitably been shaped by the city's economic collapse, not just because of the tendency to congregate in the ruined and cavernous Victorian homes abandoned by the city's depopulation, but also because of the high rates of poverty and unemployment among its members. The journalists noted the relative absence of a gay middle class, a group who, according to one person interviewed, had isolated themselves in the suburbs. As one gay resident of Toxteth put it, 'those kind of people have private dinner parties in their New Brighton homes'. Another estimated that 90 per cent of her friends were unemployed.[66]

Two months earlier, *Gay News* had published a smaller story, tucked away on page 9, about a second British gay man who had died of a mysterious disease that the paper was calling 'Gay Compromise Syndrome'. The disease, which suppressed the immune system to the point where it became vulnerable to rare forms of terminal illness, had already claimed the lives of 200 gay men in the United States.[67] The disease would, of course, eventually be renamed Acquired Immune Deficiency Syndrome, or AIDS. It was a consequence of being infected by an emergent virus that would come to be named Human Immunodeficiency Virus, or HIV. Over the following decades, this new disease would kill tens of millions of people – primarily gay men, intravenous drug users and people in the global south.

AIDS would reshape gay life in Liverpool as it would in every British town and city. HIV had incubated in primates living in the forests of francophone West Africa and had likely jumped to the human population during a period of deforestation and urbanisation. The exact moment that this happened remains murky and contested, but its deeper cause was the expansion of colonial powers into tropical Africa, a historical event at which Liverpool merchants had been at the vanguard. Had the AIDS pandemic emerged a generation earlier, when Liverpool was still a global centre for imperial maritime trade, then the city may have been among the first in the global north to witness the disease.

AIDS arrived in Britain during a period of immense turbulence when it came to the discussion and regulation of sexuality. The decriminalisation of gay sex for men over the age of 21 in 1967, coupled with the gradual undoing of the heterosexual breadwinner-homemaker household that had reigned supreme for much of the twentieth century, raised unresolved questions about the present and future of sexual and social relations.[68] The Thatcher government oversaw and helped instigate a wave of homophobic resentment in Britain. In 1987, Thatcher used her party conference speech to declare that children were being 'cheated' out of 'a sound start in life' by being taught that 'they had an inalienable right to be gay'.[69] The same year a survey of British social attitudes reported that 74 per cent of people thought that gay relationships were 'always, or mostly always wrong', up from 62 per cent just four years earlier.[70] A few months later, Thatcher's government introduced the notorious Section 28 amendment to the 1986 Local Government Act, which prohibited the 'promotion' of homosexuality in schools and other council venues, a bureaucratic tweak that effectively criminalised the merest acknowledgement of queer people's existence.

By the beginning of 1988, 2,500 people were known to be HIV-positive in Britain, roughly 70 per cent of whom had contracted the disease through sex with another man. Six hundred and ten had died and many more deaths were coming.[71] A chasm had opened between the gay men dying on the front lines of the epidemic and the politicians and many of the doctors responsible for its treatment and regulation. When it became clear that the gay community and drug users would bear the brunt of the epidemic, one reporter covering the crisis described it as like 'dealing with a foreign story, [that] happened to other people in other countries'.[72]

Like many places in Britain, Liverpool in the mid-1980s was awash with anxious rumours and false stories concerning AIDS. In a 1987 survey of Merseyside residents, more than half thought you could develop the disease after living in the same house as someone with AIDS, a third thought the disease could be transmitted by kissing and/or by drinking out of a glass that someone had used.[73] Describing AIDS as a 'killer that sails in with the tide', the *Liverpool Echo* ran stories of sex workers catching the virus from African sailors who, the paper claimed, refused to wear condoms.[74] The paper also published a sensational story about an AIDS victim who was secretly depositing used needles throughout the city to infect as many people as possible, claiming that 'used needles have been found in parks across Liverpool jutting out… like deadly spears'.[75] Meanwhile, officials uncovered a hoax in which hundreds of people in the city were sent fake letters on mocked-up official letterhead informing them they might have been exposed to the virus.[76]

The biggest concern for politicians and public health officials, however, was not so much gay men, but the tens of thousands of heroin users in the city, an unknown number of whom were using, sharing and then reusing syringes. The pathology of HIV meant that AIDS struck at the pleasure centres of late twentieth-century urban life. For prudish politicians, journalists and health officials, the disease demanded an abrupt confrontation with the precise mechanics of heroin use and gay sex. By the late 1980s, in its own fearful and confused way, Merseyside was bracing for a massive and sudden AIDS epidemic.

But the crisis never came. In 1988, to many people's astonishment, Merseyside recorded the lowest number of AIDS cases of any health authority in the country. The region had diagnosed just 21 cases compared with 304 in the greater Manchester's health authority, 324 in greater Birmingham and 2,410 in North-West London.[77] While officials were keen to emphasise that it was still early in the epidemic, these were extraordinary figures. How was it possible that a city with one of the worst heroin problems in the country could have so few cases?

These numbers were partly explained by Liverpool's newfound isolation from the global networks through which the pandemic was moving. But they were also the result of a secret project, pioneered by a radical group of public health academics and activists. Three years earlier, when awareness of AIDS was still at a relatively early stage, John Ashton and Howard Seymour, two senior public health officials from the Merseyside Regional Health Authority, happened to attend a lecture in Dublin by Glen Margo. Margo was a health activist who was working on the front lines of the AIDS epidemic in San Francisco and who was himself dying of the disease. Traumatised by what he had seen, Margo urged the officials to set up a clean needle exchange programme for heroin users to help offset a catastrophic epidemic among the city's addicts. Ashton and Seymour invited Margo to Liverpool to give a series of lectures about how to prepare for the coming AIDS crisis. In 1986, along with a community activist and former addict named Allan Perry, the two men acquired a squat, inconspicuous building on Maryland Street, just east of the city centre. There they opened the first large-scale needle exchange in Britain.[78]

Terrified of a backlash from politicians, the press and the

police, all of whom had reaffirmed their commitment to forcefully suppressing heroin use in the city, the group had to proceed in secret. One participant described its early months as like 'being in a spy thriller'.[79] The service was advertised solely by word of mouth among known communities of users. The two men met with the editor of the *Liverpool Echo*, who they persuaded to establish a temporary moratorium on any news stories about the exchange.[80] The head of the city's police Drug Squad was also informed about the scheme and was persuaded to hold off on making any arrests for possession of syringes, something that was technically an offence under the 1971 Misuse of Drugs Act.[81] The men deliberately avoided reaching out to the highly organised anti-drugs groups run by parents in the city, such as the one who confronted Richard Stevenson at his tempestuous inquest in front of the Council, knowing that they would disapprove of the scheme.[82]

Despite their secretive presence and their reluctance to advertise, the exchange was soon inundated with users. In its first sixteen months, the exchange was visited by more than 900 addicts, many of whom paid multiple visits.[83] Shortly after it opened, a dealer who ran a 'shooting gallery' – a space where addicts would inject – brought three bin bags full of used needles to the clinic and was recruited by the team to become an outreach volunteer.[84] Organisers went out of their way to expunge the criminal vocabulary associated with drug use, referring to visiting addicts as 'clients' and describing their operation as a 'consumer-advice service'.[85] When visitors arrived at the exchange, they found something resembling a cross between a supermarket and a health clinic. On arrival, they would deposit their used syringes in reinforced metal boxes that were regularly collected and destroyed by the Health Authority. Then, first-time visitors were asked to show staff the injection sites on their body to prove their eligibility for the scheme, at which time many were offered advice about safer injecting techniques. Next, visitors were given the choice of three types of needle and three sizes of barrel. Few questions were asked, and each visitor was given a unique nickname by which they could be referred without being identified.[86]

The project made a point of reaching out to sex workers in the city. Their work, coupled with the fact that many were also heroin addicts, meant that they were particularly vulnerable to catching and transmitting AIDS. A female sex worker had been one of the first victims of the disease in the city. Living criminalised and precarious lives, sex workers were attracted to the scheme by the promise of anonymity and the absence of the police. The project enlisted a former hairdresser, Lyn Matthews, to spend five months gathering evidence of drug and contraception use among the city's sex workers. Matthews established regular contact with over 100 women, to whom she would distribute free condoms and information packets about the disease.[87] The project also made connections with Liverpool's male sex workers, many of whom were servicing married men in a handful of known clubs. Some were underage and like their female counterparts were extremely nervous about establishing contact with the state in any form.[88]

Liverpool's needle exchange began its life as an insurgent, experimental scheme to uncouple the experience of addiction and, to a lesser extent, sex work from the punitive approach that had characterised much of the city's official response to the heroin crisis. As we saw in Chapter 8, the Militant Labour administration, incumbent in the city at the time, were firm advocates for the ruthless policing of drug use of all kinds, believing that drugs hindered the development of class consciousness. As one Militant activist put it, 'we need… citizens who can assist in the struggle for a more egalitarian society, rather than passive and dulled individuals… free needles are only the sharp end of a syringe filled with problems'.[89] Indeed, one of the project's organisers would later claim that the Militant Council did everything they could to torpedo the exchange, including what they described as 'personal attacks on staff'.[90]

With the exchange flourishing in the face of hostility from the Council, the project moved away from the secrecy that had characterised its first few months. In its second year of operation, its organisers published an information pack complete with a video, to distribute to health authorities across the country urging them to replicate Liverpool's needle exchange programme. In advocating for needle exchanges more broadly, the project's organisers deployed a utilitarian logic that suited the ideological climate of the 1980s. The group calculated that each AIDS patient cost £30,000 for the health service to treat, a figure comparable to the entire cost of setting up a new exchange.[91] Within a few years, Liverpool's project had ten satellite exchanges throughout Merseyside, servicing thousands of addicts, and there were needle exchanges in London, Cambridge, Swindon and Peterborough. In 1989, meanwhile, it was reported that, for the second year running, Merseyside had the lowest number of AIDS cases of any health authority in the country. With only 154 known cases, Liverpool compared favourably to cities like Edinburgh with similar heroin problems but no needle exchanges and where 60 per cent of known heroin users were estimated to be HIV positive.[92]

While Liverpool's needle exchange succeeded in heading off a significant mortality event among its heroin users, this did little to help the dozens of people, primarily gay men, who were dying of AIDS in the city in the late 1980s. By the end of the decade, many gay men with AIDS who had left Liverpool for other cities were returning to live out what remained of their lives.[93] Merseyside's initial response to the outbreak was anxious and muddled, as it was in most other places in Britain. Patients were given isolated rooms in hospitals. Ambulance drivers confided that they were nervous about taking AIDS patients.[94] Many were disowned by friends, family and lovers. In a candid interview in a local newspaper, Tom, a person with AIDS in the Wirral, described how he was fired from his job and was shunned by his two brothers when he declared his diagnosis. His parents, while supportive, gave him his own plates and cutlery to eat off.[95]

Many gay men with the disease, having already been driven to the margins of society by their sexuality, were treated as pariahs and faced lonely deaths in quarantine. Their condition necessitated radical new ways of providing care, love and support beyond the frontiers of the state and the traditional family. Importing medical and therapeutic practices from the United States, where many people with AIDS had been effectively abandoned by private healthcare companies, grassroots organisations emerged in Liverpool to fill the vacuum that had been left by an ill-prepared healthcare service, a hostile Conservative government and a homophobic society. In 1985, a group of eight volunteers set up the Merseyside AIDS Support Group (MASG), which ran one of the first anonymous AIDS phonelines in the country. The phoneline offered a makeshift form of counselling for those suffering from or living in fear of the disease. The volunteers, most of whom were women, educated themselves in 'the street language' of the city's gay community. Phoneline operators reported talking to people who were close to suicide and people who were wondering how to come out to their family, as well as men who wept with guilt because of their sexuality.[96] By the beginning of the 1990s, the group's phoneline was logging more than a thousand calls a year and was recruiting Cantonese- and Arabic-speaking counsellors.[97]

MASG also offered a service called 'buddying'. This was a radical social practice developed in the United States. Buddies were volunteers tasked with reaching out and developing relationships with individual sufferers of the disease, paying them visits at home, in hospital beds and even helping arrange their funerals. MASG had more than forty-five buddies who would perform tasks like bringing food to isolated victims, helping to look after the homes of those too ill to do so and in some instances providing childcare.[98] These relationships had no prescribed form and would vary from occasional phone calls and visits to the pub to profound, deeply felt familial connections that would last years. MASG even had their own internal counselling services for the many volunteers who had to deal with the death of their buddies.[99]

After 1987, the Mersey AIDS Support Group was joined by another support network called Mersey Body Positive (MBP). MBP, one branch of a nationwide 'Body Positive' movement, set out to forge a community among the small yet growing number of people on Merseyside who had been diagnosed with the disease. MBP had a small membership consisting mostly of gay men, almost all of whom were HIV positive and many of whom were dying of AIDS. In 1993, for example, the group had seventy-two service users, sixty-five of which were men. Over the previous year, thirteen others had died, twelve men and one woman.[100]

The group tried to ensure that those dying from the disease were able to live rich and fulfilling lives, organising art-making classes and yoga sessions and publishing recipes. It helped people who were ill with the disease navigate the often hostile and labyrinthine healthcare system, producing a glossary of terms to help sufferers understand their treatment options.[101] The MBP produced written advice for gay members on how to compose a legally binding will that would enshrine their partners rather than their blood relatives.[102] The group took an expansive and humanistic approach to care in ways that sometimes took fantastical and moving forms. For example, the group organised visits to a dolphin retreat on the West Coast of Ireland for people with AIDS. At the retreat, visitors would engage in group and individual therapy sessions interspersed with daily swims with Fungie, a dolphin that was described as a 'natural therapist.'[103]

The new organisations that flared into existence to plug the gaps in Merseyside's care infrastructure at times spoke the language of charity and at other times the language of welfare. Unlike either of these things, however, Black healthcare networks, insurgent needle exchanges, alternative therapy circles and delegations to hospital wards to visit isolated patients were sometimes implicit and sometimes explicit statements about how to make a better and more equal medical, social and political order. These groups prompted what the historian Melinda Cooper has described as the 'radical deinstitutionalization of care' and its re-making on new terms.[104] 'Care' is an ambiguous term. Depending on its use, it can refer to relationships that are intimate and enchanted or those that are bureaucratic and procedural. Via needle exchanges, phonelines and volunteer buddy systems, the various elements of care – medical expertise, practical support and unconditional, familial love – were disaggregated and reassembled in extraordinary new combinations. Care was volunteers making furtive, life-saving missions to deliver clean needles and condoms to sex workers in the dead of night and strangers sitting by the bedsides of the dying in hospital isolation wards.

Liverpool's modern skyline is cleft by two cathedrals. The city's Anglican Cathedral was commissioned in 1901 when Liverpool was a world-making imperial metropolis. It was finally completed in 1978, when the city was reaching the nadir of its vertiginous decline. Austere and brickish red, the cathedral is by some measures the fifth largest in the world – a solemn, gargantuan presence that towers over the transient borderlands between Toxteth and the rest of Liverpool. Less than a mile north is the city's Metropolitan Cathedral, the largest Catholic place of worship in England. Conceived of and built entirely during the 1960s, the Metropolitan Cathedral is dramatic and sculptural, its tower culminating in a circuit of spikes that resemble a crown or the head of a pineapple. Designed by the precocious Frederick Gibberd, the master planner of the Essex new town of Harlow, the cathedral feels tethered to a specific moment in Liverpool's history, one which has now passed away. If the Anglican Cathedral's mute, timeless monumentality felt awkward in such close proximity to the crumbling Victorian homes and bulldozed lots of Toxteth, then the Metropolitan Cathedral, now leaking and perennially refurbished, is a 1960s promise of future affluence that was never delivered.

For one week in late November 1992, both cathedrals were commandeered for an extraordinary commemoration of those who had died of AIDS in Liverpool. As with similar commemorations in the United States, its centrepiece was a vast, collectively made quilt, with individual squares designed by the family, friends and lovers of the disease's victims. The quilt was unveiled in a dramatic ceremony at the Anglican Cathedral. With balletic choreography, it was unveiled square by square by teams of volunteers folding and unfolding the fabric as the names of the dead were slowly read aloud. This was followed by three minutes of silence, poems and a talk from someone who was HIV positive, while strategically placed boxes of tissues placed among the pews caught the tears of the mourners.[105]

Like a politician lying in state, the quilt remained on display for a week, first at the Anglican and then at the Metropolitan Cathedral. While some came and went in silence, other visitors talked at length to the event's organisers about their reasons for wanting to see it. One man in his late forties who still lived with his mother and admitted to feeling extremely isolated confessed to organisers that he was positive with the disease and that this was the first time he had been able to tell anyone his situation. A family visited the quilt with their three daughters, telling organisers that the girls' uncle had died of AIDS. Meanwhile, his long-term partner, the girls' godfather and a close member of the family, was HIV positive. One recent migrant from Zimbabwe who visited with his son and daughter confessed that back in Zimbabwe 'almost all my female relatives have died' of the disease.[106]

Liverpool was grimly au fait with commemorations during these years. The intolerable losses of the Hillsborough disaster had produced their own forms of ritual and remembrance. Perhaps the most spectacular of these occurred one week after the tragedy, when people gathered across the city at 3.06pm, the time when the semi-final was stopped short by match officials, to remember the dead in various ways. At a time when politicians, the press and the police were engaged in a co-ordinated slander of the fans who had died, this felt like an act of defiance – an insistence on life's worth in the face of those who would happily abandon their memories to the abyss.[107] That day, a chain of 4,000 Liverpool FC and Everton scarfs were tied together and held aloft by fans to connect the one-mile distance between the teams' two stadiums. At the twilight of Liverpool's twentieth century, duelling sites of mass public assembly – the Anglican and Protestant Cathedral, Anfield and Goodison Park – were fleetingly commandeered to become communities of the dead, woven together by scarfs and quilts.

In the words of the great historian of culture Thomas Laqueur, 'the living need the dead far more than the dead need the living'.[108] As we will see in the next chapter, however, Liverpool's dead were about to be put to work in a much cruder and more lucrative sense.

Liverpool and Everton scarves adorn the goal mouth at Anfield to commemorate those who died in the Hillsborough disaster three days earlier.

II

The History Factory

This book opened with a description of the working life of Frank Shaw, a sea captain who had stewarded merchant ships on routes through the Mediterranean in the early twentieth century. These ships were agglomerations of steel and fuel that housed complex communities of sailors for months at a time. They had each been assembled by hundreds of specialist workers in enormous shipyards in places like Birkenhead, Glasgow or Tyneside with towering cranes that dominated their skylines. The ships were powered by coal or oil, their engines turning millions of compressed years of sunlight into propulsive power. They exhaled tall columns of black smoke from wide central chimneys. Anyone watching these ships depart Liverpool could have been forgiven for thinking that fragments of the city itself were breaking loose and drifting out to sea. As the century wore on, as Liverpool's docks closed and as traffic was redirected to the container terminals further upriver, ships of this size and sophistication progressively vanished from the lower Mersey. Those who had grown up in Liverpool in the 1950s and who were reaching middle age in the 1980s were struck by the emptiness and silence of the river.

Yet, on 4 August 1984, hundreds of thousands of people gathered on Liverpool's waterfront to watch the city's history coming over the horizon to greet them. Over the course of several hours a parade of more than sixty ships glided past the crowd. Unlike the precocious steamships that had dominated trade since the late nineteenth century, however, these were silent, delicate constructions, made of wood rather than steel and adorned with tall decorative sails. The Tall Ships Parade, the culmination of a trans-Atlantic race, was billed as part of that year's National Garden Festival, the spectacular regeneration scheme spearheaded by Michael Heseltine. It was to be, as a headline in the *Liverpool Daily Post* proclaimed, 'just like the old days'.[1]

The history that these ships signified, however, was ambient and imprecise, re-enacted rather than interrogated. It invoked the past while remaining curiously distant from the actual historical record of Britain's second city of empire. It was told from the perspective of a city for whom these ships were harbingers of wealth and pride, rather than the colonised parts of the world for whom they told a very different story. The tides that swept Frank Shaw's industrious steamships out to sea had come back in, bringing with them something twee, unthreatening and drenched in nostalgia. 'The future', as Vladimir Nabokov wrote, 'is but the obsolete in reverse.'[2]

From the 1980s to the early 2000s, elements of Liverpool's past were exhumed and put to work in the service of saving its economy. The result was a city in which the past was everywhere on display, but rarely meaningfully engaged with. Liverpool's late twentieth- and early twenty-first-century history has been an experiment in what the anthropologist Anna Lowenhaupt Tsing has called 'salvage capitalism'.[3] Littered with disused buildings, haemorrhaging people and traumatised by more than a decade of unemployment, insurrectionary violence, political conflict and mass death, Liverpool looked backwards. Its ruins were dramatised and re-purposed, preserved for display. Its obsolescence was embraced. Meanwhile, 'culture' and 'creativity' were summoned for similar ends. Art, music and football became central to the city's economy and were tasked with repurposing buildings, attracting private capital, enticing visitors and creating jobs. New 'sectors' of the economy flashed into being, each implausibly constructed from magical and intangible elements of the human condition – 'culture', 'knowledge', 'creativity' and 'heritage'.[4]

This chapter picks up where Chapter 7 left off, following the emergence of a type of 'entrepreneurial' city that the Conservative government had helped forge in Liverpool with the aid of bodies such as the MDC. With the political defeat of Militant and the expulsion of far-left councillors from the city's ruling Labour Party, the way was open for a city whose economy would be led by tourism, place-making and service work. By 1986, when the Merseyside Tourism Board was formed under the leadership of a former public relations advisor from Littlewoods, tourism was the eleventh largest industry in Liverpool, and the city was attracting nineteen million visitors a year.[5] By 2022, the city was attracting thirty-one million visitors a year, and tourism employed 35,000 people, comparable to the number of people working on the city's docks at their early twentieth-century peak.[6]

The attempt to salvage a new economy from Liverpool's debris led to two dramatic interventions in the early twenty-first century: Liverpool's European City of Culture status, bid for in 2003 and bestowed in 2008, and the city's UNESCO World Heritage status, granted in 2004 and revoked in 2021. Both initiatives coincided with and in some instances accelerated an explosion of property speculation in Liverpool's central areas and along the banks of the Mersey, including the creation of an enormous, privately run open-air shopping mall in the city centre. Liverpool, once a gateway to elsewhere, either as a port or a border, had to be remade into a destination. In a notorious editorial in 1982, the *Daily Mirror* sneeringly remarked that, such was the city's spectacular decline, 'they should build a fence around Liverpool and charge admission'.[7] By the end of the century this snide remark had been ironically realised.

Nineteen eighty-four was an *annus horribilis* for the Cammell Laird shipbuilding works in Birkenhead, across the river from Liverpool. The company, nationalised in 1977, was dependent on government defence contracts for its survival. These commissions were drying up, however, and in May that year the company announced that half of the shipyard's 3,300 workers would be laid off. The announcement prompted parts of the workforce to stage a dramatic, months-long occupation of two half-built ships that were scheduled to be completed in shipyards in France. Despite these actions, the shipyard continued to decline and in 1993 it had been effectively closed.[8] In January 1984, however, months before the layoffs and the occupations, engineers working at Cammell Laird were recruited for a special new project. Using state-of-the-art software, they were tasked with designing a prototype for a new type of vessel. Beginning the following month, the prototype was constructed by fifty-five apprentices, then floated on a barge across the river to Liverpool. Their creation was not a cargo ship, an oil tanker or a warship, all vessels that the Birkenhead shipyard had once specialised in producing. It was, instead, a vast, ornamental yellow submarine. The submarine was to be the centrepiece of a Beatles-themed maze, a temporary exhibition on a plot of land at that summer's National Garden Festival.[9] For two months Liverpool's former and future economies converged in the shipyard.

Cammell Laird apprentices wave in front of the yellow submarine they helped build, 1984.

Cammell Laird became a factory for manufacturing not ships, but history.

The historian Daniel T. Rodgers has argued that, towards the end of the twentieth century, something strange happened to history. Suddenly, the past was everywhere. History began to be woven into everyday life through political speeches, re-enactments, family history projects and tourism packages. Rather than a coherent narrative, however, the past reappeared as fragments, isolated from context and readily available. As Rodgers put it, 'the boundary between the past and present virtually dissolved. History's massive social processes disappeared. One travelled between past, present and future in a momentary blink of the imagination, through a wrinkle in time.'[10] The National Garden Festival with its eighteenth-century sailing ships, nineteenth-century steam train and 1960s Yellow Submarine was a forerunner of the light-touch collage-like approach to history that would play an important role in Liverpool's regeneration initiatives in the 1990s and early 2000s.

In the 1960s and 1970s, as the Beatles ascended to dizzying levels of success and global fame, visits to Liverpool by fans of the band were infrequent and ad hoc. The small numbers of fans who travelled to the city found no ready-made infrastructure or official guides for their visits. Instead, many made their own way, relying on informal networks of information. When these fans visited George Harrison's childhood home in Speke, for example, his parents, who still lived at the address, invited them in for tea and toast.[11] The fate of the Cavern Club, the iconic venue on Matthew Street that the Beatles, along with other Merseybeat bands such as The Chants and Gerry and the Pacemakers, played more than 200 times was perhaps the best indication of the City Council's lack of interest in cultivating these visits. When the Cavern closed in 1973, beset by economic difficulties, it was swiftly demolished to make space for a ventilation shaft for a proposed new underground railway system. Despite the band's extraordinary success, Liverpool's ambitious 1960s and early 1970s redevelopment plans had no interest in the Beatles and their fans. Hit by the recessions of the 1970s and undercut by rising levels of car ownership, however, plans for an integrated underground light rail system were heavily scaled back, and the ventilation shaft was cancelled. Instead, the ruins of the Cavern were turned into a car park.

By the 1980s, however, as alternative strategies for managing Liverpool's obsolescence – from subsidising light industrial work to the public-sector expansionism of Militant Tendency – fell by the wayside, the Beatles became increasingly central to the city's identity and its economy. John Lennon's murder by an obsessed fan outside his home in New York in 1980 saw Liverpool become a site of pilgrimage for fans. Visitors came to leave flowers for Lennon in pop-up shrines along Matthew Street where the Cavern Club had once stood.[12] In 1983, a new company, Cavern City Tours, attempted to systematise these various pilgrimages, organising official tours, promoting the annual Beatles Week festival and running a replica Cavern Club built adjacent to the original site.[13] In 1984, a new museum called Beatles City opened in the city centre, exhibiting a range of Beatles memorabilia that had been purchased at auction by a local radio station. The museum's manager Mike Byrne was a musician who had himself been fleetingly involved in the Merseybeat scene. His wife, Bernadette Byrne, was one of the first tourism officials in the city. Frustrated by the museum's awkward location, which, in his view, had stunted visitor numbers, Byrne oversaw the transfer of much of its collections to Dallas, where it attracted tens of thousands of visitors from across the United States, convincing the former musician there was money to be made from an ageing and increasingly nostalgic cohort of Beatles fans.[14]

On their return to Liverpool, Mike and Bernadette Byrne turned their attention to the Albert Dock. With a new Maritime Museum and with the Tate Liverpool art gallery soon to open, the dock was the centrepiece of Michael Heseltine's attempt to re-purpose Liverpool's waterfront into a venue for entertainment and tourism. Byrne managed to convince a group of property speculators of the enormous financial potential of a new dockside Beatles museum, taking the developers to Liverpool and leading them to a ruined and derelict part of the vaults of the Albert Dock's Britannia Pavilion. In 1990, the building was cleansed of seawater and carefully restored. The result was The Beatles Story, an enormous multi-storey immersive experience housing a dizzying juxtaposition of real and synthetic exhibitions, ranging from a replica of the Abbey Road studio to George Harrison's original guitar.[15] The attraction was a runaway success, attracting four million visitors in its first twenty-five years.[16]

While some of the Beatles had familial ties to Liverpool's ocean-going economy, they were mostly children of Liverpool's suburbs and products of its city centre nightlife scene. Their upbringings had little to do with Liverpool's increasingly remote maritime past. Nevertheless, the Victorian complex of jetties and warehouses that made up the Albert Dock became the focal point for Beatles-related tourism by the end of the century. The museum's success catalysed further waves of Beatles-related tours, gift shops, mini-museums and branded hotels and restaurants, which crashed into the city from the waterfront. In 2001, Liverpool's airport in Speke was renamed after John Lennon, and the yellow submarine, manufactured by Cammell Laird, was restored and deposited outside the entrance to its terminal. At the same time, the impact of the Beatles on Liverpool's economy was scrutinised and quantified by city officials. In 2014, a report commissioned by Liverpool City Council calculated that Beatles-related tourism had created 2,335 jobs and had attracted £81.9 million to the city that year.[17]

Meanwhile, the band's childhood homes, each of which had long been sites of pilgrimage for more obsessive fans, became incorporated into an increasingly official network of Beatles-related destinations. Paul McCartney's former home, a terraced council house in the southern suburb of Allerton, was purchased by the National Trust in 1995 and opened to the public for a modest admission fee. In 2002, the Trust also acquired John Lennon's home in the south-eastern suburb of Woolton, which had been purchased by his widow, Yoko Ono. By the early 2000s, four minibuses a day would set out from the city centre to these peripheral and unassuming suburbs, delivering visitors who had paid for scheduled tours of the two properties. By 2015, more than half of these visitors came from overseas.[18] George Harrison's family home in Speke, where small numbers of intrepid fans were once invited in for tea, is now available to rent on Airbnb.

The canonisation of the Beatles has been seen by critics and historians as part of a process by which mid-twentieth-century rock and pop music, cleansed of its insurgent, counter-cultural and anti-establishment origins, was institutionalised and severed from African American roots.[19] By the end of the century, rock music's impact had been softened by the generationally specific process of upward social mobility and affluence experienced by many of its fans in the intervening decades. Today, Matthew Street is a narrow thoroughfare crowded with Beatles-related businesses. One can visit a replica of the Cavern Club, go for drinks in the Rubber Soul bar or Sgt Pepper's pub, buy 1960s clothing in the Flares boutique or stay overnight at the Hard Day's Night Hotel, all within a few hundred feet. In photographs, statuettes, trinkets and snatches of piped music, the Beatles are an almost tangible presence, pressing in from all sides. The moment of aggressive urban redevelopment that led to the demolition of the original Cavern Club for a railway ventilation shaft, however, feels impossibly remote, bypassed by a wrinkle in time.

As Beatles-led tourism intensified, other, more distant parts of the city's history were similarly exhumed. After their first appearance during the National Garden Festival in 1984, 'Tall Ships' parades became a regular occurrence on the Mersey. These competitive races between ornately designed sail ships were a pantomime revival of the city's former maritime economy, an economy that now lay out of sight, sealed away in shipping containers behind security fencing in the Seaforth terminal, fifteen miles north of Liverpool. The most spectacular of these events was the 'Columbus Regatta' in 1992. The Regatta was part of a global event to mark the 500-year anniversary of Christopher Columbus' first journey to the Americas and involved more than a hundred enormous and ornately designed sail ships. Liverpool was selected to be the terminus of a 12,000-mile trans-Atlantic route for the ships that was loosely related to the biography of the Italian navigator, beginning in Genoa, then progressing to Cadiz and Lisbon before crossing the Atlantic to

San Juan in Puerto Rico, sailing through New York and Boston and then returning across the Atlantic to Merseyside. The arrival of the ships was greeted by an enormous outdoor opera concert on the former King's Dock in a pop-up auditorium with 15,000 seats, called the Fanfare for a New World and coinciding with a state visit from the King and Queen of Spain.

Columbus had a shadowy presence in modern Liverpool. The city was one of only a handful of places outside of the Americas to hold regular Columbus Day celebrations on 12 October each year, marking the anniversary of the navigator's first landing at Guanahani in what is now the Bahamas.[20] Throughout the twentieth century these events ranged from galas overseen by the Lord Mayor to smaller parties hosted by the city's Portuguese and Spanish communities.[21] Their focal point was usually the botanical Palm House in Sefton Park, where a bronze statue of Columbus is on display. The statue was commissioned in 1898 by the newspaper magnate and philanthropist Henry Yates Thompson, whose enormous wealth came from his father's extensive dealings in the Atlantic slave trade. An inscription on its base reads, 'The discoverer of America was the maker of Liverpool'. It was rumoured that the city's mysterious Luso-American Society would transport the statue to Pier Head each year on Columbus' birthday for an official night-time ceremony.[22]

The MDC spent more than a year lobbying the Spanish committee planning the Columbus Regatta to be part of the event. Central to their pitch was the unusually close relationship between Liverpool and Columbus. When delegates travelled to Spain to lobby for the city's inclusion, they produced a photograph of the statue, claiming it was the only statue of the man in Britain.[23] Meanwhile, across the United States and Latin America, the Columbus Quincentennial had led to a renewed scrutiny of the legacies of indigenous genocide and Black Atlantic slavery that Columbus' voyage had left in its wake. The political response to the Quincentennial in the United States led to the formation of Indigenous Peoples' Day, an alternative commemoration held on the same day as Columbus Day in October, which is now widely celebrated across the country.[24] In New York, the Regatta was greeted by hundreds of protestors who marched from City Hall to Battery Park chanting, 'Christopher Columbus, you can't hide, we charge you with genocide'.[25]

The MDC and other boosters were wilfully oblivious to the political battles that were raging elsewhere over the legacy of Columbus. For political leaders the Regatta's primary purpose was to attract visitors, market Liverpool as a tourist destination and stimulate investment from the United States.[26] In Liverpool, the event's success was to some degree predicated on weaponising not history but its opposite, a kind of structured forgetting of the consequences of the Columbian encounter among Liverpool's population. In the official publicity for the Regatta in Liverpool, Columbus' mythical status as the 'discoverer' of the 'New World' was blankly repeated.[27] As one guidebook briskly noted, 'whether you approve or not, his voyage was a turning point in history'.[28]

Columbus' complex legacy could not, however, be so easily repressed. Activists from Liverpool and from elsewhere in the world staged an all-day festival of protest at the University of Liverpool to coincide with the state visit of the King of Spain. The festival was organised by a group called 500 Years of Resistance, which had originated in Latin America to contest the Quincentennial. Speakers included Daniel Ortega, the former president of Nicaragua and Jean-Bertrand Aristide, the former president of Haiti, as well as the Guatemalan indigenous rights activist Rigoberta Menchu.[29] Meanwhile, the anthropologist Jacqueline Nassy-Brown, who authored an in-depth study of Liverpool's Black community shortly after the Regatta, recorded significant although less well-organised hostility to the event in Toxteth.[30]

As Liverpool's docks were being transformed into Beatles museums, art galleries, television studios, restaurants, bars and high-end shops, the buildings themselves and the maritime history they signified became increasingly central to the image that Liverpool wanted to project to the world. In the years up to and immediately after their closure in the early 1970s, these empty warehouses, jetties, piers and dock offices were a burden for the MDHB who owned them and were desperate to offload them. Indeed, in 1966, the chairman of the MDHB had been dismissive of the warehouses surrounding the Albert Dock. He noted that, while they were 'fine architecturally', we should anticipate 'their disappearance from the Liverpool skyline' and that it wasn't the duty of his company 'to cling to them purely for aesthetic purposes'.[31] By the end of the century, however, it was almost unanimously agreed that these ruins were to be preserved, scrubbed clean and put on display for visitors to see.

Various impulses towards heritage, preservation and tourism came together in a bid launched by the City Council for Liverpool's waterfront to become a UNESCO World Heritage Site. Since 1975, UNESCO, the United Nations agency tasked with managing arts, culture and science, had been preserving and drawing attention to historical ruins and natural environments that had been deemed to be of world historical significance. In its early years, the recipients of World Heritage status tended to be parts of the natural world (such as the Plitvice Lakes National Park in Croatia or the Sagarmatha National Park in Nepal, which contains Mount Everest), the ancient world (such as the Roman ruins of Pompeii or Machu Pichu in Peru) or the medieval world (such as Chartres Cathedral in France or the medieval city of Rhodes in Greece). Indeed, the World Heritage project had emerged out of attempts to save ancient Egyptian monuments and artifacts from the flooding of parts of the Nile during the construction of the Aswan Dam in the 1960s. Towards the end of the century, however, more modern sites had been designated, particularly in Britain, where Edinburgh's Georgian New Town had been listed in 1995 and the ironmaking works in Blaenavon in South Wales had been listed in 2000.[32]

Liverpool submitted its application with the approval of the national government in 2003. The city's application document argued that it was 'the supreme example of a commercial port at the time of Britain's greatest global influence'.[33] Liverpool, the application argued, had a significant influence on world trade (including the trade in enslaved people) and had greased the wheels of the industrial revolution. As well as the restored complex of nineteenth-century docks, the city had many well-preserved nineteenth- and twentieth-century commercial buildings and could boast the world's first commercial wet dock, built in 1715, whose walls were still visible.[34] In 2004, the bid was successfully ratified by the twenty-eighth session of the World Heritage Committee and the 'Liverpool Maritime Mercantile City' World Heritage Site was ushered into existence.

It was unclear exactly what, where and when the 'Liverpool Maritime Mercantile City' was supposed to be, an ambiguity not helped by its clumsy name. The designation, in its grandest most teleological form, preserved some of the origins of the modern world itself. One official guidebook noted how the city's eighteenth-century dock walls were 'the foundations of a civilisation – capitalist civilisation, a globalised industrial society – which has spread across and now dominates the world, even in Communist China and post-Communist Russia. It started here. With Liverpool as Ostia to Manchester's Rome.'[35] However, these grand claims were somewhat belied by Liverpool's centuries of boom, bust and capitalist restructuring, which had left a confused and cacophonous built environment, where layers of retrofitting, regeneration and property speculation had accreted without any guiding logic.

Instead, the World Heritage Site was something that had to be constructed as much as defended. While many previous UNESCO interventions were created to protect existing relics from the effects of over-development, Liverpool's Site trod a delicate tightrope between 'heritage' and regeneration. A hodgepodge of buildings from different eras, the Site had to fit into the Council's broader plans for the city's regeneration and needed to be demarcated and clearly explained to visitors. The city's application for the Site deliberately blurred the line between tourism and preservation, arguing that 'heritage can be a positive force for sustainable regeneration'.[36] Lest anyone thought the designation would stand in the way of the continued redevelopment of the city's docks as a destination for tourists, the proposal warned that 'Liverpool's renaissance is central to securing the long-term conservation of the Site and should be encouraged'.[37] In this sense, Liverpool was participating in what the Italian philosopher Marco D'Eramo has called 'UNESCOcide', in which post-industrial cities are partitioned between zones of rampant property speculation and inert, lifeless ruins carefully preserved for tourists, a dichotomy that leaves citizens, in D'Eramo's words, left to choose between 'living in a museum or in the shadow of a giant bank'.[38]

Designating the boundaries of the World Heritage Site was a complex exercise in map-making. Lines had to be drawn to mark out where the city's maritime history began and ended. The Site was divided into six 'Character Areas', which covered Pier Head, the Albert, Wapping and Stanley docks, the old commercial city around Dale Street and Victoria Street and St George's Hall, as well as Liverpool's original museum complex and the newly branded 'Ropewalks' area around Lower Duke Street.[39] These amounted to a horseshoe-shaped zone covering a strip of former dockland adjacent to the river and two prongs extending east into the city centre. Although the designation came with no restrictions, its integrity was subject to frequent and intensive monitoring by UNESCO officials, who had the right to de-list the Site at any time.[40] Liverpool Maritime Mercantile City, therefore, added another layer to Merseyside's already muddled cartography. Together with the enterprise zone in Speke, the freeport in Seaforth and the strips of land ceded to the MDC, the Site contributed to the jurisdictional quality of Liverpool's late twentieth-century regeneration. While these other spaces were, as I have argued earlier, designed to accelerate historical change – to sculpt in time – Liverpool Maritime Mercantile City was intended to do the opposite, to stop the clock and preserve the past as something lapidary and mute.

In the end, the City Council was never able – or willing – to reconcile the competing demands of development and preservation. In 2012, a UNESCO monitoring mission to Liverpool announced the designation would be added to its list of sites 'in danger'.[41] This formal warning was prompted by an intensive redevelopment scheme announced for the city's north docks. Liverpool officials were given repeated warnings by inspectors each subsequent year until 2021, when its status as a World Heritage Site was formally rescinded.[42] Of almost 1,200 sites across the world, Liverpool became one of only three to lose its status, joining a sanctuary for rare antelopes in Oman whose area had been reduced by 90 per cent to suit oil prospectors, and the Elbe Valley in Germany which had been transformed by the construction of a four-lane bridge across its width. In the end, Liverpool Maritime Mercantile City was a fragile and unwieldy construction, ultimately abolished by the stroke of a pen.

Those who sought to draw on Liverpool's past to resolve the contradictions of its present faced a problem: the actual content of this past. Much of the city's maritime history – the buildings and streets preserved by UNESCO and the journeys alluded to by the parades of Tall Ships up and down the Mersey – was fuelled by spectacular violence taking place off-stage. What Liverpool's history factory could not fully account for, in other words, was the fact that for more than half a century Liverpool was the largest slave trading port in Europe.

It is worth pausing on what this meant. In the final fifty years of Britain's involvement in the trade, before its abolition in 1807, Liverpool dominated the country's slave economy, massively outpacing rival ports such as Bristol and London. In the 1740s, the city sent out 43 per cent of the total number of slaving ships launched by Britain. Between 1791 and 1800 this rose to 77 per cent. That decade, an average of 100 ships each year would set sail from Liverpool to the West Coast of Africa, incarcerate hundreds of Africans in suffocating holds and undertake the deadly, months-long voyage to the Caribbean or North America, where the survivors were sold or traded for tropical commodities and worked to death. The total number of enslaved people transported on Liverpool ships has been estimated at a little over 1.1 million. Before the nineteenth century, no port on earth was more involved in the slave trade than Liverpool.[43] In the eighteenth century, the trade was a principal engine of growth for the city, aiding in its transformation from a village of a few thousand people that mostly traded with Ireland to England's second biggest city in 1800. As calls for abolition gathered pace from the late eighteenth century, Liverpool merchants and MPs were some of the loudest and most organised voices arguing in favour of preserving the trade. The defeat of the first abolition bill in Parliament in 1791 was a moment of jubilation in the city, prompting the ringing of church bells.[44]

As Liverpool reorganised its economy after abolition, repurposing the networks used to buy and sell enslaved people for new types of trade, the legacy and uncomfortable memory of this violence was felt in different ways. Slavery occupied an awkward, ghostly presence in centuries of official histories and guidebooks. On the one hand, local histories gave an outsized role to the Liverpool-based poet and MP William Roscoe, whose vote in favour of the Abolition Bill in 1806 meant that he was the closest thing the city had to an abolitionist activist. On the other hand, Liverpool's continued prosperity throughout the nineteenth century, in the face of abolition, was frequently cited as part of a wider story about the city's propensity to thrive in times of adversity.[45] Other accounts tried, with little success, to emphasise the relative humanity of Liverpool's slave traders. One school textbook published in 1946 noted that some Liverpool slave captains were 'remarkably kind hearted men' who allowed enslaved people to dance on deck.[46]

Most importantly, however, for much of Liverpool's modern history, the city's relationship with slavery was characterised by amnesia rather than memory, and omission rather than commemoration. In 1957, for example, local historian George Chandler's 500-page history of Liverpool, written to mark the 750-year anniversary of the city's royal charter and funded by the City Council, has just four paragraphs on slavery.[47] As we have already seen, the fact that slavery was the city's most lucrative business during the age of sail did nothing to trouble the mawkish nostalgia of the city's many 'Tall Ships' parades. Indeed, in 1984, one of the participating ships carried eight bales of cotton to celebrate the

200-year anniversary of the trans-Atlantic cotton trade between the US South and Liverpool, a commodity that, for the first half of the nineteenth century, was produced almost entirely by enslaved labour.[48]

By the time the Merseyside Maritime Museum opened on a permanent basis in 1984, these omissions were becoming more and more difficult to sustain. The museum occupied a restored warehouse on the Albert Dock. Along with Tate Liverpool and the Beatles Story, it was part of a triumvirate of tourist attractions each within a few hundred feet of the others overlooking the former dock's basin. In its early years, the city's involvement in the slave trade, arguably the biggest maritime endeavour in its history, was unsettlingly absent. Instead, the museum offered visitors an antiquarian and technical celebration of seafaring endeavour, intended, according to its founding document, to showcase the 'proud history' of Liverpool.[49] Slavery was mentioned only in a small information panel in an exhibit on the history of Liverpool's port. In a few sentences, the panel told visitors that Liverpool's prosperity 'was firmly established before it began to dominate the slave trade' and that 'sailings to Africa represented only 10% of outward bound tonnage from Liverpool'. The panel was described by the 1989 Gifford Inquiry into the causes of the Toxteth uprising as resembling 'a lawyer's plea in mitigation for Liverpool'.[50] Meanwhile, a survey of a hundred visitors to the Maritime Museum in 1993 found that a quarter knew nothing about Liverpool's relationship to slavery, an indication of how successfully the memory of one of the most significant chapters of the city's history had been repressed.[51]

In 1991, partly as a response to these criticisms, the museum announced that it would install a new, permanent exhibition about slavery. The exhibition took shape during three years of fraught discussions among intellectuals and local Black activists, including the theorist Stuart Hall; the founder of the Black Cultural Archives, Len Garrison; and the formerly Liverpool-based Black activist Dorothea Kuya.[52] In 1994, it was formally opened under the name *Transatlantic Slavery: Against Human Dignity* in a ceremony led by the American poet Maya Angelou. The gallery's ten sections told a comprehensive account of the global consequences of Atlantic slavery, through information panels, paintings and dioramas, and featured collections of objects from West Africa, some dating back to the sixteenth century, including jewellery, masks and musical instruments.[53] In 2007, the exhibition became its own separate attraction – renamed the International Slavery Museum – to coincide with the 200th anniversary of Britain's abolition of the slave trade.

The initial exhibition prompted a mixed response from the city's Black community. One Toxteth-based newsletter claimed that the museum was monetising white guilt for financial gain and tourism-led regeneration.[54] Some Black groups such as the Liverpool 8 Law Centre and the Consortium of Black Organisations distanced themselves from the project, citing the poor record of Liverpool's museums and the city's waterfront regeneration schemes in employing and welcoming Black residents of the city. At the gallery's launch event in 1991, some Black residents objected to being blindsided by the announcement and expressed anger at having not been consulted before important decisions had been made. The Merseyside African Council threatened to boycott the museum and some Black Liverpool residents refused to attend once it opened.[55] Other groups, however, such as the Federation of Liverpool Black Organisations, were more willing to participate. The Black, Liverpool-born sociologist Stephen Small, who was involved in early discussions about the gallery, remembered having 'low expectations of what a museum could achieve'. Nonetheless, he argued that 'no matter how we responded, the museum was going to go ahead with its plans and so we had to be a part of what happened'.[56]

These contradictions were never fully resolved. By offering visitors an implicit critique of the theme-park-like waterfront complex of which it is a crucial part, the International Slavery Museum occupies a paradoxical place in the city's history factory. Its galleries jar in tone and content with those of the Maritime Museum, which occupies the three floors below, where an untroubled, nostalgic and decidedly imperial story is told about the city's seafaring past.[57] Its new 'international' status is a sign of the museum's laudable ambition to summon and represent a global community of people displaced and re-made by slavery as well as an awareness of its status as one of the few dedicated slavery museums in Britain. These ambitions, however, have seen a subtle shift in the museum's purpose. The aim of drawing attention to Liverpool's history of slavery has arguably been overshadowed by the burden of telling a much bigger story. This shift in focus has allowed some white residents of the city to retreat to a state of wilful forgetting. A comment from one such resident uncovered by the historian Jessica Moody, is telling: 'I can live with an International Slavery Museum so long as [the museum] points out that internationally, over the history of mankind to the present day, slave ships sailing from Liverpool, although unsavoury, is actually a mere footnote.'[58]

Slavery, meanwhile, was a spectral presence in Liverpool's short-lived UNESCO World Heritage Site. It was rarely mentioned in the bidding documents, guidebooks and management plans produced to promote and advocate for the designation. These official publications dwelled heavily on architectural accomplishments and technical innovations in docking and trade, with only occasional digressions on the trade in enslaved people. The 2014 official guidebook to the UNESCO Site is an ideal example of this genre. In a potted history of the city, the slave trade is awarded two of seventeen paragraphs, the latter of which is entirely given over to civil rights struggles in the United States, in which the reader is informed that Michelle Obama and Duke Ellington were both descended from slaves.[59] There is no mention of the city's own Black population or its equivalent struggles for civil rights. The guide's thick descriptions of eighteenth- and early nineteenth-century architecture within the designation unfolds with few allusions to what had been a primary source of the city's wealth during the period of their construction.

Finally, while references to slavery were sparse, references to the myriad other ways in which Liverpool's history was implicated in colonial violence were almost entirely absent from the history factory's promotional material. With some exceptions, the surviving dock buildings that formed the centrepiece of the city's UNESCO-branded heritage complex were built after the abolition of slavery across the British empire in 1833. Nevertheless, these docks had their own dark story to tell. The ships they launched contributed to the under-development and ecological devastation of parts of West Africa and East Asia. Their shipping companies uprooted populations in the service of racially unequal labour regimes, in which, as we have already seen in this book, workers were underpaid, brutalised and sometimes deported. Their warehouses stored cotton grown by enslaved people in the United States, decades after the abolition of slavery in the British empire. Indeed, Liverpool elites had been enthusiastic supporters of the US slave-owning Confederacy during the Civil War, sending warships and military supplies to blockaded ports in the US South to support their war effort.[60]

Unlike Liverpool's involvement in the slave trade, the city's broader imperial ties do not have such a clear end-date. Slavery, bookended by the triumphant act of abolition, has frequently been made to bear the moral and political weight of the city's imperial history as a whole, allowing museums, guidebooks and boosters to draw on a language of heritage and pride, with slavery safely contained as a parenthetical caveat. Under these terms Liverpool's imperial past can be exhumed without qualm, shorn of its manifest inequalities and lauded as an example of the city's propensity for 'diversity' and 'innovation'. Michael Parkinson, a high-profile urbanist and a member of a mayoral task force formed to manage the city's UNESCO status, proudly declared that during the age of empire Liverpool was 'extroverted; globally connected; economically, culturally and socially diverse; self-confident and adventurous'.[61] Neil Cossons, the former chair of English Heritage, wrote that 'Liverpool's exceptionalism has been a source of wonder throughout her history, the root of the city's pride and self-esteem, the source of her wealth, and the reason she stands today as England's finest Victorian city.'[62] Those researching Liverpool's history on the third floor of the Central Library, meanwhile, work in view of a wide, recently installed plaque that reads, 'Liverpool's story is the world's glory'.[63]

All factories entail some degree of mystification. The commodities they produce circulate, for the most part, among people who know little about the conditions in which they were made. Liverpool's history factory is no different. The preservation, restoration and retrofitting of the city's maritime buildings has required isolating them from their historical context. Much has been written about Britain's troubled relationship with its own imperial past, whether this is characterised as 'amnesia' or 'nostalgia' or a heady mix of both.[64] There are many reasons why Britain has failed to fully come to terms with the scale and violence of its imperial past. In Liverpool, we find another important and often overlooked explanation: the necessity of drawing on reserves of history to rescue the city's economy.

In places like the restored Albert Dock or the self-styled Georgian Quarter or the Ropewalks district, history is everywhere, yet it is harder than ever to meaningfully connect the past with the present, to uncover, condemn and ultimately move beyond the inequalities that have been produced during Liverpool's history. Within national communities, the past has, of course, always worked in service of the present. In Liverpool as well as in many other places in Britain, however, history has been forced to be more than merely a flawed mythology around which to cohere a body politic, a highly selective 'collective social memory' to use the words of the critical theorist Stuart Hall.[65] It has been vested with a macroeconomic mission – to rescue certain populations from obsolescence, and in doing so suture some of its own wounds.

There are, of course, other ways of interrogating the past. In 1954, a statue of the Liverpool MP and President of the Board of Trade William Huskisson was moved from its location outside the Customs House to the terminus of Princes Drive, the wide boulevard that bisects Toxteth. Huskisson is perhaps best known for his spectacular death. In 1830, he became the second person ever to be killed by a train, after being haplessly caught in the path of Stephenson's Rocket on its maiden voyage between Liverpool and

Manchester. More consequentially, in 1826, beholden to plantation owners in the city, Huskisson had opposed the abolition of slavery in Britain's colonies and was widely (although inaccurately) believed by many locals to be a slave trader. In 1982, his statue was torn down by protestors, leaving only an empty plinth, which still stands. In the wake of the Black Lives Matter protests of 2020, there were concerns that the statute of Christopher Columbus in Sefton Park could meet the same fate.[66] The history factory has produced its own machine breakers. Perhaps iconoclasm rather than preservation is a better means of grasping the weight of the past as it continues to bear down on the present.

In 1990, as if by magic, a new sector of Liverpool's economy was conjured into being. That year, the Merseyside Task Force, an advisory group of civil servants appointed by Michael Heseltine, approached a somewhat eccentric London-based think tank Comedia with a specific task – to calculate the exact size and value of what were deemed to be the city's 'cultural industries'. The task required gathering data on various types of economic activity that had not previously been seen as connected. The think tank totalled the amount of money collected each year in entrance fees to the city's museums, the amount of public funding awarded to its local radio and television stations, as well as the number of people employed in cinemas and even in video rental shops. Artists, curators, journalists, receptionists and cashiers who worked incomparably different jobs suddenly found themselves bound together as part of the same economic 'sector'. Once defined and quantified, officials hoped that Liverpool's 'cultural industries' would be a platform for the city's future growth and regeneration.[67] Earlier in the century, Liverpool's enormous cultural footprint, primarily in the form of music and football, had been at best a curiosity and at worst a problem for its politicians. Now it would be central to its future. Liverpool's culture, like its history, was to be deployed in the service of reclaiming derelict buildings, creating new jobs and, perhaps most important of all, attracting visitors.

A statue of the Liverpool pro-slavery MP William Huskisson was torn down by protestors in 1982. The empty plinth where he used to stand remains to this day in Toxteth.

The idea that art and culture could be a discrete 'industry' or economic 'sector', like mining or fishing, has a relatively recent history. Comedia, the think tank employed to assess Liverpool's cultural sector, was founded in 1978 by the radical publisher Charles Landry. Landry had gained prominence by, among other things, arguing that independent arts organisations needed to develop hard-headed, Thatcherite business strategies to survive. In 1985, he developed a syllabus of airport-style business books for artists, musicians and publishers that included titles such as Tom Peters and Robert Waterman's *In Search of Excellence: Lessons from America's Best Run Companies*.[68] Along with his colleagues in Comedia, Landry argued that creative work was a growing area of employment and revenue in an increasingly post-industrial economy.[69] The cultural industries needed to be unearthed, quantified and then stimulated by the right balance of public funding and free-market incentives. This idea was quietly radical. While some of the most famous twentieth-century historians and theorists of culture, from Theodore Adorno to E. P. Thompson, had argued that capitalism had stultified and occluded creativity, here was an argument that cultural work could be central to the economy. Comedia's logic inverted the Marxist idea that art and culture were determined by a society's economic relations.[70]

By the time that Comedia's accountants rolled into Liverpool, 'cultural industries'-led regeneration strategies were already underway in several British cities. From 1983, for example, Glasgow had launched a co-ordinated programme of investment in cultural institutions such as the Scottish Ballet and the Scottish National Orchestra to rehabilitate the city's image and attract tourists.[71] Likewise, Bradford, as part of its 'Bradford's Bouncing Back' tourism campaign in the early 1980s, had sought to revive its economy by investing in cultural institutions such as the National Museum of Photography, Film and Television and the Alhambra Theatre.[72] Meanwhile, in 1985, the year before its abolition, the Greater London Council's industrial strategy featured a detailed breakdown of what it called the 'creative industries', a 'sector' that the authors calculated was worth £33.6 billion in London.[73] By the early 1990s, Cardiff, Sheffield and Newcastle had all invested heavily in institutions that later came to be recognised as part of this novel area of the economy.[74]

Unusually for a city that had been a laboratory for almost every post-war urban regeneration scheme, Liverpool was a relative latecomer to this party. The opening of a new Tate art gallery on the Albert Docks in 1988 had been a step in this direction. In 1987, meanwhile, the City Council's post-Militant Labour administration had also set up an Arts and Cultural Industries Unit in the Council's Department for Libraries.[75] In 1989, the MDC had created its own experimental 'community arts' programme in the city called Fringe. The group was given office space in the 'New Enterprise Workshops' of the remodelled Albert Dock and were sponsored by British American Tobacco. Fringe worked closely with private industry in the city, both in search of further sponsorship and with the idea that firms can learn from artists and stage performances in offices or factories.[76] Outside of the zones of redevelopment commandeered by the MDC, however, Liverpool's art scene had been savagely hit by funding cuts during the 1980s. In 1986, the abolition of the Merseyside County Council, which had funded many of the city's theatres and galleries, had plunged the city's arts scene into crisis.[77]

Perhaps unsurprisingly, Comedia's assessment of the size of Liverpool's 'cultural industries' was not very impressive. In all, this newly discovered realm of economic activity employed just 3,100 people, fewer, the report was at pains to point out, than the number employed by the Royal Insurance company in the city. The figure amounted to just 1.6 per cent of all service sector jobs in the city, and 7 per cent of the total number of unemployed people. The report also noted that most of these jobs were poorly paid. It estimated that only 5 per cent of the city's cultural workers would be classified as 'very well paid' and 30 per cent would be at or below 'the acceptable thresholds of low pay'. In more auspicious news for city leaders, however, the report found that culture and art-making was comparatively lucrative, bringing almost £100 million into the city each year, a figure equivalent to a quarter of the city's annual expenditure.[78]

To the disappointment of many cultural leaders in the city, this new sector of the economy remained relatively dormant for the subsequent decade.[79] This changed in 1998, with the election of a new Liberal Democrat Council, when attempts to stimulate the 'cultural industries' became central to the city's ongoing mission to preserve its economy in the face of obsolescence. Shortly after winning power, the new administration began drawing up an ambitious bid for the city to become Europe's 'Capital of Culture' in 2008. Founded in 1985, 'capital of culture' status was awarded to different cities in the European Union, a status that came with the promise of publicity, funding and an influx of tourists. As with the UNESCO World Heritage scheme, Liverpool's bid to be 2008's Capital was a deliberate attempt to take advantage of post-imperial global networks of tourists and capital that had previously left Liverpool behind. With its slogan 'the World in One City', Liverpool's bid was a now familiar sleight of hand, in which the city's history of imperial and unequal racial dominance was laundered into a story about diversity and cosmopolitanism.[80] Unlike the UNESCO scheme, however, Liverpool's Capital of Culture application put the city in direct competition with other parts of Britain that were similarly desperate to establish a competitive edge in a zero-sum marketplace of visitors and investors. With that year's Capital of Culture designation guaranteed to be awarded to a British city, Liverpool found itself in a race with multiple other cities including Birmingham, Cardiff and Newcastle. This was a contest that epitomised the new kind of competitive, 'entrepreneurial' urbanism of the age.

In 2003, Liverpool's award was announced live on television by Tony Blair's then Culture Secretary Tessa Jowell. The news was greeted with jubilation by city leaders, as well as surprise – Newcastle was widely considered to be the favourite to win. For Mike Storey, the Liberal leader who had sat in the Council since the party's brief electoral breakthrough in the 1970s, Liverpool's year as Capital of Culture promised to be the culmination of the city's revival and would put an end to its obsolescence. He likened it to 'Liverpool winning the Champions League, Everton winning the double and the Beatles reforming, all on the same day – and Steve Spielberg [sic] coming to the city to make a Hollywood Blockbuster about it'.[81] The local comedian Alexei Sayle was more succinct and pragmatic, claiming, during a televised show in the city, 'culture is big business... culture could be Liverpool's salvation'.[82]

Capital of Culture status entailed a constellation of disjointed set-piece events hosted throughout 2008, including a launch party that featured acrobats and live music, a festival of animatronic sculpture, a Paul McCartney show at Anfield Stadium, a performance of Benjamin Britten's 'War Requiem' in Liverpool Cathedral, a high-profile exhibition of paintings by Gustav Klimt and, predictably, yet another Tall Ships race along the Mersey. The city hosted that year's MTV Europe Music Awards in its new Arena by the waterfront and Tate Liverpool hosted the 2008 Turner Prize awards ceremony.[83] The economic impact of the year was meticulously monitored and calculated by a team of researchers at the city's two leading universities, an undertaking that dwarfed Comedia's first attempt to assess the economic value of the city's 'cultural industries'. The team calculated that 9.7 million additional visitors came to Liverpool in 2008 and the year brought an estimated £753.8 million into the city.[84]

Meanwhile, Liverpool's year as Capital of Culture coincided with a massive wave of aggressive property speculation and redevelopment. In 1999, the newly elected Labour government oversaw the creation of Liverpool Vision, one of three 'urban regeneration companies' founded across the country. The company, whose board was dominated by representatives of chain stores such as Tesco, Wimpy and Littlewoods, was tasked with attracting private capital to re-make significant areas of the city centre.[85] Over the subsequent decade, Liverpool Vision would do more than any other body to shape the look and feel of the city's central areas, having a hand in developing the Echo Arena, a new cruise-liner terminal and a string of office blocks and high-rise housing developments along the Princes Dock. While Michael Heseltine's MDC was an alien body, grafted onto the city by a government that few in the city voted for, Liverpool Vision emerged from within the city itself, arguably marking the final triumph of the experimental mode of neoliberal urban regeneration pioneered by Margaret Thatcher in the city.

By far the most spectacular of these developments was the vast Liverpool One shopping mall, which opened on the other side of the Strand from the Albert Dock in 2008, in the midst of the Capital of Culture celebrations. The mall was a sweeping complex of more than 150 shops layered over what had once been a transient and heavily bombed hinterland between the docks and the rest of the city. It was open-air and seamlessly integrated into the city's pre-existing street plan. Pedestrians walking through the city centre were deliberately left uncertain about where it began and ended.[86] The mall's origins dated from 1999, when the Council began casting around for private developers to re-make the neighbourhood, with adverts in the *Financial Times* and the *Estates Gazette*.[87] The sale of the land marked an extraordinary transfer of power. Thirty-four streets in the city centre were ceded to the Grosvenor Group, a Mayfair-based property developer owned by Gerald Cavendish, the then Duke of Westminster. While Liverpool's mid-twentieth-century expansion had seen the Council annex surrounding land from rural aristocrats to develop places like Speke and Kirkby, Liverpool One amounted to an unexpected act of retrocession, where some of the oldest and most central areas of the city were returned to the landed gentry.

Liverpool One's architects deliberately distanced themselves from the massive peripheral shopping malls that had clustered on the outskirts of post-industrial British cities in the late twentieth century – places like Merry Hill in Greater Birmingham, the MetroCentre in Gateshead or the Trafford Centre in Manchester. The aim was to create something lively, porous, urbane and open to nightlife as well as shopping.[88] Nevertheless, the development saw many of the subtle attempts used to manipulate the movement of shoppers through suburban malls creep into the heart of the city. The mall's architects devised a lighting scheme that was, in their description, 'phototropic', modelled on the 'way that plants are drawn towards the light' and thus 'encouraging movement' between different shopping areas.[89] The mall also followed a model, widely used in British and American suburban shopping malls, whereby large department stores, in this case John Lewis and Debenhams, anchored each of its ends, encouraging shoppers to flow across its entire length to move between them. More consequentially, Liverpool One also saw some of the same processes of securitisation and policing that had characterised shopping malls elsewhere. As part of their agreement with the City Council, Grosvenor were given exceptional powers to curtail rights enjoyed by pedestrians in other parts of the city. Begging, skateboarding and rollerblading were banned and any form of protest would require special police permission.[90]

Liverpool One revealed the shallowness of the city's attempts to draw on 'culture' in the service of regeneration and economic development. While not formally part of the Capital of Culture celebrations, its construction was accelerated to coincide with the designation, and its opening that year was heavily touted as part of the city's revival. The development, however, amounted to little more than a blankly repetitive sequence of chain stores – homogenous, intensively surveilled and stripped of the kinds of organic spontaneity that are the breeding ground for the kinds of culture that the city leadership was professing to cultivate. Assessing the development in 2008, the *Architectural Review* described the mall as an 'endless Modernist Esperanto of polite retail boringness'.[91] Its construction also entailed the quiet erasure of one of the city's most popular grassroots cultural institutions. Since 1988, a ramshackle and labyrinthine market called Quiggins had formed in a handful of former warehouses in the heart of the area that would be ceded to Grosvenor. The market was a dense warren of more than forty antique stores, pop-up art galleries, cafés, pubs, studios, tattoo parlours and music venues. It was an established part of the city's lively punk and metal music scenes that had its own free magazine, offering extensive reviews of local shows and independent films.[92] As an insurgent, ungovernable space, Quiggins had acted as an engine room for producing the culture that Liverpool's city leaders were hoping to capitalise on. Despite an organised campaign of resistance and a petition with 150,000 signatures, however, Quiggins was demolished in 2006 to make way for Liverpool One, and all its independent businesses were evicted.[93] The block that it used to occupy was seamlessly integrated into the mall's master plan. It now houses a Levi's store, a Ralph Lauren and a Starbucks.

On 11 October 2008, thousands of architects, critics, town planners and property developers descended on Liverpool to attend Britain's most prestigious architecture award ceremony. The Stirling Prize was to be held in Liverpool's Echo Arena, which had opened just a few months earlier on a sheer stretch of riverbank by the former Wapping Dock. The event, which was televised live on Channel 4, was an important part of the Capital of Culture celebrations and was intended to further cement Liverpool's reputation as a new centre of gravity for the arts. In the autumn-evening gloom, the stadium, curvaceous and brightly lit, would have appeared otherworldly next to the silent and dark expanse of the Mersey. Queuing to enter the Arena, the attendees would have been able to trace the lights of Birkenhead out to the north and to the edge of the river's mouth, after which they vanished into the black hole of the Atlantic.

The prize was awarded to a neat, high-density housing development in Cambridge with communal gardens and delicate wooden panelling called Accordia. That evening, however, many of the attendees would have had other things on their mind. Some would have been engaging in hushed, half-distracted conversations. Their attention, while mostly fixed on the ceremony, would have occasionally drifted to the news coming from the other side of the Atlantic. Earlier that day, in Washington DC, Dominique Strauss-Kahn, the then head of the International Monetary Fund, had warned that 'the global financial system' was on the 'brink of systemic meltdown'.[94] A rash of foreclosures in the United States' unequal and heavily indebted mortgage market were burning through the balance-sheets of the world's financial organisations. Three weeks earlier, the collapse of Lehman Brothers, one of the world's biggest investment banks, had unleased a phase of acute economic crisis the scale of which few had ever seen. The day before the ceremony, the FTSE 100 had closed nearly nine points down, the biggest one-day fall since 1987. Alistair Darling, Britain's Chancellor, was spending that weekend drafting emergency measures to offset economic Armageddon when the markets re-opened on Monday. What was at stake that weekend, according to *The Guardian*'s chief economics correspondent, was nothing less than 'the collapse of the western banking system'.[95] To the attendees of the Stirling Prize, the future had never been less certain. History, once safely contained and statically preserved in the warehouses and jetties of the restored docklands, was suddenly returning with an incredible, jarring force.

The 2008 crisis and its long aftermath brought an end to almost fifteen years of economic stability, sometimes referred to as the 'Great Moderation'. The following year, the Centre for Cities think tank would issue a 'red alert' for Liverpool, warning that its fragile recovery was particularly vulnerable to the economic disaster that was engulfing large parts of the world.[96] According to the 'social deprivation index', a holistic measure of poverty that considers income, employment, health, education and environment, Liverpool had become the poorest city in Britain by the end of 2009.[97] Some inner-city wards such as Granby in Toxteth, where unemployment was at 13.5 per cent – twice the national rate – had never fully recovered from their post-war collapse.[98] A new Conservative government, elected in 2010, began, once again, to starve Liverpool and other British cities of money. Between 2009 and 2019, council spending in Liverpool fell by £441 million, almost a third of its total, an effective reduction of £816 in spending per person.[99] Defeated, disorganised and co-opted, Liverpool's various radical traditions were unable, this time, to mount an effective resistance. While Britain's economic infrastructure survived the weekend of 11–12 October, the crisis also revealed that Liverpool's turn-of-the-century regeneration would not, at least any time soon, rescue the city from its obsolescence.

Epilogue

Liverpool Waters

Depending on the time of day, four or five trains leave each hour from Liverpool's Lime Street station bound for Manchester. The trains depart through a gloomy channel cut deep into the limestone bedrock before emerging into the suburbs and then eventually accelerating into flat Lancashire farmland. The northern route to Manchester follows the same path set out in 1830 by Stephenson's Rocket, the first inter-city railway journey in the world. Twenty minutes out of Liverpool, the train flashes past the site of the long-closed Parkside station on the fringes of the small market town of Newton-le-Willows, the spot where the hapless Liverpool MP William Huskisson was killed by the Rocket's first journey. As the train passes through Eccles, Salford and into the heart of Manchester, weaving through a familiar patchwork of glossy, hastily built private flats, flyovers and business parks, attentive passengers might notice a proliferation of similar-looking buildings. Clustered along canals, nestled in distant valleys and sometimes partially occluded by new office developments, the landscape is punctuated by former textile mills – large, squat, brick buildings, usually four or five storeys high, sometimes more, with tall, slender chimneys.

Lancashire's textile mills were once at the avant-garde of Britain's economy. With their globally sourced inventories, their innovative methods of workplace discipline and their deployment of sophisticated machines powered by water or steam, they came, for many, to represent nineteenth-century industrial modernity as a whole. It was, for example, primarily by studying these buildings and their brutalised workforces that Karl Marx and Friedrich Engels honed their theories and critiques of capitalism. The precocious train line between Manchester and Liverpool was once a short but significant artery of imperial trade – a hypodermic needle through which cotton grown in the fields of Alabama, Egypt or the Punjab was injected from Liverpool's docks directly into Lancashire's mills.

There are 540 mills still standing in Greater Manchester, almost all of which are now obsolete.[1] While some mills have been repurposed into luxury flats, offices, workshops or community centres, many are empty, ruined and shuttered. One recent survey calculated that in Greater Manchester alone there are more than 1.1 million square metres of derelict floorspace in former mills, the equivalent of 160 football fields of silent, crumbling rooms where vast machines serviced by hundreds of workers once operated.[2] Among these ruins are the Peel Mills in Bury. Although parts of the surviving mill-complex are available to rent, it is mostly empty, its glass windows shattered and partially boarded up. On the confluence of the River Irwell and the River Roch, Bury was one of the first places in Britain to develop a textile economy. In the late eighteenth century, Robert Peel, father of the Conservative Prime Minister and economic liberal of the same name, founded the first mills in the area, which were powered by water from the two rivers and mostly employed children from nearby villages. The Peel Mills cotton spinning complex in Bury, named as an homage to the same family, was built in stages from 1885. Undercut by cheaper textiles manufactured overseas, its operation eventually ceased in 1977.

Four years before Peel Mills closed, it was purchased by a local businessman named John Whittaker. One might assume that Whittaker's story would be an unremarkable and provincial tale of post-industrial decline and foreclosure, a reckless mistaken gamble on a dying trade. Instead, it was quite the opposite. Whittaker and his son, also named John, would, over the course of half a century, use this run-down, unproductive complex of Victorian mills as the basis for massing a vast fortune of more than £1.7

billion.[3] Whittaker realised that while textile spinning was a dying trade, textile companies had another vital commodity that, if used correctly, could be even more lucrative: land. The textile companies that were falling into disuse across the former heartlands of the industrial revolution owned prime real estate in multiple British cities in the form of mills, warehouses and ancillary buildings. Peel began buying up dead or dying textile firms primarily for their land, initially building cheap pop-up warehouses on the outskirts of major towns.[4]

After two decades of buying and selling or leasing land across northern England, Whittaker's company, renamed Peel Holdings and then, more recently, the Peel Group, have accumulated a dazzling and lucrative property portfolio. In 1987, the company purchased the Manchester Ship Canal, interested less in profiting from its traffic and more from the redevelopment opportunities afforded by the land that the canal abutted. Peel then expanded to purchase several provincial airports, including Doncaster-Sheffield Airport and Teeside International Airport. In 1997, the company purchased Liverpool's airport in Speke. By the early 2000s, the company owned Clydeport in Western Scotland, Great Yarmouth's harbour, parts of the dockland along the Tyne and the Tees, Falmouth port in Cornwall, the Bridgewater Canal between Liverpool and Manchester, the Media City complex in Salford that houses the regional headquarters of the BBC and ITV, the enormous Scout Moor Wind Farm that covers more than 1,300 acres of Lancashire countryside and the Trafford Centre shopping mall on the outskirts of Manchester. By 2019, it was estimated that Peel owned more than 1,000 discrete pieces of land in Britain.[5] Despite its massive footprint, Peel is opaque and unaccountable, operating through concentric chains of similarly named holding companies, likened by one journalist to 'a series of Russian dolls, one nested inside another'.[6] John Whittaker, now in his eighties, still owns the company, but lives on the Isle of Man where he helicopters out for board meetings and where residents are exempted by local laws from paying capital gains tax, inheritance tax or stamp duty.[7]

Peel have become experts at managing Britain's obsolescence. The company have earned a fortune from the discarded residues left behind by Britain's nineteenth- and twentieth-century economy: polluted land, rotting buildings and surplus workers. They are drawing down the last reserves of Britain's extinguished industrial past, salvaging wealth from disorganised ruins. It is unsurprising, then, that their most substantial and notorious acquisitions have been in Liverpool. In 2005, Peel purchased the MDHC, the body that had owned and managed Liverpool and Birkenhead's docks since the mid-nineteenth century. In 1970, containerisation and Liverpool's collapsing share of world trade had bankrupted the Company. In the intervening thirty years, however, its fortunes had been revived by a mixture of property development, consultancy and a new container terminal built to the north of the city. When Peel bought the MDHC for £770 million, it had become the second largest ports operator in Britain and had expanded to include Medway Ports in Kent and a container terminal in Dublin.[8]

Like most of Peel's acquisitions, the deal came with land – in this case a long strip of former docks, still derelict, running along Liverpool's northern riverfront. In 2007, Peel announced a spectacular redevelopment plan for this neglected stretch of riverbank, a proposal that dwarfed all the city's previous regeneration schemes. Called 'Liverpool Waters', the development is nothing less than a city within a city – a mixed-use waterside complex that, in its scale and plasticity, resembles pop-up Middle Eastern metropoles such as Dubai or the planned city of Neom in the Saudi Arabian desert. The initial proposal included a forest of high-rise towers stretching for two kilometres along the riverbank studded with squares, parks, offices, luxury homes and hotels.[9] There are plans for a 55-storey 'Shanghai Tower' inspired by the skyline of the Chinese city, which had been such an important source of trade and labour during Liverpool's imperial history. If built, the tower will be the tallest in Britain outside of London. Liverpool Waters also features a new, £500 million stadium for Everton Football Club on the site of the old Bramley Moore Dock jutting out into the river. The stadium will replace the 130-year-old Goodison Park, now set to be demolished and built over with a bland mixed-use complex of houses and offices.[10]

Liverpool Waters is still in its early stages and Peel's proposals continue to be contested and redrafted. According to the company, it might be another fifty years before the development is complete. By that time, Liverpool's coastline will be an increasingly precarious place to live and work. According to the most recent report of the International Panel on Climate Change, the world is on course for between one and three feet of sea level rise by 2100, though some more pessimistic models predict more than six feet of rising.[11] Even if we see dramatic global measures enacted to suppress the emission of fossil fuels, the city's waters will continue to rise into the next century and beyond. It is possible that Liverpool Waters will be uninhabitable within less than a generation of its delayed completion.[12] Liverpool's imperial history has contributed to a warming world that may, eventually, subsume parts of the city itself. The most dramatic consequences of the global, industrial economy that Liverpool helped forge may yet be felt. While a child born in Liverpool in 1920 would have lived long enough to witness a city that outlived its purpose, a child born a hundred years later may live long enough to watch parts of the city disappear forever.

In this book I have argued that Liverpool's history is where we need to look to understand the present and the future of Britain, as well as many other parts of the global north that have outlived their original purpose and have inherited decaying infrastructures from a previous era of aggressive, developmental modernity. Liverpool's prophecy of a coming age of entropy and decline requires a new political vocabulary. As early as the 1960s, James Boggs, a Black writer, civil rights activist and autoworker, saw how changes in the industrial economy of his hometown of Detroit threatened to render workers surplus on a vast scale. Boggs imagined a future where millions of 'outsiders' were assembled on the margins of the productive economy, a disorganised and surplus constituency excluded from the unions and political movements that fought to secure the futures of the stably employed. For Boggs, these outsiders were the permanently unemployed, but this group might now also include a host of other refugees from the productive orders of the past: prisoners, the homeless, displaced migrants and perhaps even those who are today currently working precarious, contingent and underpaid jobs – food delivery workers, Uber drivers, low-paid care workers and countless others. Boggs argued that the existence of these outsiders required a new kind of humanism, the making of 'radical concepts beyond the imagination of us all but certainly founded on the principle that people should be able to enjoy everything in life and from life'.[13]

In telling the history of post-war Liverpool, this book has attempted to transplant Boggs' hopeful demands from the car plants of 1960s Detroit to the streets of early twenty-first-century Liverpool. That whole populations are outliving the productive regimes that summoned them into being should not make them surplus or disposable. The unmaking of many of the features of Britain's nineteenth and twentieth centuries – imperial trading networks patched together by exploitative shipping companies, punitive forms of industrial work, sprawling and isolated suburbs, segregated and brutally policed inner cities – can be a source of possibility, even hope. Journalists, politicians and even historians often call on history to constrain the options available to us in the present, dulling our political imagination. History is frequently taught as a menu of 'lessons' and 'warnings' – 'mistakes' that must be avoided rather than repeated. Instead, I want to argue the opposite. Liverpool's history has only one 'lesson' and it is that the future is less certain and more open to possibilities than we can presently imagine.

Notes

Introduction

1 Frank Shaw, 'Liverpool Dockland: A Seven Mile Pageant of Empire', *Liverpool Echo*, 15 July 1952.

2 Bill Hunter, *They Knew Why They Fought: Unofficial Struggles & Leadership on the Docks 1945–1989* (London: Index, 1994), 135.

3 Tony Dickson and David Judge eds., *The Politics of Industrial Closure* (London: Macmillan, 1987), 29.

4 Tony Gifford, Wally Brown and Ruth Bundey, *Loosen the Shackles: First Report of the Liverpool 8 Enquiry into Race Relations in Liverpool* (London: Kaira, 1989), 40–41.

5 Erik Linstrum, 'Domesticating Chemical Weapons: Tear Gas and the Militarization of Policing in the British Imperial World, 1919–1981', *The Journal of Modern History* 91, no. 3 (September 2019): 557–585, 574.

6 Geoffrey Howe to Margaret Thatcher, memo, 11 August 1981, The National Archives, PREM 19/578.

7 This book sits alongside other recent works on post-war Britain in which detailed histories of specific places are used to tell national and even global stories about themes such as social democracy, political culture, decolonisation, race and neoliberalism. Some examples include James Vernon, 'Heathrow and the Making of Neoliberal Britain', *Past and Present* 252, no. 1 (August 2021): 213–247; Kennetta Hammond Perry, *London is the Place for Me: Black Britons, Citizenship and the Politics of Race* (Oxford: Oxford University Press, 2015); Daisy Payling, *Socialist Republic: Remaking the British Left in 1980s Sheffield* (Manchester: Manchester University Press, 2023); Guy Ortolano, *Thatcher's Progress: From Social Democracy to Market Liberalism Through an English New Town* (Cambridge: Cambridge University Press, 2019). Three recent studies of Liverpool have placed the city at the centre of debates about inner-city crisis, urban regeneration, class formation and property speculation in the post-war era: Abi O'Connor, 'Saving the City? Neoliberal Stigma, the State and "Socialism" in Liverpool' (PhD diss.,

University of Liverpool, 2024); Aaron Andrews, 'Decline and the City: The Urban Crisis in Liverpool c. 1968 to 1986' (PhD diss., University of Leicester, 2018); Daniel Warner, 'Working-Class Culture and Practice amid Urban Renewal and Decline: Liverpool c. 1986–1985' (PhD diss., University of Liverpool, 2018).

8 For the most coherent expression of Liverpool as a national exception see John Belchem's argument that Liverpool stands 'outside the main narrative frameworks of modern British history'. John Belchem, *Merseypride: Essays in Liverpool Exceptionalism* (Liverpool: Liverpool University Press, 2006), xxx. For the distinctiveness of Liverpool within Britain's broader Black history see Jacqueline Nassy Brown, *Dropping Anchor, Setting Sail: Geographies of Race in Black Liverpool* (Princeton, NJ: Princeton University Press, 2005).

9 The idea of a place 'producing more history than it can consume' was originally applied by the Victorian short-story writer H. H. Munro (known by the pen name Saki) to Crete. It is frequently misattributed to Winston Churchill.

10 Svetlana Alexievich, *Secondhand Time: The Last of the Soviets* (New York: Random House, 2017), 11.

11 For a more technical history of obsolescence as a problem for architectural theory and practice see Daniel M. Abramson, *Obsolescence: An Architectural History* (Chicago: University of Chicago Press, 2016).

12 Originally from Henry James, *The American Scene* (1907), this is quoted in Max Page, *The Creative Destruction of Manhattan: 1900–1940* (Chicago: Chicago University Press, 1999), 1.

13 Karl Marx and Friedrich Engels, *The Communist Manifesto* (London: Penguin, 2002), 223.

14 For a critical summary of the 'decline' thesis see Jim Tomlinson, 'Inventing "Decline": The Falling Behind of the British Economy in the Postwar Years', *The Economic History Review* 49, no. 4 (November 1996): 731–757; David Edgerton, 'Why the Left Must Abandon the British Myth of Decline', *The New Statesman*, 5 October 2021. For 'decline' seen from a wider imperial lens see Stuart Ward, *Untied Kingdom: A Global History of the End of Britain* (Cambridge: Cambridge University Press, 2023), Ch. 11.

15 A version of this argument has been made by Mike Savage, *The Return of Inequality: Social Change and the Weight of the Past* (Cambridge, MA: Harvard University Press, 2021), Ch. 4.

16 Tony Lane, *Liverpool: City of the Sea* (Liverpool: Liverpool University Press, 1997), 46.

17 The argument that welfare provision policed the boundaries of whiteness in modern Britain is (along with so much else in this book) indebted

to the work of the political theorist Robbie Shilliam. In particular, see Robbie Shilliam, *Race and the Undeserving Poor: From Abolition to Brexit* (New York: Columbia University Press, 2018).

18 There are too many iterations of this argument to form a comprehensive list in this endnote. In its typical expression, historians have argued that Britain's eighteenth- and nineteenth-century Atlantic slave economy, an economy for which Liverpool was central, prefigured the technological sophistication of, established the trade routes for and, most importantly, generated the wealth that underpinned Britain's rapid industrialisation. Three of the most significant versions of this argument would be Eric Williams, *Capitalism and Slavery* (London: Penguin, 1944, 2022); Sydney Mintz, *Sweetness and Power: The Place of Sugar in Modern History* (London: Penguin, 1986); Catherine Hall et al., *Legacies of British Slave Ownership: Colonial Slavery and the Formation of Victorian Britain* (Cambridge: Cambridge University Press, 2016).

19 Historical and theoretical works in this vein that have been influential on this book include Cedric Robinson, *Black Marxism: The Making of the Black Radical Tradition* (Chapel Hill: University of North Carolina Press, 1983, 2021). Various writings by Stuart Hall but particularly 'Race, Articulation and Societies Structured in Dominance' and 'New Ethnicities', in Stuart Hall, Paul Gilroy and Ruth Wilson Gilmore eds., *Selected Writings on Race and Difference* (Durham, NC: Duke University Press, 2021); Ruth Wilson Gilmore, *Golden Gulag: Prisons, Surplus, Crisis and Opposition in Globalizing California* (Oakland: University of California Press, 2007); Shilliam, *Race and the Undeserving Poor.*

20 An important exception can be found in the work of Arun Kundnani, who argues that neoliberalism has its own distinctive racial formation arising out of the exploitation and management of surplus populations. Arun Kundnani, 'The Racial Constitution of Neoliberalism', *Race and Class* 61, no. 1 (April 2021): 51–69.

21 Or, as Stuart Hall put it when referring to domestic post-war British racism, it is the racism 'not of a dominant, but a declining social formation'. Stuart Hall, 'Race and "Moral Panics" in Postwar Britain', in Hall et al. eds., *Selected Writings on Race and Difference*, 59.

22 For 'working-class' histories of Liverpool that tend to privilege the experiences and political activism of white men, see Brian Marren, *We Shall Not Be Moved: How Liverpool's Working Class Fought Redundancies, Closures and Cuts in the Age of Thatcher* (Manchester: Manchester University Press, 2016); Peter Taafe and Tony Mulhearn, *Liverpool: A City that Dared to Fight* (London: Fortress, 1988); Hunter, *They Knew Why They Fought.* A richer social picture can be found in Alice Mah, *Port Cities and Global Legacies: Urban Identity, Waterfront Work*

and Radicalism (Basingstoke: Palgrave, 2018). For a recent overview of Britain's post-war 'imperial racial formation' see Marc Matera, Radhika Natarajan, Kennetta Hammond Perry, Camilla Schofield and Rob Waters, 'Marking Race in Twentieth Century British History', *Twentieth Century British History* 34, no. 3 (September 2023): 407–414.

23 Nadine El-Enany, *Bordering Britain: Law, Race and Empire* (Manchester: Manchester University Press, 2020); Ian Patel, *We're Here Because You Were There: Immigration and the End of Empire* (London: Verso, 2021).

24 Many activists and theorists in the 1970s and 1980s were making arguments in favour of an expansive, 'political' Blackness or against an essential, fixed notion of Blackness. For an influential example of each of these see A. Sivanandan, 'From Resistance to Rebellion: Asian and Afro-Caribbean Struggles in Britain', *Race & Class* 23, no. 2–3 (1981): 111–152; Hall, 'New Ethnicities'. For a history of this moment see Rob Waters, *Thinking Black: Britain, 1964–1985* (Oakland, CA: University of California Press, 2019).

25 Gilmore, *Golden Gulag*, 179.

Prelude: The World that Liverpool Made

1 Gabriel Winant and Alex Press, hosts, 'Casualties of History', Podcast, 25 June 2020.

2 For a succinct account of Liverpool's involvement in the trans-Atlantic slave trade see Kenneth Morgan, 'Liverpool's Dominance in the British Slave Trade, 1740–1807', in David Richardson, Suzanne Schwarz and Anthony Tibbles, *Liverpool and Transatlantic Slavery* (Liverpool: Liverpool University Press, 2007).

3 Anthony Tibbles, '"My Interest Be Your Guide": Richard Watt (1724–1796), Merchant of Liverpool and Kingston, Jamaica', *Transactions of the Royal Historical Society of Lancashire and Cheshire* 166 (January 2017): 25–44.

4 Richard Watt III, who owned Speke Hall, is recorded in University College London's Legacies of British Slave Ownership online database as having received £4,485 4s 9d in compensation when slavery was abolished, www.ucl.ac.uk/lbs/person/view/13160.

5 Max Haven, *Palm Oil: The Grease of Empire* (London: Pluto, 2022).

6 Marika Sherwood, 'Elder Dempster and West Africa 1891–c. 1914: The Genesis of Underdevelopment?' *The International Journal of African Historical Studies* 30, no. 2 (1997): 253–276.

7 For the New Orleans slave market see Walter Johnson, *Soul by Soul: Life Inside the Antebellum Slave Market* (Cambridge, MA: Harvard University Press, 1999).

8 Sven Beckett, *Empire of Cotton: A Global History* (New York: Knopf, 2014), Ch. 8.

9 Ibid., 260.

10 James L. Watson, *Emigration and the Chinese Lineage: The Mans in Hong Kong and London* (Berkeley: University of California Press, 1975), 60–61.

11 The figure of five million is estimated in Donald M. MacRaild, *Irish Migrants in Modern Britain, 1750–1922* (Basingstoke: Palgrave, 1999), 9. For the Irish experience in Liverpool see John Belchem, *Irish, Catholic, and Scouse: The History of the Liverpool Irish 1800–1939* (Liverpool: Liverpool University Press, 2007).

12 Pat O'Mara, *The Autobiography of a Liverpool Irish Slummy* (Liverpool: Bluecoat, 2007), 5.

13 Tony Lane, *City of the Sea* (Liverpool: Liverpool University Press, 1997), 1.

1. Departures

1 Local journalist Laura Davis has compiled a list of events that took place in the city on that day using historical newspaper reports. Laura Davis, '50 Things that Happened in Merseyside on VE Day 1945', *Liverpool Echo*, 8 May 2020; Bryan Perrett, *Liverpool: A City at War* (Liverpool: Robert Hale, 1990), 162.

2 Perrett, *Liverpool: A City at War*, 151. For international communities in Britain during the war see Wendy Webster, *Mixing it: Diversity in World War Two Britain* (Oxford: Oxford University Press, 2018).

3 The schedule of events held at Allied House during and immediately after the war has been largely preserved in the National Archives (henceforward TNA:PRO), BW 3/3.

4 Historians have been increasingly conscious of the ways that the creation of Britain's 'welfare state' was inseparable from broader histories of empire, citizenship and domestic race relations during this period. See, for example, Robbie Shilliam, *Race and the Undeserving Poor: From Abolition to Brexit* (New York: Columbia University Press, 2018); Kennetta Hammond Perry, *London is the Place for Me: Black Britons, Citizenship and the Politics of Race* (Oxford: Oxford University Press, 2016); Jordanna Bailkin, *Afterlife of Empire* (Oakland: University of California Press, 2012).

5 Report from H. M. Chief Inspector, 12 December 1945, TNA:PRO, HO 213/926.

6 The best account of the economic and environmental carnage wrought by late nineteenth-century globalisation on China remains Mike Davis, *Late Victorian Holocausts: El Niño Famines and the Making of the Third World* (London: Verso, 2000), esp. Ch. 11. For the migration of Chinese

workers to white settler colonial states in the late nineteenth and early twentieth centuries see Marilyn Lake and Henry Reynolds, *Drawing the Global Colour Line: White Men's Countries and the International Challenge of Racial Equality* (Cambridge: Cambridge University Press, 2008), Chs. 1 and 6.

7 Maria Lin Wong, *Chinese Liverpudlians: A History of the Chinese Community in Liverpool* (Liverpool: Liver Press, 1989), 4.

8 These details come from oral histories collected by Maria Lin Wong in the 1980s in ibid., 15–21, 25. For other accounts of the Chinese community in mid-century Liverpool see Irene Loh Lynn, *The Chinese Community in Liverpool: Their Unmet Needs with Respect to Education, Social Welfare and Housing* (Liverpool: Merseyside Area Profile Group, 1982); S. Craggs and I. Loh Lynn, *A History of the Chinese Community* (Liverpool: Merseyside Community Relations Council, 1985); Maurice Broady, 'The Social Adjustment of Chinese Immigrants in Liverpool', *The Sociological Review* 3, no. 1 (1955): 65–75.

9 Craggs and Loh Lynn, *A History of the Chinese Community*, 3.

10 For example: Memo, 'Chinese', 2 November 1945, Liverpool Maritime Museum Archives (henceforward LMM) OA 1088.

11 Loh Lynn, *The Chinese Community*, 14. Wong, *Chinese Liverpudlians*, 10–15.

12 Wong, *Chinese Liverpudlians*, 29–32, 36–40.

13 John Seed, 'Limehouse Blues: Looking for Chinatown in the London Docks, 1900–40', *History Workshop Journal* 62, no. 1 (October 2006): 58–85.

14 Some of these reports are detailed in Wong, *Chinese Liverpudlians*, Ch. 4.

15 Douglas Jones, 'The Chinese in Britain: Origins and Development of a Community', *Journal of Ethnic and Migration Studies* 7, no. 3 (1979): 397–402, 400.

16 M. Perks, memo, 12 February 1945, TNA:PRO, HO 213/808.

17 B. Hawkins, memo, 30 May 1947, TNA:PRO, 213/809.

18 Memo, 28 May 1945, TNA:PRO, HO 213/808.

19 Memo, 7 March 1945, TNA:PRO, HO 213/808.

20 Note of meeting held at Home Office, 19 October 1945, TNA:PRO, HO 213/926.

21 Memo, 30 August 1945, TNA:PRO, HO 213/808.

22 Note of meeting held at Home Office, 19 October 1945, TNA:PRO, HO 213/926. This meeting, and this file in the National Archives, has been the focus of a substantial amount of activism and attention from Liverpool's Chinese community. *HO 213/926* is even the title of a poem published by the Singaporean poet Theophilus Kwek in 2017.

23 The rounding-up process is described in H. M. Chief Inspector, 'Repatriation of Chinese Seamen', report, TNA:PRO, HO 213/926.

24 Ibid.

25 This activism has taken several forms including a multimedia heritage project at the Williamson Art Gallery in Birkenhead organised by a group called Dragons of the Pool. In May 2021, the Labour MP for Liverpool Riverside Kim Johnson called on the then Prime Minister Boris Johnson to issue a formal apology for the deportations, a call that Johnson deflected.

26 Dan Hancox, 'The Secret Deportations', *The Guardian*, 25 May 2021.

27 For an example of a narrative of this sort that begins with the *Windrush* see Mike Phillips and Trevor Phillips, *Windrush: The Irresistible Rise of Multi-Cultural Britain* (London: HarperCollins, 2009). For the myth of the *Windrush* see Simon Peplow, '"In 1997 Nobody Had Heard of the Windrush": The "Windrush Narrative" in British Newspapers', *Immigrants & Minorities* 37, no. 3 (July 2020): 211–237.

28 Transcribed interview with Captain Clifford Sullivan, 30 November 1982, LMM Merseyside Docklands History Survey, SA/4. See also Tony Lane, *The Merchant Seamen's War* (Liverpool: Bluecoat, 1990).

29 Diane Frost, *Work and Community Among West African Migrant Workers Since the Nineteenth Century* (Liverpool: Liverpool University Press, 1999), 62.

30 Memo, 1 March 1941, TNA:PRO, CO 859/40/2.

31 John Belchem, *Before the Windrush: Race Relations in 20th-Century Liverpool* (Liverpool: Liverpool University Press, 2014), 100. For an authoritative account of Black sailors in Britain see Ray Costello, *Black Salt: Seafarers of African Descent on British Ships* (Liverpool: Liverpool University Press, 2012).

32 Diane Frost, 'Racism and Social Segregation: Settlement Patterns of West African Seamen in Liverpool Since the Nineteenth Century', *Journal of Ethnic and Migration Studies* 22, no. 1 (1996): 85–95, 90–91.

33 On the 1919 riots see Laura Tabili, *Global Migrants, Local Culture: Natives and Newcomers in Provincial England, 1841–1939* (Basingstoke: Palgrave Macmillan, 2011), Ch. 8; Belchem, *Before the Windrush*, Ch. 2. On the Coloured Alien Seamen Order see Nadine El-Enany, *Bordering Britain: Law, Race and Empire* (Manchester: Manchester University Press, 2020), 67–68; Laura Tabili, 'The Construction of Racial Difference in Twentieth-Century Britain: The Special Restriction (Coloured Alien Seamen) Order, 1925', *Journal of British Studies* 33, no. 1 (January 1994): 54–98.

34 Chris Renwick, 'Eugenics, Population Research and Social Mobility Studies in Early and Mid-Twentieth Century Britain', *The Historical*

Journal 59, no. 3 (September 2016): 845–867. For race and eugenics in inter-war Britain see Alison Bashford, *Global Population: History, Geopolitics and Life on Earth* (New York: Columbia University Press, 2016); Shilliam, *Race and the Undeserving Poor*; Gavin Schaffer, *Racial Science and British Society 1930–62* (New York: Palgrave Macmillan, 2008).

35 Muriel Fletcher, *Report on an Investigation into the Colour Problem in Liverpool and Other Ports* (Liverpool: Liverpool Association for the Welfare of Half-Caste Children, 1930).

36 For a detailed debunking of Fletcher's methodology see Mark Christian, 'The Fletcher Report 1930: A Historical Case Study of Contested Black Mixed Heritage Britishness', *Journal of Historical Sociology* 21, no. 2–3 (June 2008): 213–241.

37 Fletcher, *Report*, 38.

38 Ibid., 21, 38.

39 Paul Gilroy, *The Black Atlantic: Modernity and Double-Consciousness* (Cambridge, MA: Harvard University Press, 1995).

40 Tabili, 'The Construction of Racial Difference in Twentieth Century Britain', 54–98, 60.

41 Belchem, *Before the Windrush*, 82–85.

42 Memo, 1 March 1941, TNA:PRO, CO 859/40/2.

43 Anthony Richmond, *Colour Prejudice in Great Britain: A Study of West Indian Workers in Liverpool, 1941–51* (London: Routledge, 1954).

44 Ibid., 36–48, 59.

45 Ibid., 49, 61.

46 Report prepared for the Advisory Committee on the Welfare of Coloured Peoples in the UK, quoted in Belchem, *Before the Windrush*, 83.

47 Richmond, *Colour Prejudice*, 73.

48 Ibid., 74, 97.

49 Ibid., 78.

50 Cebert Lewis signed statement, 1 December 1941, TNA:PRO, HO 45/24471.

51 Richmond, *Colour Prejudice*, 139.

52 Ibid., 141–142.

53 Employment of Colonial Seamen in the United Kingdom, Circular Dispatch, 9 June 1950, TNA:PRO, CO 876/233.

54 Colonial Peoples' Defence Association, 'Report of Activity: 1950–1952', Liverpool Record Office, 329 COM/14, 10.

55 J. E. Thomas to E. Y. Bannard, letter, 13 February 1950, TNA:PRO, CO 876/233.

56 These details are from Marika Sherwood, *Pastor Daniels Ekarte and the*

African Churches Mission, Liverpool 1931–64 (London: Savannah Press, 1964), 29–35, 85.

57 Adom Getachew, *Worldmaking After Empire: The Rise and Fall of Self-Determination* (Princeton, NJ: Princeton University Press, 2019); Lydia Walker, 'Decolonization in the 1960s: On Legitimate and Illegitimate Nationalist Claims-Making', *Past and Present* 242, no. 1 (February 2019): 227–264. For alternatives to nationalism in Africa see Frederick Cooper, 'Reconstructing Empire in British and French Africa', *Past and Present*, 210, no. 6 (2011): 196–210. For alternatives in South Asia see Manu Goswami and Mrinalini Sinha eds., *Political Imaginaries in Twentieth-Century India* (London: Bloomsbury, 2022).

58 Getachew describes worldmaking as a process of 'international non-domination', a project of 'overcoming international hierarchy and constituting a postimperial world'. Getachew, *Worldmaking After Empire*, 23.

59 Sherwood, *Pastor Daniels Ekarte*, 24–29.

60 St Clair Drake, 'The African Churches Mission and the Issue of the Negro Babies', St Clair Drake Archives, Schomburg Center for Research in Black Culture (henceforward SCDA), Box 61, Folder 1–2.

61 Daniels Ekarte, letter, 24 August 1940, TNA:PRO, CO 859/40/2.

62 N. A. Guttery to J. A. Paskin, 1 October 1940, TNA:PRO, CO 859/40/2.

63 For the experiences of and reactions to Black US servicemen see Graham Smith, *When Jim Crow Met John Bull* (New York: St Martin's Press, 1987); Webster, *Mixing It*, Ch. 6.

64 Liverpool Assistant Chief Constable to Mrs J. Hart, letter, 19 April 1944, TNA:PRO, HO 45/24471.

65 Lucy Bland, *Britain's 'Brown Babies': The Stories of Children Born to Black GIs and White Women in the Second World War* (Manchester: Manchester University Press, 2019), 33.

66 St Clair Drake, 'A Report on the Brown Britishers', SCDA, Box 61, Folder 14.

67 Hazel V. Carby, *Imperial Intimacies: A Tale of Two Islands* (London: Verso, 2019), 100–114.

68 St Clair Drake, 'League of Coloured Peoples in Liverpool', SCDA, Box 61, Folder 16.

69 Sherwood, *Pastor Daniels Ekarte*, 32–33.

70 St Clair Drake, 'The African Churches Mission and the Issue of the Negro Babies', SCDA, Box 61, Folder 1–2.

71 Marc Matera, *Black London: The Imperial Metropolis and Decolonisation in the Twentieth Century* (Oakland: University of California Press, 2015), 37–45.

72 For mid-twentieth-century liberal anti-racism see Rob Waters,

Colonized by Humanity: Caribbean London and the Politics of Integration at the End of Empire (Oxford: Oxford University Press, 2023).

73 *The League of Coloured People Newsletter*, No. 42, March 1943, TNA:PRO, HO 45/24471, 163.

74 Bland, *Britain's 'Brown Babies'*, 101.

75 St Clair Drake, 'The 'American Campaign' Debacle', SCDA, Box 61, Folder 1–2; Bland, *Britain's 'Brown Babies'*, 101–104.

76 Bland, *Britain's 'Brown Babies'*, 103.

77 Ibid., 102–103.

78 Sherwood, *Pastor Daniels Ekarte*, 63. St Clair Drake, 'The Genesis of the Brown Baby Problem', SCDA, Box 61, Folder 1–2.

79 Sherwood, *Pastor Daniels Ekarte*, 66–67.

80 St Clair Drake, 'Rainbow Homes Fiasco', SCDA, Box 61, Folder 1–2; Bland, *Britain's 'Brown Babies'*, 106–110.

81 St Clair Drake, 'League of Coloured Peoples in Liverpool', SCDA, Box 61, Folder 16.

82 St Clair Drake, 'The Liverpool Disturbances', SCDA, Box 61, Folder 15; Belchem, *Before the Windrush*, 139–140.

83 Belchem, *Before the Windrush*, 140.

84 St Clair Drake, 'The Liverpool Disturbances', SCDA, Box 61, Folder 15.

85 Ibid.

86 According to the 2011 Census, Liverpool's population was 91 per cent white compared with 87.2 per cent of Britain as a whole.

2. The Rescue Mission

1 Daniel Caradog Jones ed., *The Social Survey of Merseyside vol. 2* (Liverpool: Liverpool University Press, 1934), 390–403; Caradog Jones ed., *Social Survey vol. 3* (Liverpool: Liverpool University Press, 1934), 479, 515, 547.

2 Frances E. Hyde, *Liverpool and the Mersey: An Economic History of a Port, 1700–1970* (Newton Abbott: David and Charles, 1971), 160; D. E. Baines, 'Merseyside in the British Economy: The 1930s and the Second World War', in Richard Lawton and Catherine Cunningham eds., *Merseyside Social and Economic Studies* (Harlow: Longman, 1970), 62.

3 Transcribed interview with Herbert Crosbie, 9 February 1982, Liverpool Maritime Museum Archives Centre (henceforth LMM), Merseyside Docklands History Survey, SA/4.

4 16,500 was the size of Liverpool's register of workers permitted by the National Dock Labour Board between 1953 and 1958.

5 Michael B. Miller, *Europe and the Maritime World: A Twentieth-Century History* (Cambridge: Cambridge University Press, 2012), 50.

6 For Liverpool's port pre-1945 see Sheila Marriner, *The Economic and Social Development of Merseyside* (London: Croom Helm, 1982).

7 The idea that dock workers were a dangerous underclass or a social 'residuum' was particularly prominent in London. See Gareth Stedman Jones, *Outcast London: A Study in the Relationship Between Classes* (London: Verso, 1971, 2014), esp. Part 1; Judith Walkowitz, *City of Dreadful Delight: Narratives of Sexual Danger in Late-Victorian London* (Chicago: Chicago University Press, 1992), esp. Chs. 1–2. Distinctions between the respectable working class and a casualised 'residuum' that included dock workers were made in the second half the nineteenth century by the philanthropist Charles Booth, the popular journalist Andrew Mearns and the economist Alfred Marshall. For Irish migration in nineteenth-century Liverpool see John Belchem, *Irish, Catholic and Scouse: A History of the Liverpool Irish* (Liverpool: Liverpool University Press, 2007).

8 Greig Taylor, 'The Dynamics of Labour Relations at the Port of Liverpool, 1967–1989' (PhD diss., Manchester Metropolitan University, 2012), 60.

9 Tony Lane, *Liverpool: City of the Sea* (Liverpool: Liverpool University Press, 1997), 86.

10 The two classic accounts of this strike within the context of the wider trade union movement remain Eric Hobsbawm, 'The "New Unionism" in Perspective', in Hobsbawm ed., *Worlds of Labour: Further Studies in the History of Labour* (London: Weidenfeld & Nicolson, 1984); Ben Tillet, *Memories and Reflections* (London: J. Long, 1973), 119–147.

11 David F. Wilson, *Dockers: The Impact of Industrial Change* (London: Fontana Collins, 1972), 69.

12 Quoted in ibid., 72.

13 Parliamentary Papers, 'Transport Workers – Court of Inquiry. Vol. 1 Report and Minutes of Evidence of the Inquiry', 1920, cmnd. 936, 384.

14 Ibid., 44.

15 Vernon H. Jensen, *Hiring of Dockworkers and Employment Practices in the Ports of New York, Liverpool, London, Rotterdam and Marseille* (Cambridge, MA: Harvard University Press, 1964), 34.

16 Wilson, *Dockers*, 95–97; Jensen, *Hiring of Dockworkers*, 143–153.

17 National Dock Labour Board, *Review of the National Dock Labour Board 1947–1949* (London: National Dock Labour Board, 1950), 14, 16.

18 Peter Kilfoyle, *Left Behind: Lessons from Labour's Heartlands* (London: Politico's, 1999), 134.

19 Baines, 'Merseyside in the British Economy', 64.

20 National Dock Labour Board (Liverpool Group), 'New Entrants Training', 10 March 1952, LMM, P/NDLB/L/1/2.

21 Much of what follows draws on interviews with dock workers who

worked in the years immediately before and after the Second World War in Liverpool. The interviews were conducted in 1982 as part of the Merseyside Docklands History Survey. The account also draws on the labour relations expert Vernon Jensen's detailed investigation into the lives and working practices of Liverpool dock workers under the NDLB scheme, Jensen, *Hiring of Dockworkers*.

22 For an account of the open-air system in pre-war Liverpool see transcribed interview with Frank Dooley, 6 April 1982, LMM, Merseyside Docklands History Survey, SA/4. For the rebuilding of stands see Jensen, *Hiring of Dockworkers*, 95.

23 Transcribed interview with Charlie Fane, 15 March 1982, LMM, Merseyside Docklands History Survey, SA/4; Jensen, *Hiring of Dockworkers*, 163, 176.

24 Transcribed interview with Frank Dooley, 2 February 1982, LMM, Merseyside Docklands History Survey, SA/4.

25 Wilson, *Dockers*, 50.

26 Jensen, *Hiring of Dockworkers*, 171– 172.

27 These details come respectively from the interviews with Brian Jacques, Herbert Crosbie and Frank Dooley.

28 Taylor, 'The Dynamics of Labour Relations', 40.

29 Emma Copestake, 'Love, Laughter and Solidarity on the Docks in Liverpool, c. 1950s–1990s', *The Sociological Review* 7, no. 2 (March 2023), 441–457, 446.

30 Interview with Brian Jacques.

31 For organised sport see National Dock Labour Board (Liverpool Group), 'Welfare Report for the Quarter Ended 31st March 1954', April 1954, LMM, P/NDLB/L/1/2. For Breck Park see National Dock Labour Board, *Welfare Among Dockworkers* (London: National Dock Labour Board, 1951), 26. For further education see, for example, National Dock Labour Board (Liverpool Group), 'Minutes of a Meeting of the Welfare Sub-Committee', 9 June 1952, LMM, P/NDLB/L/1/2. For canteens see, for example, National Dock Labour Board (Liverpool Group), 'Minutes of a Meeting of the National Dock Labour Board (Liverpool Group), 30 July 1951', LMM, P/NDLB/L/1/2.

32 Quoted in Brian Marren, *We Shall Not Be Moved: How Liverpool's Working Class Fought Redundancies, Closures and Cuts in the Age of Thatcher* (Liverpool: Liverpool University Press, 2016), 204–205. For the intense bonds of male solidarity felt between dock workers see Copestake, 'Love, Laughter and Solidarity on the Docks'.

33 Interview with Frank Dooley.

34 Jim Phillips, 'Decasualization and Disruption: Industrial Relations in

the Docks, 1945–79', in Chris Wrigley ed., *A History of British Industrial Relations 1939–1979* (Cheltenham: Edward Elgar, 1996), 168.

35 Bill Hunter, *They Knew Why They Fought: Unofficial Struggles & Leadership on the Docks 1945–1989* (London: Index, 1994), 25–27.

36 Jim Phillips, 'Class and Industrial Relations in Britain: The "Long" Mid-Century and the Case of Port-Transport, c. 1920–70', *Modern British History* 16, no. 1 (March 2005): 52–73; Jensen, *Hiring of Dockworkers*, 141–142.

37 Gordon Phillips and Noel Whiteside, *Casual Labour: The Unemployment Question in the Port Transport Industry 1880–1970* (Oxford: Clarendon Press, 1985), 246–247.

38 National Dock Labour Board (Liverpool Group), 'Statement Issued to the Press', 4 July 1950, LMM, P/NDLB/L/1/1.

39 National Dock Labour Board (Liverpool Group), 'Memorandum', 19 September 1951, LMM, P/NDLB/L/1/1.

40 For example, National Dock Labour Board (Liverpool Group), 'Minutes of a Meeting of the Local Dock Labour Board (Liverpool Group)', 30 November 1954, LMM, P/NDLB/L/1/3; National Dock Labour Board (Liverpool Group), 'Minutes of a Meeting of the Local Dock Labour Board (Liverpool Group)', 8 July 1954, LMM, P/NDLB/L/1/3.

41 Women's History – Women's Lives, 'Women's Work on the Liverpool Docks and Waterfront, 1916–1987', 1987, available in the Liverpool Records Office, 12.

42 Miriam Glucksmann, *Women Assemble: Women Workers and the New Industries in Inter-War Britain* (London: Routledge, 1990); Vicky Long, 'Industrial Homes and Domestic Factories: The Convergence of Public and Private Space in Interwar Britain', *Journal of British Studies* 50, no. 2 (April 2011): 434–464; Sally Alexander, 'Becoming a Woman in London in the 1920s and 1930s', in Sally Alexander ed., *Becoming a Woman and Other Essays in 19th and 20th Century Feminist History* (New York: NYU Press, 1995); Birgitte Søland, *Young Women and the Reconstruction of Womanhood in the 1920s* (Princeton, NJ: Princeton University Press, 2000). One historian's contribution to this field has been omitted in solidarity with trans students and colleagues.

43 Linda May Grant, 'Women Workers and the Sexual Division of Labour: Liverpool 1890–1930' (PhD diss., University of Liverpool, 1987), 106, 105–124.

44 Until moving to Birkenhead in the 1960s, the main office of the Liverpool branch of the NDLB was located in the Exchange Buildings on Chapel Street built in 1937.

45 Mar Hicks, *Programmed Inequality: How Britain Discarded Women*

Technologists and Lost its Edge in Computing (Cambridge, MA: MIT Press, 2017).

46 A list of the names of all the Liverpool NDLB's clerical staff detailing their salaries and marital status can be found at National Dock Labour Board (Liverpool Group), 'Accounting Establishment', 9 November 1948. For the average dock worker's salary in 1948 see Jensen, *Hiring of Dockworkers*, 153.

47 Quoted in Laura Balderstone, Graeme J. Milne and Rachel Mulhearn, 'Memory and Place on the Liverpool Waterfront in the Mid-Twentieth Century', *Urban History* 43, no. 3 (August 2014): 478–496, 487.

48 These details are from interviews with an unnamed dock worker, Catherine Tipping, Florence Martinfield, Mrs Redmond and Nora McGrady recorded in Women's History – Women's Lives, 'Women's Work on the Liverpool Docks', 12, 39–40, 42, 44, 45.

49 Balderstone et al., 'Memory and Place on the Liverpool Waterfront', 488.

50 Jo Stanley, 'Women at Sea: Four Liverpool Stewardesses in the 1930s', 1987, available in the Liverpool Records Office.

51 These details are from interviews with Mary Malloy and 'Lizzie', in Women's History – Women's Lives, 'Women's Work on the Liverpool Docks', 25–27, 30–32.

52 These details are from interviews with 'Lizzie' and Mary Malloy, ibid., 30–32, 25–27.

53 For example, the interview with the cleaner Anne Tidmarsh in the early 1950s, ibid., 29.

54 For Merseyside's industrial base see Marriner, *Economic and Social Development of Merseyside*, Ch. 7; Wilfred Smith, 'The Location of Industry', in Wilfred Smith ed., *A Scientific Survey of Merseyside* (Liverpool: Liverpool University Press, 1953). For shipbuilding see Kenneth Warren, *Steel, Ships and Men: Cammell Laird 1824–1993* (Liverpool: Liverpool University Press, 1998), 158.

55 Stuart Wilks-Heeg, 'From World City to Pariah City? Liverpool and the Global Economy, 1850–2000', in Ronaldo Munck ed., *Reinventing the City? Liverpool in Comparative Perspective* (Liverpool: Liverpool University Press, 2003), 47.

56 Baines, 'Merseyside in the British Economy', 60.

57 Warren, *Steel Ships and Men*, 252– 253.

58 Glucksmann, *Women Assemble*; Denis Linehan, 'A New England: Landscape, Exhibition and Remaking Industrial Space in the 1930s', in David Gilbert et al. ed., *Geographies of British Modernity: Space and Society in the Twentieth Century* (Oxford: Blackwell, 2003); Peter Scott, *The Triumph of the South: A Regional Economic History of Early Twentieth*

Century Britain (London: Routledge, 2007). The statistic is from Scott, *Triumph of the South*, 77.

59 For the services offered at Speke and Fazakerley and the development's tenants see 'Liverpool & Industry: Brochure Outlining the Development of the Speke, Fazakerley and Kirkby Trading Estates', Liverpool Record Office (henceforward LRO), 388 LIV, 1950. For the attempt to attract male labour see George Mercer, 'Speke as a New Town: An Experimental Industrial Study', *The Town Planning Review* 24, no. 3 (October 1953): 215–238, 221. The urbanist John Boughton, who grew up in Speke, has written a vivid account of the suburb's history and development, 'Speke, Liverpool, Part II, Reflections on Time Spent', Municipal Dreams Blog, https://municipaldreams.wordpress.com/2020/06/30/speke_liverpool_part_ii/. For attempts by local authorities to build industrial estates in the mid-twentieth century see Alistair Kefford, 'Disruption, Destruction and the Creation of "the Inner Cities": The Impact of Urban Renewal on Industry, 1945–1980', *Urban History* 44, no. 3 (August 2017): 492–515. For the evolution of industrial estates as a type of urban space see Sam Wetherell, *Foundations: How the Built Environment Made Twentieth-Century Britain* (Princeton, NJ: Princeton University Press, 2020), Ch. 1.

60 Charlotte Wildman, *Urban Redevelopment and Modernity in Liverpool and Manchester, 1919–1939* (London: Bloomsbury, 2018), 28–33; Madeline McKenna, 'The Development of Suburban Council Housing Estates in Liverpool Between the Wars' (PhD diss., University of Liverpool, 1986), 178–218.

61 P. H. Lister, 'Regional Policies and Industrial Development on Merseyside, 1930–60', in B. L. Anderson and P. J. M. Stoney, *Commerce, Industry and Transport: Studies in Economic Change on Merseyside* (Liverpool: Liverpool University Press, 1983), 157–159; H. Gentleman, 'Kirkby Industrial Estate: Theory versus Practice', in Cunningham et al. eds., *Merseyside Social and Economic Studies*; 'Liverpool & Industry'. For accounts of the purchase of the land, the scale of the housing project and the labour employed in construction see 'The Vision Splendid at Kirkby', *Liverpool Daily Post*, 14 October 1952; 'Kirkby to Get 30 New Houses a Week', *Liverpool Echo*, 5 March 1954.

62 Francis Longstreth-Thompson, *Merseyside Plan 1944* (London: HMSO, 1944). The drive towards decentralisation was also a key part of Liverpool's 1952 Development Plan. Aaron Andrews, 'Decline and the City: The Urban Crisis in Liverpool' (PhD diss., University of Leicester, 2018), 25–27.

63 Wilfred Smith, 'Present Distribution of Population', in Smith ed., *A Scientific Survey of Merseyside*, 134–135.

64 Richard Meegan, 'Paradise Postponed: The Growth and Decline

of Merseyside's Outer Estates', in Phillip Cooke ed., *Localities: The Changing Face of Urban Britain* (London: Hutchinson, 1989), 202; Kathleen G. Pickett and David K. Boulton, *Migration and Social Adjustment: Kirkby and Maghull* (Liverpool: Liverpool University Press, 1974).

65 Taylor, 'The Dynamics of Labour Relations', 65.

66 I am indebted to the work of Madeline McKenna, whose unpublished PhD thesis contains transcriptions of fifty-eight interviews with people who moved to new suburban housing estates in Liverpool between the wars in its appendix. McKenna, 'The Development of Suburban Council Housing.'

67 Respectively, these details are from McKenna, 'The Development of Suburban Council Housing', 403, 471, 608–609, 292–293, 487.

68 Ibid., 451.

69 George Orwell, *Keep the Aspidistra Flying* (London: Secker and Warburg, 1969), 84. The stultifying effects of new middle-class suburbs in the south were an obsession of inter-war writers such as Orwell, J. B. Priestley, Clough Williams-Ellis and John Betjeman.

70 McKenna, 'The Development of Suburban Council Housing', 470, 490, 541–542.

71 For the modernisation of domestic work and the subsequent entrenchment of gendered divisions of labour in the household in the inter-war period see Judy Giles, *The Parlour and the Suburb: Domestic Identities, Class, Femininity and Modernity* (Oxford: Berg, 2004); Deborah Sugg Ryan, *Ideal Homes: 1918–1939: Domestic Design and Suburban Modernism* (Manchester: Manchester University Press, 2018); David Jeremiah, *Architecture and Design for the Family in Britain, 1900–1970* (Manchester: Manchester University Press, 2000), Chs. 1–3.

72 *Homes For Workers*, North-West Film Archive, 1938, https://vimeo.com/464276971.

73 McKenna, 'The Development of Suburban Council Housing', 514 and, for example, 268, 424. For fear of electricity see 451.

74 Details respectively from ibid., 536, 85–90, 166.

75 Parliamentary Papers, 'Royal Commission on the Distribution of the Industrial Population', 1940, cmnd. 6153. The Report refers to Speke on pages 9, 116, 128–135, 282–283.

76 Parliamentary Papers, 'Distribution of Industry: A Bill to Provide for the Development of Certain Areas. For Controlling the Provision of Industrial Premises with a View to Securing the Proper Distribution of Industry', 1944–5; D. W. Parsons, *The Political Economy of British Regional Policy* (London: Croom Helm, 1986).

77 Parliamentary Papers, 'Distribution of Industry', 1948, cmnd. 7540.
78 P. E. Lloyd, 'The Impact of Development Areas Policies on Merseyside, 1949–1967', in Cunningham et al. eds., *Merseyside Social and Economic Studies*, 379.
79 Lloyd, 'The Impact of Development Areas Policies', 376; Peter Scott, 'Worst of Both Worlds: British Regional Policy, 1951–64', *Business History* 38, no. 4 (October 1996): 41–64.
80 Robbie Shilliam, *Race and the Undeserving Poor: From Abolition to Brexit* (New York: Columbia University Press, 2018).

3. Britain's Detroit

1 Alfred Hickling, 'It's Like San Francisco – With Greyer Weather', *The Guardian*, 21 February 2007. Brian Patten, the Liverpool poet with whom Ginsberg was staying at the time, noted, 'I think Allen believed the centre of human consciousness to be wherever he was at the time.'
2 Brian Marren, *We Shall Not Be Moved: How Liverpool's Working Class Fought Redundancies, Closures and Cuts in the Age of Thatcher* (Manchester: Manchester University Press, 2016), 24.
3 This quote by Starr comes from the local historian David Bedford, https://davidabedford.com/10th-july-1964-the-beatles-civic-reception-at-liddypool-town-hall/.
4 Hunter Davies, *The Beatles: The Only Ever Authorised Biography* (London: Ebury, 2009, 1968), 271.
5 For an overview of the Beatles' respective childhoods and the formation of the band in their early years see Dave Laing, 'Six Boys, Six Beatles: The Formative Years, 1950–1962', in Kenneth Womack ed., *The Cambridge Companion to the Beatles* (Cambridge: Cambridge University Press, 2009). For a history that places the Beatles in the context of 1960s Britain see Marcus Collins, *The Beatles and Sixties Britain* (Cambridge: Cambridge University Press, 2020).
6 Sara Cohen, *Decline, Renewal and the City in Popular Music Culture: Beyond the Beatles* (London: Routledge, 2007), 81–82. The *Guardian* journalist Tim Jonze has interviewed people from the Liverpool scene during those years who were influenced by imported US music. Tim Jonze, 'Cunard Yanks: The Sailors who Taught Britain how to Rock'n'Roll', *The Guardian*, 1 July 2015.
7 For the Beatles' relationships with their mothers and aunts see Christine Feldman-Barrett, *A Women's History of the Beatles* (London: Bloomsbury, 2021), 22–26.
8 'Night of 100,000 Screams', *Liverpool Daily Post*, 10 July 1964.
9 Ibid.

10 City Centre Planning Group, *Liverpool City Centre Plan* (Liverpool: Liverpool City Planning Department, 1966), 53.

11 Gordon Stephenson, 'The Planning Schools: 7. The University of Liverpool', *The Town Planning Review* 22, no. 1 (April 1957): 84–87.

12 Charlotte Wildman, *Urban Redevelopment and Modernity in Liverpool and Manchester, 1918–1939* (Manchester: Manchester University Press, 2018), 41–46, 96–109.

13 F. T. Burnett and Shelia F. Scott, 'A Survey of Housing Conditions in the Urban Areas of England and Wales: 1960', *The Sociological Review* 10, no. 1 (March 1962): 35–79, 39.

14 John Barron Mays, *Growing Up in the City: A Study of Juvenile Delinquency in an Urban Neighbourhood* (Liverpool: Liverpool University Press, 1964), 37.

15 Catherine Flinn, *Rebuilding Britain's Blitzed Cities: Hopeful Dreams, Stark Realities* (London: Bloomsbury, 2020), 110.

16 Quoted in Laura Balderstone, Graeme J. Milne and Rachel Mulhearn, 'Memory and Place on the Liverpool Waterfront in the Mid-Twentieth Century', *Urban History* 43, no. 3 (August 2014): 478–496, 485.

17 Mays, *Growing Up in the City*, 3.

18 Charles Vereker and John Barron Mays with the assistance of Elizabeth Gittus and Maurice Broady, *Urban Redevelopment and Social Change: A Study of Social Conditions in Central Liverpool, 1955–56* (Liverpool: Liverpool University Press, 1961), 93.

19 Ibid., 121.

20 Michael Young and Peter Willmott, *Family and Kinship in East London* (London: Routledge & Kegan Paul, 1957). For the ways in which Young and Wilmott's sociological work was imbued with communitarian nostalgia see Jon Lawrence, 'Inventing the "Traditional Working Class": A Re-Analysis of Interview Notes from Young and Wilmott's *Family and Kinship in East London*', *The Historical Journal* 59, no. 2 (June 2016): 567–593.

21 Madeline Kerr, *The People of Ship Street* (London: Routledge, 1958), 4–5.

22 'Night of 100,000 Screams'.

23 For the best summary of Shankland's career and his politics see Otto Saumarez Smith, 'Graeme Shankland: A Sixties Architect Planner and the Political Culture of the British Left', *Architectural History* 57 (2014): 393–422.

24 City Centre Planning Group, *Liverpool City Centre Plan*, 53.

25 Ibid., 28.

26 Saumarez Smith, 'Graeme Shankland: A Sixties Architect Planner', 406.

27 Alistair Kefford, *The Life and Death of the Shopping City: Public Planning*

and Private Redevelopment in Britain Since 1945 (Cambridge: Cambridge University Press, 2022), 139–142.

28 Stanley's memories of working in the pub were recorded by the Museum of Liverpool to accompany an artwork made of its interior. For the artwork and the interview with Stanley: www.liverpoolmuseums.org.uk/stories/frontstage-and-backstage-magic-clock-easter-lunchtime-1969. With thanks to Tom Ward and Tess Wingard.

29 City Centre Planning Group, *Liverpool City Centre Plan*, 7.

30 Jacqueline Nassy Brown, *Dropping Anchor, Setting Sail: Geographies of Race in Black Liverpool* (Princeton, NJ: Princeton University Press, 2005), 43–44.

31 Cohen, *Decline, Renewal and the City*, 20, 31.

32 Ed Vulliamy, 'The Real Thing: Soudtrack to the Toxteth Riots', *The Guardian*, 3 July 2011.

33 Cohen, *Decline, Renewal and the City*, 20, 25.

34 Martin Dodge and Richard Brook, 'Dreams of Helicopter Travel in the 1950s and Liverpool's Undeveloped Plans for a City Centre Heliport', *Transactions of the Royal Historical Society of Lancashire and Cheshire* no. 163 (January 2014): 111–125.

35 J. S. Dodgson, 'The Development of Transport on Merseyside since 1945', in B. L. Anderson and P. J. M. Stoney eds., *Commerce, Industry and Transport: Studies in Economic Change on Merseyside* (Liverpool: Liverpool University Press, 1983), 189–190.

36 Quoted in Simon Gunn and Susan C. Townsend, *Automobility in the City in Twentieth Century Britain and Japan* (London: Bloomsbury, 2020), 98.

37 For a detailed description of Liverpool's tram network see Charles Klapper, *The Golden Age of Tramways* (London: Routledge & Kegan Paul, 1961), 83–92.

38 Madeline McKenna, 'The Development of Suburban Council Housing Estates in Liverpool Between the Wars' (PhD diss., University of Liverpool, 1986). See, for example, 388–389, 395, 397, 407, 411.

39 Dodgson, 'The Development of Transport on Merseyside', 187.

40 'New Model Trains for "Overhead"', *Liverpool Daily Post*, 9 February 1946; John Gahan, *Seventeen Stations to the Dingle: The Liverpool Overhead Railway Remembered* (Weston-super-Mare: Avon Anglia, 1982).

41 Charles E. Box, *The Liverpool Overhead Railway 1893–1956* (London: Railway World Limited, 1959), 147–150.

42 Dodgson, 'The Development of Transport on Merseyside', 187–189.

43 Hugh Wilson and Lewis Womersley, *Liverpool: Economic Development of the Inner Area* (London: Department of the Environment, 1977).

44 Jon Murden, 'City of Change and Challenge', in John Belchem ed., *Liverpool 800: Culture, Character and History* (Liverpool: Liverpool University Press, 2006), 414.

45 Chris Couch, *City of Change and Challenge: Urban Planning and Regeneration in Liverpool* (Abingdon: Routledge, 2003, 2018), 43–50.

46 Dodgson, 'The Development of Transport on Merseyside', 192–193.

47 Merseyside Area Land Use Transportation Study, *Final Report* (Liverpool: Traffic Research Corporation Ltd, 1969), 23–31.

48 A call for an improved road network in the wake of the M6 can be found in City Centre Planning Group, *Liverpool City Centre Plan*, 7.

49 Dodgson, 'The Development of Transport on Merseyside', 193.

50 'Men who "Live" Beneath the Mersey', *Liverpool Weekly News*, 13 October 1966. For a technical account of the planning and construction of the tunnel see T. M. Megaw and C. D. Brown, 'Mersey Kingsway Tunnel: Planning and Design', *Proceedings of the Institution of Civil Engineers* 51 (1972): 479–502.

51 'River Task for Mighty Mole', *Liverpool Daily Post*, 9 March 1967.

52 'Handshakes that Made History', *Liverpool Echo*, 17 January 1967.

53 'Flaw in Work: Tunnel Work Stopped', *Liverpool Echo*, 19 November 1968; 'A Question Still to Settle: Who Pays?' *Liverpool Daily Post*, 13 February 1974.

54 'Houses Demolished to Make Way for New Tunnel', *Liverpool Daily Post*, 12 November 1968. For the longer histories of the communities displaced by the tunnel see Matthew Thompson, *Reconstructing Public Housing: Liverpool's Hidden History of Collective Alternatives* (Liverpool: Liverpool University Press, 2020), Ch. 8.

55 'Heartache as Wallasey Homes Make Way for Second Tunnel', *Liverpool Daily Post*, 10 January 1966.

56 'Mothers Threaten to Barricade Roads', *Liverpool Weekly News*, 2 May 1968.

57 Krista Cowman, 'Play Streets: Women, Children and the Problem of Urban Traffic, 1930–1970', *Social History* 42, no. 2 (2017): 233–256, 246–253.

58 David Butler and Gareth Butler, *British Political Facts*, 10th ed. (Basingstoke: Palgrave Macmillan, 2011), 399–400.

59 Paul Warde, *Energy Consumption in England and Wales 1560–2000* (Rome: National Research Council, Institute of Studies on Mediterranean Societies, 2007), 115–130.

60 With thanks to Harry Kennard for collating this information from the International Energy Agency's data on world energy balance, www.iea.org/data-and-statistics/data-product/world-energy-balances.

61 James Marriott and Terry Macalister, *Crude Britannia: How Oil Shaped a Nation* (London: Pluto, 2021), 13–31.

62 Merseyside Dock and Harbour Board, 'Annual Reports and Accounts for the Year Ended 1962', Liverpool Maritime Museum Archives (henceforward LMM), MDHB/FIN/1/2/22, 4, 48.

63 Merseyside Dock and Harbour Board, 'Annual Reports and Accounts for the Year Ended 1968', LMM, MDHB/FIN/1/2/29, 12.

64 Marriott et al., *Crude Britannia*, 30.

65 P. E. Lloyd, 'The Impact of Development Areas on Merseyside, 1949–1967', in Lawton et al. eds., *Merseyside Social and Economic Studies*, 395–397; John Salt, 'The Impact of the Ford and Vauxhall Plants on the Employment Situation of Merseyside, 1962–1965', *Journal of Economic and Human Geography* 58, no. 5 (September 1967): 255–264.

66 Aaron Andrews, 'Decline and the City: The Urban Crisis in Liverpool c. 1968 to 1986' (PhD diss., University of Leicester, 2018), 59–61.

67 Huw Beynon, *Working for Ford* (London: Allen Lane, 1973), 11; Roy Church, *The Rise and Decline of the British Motor Industry* (Cambridge: Cambridge University Press, 1995).

68 Jack Saunders, 'The Untraditional Worker: Class Re-Formation in Britain, 1945–65', *Modern British History* 26, no. 2 (June 2015): 225–248.

69 Beynon, *Working for Ford*, 66.

70 Pat Ayers, 'Work, Culture and Gender: The Making of Masculinities in Post-War Liverpool', *Labour History Review* 69, no. 2 (August 2004): 153–167, 157.

71 For a retrospective of Beynon's research see Ralph Darlington, 'Shop Stewards' Organisation in Ford Halewood: from Beynon to Today', *Industrial Relations Journal* 25, no. 2 (June 1994): 136–149.

72 Beynon, *Working for Fords*, 118, 131.

73 Ibid., 139.

74 Ayers, 'Work, Culture and Gender', 157.

75 Andrew Gorz, 'The Social Ideology of the Motorcar', 1973. The essay was originally published in French in *Le Sauvage*. A translation is available here: www.worldcarfree.net/resources/freesources/TheSocialIdeology.rtf.

76 For the revival of Welsh nationalism in the post-war period see Martin Johnes, 'A Prince, a King, and a Referendum: Rugby, Politics and Nationhood in Wales, 1969–1979', *Journal of British Studies* 47, no. 1 (January 2008): 129–148; Kenneth Morgan, *Re-birth of a Nation: Wales 1880–1980* (Oxford: Oxford University Press, 1980), Ch. 13. Scholarly accounts of Capel Celyn and the political response to the dam are few. Some exceptions are Hywel M. Griffiths, 'Water Under the Bridge? Nature, Memory and Hydropolitics', *Cultural Geographies* 21, no. 3 (July 2014): 449–474; Michael Cunningham, 'Public Policy and Normative Language: Utility, Community and Nation in the Debate over the Construction of Tryweryn Reservoir', *Parliamentary Affairs* 60, no. 4

(2007): 625–636; Ed Atkins, 'Building a Dam, Constructing a Nation: The "Drowning" of Capel Celyn', *Journal of Historical Sociology* 31 (2018): 455–468; Mark Whitehead, Rhys Jones and Martin Jones, *The Nature of the State: Excavating the Political Ecologies of the Modern State* (Oxford: Oxford University Press, 2007), 56–75. For a non-academic history of the events drawing on contemporary interviews see Wyn Thomas, *Hands Off Wales: Nationhood and Militancy* (Llandysul: Gomer, 2013).

77 Whitehead et al., *The Nature of the State*, 70–72.

78 Thomas, *Hands Off Wales*, 399.

79 Griffiths, 'Water Under the Bridge?', 451.

80 Cunningham, 'Public Policy', 632–633. For photographs of the Liverpool protest see Vaughan Roderick, 'Tryweryn: How Reservoir of Anger "Fuelled Nationalist Cause",' *BBC News*, 21 October 2015.

81 Atkins, 'Building a Dam, Constructing a Nation'.

82 Quoted in Cunningham 'Public Policy', 631.

83 Atkins, 'Building a Dam, Constructing a Nation', 462.

84 Quoted in Griffiths, 'Water Under the Bridge', 458.

85 Cunningham, 'Public Policy', 626–627.

86 *Tryweryn, the Story of a Valley*, was produced by the staff and students at Friars School in Bangor and has been archived by the British Film Institute: https://player.bfi.org.uk/free/film/watch-tryweryn-the-story-of-a-valley-1965-online.

87 Thomas, *Hands Off Wales*, 402–403.

88 Eryl Crump, 'Gwynedd Bomber Relives the Night he Tried to Blow Up Dam', *Daily Post*, 18 October 2015.

89 For MAC in the context of other terrorist movements see Nick Brooke, 'Learning the Lessons of Terrorist Failure: The Dogs that Didn't Bark in Scotland and Wales', ICCT Policy Brief, March 2019. Many Toxteth protestors received prison sentences of four years or longer for riot charges after 1981. Liverpool 8 Law Centre, 'Court Data', Liverpool Record Office, 340 LAW 1/3/3.

90 John Jenkins and Rhodri Williams, *Prison Letters* (Talybont: Y Lolfa Cyf, 2019), 6, 25.

91 *Tryweryn, the Story of a Valley*.

92 Matthew Weaver, 'Summer of 2018 was UK's Joint Hottest on Record, Met Office Says', *The Guardian*, 3 September 2018; Damian Carrington, 'Climate Change Made UK Heatwave 30 Times More Likely', *The Guardian*, 6 December 2018.

93 Public Health England, 'PHE Heatwave Mortality Monitoring, Summer 2018', 4.

94 Katie Bellis, 'The Lost Village of Tryweryn Becomes Visible for the First Time in Decades in the Heatwave', *Wales Online*, 12 August 2018.

95 Andreas Malm, *Fossil Capital: The Rise of Steam Power and the Roots of Global Warming* (London: Verso, 2016), 10.

96 'Official Apology Over Tryweryn', *BBC News*, 19 October 2005.

4. The Music of the World

1 Brian Marren, *We Shall Not Be Moved: How Liverpool's Working Class Fought Redundancies, Closures and Cuts in the Age of Thatcher* (Manchester: Manchester University Press, 2016), 206.

2 John Belchem, *Before the Windrush: Race Relations in 20th-Century Liverpool* (Liverpool: Liverpool University Press, 2014), 238.

3 From census data available at: www.visionofbritain.org.uk/unit/10105821/cube/TOT_POP.

4 Merseyside Socialist Campaign Group, *Merseyside in Crisis* (Liverpool: Merseyside Socialist Campaign Group, 1980), 9.

5 Tony Lane, 'Liverpool: City of Harder Times to Come', *Marxism Today*, November 1978, 342.

6 Quoted in Laleh Khalili, *Sinews of War and Trade: Shipping and Capitalism in the Arabian Peninsula* (London: Verso, 2021), 76.

7 For classic accounts of the re-making of port cities in the late twentieth century see Michael B. Miller, *Europe and the Maritime World: A Twentieth-Century History* (Cambridge: Cambridge University Press, 2012); Khalili, *Sinews of War and Trade*; Deborah Cowan, *The Deadly Life of Logistics: Mapping Violence in Global Trade* (Minneapolis: University of Minnesota Press, 2014); Alice Mah, *Port Cities and Global Legacies: Urban Identity, Waterfront Work and Radicalism* (Basingstoke: Palgrave Macmillan, 2014).

8 Marc Levinson, *The Box: How the Shipping Container Made the World Smaller and the World Economy Bigger* (Princeton, NJ: Princeton University Press, 2016), 66–69.

9 Ibid., 47–63.

10 Transcribed interview with Alec Grant, 10 March 1982, Liverpool Maritime Museum Archives (henceforth LMM), Merseyside Docklands History Survey, SA/4. For the intense social worlds and masculine bonds of solidarity formed in dockland communities see Emma Copestake, 'Love, Laughter and Solidarity on the Docks in Liverpool, c. 1950s–1990s', *The Sociological Review* 7, no. 2 (March 2023), 441–457.

11 Transcribed interview with Billy Cliff, 21 April 1983, LMM, Merseyside Docklands History Survey, SA/4.

12 Transcribed interview with Jack Chester, 8 November 1982, LMM, Merseyside Docklands History Survey, SA/4.

13 Quoted in Laura Balderstone, Graeme J. Milne and Rachel Mulhearn,

'Memory and Place on the Liverpool Waterfront in the Mid-Twentieth Century', *Urban History* 43, no. 3 (August 2014): 478–496, 487.

14 Liverpool was the first port in Britain and the fourth in the world to install an electronic computer, which was initially used to process the salaries of the employees of the Merseyside Dock and Harbour Board. For information about the computer, eventually called PORTIA, see Merseyside Dock and Harbour Board, 'Annual Reports and Accounts for the Year Ended 1962', LMM, MDHB/FIN/1/2/22, 55.

15 Vernon H. Jensen, *Hiring of Dockworkers and Employment Practices in the Ports of New York, Liverpool, London, Rotterdam and Marseille* (Cambridge, MA: Harvard University Press, 1964), 153.

16 Gordon Phillips and Noel Whiteside, *Casual Labour: The Unemployment Question in the Port Transport Industry 1880–1970* (Oxford: Clarendon Press, 1985), 246.

17 Quoted in Marren, *We Shall Not Be Moved*, 202.

18 David F. Wilson, *Dockers: The Impact of Industrial Change* (London: Fontana Collins, 1972), 117.

19 Ibid., 112.

20 Ibid., 111–115; Phillips and Whiteside, *Casual Labour*, 261–268.

21 Transcribed interview with Alec Grant. For the importance of nicknames among dock workers see Copestake, 'Love, Laughter and Solidarity on the Docks in Liverpool', 450–451.

22 Levinson, *The Box*, 79–89, 97–99.

23 Ibid., 170–201; Keller Easterling, *Extrastatecraft: The Power of Infrastructure Space* (London: Verso, 2014), Ch. 5.

24 McKinsey and Co., 'Containerisation: The Key to Low-Cost Transport' (British Transport Docks Board, 1967), 3–4.

25 National Ports Council, 'Containerisation on the North Atlantic: A Port to Port Analysis & Outlook for Deep Sea Container Services' (London: National Ports Council, 1967), 2.

26 Merseyside Dock and Harbour Board, 'Annual Reports and Accounts for the Year Ended 1967', LMM, MDHB/FIN/1/2/27, 21.

27 Wilson, *Dockers*, 133–137.

28 Ibid., 139–141.

29 Ibid., 146–150.

30 Ibid., 146–147, 150; National Dock Labour Board (Liverpool Group), 'Minutes of a Special Meeting of the Liverpool Board Held at Sefton House, Liverpool', 9 December 1969', LMM, P/NDLB/L/1/10; Greig Taylor, 'The Dynamics of Labour Relations at the Port of Liverpool, 1967–1989', (PhD diss., Manchester Metropolitan University, 2012), 96–100.

31 For the role of shipping and logistics in enabling global supply chains

and 'just-in-time' production see Cowan, *The Deadly Life of Logistics*, Ch. 2; Levinson, *The Box*, Ch. 14.

32 Quoted in Wilson, *Dockers*, 153–154.

33 From an interview with Diane Frost, whose account of the Kru diaspora in Britain remains definitive. Diane Frost, *Work and Community Among West African Migrant Workers since the Nineteenth Century* (Liverpool: Liverpool University Press, 1999), 51.

34 Perhaps the most striking example of this type of analysis can be found in Michael Young, Kate Gavron, Geoff Dench, *The New East End: Kinship, Race and Conflict* (London: Profile, 2011), a work of sociology conducted in the former docklands of London, where white 'indigenous' working-class former dock workers and their families are described as competing for housing and work with recent migrants from South Asia. For one of the few historians to put containerisation in the context of decolonisation see Nicholas J. White, 'Thinking Outside "The Box": Decolonisation and Containerization', in Niels. P. Petersson, Stig Tenold and Nicholas J. White, *Shipping and Globalization in the Post-War Era: Contexts, Companies, Connections* (Cham: Palgrave, 2019).

35 Jane Martin, 'Krumen Down the Coast: Liberian Migrants on the West African Coast in the 19th and Early 20th Centuries', *International Journal of African Historical Studies* 18, no. 3 (1985): 401–423; Frost, *Work and Community*, 15–27.

36 Frost, *Work and Community*, 10.

37 Ibid., 149–150.

38 Ibid., 102; transcribed interview with Clifford Sullivan, 30 November 1982, LMM, Merseyside Docklands History Survey, SA/4.

39 Nicholas J. White, '"Ferry off the Mersey": The Business Impact of Decolonisation in Liverpool', *History: Journal of the Historical Association* 96, no. 2 (April 2011): 188–204, 196–197.

40 Sarah Stockwell, *The Business of Decolonisation: British Business Strategies in the Gold Coast* (Oxford: Oxford University Press, 2000), 140, 142.

41 Ibid., 101–102, 158–160.

42 White, '"Ferry off the Mersey"', 192.

43 Nicholas White, 'Liverpool Shipping and the End of Empire: The Ocean Group in East and Southeast Asia c. 1945–73', in Sheryllynne Haggerty, Anthony Webster and Nicholas J White eds., *The Empire in One City: Liverpool's Inconvenient Imperial Past* (Manchester: Manchester University Press, 2008), 169.

44 White, 'Thinking Outside "The Box"', 69.

45 After 1965, the Blue Funnell Line and Elder Dempster belonged to the same consortium called the Ocean Group.

46 John Brunskill to the Managing Directors of the Ocean Company, letter, 7 March 1970, LMM, OA 1713/3.
47 White, 'Liverpool Shipping and the End of Empire', 175–178.
48 Richard Saundry and Peter Turnbull, 'Melee on the Mersey: Contracts, Competition and Labour Relations on the Docks', *Industrial Relations* 27 no. 4 (1996): 275–288, 279.
49 White, 'Ferry off the Mersey', 197.
50 Full interview from Frost, *Work and Community*, 212–219.
51 Ibid., 231–232. See also forthcoming work on modern Freetown by Nile Davis, a conversation with whom was essential for fleshing out some of the ideas of the above.
52 For Elder Dempster's role in under developing the economies of British West African colonies see Marika Sherwood, 'Elder Dempster and West Africa 1891–c. 1940: The Genesis of Underdevelopment?' *International Journal of African Historical Studies* 30, no. 2 (1997): 253–276.
53 For descriptions of the south docks customs operation post-1972 and beached ships from undredged mud see transcribed interview with Bill Cullington (Part 1), 3 August 1982, LMM, Merseyside Docklands History Survey, SA/4.
54 Quoted in Balderstone et al., 'Memory and Place on the Liverpool Waterfront', 494.
55 David Robinson, 'Rebirth – for Marie Celeste Hi-Tech Future', *Liverpool Daily Post*, 23 December 1985.
56 Department of the Environment, 'Cleaning up the Mersey: A Consultation Paper on Tackling Water Pollution in the Rivers and Canals of the Mersey Catchment, and Improving Appearance and Use of their Banks' (London: Great Britain, Department of the Environment: 1982), 3.
57 Merseyside County Council, 'Report of Survey: Environmental Pollution and Condition of Land', June 1979, Liverpool Record Office (henceforward LRO), HQ711 309 425 MER, 67.
58 Department of the Environment, 'Cleaning up the Mersey', 4.
59 The problem of radiation in the Irish Sea was highlighted by a conference in 1985 held by a group called the Celtic League including representatives from Liverpool, Northern Ireland, Scotland, Wales and the Isle of Man as well as the Connolly Association of Irish migrants to Britain. Connolly Association Liverpool Branch, 'Irish Sea: Nuclear Cesspool', 1985, LRO, 363.73940916337 CON.
60 Aaron Andrews, 'Decline and the City: The Urban Crisis in Liverpool c. 1968 to 1986' (PhD diss., University of Leicester, 2018), 109–110.
61 Hugh Wilson and Lewis Womersley, *Vacant Land: Report by Consultants, IAS/LI/11* (London, 1976), a.

62 Hugh Wilson and Lewis Womersley, *Change or Decay: Final Report of the Liverpool Inner Area Study* (London: Department of the Environment, 1977), 47.
63 Wilson, *Dockers*, 117–120.
64 National Dock Labour Board (Liverpool Group), 'Minutes of a Meeting of the Liverpool Board Held at Sefton House, Liverpool', March 9, 1976', LMM, P/NDLB/L/1/13.
65 Merseyside Dock and Harbour Company, 'Annual Reports and Accounts for the Year Ended 1980', LMM, MDHB/FIN/1/2/41, 3.
66 E. S. P. Evans, *The Inner Area District Statements: Proposals for the Development of the Land Resource* (Liverpool, 1976), LRO, 333.77 CRT, 9.
67 Merseyside Dock and Harbour Company, 'Annual Reports and Accounts for the Year Ended 1976', LMM, MDHB/FIN/1/2/37, 4.
68 Martin Adeney, 'Sir John Page', *The Guardian*, 3 March 2006.
69 Merseyside Dock and Harbour Company, 'Annual Reports and Accounts for the Year Ended 1978', LMM, MDHB/FIN/1/2/39, 7.
70 Merseyside Dock and Harbour Company, 'Annual Reports and Accounts for the Year Ended 1991', LMM, MDHB/FIN/1/2/52, 10.
71 Merseyside Dock and Harbour Company, 'Annual Reports and Accounts for the Year Ended 1980', 6.
72 Merseyside Dock and Harbour Company, 'Annual Reports and Accounts for the Year Ended 1988', LMM, MDHB/FIN/1/2/49, 4.
73 Patrick Keiller, 'Port Statistics', in Patrick Keiller ed., *A View from the Train: Cities and other Landscapes* (London: Verso, 2013), 42–43.
74 Valerie Sweeny, *Shannon Airport: A Unique Story of Survival* (Shannon: Valerie Sweeny, 2004), 231–241; Brian Callanan: *Ireland's Shannon Story: Leaders, Visions and Networks: A Case Study of Local and Regional Development* (Dublin: Irish Academic Press, 2000), 41–46.
75 Sweeny, *Shannon Airport*, 232.
76 In 2008, the World Bank estimated that there were more than 2,000 such zones across the world: Gokhan Akinci et al., *Special Economic Zones: Performance, Lessons Learned and Implications for Zone Development* (World Bank Group, 2008), 3. For special economic zones in South Asia see Aihwa Ong, *Neoliberalism as Exception: Mutations in Citizenship and Sovereignty* (Durham, NC: Duke University Press, 2006), 97–121. For a broad history of zonal policies see Patrick Neveling, 'Export Processing Zones, Special Economic Zones, and the Long March of Capitalist Development Policies during the Cold War', in Leslie James and Elisabeth Leake, eds., *Negotiating Independence: New Directions in the History of the Cold War and Decolonization* (London: Bloomsbury Academic, 2015).
77 Quinn Slobodian, *Crack-Up Capitalism: Market Radicals and the Dream*

of a World Without Democracy (London: Penguin, 2023); Vanessa Ogle, 'Archipelago Capitalism: Tax Havens, Offshore Money and the State', *American Historical Review* 122, no. 5 (December 2017): 1431–1458; Sam Wetherell, 'Freedom Planned: Enterprise Zones and Urban Non-Planning in Post-War Britain', *Modern British History* 27, no. 2 (June 2016): 266–289.

78 Barney Heyhoe, 'Statement on Freeports', Hansard, HC Deb, vol. 53, col. 411.

79 This was the argument, for example, of the Adam Smith Institute: Adam Smith Institute, *A Proposal for the Establishment of Freeports in the United Kingdom* (London: Adam Smith Institute, 1981), 2. For a more sophisticated analysis of the medieval genealogy of freeports see Stefan Schwarzkopf and Jessica Inez Backsell, 'The Nomos of the Freeport', *EPD: Society and Space* 39, vol. 2 (September 2020): 328–346.

80 Merseyside Dock and Harbour Company, 'Annual Reports and Accounts for the Year Ended 1984', LMM, MDHB/FIN/1/2/45, 7.

81 See, for example, Merseyside Dock and Harbour Company, 'Annual Reports and Accounts for the Year Ended 1986', LMM, MDHB/FIN/1/2/47, 6.

82 Quoted in Matt Kennard and Claire Provost, 'Shannon: A Tiny Irish Town Inspires China's Economic Boom', *The Guardian*, 19 April 2016.

83 Merseyside Dock and Harbour Company, 'Annual Reports and Accounts for the Year Ended 1990', LMM, MDHB/FIN/1/2/51, 8.

84 Keiller, 'Port Statistics', 45.

85 Quoted in Jim Phillips, 'Decasualization and Disruption: Industrial Relations in the Docks, 1945–79', in Chris Wrigley ed., *A History of British Industrial Relations 1939–1979: Industrial Relations in a Declining Economy* (Cheltenham: Elgar, 1996), 165.

86 Merseyside Dock and Harbour Company, 'Annual Reports and Accounts for the Year Ended 1989', LMM, MDHB/FIN/1/2/50, 4. Its chairman noted that abolition presented 'an opportunity... to maximise efficiency and sharpen the ability to compete'. For a similarly triumphant retrospective see Peter Stoney, 'The Abolition of the National Dock Labour Scheme and the Revival of the Port of Liverpool', *Economic Affairs* 19, no. 2 (June 1999): 18–22.

87 Merseyside Dock and Harbour Company, 'Annual Reports and Accounts for the Year Ended 1990', 10.

88 Marren, *We Shall Not Be Moved*, 211.

89 Ibid., 212–213.

90 Ibid., 211–212.

91 Saundry and Turnbull, 'Melee on the Mersey', 286.

92 Marren, *We Shall Not Be Moved*, 213. Similar accounts are reported

in Michael Lavalette and Jane Kennedy, 'Casual Lives? The Social Effects of Work Casualization and the Lock Out on the Liverpool Docks', *Critical Social Policy* 48, no. 16 (1996): 95–107; Peter Turnbull and Victoria Wass, 'The Greatest Game No More: Redundant Dockers and the Demise of "Dock Work"', *Work, Employment and Society* 8, no. 4 (December 1994): 487–506.

93 Gareth Stedman Jones, *Outcast London: A Study in the Relationship Between Classes in Victorian Society* (London: Verso, 2003, 1971).

94 Mah, *Port Cities*, 121.

95 Ibid., 122, 126–127; Marren, *We Shall Not Be Moved*, 222. For women in the Miners' Strike see Florence Sutcliffe-Braithwaite and Natalie Thomlinson, 'National Women Against Pit Closures: Gender, Trade Unionism and Community Activism in the Miners' Strike, 1984–5', *Contemporary British History* 32, no. 1 (December 2017): 78–100.

96 Chris Carter, Stewart Clegg, John Hogan and Martin Kornberger, 'The Polyphonic Spree: The Case of the Liverpool Dockers', *Industrial Relations Journal* 34, no. 4 (October 2003): 290–304. The website is still live and the relevant material on the dock strike is archived at: www.labournet.net/docks2/other/archive.htm.

97 Ibid., 299.

98 Ibid., 302.

5. Made Surplus

1 Tony Dickson and David Judge eds., *The Politics of Industrial Closure* (London: Macmillan, 1987), 29.

2 For the collapse of Standard-Triumph in Speke see Brian Marren, *We Shall Not Be Moved: How Liverpool's Working Class Fought Redundancies, Closures and Cuts in the Age of Thatcher* (Manchester: Manchester University Press, 2016), Ch. 2.

3 Merseyside Area Land Use Transportation Study, *Final Report* (Liverpool: Traffic Research Corporation Ltd, 1969), 25.

4 I am grateful to Brian Marren for assembling these comprehensive statistics on Liverpool's unemployment in Marren, *We Shall Not Be Moved*, 25, 36, 43.

5 Kerrie McGiveron, '"Notes on a Community Struggle": Big Flame, the Kirkby Rent Strike and the "Mass Struggle of Housewives"', *Women's History Review* 32, no. 4 (September 2022): 517–539, 520–521; Kathleen G. Pickett and David K. Boulton, *Migration and Social Adjustment: Kirkby and Maghull* (Liverpool: Liverpool University Press, 1974), 19–20.

6 Richard Meegan, 'Paradise Postponed: The Growth and Decline of Merseyside's Outer Estates', in Phillip Cooke ed., *Localities: The Changing Face of Urban Britain* (London: Hutchinson, 1989), 198–234, 202.

7 Pickett and Boulton, *Migration and Social Adjustment*, 61.
8 Ibid., 39.
9 Merseyside Socialist Campaign Group, *Merseyside in Crisis* (Birkenhead: Merseyside Socialist Campaign Group, 1980), 18.
10 Meegan, 'Paradise Postponed', 207–208.
11 Ibid., 215.
12 Ibid., 214–215.
13 Interviewed in *Behind the Rent Strike*, dir. Nick Broomfield, 1974.
14 Meegan, 'Paradise Postponed', 214.
15 McGiveron, '"Notes on a Community Struggle"', 521.
16 Ian Williams, 'Liverpool', *New Statesman*, 4 October 1985.
17 Peter Kilfoyle, *Left Behind: Lessons from Labour's Heartlands* (London: Politico's, 1999), 27.
18 George Mercer, 'Speke as a New Town: An Experimental Industrial Study', *The Town Planning Review* 24, no. 3 (October 1953): 215–238, 221.
19 For women workers in light industry in mid-twentieth-century Britain see Miriam Glucksmann, *Women Assemble: Women Workers and the New Industries in Inter-War Britain* (London: Routledge, 1990); Ruth Cavendish, *Women on the Line* (London: Routledge, 1982); Sue Bruley, 'Sorters, Pipers and Packers: Women in Light Industry in South London 1920–1960', *Oral History* 25, no. 1 (April 1997): 75–82; Bruley, '"A Very Happy Crowd": Women in Industry in South London in World War Two', *History Workshop Journal* 44 (October 1997): 59–76.
20 Interviewed in *Behind the Rent Strike*.
21 Meegan, 'Paradise Postponed', 207.
22 Sarah Stoller, 'Forging a Politics of Care: Theorizing Household Work in the British Women's Liberation Movement', *History Workshop Journal* 85 (Spring 2018): 95–119; Katrina Forrester, 'Feminist Demands and the Problem of Housework', *American Political Science Review* 116, no. 4 (November 2022): 1278–1292.
23 Mariosa Dalla Costa and Selma James, *The Power of Women and the Subversion of Community* (London: Facing the Wall, 1972, 1975), 38.
24 Forrester, 'Feminist Demands and the Problem of Housework'.
25 Silvia Federici, *Wages Against Housework* (Bristol: Power of Women Collective, 1975), 7.
26 The organisation's support for Wages for Housework at the Liverpool meeting of the Big Flame Women's Group prompted an intense debate about the nature of work and the family. See, for example, 'Wages for Housework is Not Enough but it's Necessary' and 'A. A.'s Reply to C. D.'s Document on Wages for Housework', *Big Flame Internal Bulletin*, May 1976, Big Flame Archive, May Day Rooms, London.
27 'Housework: The Longest Day', *Big Flame: Merseyside Edition*,

November 1973. Much of Big Flame's print material, including its Merseyside paper, has been digitised at: https://archive.leftove.rs/. For Big Flame's activism in Kirkby and the organisation's feminist politics see Kerrie McGiveron, '"Notes on a Community Struggle"'.

28 'Kirkby's Gas Blast', *Big Flame: Merseyside Edition*, June 1975.

29 McGiveron, '"Notes on a Community Struggle"', 519.

30 'Kirkby Women's Victory', *Big Flame: Merseyside Edition*, April 1975.

31 Meegan, 'Paradise Postponed', 213.

32 Interviewed in *Behind the Rent Strike.*

33 McGiveron, '"Notes on a Community Struggle"'; Big Flame, 'We Won't Pay, Women's Struggle on Tower Hill (A New Housing Estate Near Liverpool)', reproduced at: https://bigflameuk.files.wordpress.com/2009/05/tower-all.pdf.

34 'Kirkby: Barricades Against the Cuts', *Big Flame: Merseyside Edition*, July 1976; 'Kirkby Women's Victory', *Big Flame: Merseyside Edition.*

35 McGiveron, '"Notes on a Community Struggle"', 523.

36 'Tower Hill Diary', *Big Flame: Merseyside Edition*, December 1973.

37 Kerrie McGiveron, 'Big Flame and the Kirkby Rent Strike', *Social History Society*, https://socialhistory.org.uk/shs_exchange/big-flame-and-the-kirkby-rent-strike/; 'We Won't Pay: Women's Struggles on Tower Hill'. For the ways in which rent strikes opened up a new domain of political struggle for women in the global north see Manuel Castells, 'The Industrial City and the Working Class: The Glasgow Rent Strike of 1915', in Manuel Castells, *The City and the Grassroots: A Cross Cultural Theory of Urban Social Movements* (Oakland: University of California Press, 1983).

38 'We Won't Pay', *Big Flame: Merseyside Edition*, June 1973.

39 Interviewed in *Behind the Rent Strike.*

40 This process is laid out in 'Liverpool Abortion Action Service', information sheet, Liverpool Record Office (henceforward LRO), 305 WLM/2/8.

41 Despite legalisation, abortion in Northern Ireland remains extremely rare and difficult to access. Rory Carroll, 'Abortion Services in Northern Ireland almost Nonexistent despite Legalisation', *The Guardian*, 4 May 2022.

42 Lindsey Earner-Byrne, 'The Boat to England: An Analysis of the Official Reactions to the Emigration of Single Expectant Irishwomen to Britain 1922–1972', *Irish Economic and Social History* 30 (2003): 52–72; Jennifer Redmond, 'In the Family Way and Away from the Family: Examining the Evidence in Irish Unmarried Mothers in Britain 1920–1940s', in Elaine Farrell ed., *She Said She was in the Family Way: Pregnancy and Infancy in Modern Ireland* (London: University of London Press, 2012).

43 The figure of 170,000 was calculated by the Irish Solidarity Party based on publicly available information from Britain's Department of Health. For a full breakdown of the numbers see Sarah Bardon, 'Fact Check: Have More than 170,000 Irish Women Travelled Abroad for an Abortion?' *Irish Times*, 2 May 2018.

44 For 'abortion corridors' between Ireland and Britain see Lindsey Earner-Byrne and Diane Urquhart, *The Irish Abortion Journey, 1920–2018* (Cham: Palgrave Pivot, 2019).

45 'LASS: One Year Old', Newsletter, LRO, 305 WLM/2/8.

46 'Should We Be Organising a Support Network for Women Coming from Ireland to England for Abortions?' Pamphlet, LRO, 305 WLM/2/8. For the distinctive encounters produced by abortion networks see Ruth Fletcher, 'Negotiating Strangeness on the Abortion Trial', in Rose Harding ed., *Revaluing Care in Theory, Law and Policy* (London: Routledge, 2018).

47 Deirdre Niamh Duffy has likened this practice to a kind of 'feminist anarchy'. Deirdre Niamh Duffy, 'From Feminist Anarchy to Decolonisation: Understanding Abortion Health Activism Before and After the Repeal of the 8th Amendment', *Feminist Review* 124 (January 2020): 60–85.

48 Lucy Delap, *Feminisms: A Global History* (Chicago: University of Chicago Press, 2020), 83–94. For the origins of the Women's Liberation Movement in Britain see Margaretta Jolly, *Sisterhood and After: An Oral History of the UK Women's Liberation Movement, 1968–present* (Oxford: Oxford University Press, 2021); Sue Bruley, 'Consciousness-Raising in Clapham; Women's Liberation as "Lived Experience" in South London in the 1970s', *Women's History Review* 22, no. 5 (April 2013): 717–738; Eve Setch, 'The Face of Metropolitan Feminism: The London Women's Liberation Workshop 1969–1979', *Modern British History* 12, no. 2 (2002): 171–190; Lucy Delap, 'Feminist Bookshops, Reading Cultures and the Women's Liberation Movement in Great Britain, c. 1974 – 2000', *History Workshop Journal* 81, no. 1 (April 2016): 171–196.

49 Information about the early years of the Merseyside Women's Liberation Movement, including meeting locations and the names of participants, have been collected in the movement's archive, LRO, 305 WLM/1/2.

50 'The Merseyside Women's Liberation Movement Demand', Pamphlet, LRO, 305 WLM/1/1.

51 Ibid.

52 For delivering pamphlets to doctors see 'Merseyside Women's Liberation Movement: Minutes of Meeting 17th August 1970', LRO, 305 WLM/1/2. For the rape crisis centre see 'Merseyside Women's Liberation Movement: October 1979', LRO, 305 WLM/1/7.

53 For the Lesbian Feminist Group that met at the Women's Centre see 'Merseyside Women's Liberation Movement: January 1980', LRO, 305 WLM/1/7.

54 'Merseyside Women's Centre, July 1978', LRO, 305 WLM/1/7.

55 'Women's Education Centre Newsletter', LRO, 305 WLM/1/7.

56 This slip of paper has been archived in LRO, 305 WLM/1/2.

57 For the origins and history of News From Nowhere see Mandy Vere, 'News from Nowhere', in Ross Bradshaw ed., *Utopia* (London: Five Leaves, 2013), 50–55; Alice Mah, *Port Cities and Global Legacies: Urban Identity, Waterfront Work and Radicalism* (London: Palgrave, 2014), 182–186. For the significance of feminist bookshops to the Women's Liberation Movement see Lucy Delap, 'Feminist Bookshops'.

58 Vere, 'News from Nowhere', 54–55.

59 Ibid., 60; Mah, *Port Cities*, 185–186.

60 'Merseyside Campaign to Free Angela Davis', Pamphlet, LRO, 305 WLM/3/4; 'International Women's Day', Pamphlet, LRO, 305 WLM/3/4. The Liverpool-based feminist activist Jo Stanley, for example, remembered that most of the meetings she attended were exclusively white. Natalie Thomlinson, 'The Colour of Feminism: White Feminists and Race in the Women's Liberation Movement', *History* 97, no. 3 (July 2012): 453–475, 463.

61 Mandy Vere interviewed in Natalie Thomlinson, *Race, Ethnicity and the Women's Movement in England 1968–1993* (London: Palgrave, 2016), 188.

62 Ibid.

63 Hazel V. Carby, 'White Women Listen! Black Feminism and the Boundaries of Sisterhood', in Centre for Contemporary Cultural Studies ed., *Empire Strikes Back: Race and Racism in 70s Britain* (London: Hutchinson, 1982); Beverley Bryan, Stella Dadzie and Suzanne Scafe, *Heart of the Race: Black Women's Lives in Britain* (London: Verso, 1985, 2018).

64 Stephen Small and Jimi Jagne, *1981 – Black Liverpool Past and Present* (Leicester: Serendipity, 2022), 58–59.

65 For works that deal with the Liverpool Black Sisters alongside other Black organisations see Julie Sudbury, *Other Kinds of Dreams: Black Women's Organisations and the Politics of Transformation* (London: Routledge, 1998), 122, 243; William E. Nelson, *Black Atlantic Politics: Dilemmas of Political Empowerment in Boston and Liverpool* (Albany: State University of New York Press, 2000), 272. See also Stephen Small, 'Black Women and Black Sisters in Liverpool', *The Writing on the Wall*, https://writingonthewall.org.uk/wp-content/uploads/2021/06/05_Black-Women-and-Black-Sisters-in-Liverpool_01.pdf; Small and Jagne, *1981 – Black Liverpool Past and Present*, 56–64.

66 'Liverpool Black Women's Group', *Black Linx*, November 1983; Nelson, 'Black Atlantic Politics', 174.

67 The exact border between Toxteth and the Dingle continues to be a source of debate in Liverpool. Lisa Rand, 'We Try to Find Out Where Exactly is Toxteth', *Liverpool Echo*, 30 October 2019.

68 Michel de Certeau, *The Practice of Everyday Life*, trans. Steven Rendall (Berkeley: University of California Press, 1984), 93.

69 Rob Waters, *Thinking Black: Britain, 1964–1985* (Oakland: University of California Press, 2019), 182.

70 John Belchem, *Before the Windrush: Race Relations in 20th-Century Liverpool* (Liverpool: Liverpool University Press, 2014), 25–26.

71 Diane Frost, 'Racism and Social Segregation: Settlement Patterns of West African Seamen in Liverpool Since the Nineteenth Century', *Journal of Ethnic and Migration Studies* 22, no. 1 (1996): 85–95, 91–93.

72 For discussions of the size of Liverpool's Black community citing different upper and lower threshold figures see Stephen Small, 'Racialised Relations in Liverpool: A Contemporary Anomaly', *New Community* 17, no. 4 (July 1991): 511–537, 514; Tony Gifford, Wally Brown and Ruth Bundey, *Loosen the Shackles: First Report of the Liverpool 8 Inquiry into Race Relations in Liverpool* (London: Kaira, 1989), 37–40.

73 'Minutes of the Meeting to Consider Colonial Welfare', 22 March 1954, LRO, M364 PSS 711.

74 D. R. Manley, 'The Social Structure of the Liverpool Negro Community, with Special Reference to the Development of Formal Associations', (PhD diss., University of Liverpool, 1959), 90–91.

75 Shelter Neighbourhood Action Project, *Another Chance for Cities: SNAP 69–72* (Liverpool: SNAP, 1973), 54–55.

76 Ibid., 55.

77 Gifford et al., *Loosen the Shackles*, 40–41.

78 Sam Wetherell, '"Redlining" the British City', *Renewal* 28, no. 2 (2020): 81–89; Sam Wetherell, *Foundations: How the Built Environment Made Twentieth-Century Britain* (Princeton, NJ: Princeton University Press, 2020), 98–100. For a contemporary account of racism in local authority housing departments see Elisabeth Mary Burney, *Housing on Trial: A Study of Immigrants and Local Government* (Oxford: Oxford University Press, 1967). With thanks to Claire Wrigley for sharing ideas and citations about her forthcoming work on this topic.

79 Commission for Racial Equality, *Race and Housing in Liverpool: A Research Report* (London: Commission for Racial Equality, 1986); Commission for Racial Equality, *Racial Discrimination in Liverpool City Council: A Formal Investigation into the Housing Department* (London: Commission for Racial Equality, 1989).

80 Commission for Racial Equality, *Race and Housing*, 79, 80.
81 Parliamentary Papers, 'Report of the Race Relations Board for 1974', 36–37.
82 Some of these practices are detailed in Diane Frost, 'Racism and Social Segregation'.
83 A detailed account of the unrest around the Falkner Estate can be found in a Thames Television documentary, *Racial Tension*, which aired 17 August 1972.
84 Ibid.
85 Merseyside Community Relations Council, '11th Annual Report', 1981, LRO, H.301.34 MER, 17.
86 Gifford et al., Loosen the Shackles, 67–69.
87 Liverpool Youth Organisation Committee, 'A Report of the Working Party About the Situation of Young Coloured People in Liverpool', 1969, LRO, M364 PSS/5/1/4.
88 Belchem, *Before the Windrush*, 208.
89 Gifford et al., *Loosen the Shackles*, 53.
90 Nelson, *Black Atlantic Politics*, 220–221.
91 Simon Hughes, 'Liverpool, Howard Gayle and the Harsh Lessons Football Can Still Learn from his Story', *Liverpool Echo*, 16 April 2019; Howard Gayle and Simon Hughes, *61 Minutes in Munich* (Liverpool: DeCoubertin, 2016), 95–99.
92 Stuart Hall, 'Race and Moral Panics in Post-War Britain', in Paul Gilroy and Ruth Wilson Gilmore eds., *Stuart Hall: Selected Writings on Race and Difference* (Durham, NC: Duke University Press, 2021), 59.
93 Parliamentary Papers, 'Report of the Race Relations Board for 1967–68', 27.
94 Gifford et al., *Loosen the Shackles*, 82–83.
95 Jacqueline Nassy Brown, *Dropping Anchor, Setting Sail: Geographies of Race in Black Liverpool* (Princeton, NJ: Princeton University Press, 2005), esp. Ch. 4.
96 Manley, 'The Social Structure of the Liverpool Negro Community', 190.
97 Ibid., 189–190.
98 Colonial Peoples' Defence Association, 'Report of Activity: 1950–1952', 10, LRO, 329 COM/14.
99 Manley, 'The Social Structure of the Liverpool Negro Community', 283–286. According to Manley this organisation was founded by a con man who falsely claimed to be a relative of Kwame Nkrumah.
100 Ibid., 97.
101 Colonial Peoples' Defence Association, 'Report of Activity: 1950–1952', 5.
102 Manley, 'The Social Structure of the Liverpool Negro Community', 261.

103 Ibid., 267–271; Belchem, *Before the Windrush*, 102–107.

104 Belchem, *Before the Windrush*, 199–201.

105 Michael Romyn, '"For them it was Just a Game, but for us was More": Black Identity and the Making of Basketball in Urban Britain', *History Workshop Journal* 93, no. 1 (Spring 2022): 69-94.

106 For the turn towards 'community' in post-war race relations see Camilla Schofield and Ben Jones, '"Whatever Community Is, This Is Not It": Notting Hill and the Reconstruction of "Race" in Britain After 1958', *Journal of British Studies* 58, no. 1 (January 2019): 142–173; Radhika Natarajan, 'Organising Community: Commonwealth Citizens and Social Activism in Britain, 1948–1982' (PhD diss., University of California Berkeley, 2013).

107 Ambalavaner Sivanandan, the critical theorist and chair of the Institute of Race Relations, for example, denounced the councils for 'minimis[ing] the social and political cost of racial exploitation. Ambalavaner Sivanandan, *Communities of Resistance: Writings on Black Struggles for Socialism* (London: Verso, 1990, 2019), 80.

108 See, for example, Merseyside Community Relations Council, 'Seventh Annual Report', 1977, LRO, H.301.34 MER, 16, 42; Merseyside Community Relations Council, 'Sixth Annual Report', 1976, LRO, H.301.34.

109 Irene Loh Lynn, *The Chinese Community in Liverpool: Their Unmet Needs with Respect to Education, Social Welfare and Housing* (Liverpool: Merseyside Area Profile Group, 1982), 16–17. For Chinese restaurants in Britain see James L. Watson, 'The Chinese: Hong Kong Villagers in the British Catering Trade', in James L. Watson ed., *Between Two Cultures: Migrants and Minorities in Britain* (Oxford: Blackwell, 1977).

110 Loh Lynn, *The Chinese Community in Liverpool*, 17, 51–56.

111 Ibid., 39–44, 67–69.

112 Merseyside Community Relations Council, 'Seventh Annual Report', 25.

113 S. Craggs and I. Loh Lynn, *A History of the Chinese Community* (Liverpool: Merseyside Community Relations Council, 1985).

114 'Introducing Black Studies to the Curriculum', Pamphlet, LRO, VAS 2/7/2.

115 Waters, *Thinking Black*, Ch. 4.

116 Gifford et al., *Loosen the Shackles*, 150.

117 Many activists and theorists in the 1970s and 1980s were making arguments in favour of an expansive, 'political' Blackness or against an essential, fixed notion of Blackness. For an influential example of each of these see A. Sivanandan, 'From Resistance to Rebellion: Asian and Afro-Caribbean Struggles in Britain', *Race & Class* 23, no. 2–3 (1981):

111–152; Stuart Hall, 'New Ethnicities', in Paul Gilroy and Ruth Wilson Gilmore eds., *Selected Writings on Race and Difference* (Durham, NC: Duke University Press, 2021). For a history of this turn see John Narayan, 'British Black Power: The Anti-Imperialism of Political Blackness and the Problem of Nativist Socialism', *The Sociological Review* 67, no. 5 (2019): 945–967; Waters, *Thinking Black.*

118 Clive Emsley, *The English Police: A Social History* (London: Routledge, 1997), 175–177, 179.

6. The Uprising

1 There are many descriptions of this evening's events. One of the best is the recent account by the journalist Andy Beckett, which is based on interviews with participants in the uprising. Andy Beckett, *Promised You a Miracle: UK 80–82* (London: Allen Lane, 2015), Ch. 4.

2 'Leave Us Alone: A Special Report on the Cooper Family', *Black Linx*, February 1984; P. J. Waller, 'The Riots in Toxteth, Liverpool: A Survey', *Journal of Ethnic and Migration Studies* 9, no 3 (1981): 344–353.

3 'MPs Demand Probe into City Riots', *Liverpool Echo*, 30 July 1981.

4 Figure cited by Councillor Margaret Simey in Michael T. Kaufmann, 'In Liverpool, Many Blame the Police, Not Poverty Conditions, For Unrest', *New York Times*, 18 July 1981.

5 Martin Kettle and Lucy Hodges, *Uprising! The Police, the People and the Riots in British Cities* (London: Pan Books, 1982), 91.

6 John Belchem, *Before the Windrush: Race Relations in Twentieth-Century Liverpool* (Liverpool: Liverpool University Press, 2014), 242–243.

7 Derek Humphrey, *Police Power and Black People* (London: Panther, 1972), 18.

8 Tony Gifford, Wally Brown and Ruth Bundey, *Loosen the Shackles: First Report of the Liverpool 8 Inquiry into Race Relations in Liverpool* (London: Kaira, 1989), 79–80.

9 Liverpool 8 Defence Committee, 'Why Oxford Must Go', Liverpool Record Office (henceforward LRO), 920 VAS 272.

10 David Sheppard, *Steps Along Hope Street* (London: Darton, Longman & Todd, 2013), 214.

11 Liverpool 8 Defence Committee, 'Why Oxford Must Go'.

12 This is implied in ibid.

13 See, for example, Kennetta Hammond Perry, *London is the Place for Me: Black Britons, Citizenship and the Politics of Race* (Oxford: Oxford University Press, 2015); Adam Elliot Cooper, *Black Resistance to British Policing* (Manchester: Manchester University Press, 2021), Ch. 1; Cedric Robinson, 'An Inventory of Contemporary Black Politics', *Emergency* 2 (1984); Paul Gilroy, 'Police and Thieves', in Centre for Contemporary

Cultural Studies, *The Empire Strikes Back: Race and Racism in 70s Britain* (London: Routledge, 1982).

14 Kennetta Hammond Perry, 'Sights and Sounds of the Archive of State Violence: Encounters with the Archive of David Oluwale', *Modern British History*, 34, no. 3 (September 2023): 467–490.

15 For a detailed account of the St Pauls uprising see S. D. Reicher, 'The St. Pauls' Riot: An Explanation of the Limits of Crowd Action in Terms of a Social Identity Model', *European Journal of Social Psychology* 14, no. 1 (1984): 1–21.

16 Simon Peplow, *Race and Riots in Thatcher's Britain* (Manchester: Manchester University Press, 2021), 65.

17 Ibid., 66.

18 Parliamentary Papers, 'The Brixton Disorders: 10–12 April 1981', 1981, cmnd. 8427, 10.

19 Peplow, *Race and Riots*, 102–110; Kettle and Hodges, *Uprising!* 93–97.

20 Aaron Andrews, 'Truth, Justice, and Expertise in 1980s Britain: The Cultural Politics of the New Cross Massacre, *History Workshop Journal* 91, no. 1 (2021): 182–209.

21 Peplow, *Race and Riots*, 108–109.

22 Margaret Thatcher, 'TV Interview for Granada World in Action', 27 January 1978, Margaret Thatcher Archive (henceforward MT).

23 'The Brixton Disorders', 17–41.

24 Liverpool Teachers Association, 'Bristol!! Can it Happen Here?' in 'Before the Fire', LRO, HQ 371.97 LIV.

25 Beckett, *Promised You a Miracle*, 64.

26 Humphrey, *Police Power and Black People*, 13.

27 Kettle and Hodges, *Uprising!* 172.

28 Belchem, *Before the Windrush*, 252. For figures on Brixton and St Pauls see Kettle and Hodges, *Uprising!* 29, 114; Peplow, *Race and Riots*, 114.

29 Charles Tilly, *The Politics of Collective Violence* (Cambridge: Cambridge University Press, 2003).

30 'Summary of the Report of the Chief Constable to the Secretary of State for the Home Department as Presented by the Chief Constable in his Report to the Merseyside Police Committee', The National Archives (henceforward TNA:PRO), HO 287/2978; Diane Frost and Richard Phillips eds., *Liverpool '81: Remembering the Riots* (Liverpool: Liverpool University Press, 2011), 7–8.

31 Kettle and Hodges, *Uprising!* 161–162.

32 Frost and Phillips eds., *Liverpool '81*, 9.

33 Colin Bedford, *Weep for the City* (Tring: Lion Publishing, 1982), 7.

34 Interview reproduced in Timeri Murari, *The New Savages* (London: Macmillan, 1975), 55.

35 Frost and Phillips eds., *Liverpool '81*, 105–106.
36 Ibid., 26; Reicher, 'The St. Pauls' Riot', 10.
37 HC Deb, 16 July 1981, vol. 8, col. 1427.
38 Jeremy Hawthorne to Antony Wilson, Memo, 'Liverpool 8 Defence cttee', 28 August 1981, LRO, 340 LAW 1/4.
39 Frost and Phillips eds., *Liverpool '81*, 11.
40 Ian Ross, 'Night of Fear and Theft on Streets of Violence', *Liverpool Daily Post*, 7 July 1981.
41 Beckett, *Promised You a Miracle*, 65.
42 Frost and Phillips eds., *Liverpool '81*, 18.
43 Sheppard, *Steps Along Hope Street*, 212–213.
44 'Liverpool 8 Defence cttee'; Liverpool 8 Defence Committee, 'Why Oxford Must Go'.
45 Beckett, *Promised You a Miracle*, 66; Brian Roberts, 'Out of the Sunshine and into the Riots', *Liverpool Echo*, 8 July 1981.
46 Roberts, 'Out of the Sunshine and into the Riots'.
47 'Summary of the Report of the Chief Constable to the Secretary of State for the Home Department as Presented by the Chief Constable in his Report to the Merseyside Police Committee'.
48 William Whitelaw, *The Whitelaw Memoirs* (London: Aurum, 1989), 189.
49 Rob Rohrer, 'Police Open Fire on Civilians', *New Statesman*, 17 July 1981.
50 Ibid.
51 Ibid.
52 Erik Linstrum, 'Domesticating Chemical Weapons: Tear Gas and the Militarization of Policing in the British Imperial World, 1919–1981', *The Journal of Modern History* 91, no. 3 (September 2019): 557–585, 574; Anna Feigenbaum, *Tear Gas: From the Battlefields of World War I to the Streets of Today* (London: Verso, 2017).
53 Peplow, *Race and Riots*, 62; Whitelaw, *The Whitelaw Memoirs*, 189–190.
54 Howard Tumber, 'A Report on the Television Coverage of the July 1981 Riots in Inner City Areas', Broadcasting Research Unit, 1982, LRO, 340 LAW 11/1/5/2–5.
55 Peplow, *Race and Riots*, 168.
56 Gilroy, 'Police and Thieves', 153.
57 E. J. Hobsbawm, 'The Machine Breakers', *Past and Present* 1 (February 1952): 57–70, 59. See also E. P. Thompson, 'The Moral Economy of the English Crowd in the Eighteenth Century', *Past and Present* 50 (February 1971): 76–136; George Rudé and Eric Hobsbawm, *Captain Swing* (London: Lawrence & Wishart, 1969). These scholars have been cited by historians of the 1981 uprising such as Simon Peplow and Brian Marren as well as contemporaries such as Lucy Hodges and Martin Kettle.

58 Nasser Hussain, *The Jurisprudence of Emergency: Colonialism and the Rule of Law* (Ann Arbor: University of Michigan Press, 2003); Erik Linstrum, *Age of Emergency: Living with Violence at the End of the British Empire* (Oxford: Oxford University Press, 2022).
59 Rohrer, 'Police Open Fire on Civilians'.
60 Peplow, *Race and Riots*, 158–171; Kettle and Hodges, *Uprising!* 162–165.
61 'Toxteth on a Knife Edge', *Liverpool Daily Post*, 7 July 1981.
62 HC Deb, 7 July 1981, vol. 8, col. 29–30.
63 'Press Conference Visiting Liverpool (Toxteth Riot)', 13 July 1981, MT. For explicit references to tactics including rubber bullets see HC Deb. 14 July 1981, vol. 8, col. 973–978.
64 Aileen Ballantyne, 'Prison Officers Surprised by Camp Solution for Rioters', *The Guardian*, 15 July 1981; HC Deb, 15 July 1981, vol. 8, col. 1177.
65 Stuart Hall, Chas Critcher, Tony Jefferson, John Clarke and Brian Roberts, *Policing the Crisis: Mugging the State, Law and Order* (London: Bloomsbury, 1978, 2013).
66 HC Deb, 9 July 1981, vol. 8, col. 575.
67 'Party Political Broadcast', 8 July 1981, MT.
68 Martin Kettle, 'The Evolution of an Official Explanation', *New Society*, 3 December 1981.
69 'Riots Fury: Calls to Bring Back Enoch', *Liverpool Echo*, 24 September 1981.
70 Michael Heseltine, *Life in the Jungle: My Autobiography* (London: Coronet, 2001), 215.
71 Brian James, 'Don't Their Parents Care?' *Daily Mail*, 8 July 1981.
72 'We Must Not Fail', *Liverpool Daily Post*, 11 July 1981.
73 'The Balance of Order', *Liverpool Daily Post*, 7 July 1981.
74 'Riot City in Flames', *Daily Mail*, 8 July 1981; 'I had no Chance, they were like a Pack of Hyenas', *Daily Mail*, 17 August 1981.
75 'Riot City in Flames.'
76 Michael Parry and David Stoakes, 'Looters in New Riots', *Daily Express*, 6 July 1981.
77 M. O'Reilly, Statement, LRO, 340 LAW 1/2/1.
78 Liverpool 8 Defence Committee, 'Why Oxford Must Go'.
79 Jack Ashton, 'Stand Up and Back Police, Demands Tory', *Liverpool Echo*, 18 August 1981.
80 A. Kanwa, Statement, LRO, 340 LAW 1/2/1.
81 Teresa Riley, Statement, LRO, 340 LAW 1/2/1.
82 Patricia Fearon, Statement, LRO, 340 LAW 1/2/1.
83 Bendeli Akinyani, Statement, LRO, 340 LAW 1/2/1.
84 E. Walters, Statement, LRO, 340 LAW 1/2/1.

85 Mr Jones, Statement (taken at CRC), LRO, 340 LAW 1/2/1.
86 John Neil, Statement, LRO, 340 LAW 1/2/1.
87 Kettle and Hodges, *Uprising!* 171.
88 Kettle, 'The Evolution of an Official Explanation'. See also Peter Kilfoyle, *Left Behind: Lessons from Labour's Heartlands* (London: Politico's, 1999), 60–61.
89 See, for example, Peter Taaffe and Tony Mulhearn, *Liverpool: A City that Dared to Fight* (London: Fortress, 1988), 52.
90 Kettle, 'The Evolution of an Official Explanation'; Parliamentary Papers, 'The Brixton Disorders: 10–12 April 1981'. For a more recent account of the uprising that emphasises poverty rather than racial inequality see Brian Marren, *We Shall Not Be Moved: How Liverpool's Working Class Fought Redundancies, Closures and Cuts in the Age of Thatcher* (Manchester: Manchester University Press, 2016), Ch. 5.
91 Tumber, 'A Report on the Television Coverage of the July 1981 Riots', 60.
92 Kettle, 'The Evolution of an Official Explanation'.
93 Aileen Ballantyne, 'Police Accused of Taking Vengeance Over Criticism', *The Guardian*, 25 February 1982.
94 Jacqueline Nassy Brown, *Dropping Anchor, Setting Sail: Geographies of Race in Black Liverpool* (Princeton, NJ: Princeton University Press, 2005), 66.
95 Stuart Hall, 'Summer in the City', in Paul Gilroy and Ruth Wilson Gilmore eds., *Selected Writings on Race and Difference* (Durham, NC: Duke University Press, 2021), 75–76.
96 Reicher, 'The St. Pauls' Riot', 15.
97 Geoffrey Howe to Margaret Thatcher, Memo, 11 August 1981, TNA:PRO, PREM 19/578.
98 'Southend 81 to Toxteth 83', *Black Linx*, September 1983.

7. Disneypool

1 China Miéville, *The City and the City* (New York: Del Rey/Ballantine, 2010).
2 Andrei Tarkovsky, *Sculpting in Time: Reflections on the Cinema* (London: Faber, 1989).
3 For an early confrontation between Heseltine on the one side and Howe and Joseph on the other see Michael Heseltine, *Life in the Jungle: My Autobiography* (London: Coronet, 2001), 212–213.
4 Ibid, 219.
5 Ibid., 219–221.
6 Ibid., 218.
7 Ibid., 217.

8 Michael Heseltine, 'It Took a Riot', Memo, The National Archives (henceforward TNA:PRO), PREM 19/578.

9 For overviews of Margaret Thatcher's urban policy during the early years of her premiership see Michael Parkinson, 'The Thatcher Government's Urban Policy, 1979–1989, a Review', *The Town Planning Review* 60, no. 4 (October 1989): 421–440; Otto Saumerez Smith, 'Action for Cities: The Thatcher Government and Inner City Policy', *Urban History* 47, no. 2 (May 2019): 1–18; Sam Wetherell, *Foundations: How the Built Environment Made Twentieth-Century Britain* (Princeton, NJ: Princeton University Press, 2020), 9–11.

10 Mark Thomas, 'Top Money Men Back City Plan', *Liverpool Post*, 5 August 1981; Heseltine, *Life in the Jungle*, 223–224; Michael Crick, *Michael Heseltine: A Biography* (London: Hamish Hamilton, 1997), 225–226.

11 Parkinson, 'The Thatcher Government's Urban Policy', 435–438; Nicholas Deakin and John Edwards, *Enterprise Culture and the Inner City* (London: Routledge, 1993), 34–38; Chris Couch, *City of Change and Challenge: Urban Planning and Regeneration in Liverpool* (Abingdon: Routledge, 2003, 2018), 118–125.

12 For the London Docklands Development Corporation see Peter Hall, *Cities of Tomorrow: An Intellectual History of Urban Planning and Design Since 1880* (Oxford: Wiley, 2002), Ch. 11; Anna Minton, *Ground Control: Fear and Happiness in the Twenty-First Century City* (London: Penguin, 2012), Ch. 1.

13 Diana Pulson, 'Sticking Up for Scousers', *Liverpool Echo*, 4 October 1983.

14 Brian Adcock, 'Regenerating Merseyside Docklands: The Merseyside Development Corporation, 1981–1984', *The Town Planning Review* 55, no. 3 (July 1984): 265–289.

15 Merseyside Development Corporation, 'First Annual Report and Financial Statements: 31 March 1982', Liverpool Records Office (henceforward LRO), M 352 MDC 1/1/1, 6.

16 The Corporation's initial development strategy declared that its primary aim was 'to create the climate of confidence necessary to attract private investment'. Quoted in Aaron Andrews, 'Decline and the City: The Urban Crisis in Liverpool: c. 1968 to 1986' (PhD diss., University of Leicester, 2018), 109.

17 Adcock, 'Regenerating Merseyside Docklands', 272.

18 Merseyside Development Corporation, 'First Annual Report and Financial Statements: 31 March 1982', 7.

19 Quentin Hughes, *Seaport: Architecture and Townscape in Liverpool* (London: L. Humphries, 1964).

20 For redevelopment proposals in the 1970s see Couch, *City of Change and*

Challenge, 118–119; Merseyside Dock and Harbour Company, 'Annual Reports and Accounts for the Year Ended 1976', Liverpool Maritime Museum Archives, MDHB/FIN/1/2/37, 4.

21 Andrew Morgan, 'Today's Tate Comes North to Drop a Few Bricks', *Liverpool Daily Post*, 18 September 1988, LRO, MDC 8/2.

22 Waldemar Januszczak, 'Tate Goes North', *The Guardian*, 23 March 1988, LRO, MDC 8/2.

23 Respectively: 'Reserved Welcome for New City Gallery', *Liverpool Echo*, 12 March 1988, LRO, MDC 8/2; 'Gallery', *Liverpool Daily Post*, 18 March 1988, LRO, MDC, 8/2; Letter from George Barnes, *Liverpool Echo*, 13 March 1988, LRO, MDC 8/2.

24 For example, William Hunter, 'Mersey Tate? Give us Cash', *Daily Express*, 9 March 1985, LRO, MDC 8/2.

25 David Robinson, 'Rebirth – for Marie Celeste Hi-Tech Future', *Liverpool Daily Post*, 23 December 1985, LRO, MDC 8/3.

26 William E. Nelson, *Black Atlantic Politics: Dilemmas of Political Empowerment in Boston and Liverpool* (Albany: State University of New York Press, 2000), 129.

27 Parliamentary Papers, 'Employment Select Committee: Discrimination in Employment. Minutes of Evidence', 10 February 1986, 78.

28 For example, Tony Gifford, Wally Brown and Ruth Bundey, *Loosen the Shackles: First Report of the Liverpool 8 Inquiry into Race Relations in Liverpool* (London: Kaira, 1989), 51; Jacqueline Nassy Brown, *Dropping Anchor, Setting Sail: Geographies of Race in Black Liverpool* (Princeton, NJ: Princeton University Press, 2005), 11.

29 Paul Barker, 'Thinking the Unthinkable', in Jonathan Hughes and Simon Sadler eds., *Non-Plan: Essays on Freedom, Participation and Change in Modern Architecture and Urbanism* (London: Routledge, 2000). For the link between the non-plan experiment and the enterprise zone and some examples of its use see Sam Wetherell, 'Freedom Planned: Enterprise Zones and Urban Non-Planning in Post-War Britain', *Modern British History* 27, no. 2 (June 2016): 266–289.

30 Reyner Banham, Paul Barker, Peter Hall and Cedric Price, 'Non-Plan: An Experiment in Freedom', *New Society*, 20 March 1969, 435–443.

31 Colin Ward's support was pledged in person to Paul Barker, as mentioned in Paul Barker, 'Thinking the Unthinkable', 5. Michael Young's support came from his writings in Open Group, *Social Reform in the Centrifugal Society* (London: New Society, 1969); Alfred Sherman, Letter, *New Society*, 17 April 1969, 610.

32 Peter Hall, 'Green Fields, and Grey Areas', 15 June 1977. Reprinted in *Proceedings of the RTPI Annual Conference* (Chester: Royal Town Planning Institute, 1977).

33 We will never know for certain whether enterprise zones would have existed without the inspiration of the Non-Plan movement, or without Peter Hall's input. We do know, however, that a link between enterprise zones and Peter Hall's anti-planning ideas was made repeatedly and explicitly by Geoffrey Howe, who credited Hall for the policy both in his 1978 Isle of Dogs speech, and in Parliament when introducing enterprise zone legislation for the first time. Peter Hall passionately defended the policy throughout the 1980s, in the pages of an international planning journal, and, later, from his post as Special Advisor to Conservative Environment Minister Michael Heseltine. This link is fleshed out in more detail in Sam Wetherell, 'Freedom Planned', 275–276.

34 Geoffrey Howe, 'Liberating Free Enterprise: A New Experiment', Speech to the Bow Group, 26 June 1978, Margaret Thatcher Archive (henceforward MT), THCR 2/1/1/39.

35 Memo, Keith Joseph to Margaret Thatcher, 7 July 1978, MT, THCR 2/1/1/39.

36 'Enterprise Zones', Memo, John Hunt to Margaret Thatcher, TNA:PRO, PREM 19/105.

37 'Ministerial Committee on Economic Strategy: Enterprise Zone Report', Report, 21 September 1979, TNA:PRO, CAB 134/4336, 8; 'Official Group on the Impact of Government on Industry Sub Group on Enterprise Zones/Pilot Areas', Report, 30 July 1979, TNA:PRO, T 277/3500.

38 Richard Meegan, 'Paradise Postponed: The Growth and Decline of Merseyside's Outer Estates', in Phillip Cooke ed., *Localities: The Changing Face of Urban Britain* (London: Hutchinson, 1989), 199–200.

39 For a history of the rise and fall of British Leyland in Speke see Brian Marren, *We Shall Not Be Moved: How Liverpool's Working Class Fought Redundancies, Closures and Cuts in the Age of Thatcher* (Manchester: Manchester University Press, 2016), Ch. 3.

40 Meegan, 'Paradise Postponed', 207–209.

41 'Speke Enterprise Zone No. 1', LRO, HQ 338 CIT, 1–2.

42 'Speke Enterprise Zone: Monitoring Report', LRO, HQ 338 CIT; Couch, *City of Change and Challenge*, 113.

43 'Speke Enterprise Zone: Monitoring Report'.

44 Ibid.

45 Roger Tym and Partners, *Monitoring Enterprise Zones: Three Year Report* (London: HMSO, 1984).

46 'Speke Enterprise Zone: Monitoring Report'.

47 Geoffrey Howe, 'Enterprise Zones and Enterprise Culture: Enterprise Zones Ten Years On', 26 June 1988, reprinted in Geoffrey Howe,

Enterprise Zones and Enterprise Culture (London: The Bow Group, 1988), 16–17.

48 For the definitive history of this event, see Jeffrey A. Auerbach, *The Great Exhibition of 1851: A Nation on Display* (New Haven, CT: Yale University Press, 1999). See also Jeffrey A. Auerbach and Peter H. Hoffenberg, eds., *Britain, the Empire, and the World at the Great Exhibition of 1851* (London: Routledge, 2013); Louise Purbrick, ed., *The Great Exhibition of 1851: New Interdisciplinary Essays* (Manchester: Manchester University Press, 2001).

49 Becky E. Conekin, *The Autobiography of a Nation: The 1951 Festival of Britain* (Manchester: Manchester University Press, 2003).

50 For garden festivals see Sam Wetherell, 'Sowing Seeds: Garden Festivals and the Remaking of British Cities after Deindustrialization', *Journal of British Studies* 61, no. 1 (January 2022): 83–104; C. Theokas, *Grounds for Review: The Garden Festival in Urban Planning and Design* (Liverpool: Liverpool University Press, 2004).

51 Department of the Environment, *An Evaluation of Garden Festivals* (London: HMSO, 1990).

52 The figure of one person in every ten is a rough estimate. While there were close to fifteen million total visits to the five events (Liverpool, 3.4 million; Stoke-on-Trent, 2.2 million; Glasgow, 4.3 million; Gateshead, 3 million; Ebbw Vale, 2 million), these numbers include repeat visits. The sale of season tickets at many events, and a handful of news stories of visitors claiming to have attended every day the festival was open (in Glasgow and in Ebbw Vale), suggests that repeated visits were not insignificant but probably did not amount to more than a third of all visits. With the population of Britain between 1981 and 1991 being somewhere between fifty-six million and fifty-eight million people, the figure of one in ten is a likely, if not even a conservative, one.

For the attendance figures for Liverpool, Glasgow and Stoke-on-Trent see ibid. For Gateshead see Tony Henderson, 'Gateshead National Garden Festival: 25 Years since the Event on Tyneside', *Evening Chronicle* (London), 13 May 2015. For Ebbw Vale see Lewis Smith, 'The Scorched Legacy and Sorry Sight of Ebbw Vale's Festival Park', *Wales Online*, 27 June 2020.

53 One year before the announcement of British National Garden Festivals, the Department of the Environment conducted a detailed in-house report on German *Bundesgartenschau*. See 'German Federal Garden Shows', 11 March 1980, TNA:PRO, AT 42/75.

54 Heseltine, *Life in the Jungle*, 226–228.

55 Anne Jones, 50,000 *Bluebells: The Story of Liverpool's International Garden Festival* (Leicester: Windward, 1984).

56 Department of the Environment, *An Evaluation of Garden Festivals*, 7.
57 Jones, *50,000 Bluebells*, 94.
58 'Festival Guide', Promotional Pamphlet, 1984, LRO, 712.50942753 INT, 107.
59 Jones, *50,000 Bluebells*, 16.
60 'Landform', International Garden Festival: Liverpool 1984 press release, 22 June 1982, LRO, HQ 635 INT.
61 Elsewhere I have described the politics of British garden festivals as a kind of 'market environmentalism'. Sam Wetherell, 'Sowing Seeds', 86–91. See also Chris Otter, 'Liberty and Ecology: Resources, Markets, and the British Contribution to the Global Environmental Crisis', in Simon Gunn and James Vernon eds., *The Peculiarities of Liberal Modernity in Imperial Britain* (Berkeley: University of California Press, 2011).
62 Jones, *50,000 Bluebells*, 12.
63 'Festival Guide', 33.
64 'Home Is Where the Park Is', *Liverpool Echo*, International Garden Festival Pre-opening Supplement, 25 April 1984.
65 Laura Davis, 'Flower Power', *Liverpool Daily Post*, 2 December 2006.
66 Memo, M. R. Fawcett to Mr Peck, 17 August 1983, TNA:PRO, AT 81/307.
67 'Survey of Visitors to the Liverpool Garden Festival: Final Report', LRO, HQ 712.5 NOP. The survey recorded that 54 per cent of adult visitors were from ABC1 (white collar) households (compared with 39 per cent across the country as a whole), and that only 9 per cent of visitors were ages 15 to 24 (compared with 16 per cent nationally).
68 HC Deb, 29 February 1984, vol. 55, col. 237.
69 'Gollywog Garden', *Black Linx*, June 1984.
70 Theokas, *Grounds for Review*, 10.
71 'Worldwide Lure of the Greenest Show on Earth', *Liverpool Echo* (Festival Supplement), 21 September 1983.
72 Memo, C. H. Stubbs, 4 July 1984, TNA:PRO, FCO 21/2705.
73 '[Liverpool] Festival Guide', 188.
74 Peter Wynn Jones, *Oliver and Simon at the International Garden Festival: Liverpool '84* (Liverpool: P. Wynn Jones, 1984), n.p.
75 Phil Miller, 'Garden Festival "Can Get By without City",' *Liverpool Daily Post*, 7 October 1982.
76 Peter Surridge, 'Disneypool', *The Liverpool Post*, 23 June 1984.
77 Ibid.
78 'Disney "No" to City Site', *Liverpool Echo*, 26 February 1985.
79 David Harvey, 'From Managerialism to Entrepreneurialism: The Transformation of Urban Governance in Late Capitalism', *Geografiska Annaler*, Series B: *Human Geography* 71, no. 1 (1989): 3–17. For a historical

account of how this way of conceiving the city played out in a different national context, see Kim Phillips-Fein, *Fear City: New York's Fiscal Crisis and the Rise of Austerity Politics* (New York: Metropolitan, 2017).

8. Structural Adjustment

1 Neil Kinnock, 'Leader's Speech', Bournemouth, 11 October 1985.

2 The classic example of this genre, written by a Labour MP, is Peter Kilfoyle, *Left Behind: Lessons from Labour's Heartlands* (London: Politico's, 1999). Many of the events of the 1983–7 Labour administration in Liverpool were rehashed in 2019 when Derek Hatton was readmitted to the Labour Party. See, for example, Rajeev Sayal, Josh Halliday and Poppy Noor, '"He did a lot of Damage": Liverpool Reacts to the Return of Derek Hatton', *The Guardian*, 19 February 2019; Kate Devlin, 'Labour's Split: Militant Derek Hatton is Welcomed Back into the Fold', *The Times*, 19 February 2019.

3 For example, the chapter of Michael Parkinson's recent hagiography of modern Liverpool that covers the post-Militant years is titled 'Liverpool Begins to Become Normal'. Michael Parkinson, *Liverpool Beyond the Brink: The Remaking of a Post Imperial City* (Liverpool: Liverpool University Press, 2019).

4 For a detailed account of the rise and fall of the Conservative Party in Liverpool see David Jeffrey, *Whatever Happened to Tory Liverpool? Success, Decline and Irrelevance since 1945* (Liverpool: Liverpool University Press, 2023).

5 Various social and political historians have tried to account for the Labour Party's electoral failures in Liverpool until the 1950s. See, for example, Joan Smith, 'Labour Tradition in Liverpool and Glasgow', *History Workshop Journal* 17 (Spring 1984): 32–56; Sam Davies, *Liverpool Labour: Social and Political Influences on the Development of the Labour Party in Liverpool, 1900–1939* (Keele: Keele University Press, 1996).

6 The figure is estimated in Donald M. MacRaild, *Irish Migrants in Modern Britain, 1750–1922* (Basingstoke: Palgrave, 1999), 9. For the Irish experience in Liverpool see John Belchem, *Irish, Catholic, and Scouse: The History of the Liverpool Irish 1800–1939* (Liverpool: Liverpool University Press, 2007).

7 For residual displays of organised Protestant radicalism in post-war Liverpool see Daniel Warner, 'Working Class Culture and Practice amid Urban Renewal and Decline: Liverpool, c. 1965–1985' (PhD diss., University of Liverpool, 2018), 87–126; Daniel Warner, 'When Two Tribes Go to War: Orange Parades, Religious Identity and Urban Space in Liverpool, 1965–1985', *Oral History* 47, no. 2 (2019): 30–42.

8 Smith, 'Labour Tradition in Liverpool and Glasgow', 50. In her exact words, 'Glasgow working men were good socialists but lousy rioters; Liverpool working men were quite the reverse.'

9 Daniel Warner has argued that the decline of Liverpool's sectarianism, despite these political transformations, has been overstated. Warner, 'Working Class Culture and Practice amid Urban Renewal and Decline', 87–126.

10 For a nostalgic local history of Scotland Road and its post-war redevelopment see Colin Hunt and Paul Dove, *Scottie Road: A City Within a City* (Liverpool: Trinity, 2010).

11 Kilfoyle, *Left Behind*, 2–9; Anthony Howard, 'Cook County UK', *New Statesman*, 31 July 1964.

12 Kilfoyle, *Left Behind*, 6.

13 Ibid., 7.

14 Michael Crick, *The March of Militant* (London: Faber & Faber, 1986), 221.

15 See, for example, Tony Lane, *City by the Sea* (Liverpool: Liverpool University Press, 1997), 29–59.

16 Kilfoyle, *Left Behind*, 28–29; Peter Sloman, '"Take Power – Vote Liberal": Jeremy Thorpe, the 1974 Liberal Revival and the Politics of 1970s Britain', *English Historical Review* 137, no. 588 (October 2022): 1462–1492.

17 Crick, *March of Militant*, 50–58.

18 Ibid., 60–64.

19 Ibid., 123.

20 These demands were laid out in a canonical text for the movement, authored by the Liverpool-based Militant Peter Taaffe. Peter Taaffe, *What We Stand For* (London: Militant, 1981).

21 For Northern Ireland and Gay Rights see Crick, *The March of Militant*, 88, 90. For Militant's tough stance on drugs see the undated statements authored by Brian O'Neill and Janet Ruth in Liverpool Records Office (henceforward LRO), ACC 6204, Box 13, Item 3.

22 Crick, *March of Militant*, 90–91.

23 Ibid., 143.

24 Derek Hatton, *Inside Left: The Story so Far…* (London: Bloomsbury, 1988), 40.

25 Ibid., 112–113.

26 Kilfoyle, *Left Behind*, 88.

27 Jonny Ball, '"Militant Liverpool" as Liverpool Exceptionalism: The Rise, Fall and Character of the City Council, 1983–1987', *Transactions of the Royal Historical Society of Lancashire and Cheshire* 166 (2017): 145–186, 178.

28 Hatton, *Inside Left*; Peter Taaffe and Tony Mulhearn, *Liverpool: A City that Dared to Fight* (London: Fortress, 1988).

29 Crick, *March of Militant*, 229.

30 Hatton, *Inside Left*, 56–57.

31 City of Liverpool, 'Local Economic Trends and Future Prospects', Report of the City Planning Officer as Submitted to the Employment Subcommittee, 1981, LRO, Hq330 CIT.

32 Ibid.; Michael Parkinson, *Liverpool on the Brink: One City's Struggles Against Government Cuts* (London: Hermitage, 1985), 14–15.

33 Parkinson, *Liverpool on the Brink*, 13.

34 Ibid., 10.

35 Councils in Britain were required by law to meet certain spending limits. Failure to do this left individual councillors legally liable.

36 For the disciplining of municipal budgets by bond markets in the United States, see Destin Jenkins, *The Bonds of Inequality: Debt and the Making of the American City* (Chicago: Chicago University Press, 2021). The political theorist Alasdair Roberts has referred to this as the 'logic of discipline'. Alasdair Roberts, *The Logic of Discipline* (Oxford: Oxford University Press, 2010).

37 Kim Phillips-Fein, *Fear City: New York's Fiscal Crisis and the Rise of Austerity Politics* (New York: Metropolitan, 2017).

38 For Clay Cross and the history of resistance to the Housing Finance Act see J. A. Chandler, *Explaining Local Government: Local Government in Britain Since 1800* (Manchester: Manchester University Press, 2007), 211–213.

39 Parkinson, *Liverpool on the Brink*, 32.

40 Diane Frost and Peter North, *Militant Liverpool: A City on the Edge* (Liverpool: Liverpool University Press, 2013), 72.

41 Parkinson, *Liverpool on the Brink*, 42.

42 Taaffe et al., *The City that Dared to Fight*, 120.

43 Parkinson, *Liverpool on the Brink*, 42.

44 Frost et al., *Militant Liverpool*, 73.

45 Ibid., 78.

46 Parkinson, *Liverpool on the Brink*, 64.

47 This is the implication, for example, of Alan Bleasdale's TV series *GBH*, a thinly veiled satire of Derek Hatton and Militant.

48 For interviews with participants in the Budget Day see Frost et al., *Militant Liverpool*, 76–80.

49 Parkinson, *Liverpool on the Brink*, 55–56.

50 Hatton, *Inside Left*, 77.

51 Frost et al., *Militant Liverpool*, 81.

52 Ibid., 81–82.
53 Hatton, *Inside Left*, 78.
54 Parkinson, *Liverpool on the Brink*, 121.
55 For the technical details of the agreement see ibid., 113–122.
56 Ibid., 108.
57 Chandler, *Explaining Local Government*, 250–253.
58 Derek Hatton claims that following a TV interview, the Tory MP Teddy Taylor told him, 'At this stage we want Scargill. He's our priority. But we'll come for you after.' Hatton, *Inside Left*, 85.
59 Ibid., 87–88.
60 Frost et al., *Militant Liverpool*, 85.
61 Quoted in Brian Marren, *We Shall Not Be Moved: How Liverpool's Working Class Fought Redundancies, Closures and Cuts in the Age of Thatcher* (Manchester: Manchester University Press, 2016), 169.
62 Parkinson, *Liverpool on the Brink*, 140.
63 Frost et al., *Militant Liverpool*, 98.
64 Two of the 'Priority Areas' for the Militant administration's Urban Regeneration Strategy – Priority Area 1 and Priority Area 10 – were in Vauxhall, a short walk from the Stanley Docks. Economic Development Committee and Housing Building Committee, 'Liverpool Inner City Partnership: 1983/84 Programme', 1983, LRO HQ 309.INN. Priority Area 1, for example, was bounded by Vauxhall Road, Great Mersey Street, Stanley Road and Eldon Street. Liverpool City Council, 'Urban Regeneration Strategy: Declaration of Priority Area 1', LRO Hq11 409 427 53 CIT. For the figure of 5,000 see Taaffe and Mulhearn, *The City that Dared to Fight*, 159. Michael Parkinson notes that the target of the Urban Regeneration Strategy was 6,000. Parkinson, *Liverpool on the Brink*, 130. For URS and co-operative housing see Matthew Thomson, *Reconstructing Public Housing: Liverpool's Hidden History of Collective Alternatives* (Liverpool: Liverpool University Press, 2020), 103–120.
65 Liverpool City Council, 'Success Against the Odds', LRO, LCC ACC 6204, Box 129, Item 1.
66 Ibid.; Liverpool City Council, 'Urban Regeneration Strategy: Declaration of Priority Area 1'.
67 Both Hatton and Mulhearn claim that close to 6,500 new jobs were created. Taaffe and Mulhearn, *The City that Dared to Fight*, 159. Hatton, *Inside Left*, 62.
68 Michael Parkinson, *Liverpool on the Brink*, 130.
69 Alice Coleman, *Utopia on Trial: Vision and Reality in Planned Housing* (London: Hilary Shipman, 1985). For Alice Coleman's ideas and her centrality to Thatcherite urban policy see Sam Wetherell, *Foundations: How the Built Environment Made Twentieth-Century Britain* (Princeton,

NJ: Princeton University Press, 2020), 115–126. Coleman was warmly received in Downing Street by Margaret Thatcher in 1988.

70 Coleman, *Utopia on Trial*, 157.

71 Liverpool City Council, 'Urban Regeneration Strategy', 1987, LRO, LCC 711.40942753 COU.

72 See, for example, Taaffe and Mulhearn, *The City that Dared to Fight*, 158.

73 The architecture critic Owen Hatherley has written an excoriating critique of Militant's suburban housing along these lines. Owen Hatherley, *The New Ruins of Great Britain* (London: Verso, 2010), Ch. 12.

74 Liverpool City Council, 'Urban Regeneration Strategy'.

75 Ibid.

76 Hatton, *Inside Left*, 30.

77 For Sheffield during this period see Daisy Payling, '"Socialist Republic of South Yorkshire": Grassroots Activism and Left-Wing Solidarity in 1980s Sheffield', *Modern British History* 25, no. 4 (December 2014): 602–627. For the GLC see Owen Hatherley, *Red Metropolis: Socialism and the Government of London* (London: Repeater, 2020); Stephen Brooke, *London 1984: Conflict and Change in the Radical City* (Oxford: Oxford University Press, 2024).

78 Hatton, *Inside Left*, 91.

79 A whole chapter of Michael Crick's history of Militant is dedicated to 'Hatton's Army'. Crick, *March of Militant*, Ch. 13.

80 Hatton, *Inside Left*, 91.

81 Crick, *March of Militant*, 89–90.

82 The best history of the Liverpool Black Caucus can be found in their own publication critiquing Militant. Liverpool Black Caucus, *The Racial Politics of Militant: The Black Community's Struggle for Participation in Local Politics 1980–1986* (Liverpool: Merseyside Area Profile Group and Runnymede Trust, 1986).

83 Ibid., 44–45.

84 Paul Gilroy derided this approach as the 'Black and White Unite and Fight' school of anti-racism. Paul Gilroy, *There Ain't No Black in the Union Jack: The Cultural Politics of Race and Nation* (London: Routledge, 1987, 2002), 13.

85 Liverpool Black Caucus, *The Racial Politics of Militant*, 61.

86 Ibid., 46.

87 Ibid., 37; Tony Gifford, Wally Brown and Ruth Bundey, *Loosen the Shackles: First Report of the Liverpool 8 Inquiry into Race Relations in Liverpool* (London: Kaira, 1989), 53, 57.

88 Commission for Racial Equality, *Race and Housing in Liverpool: A Research Report* (London: Commission for Racial Equality, 1984).

89 Ibid., 10–11.

90 *Racial Discrimination in Liverpool City Council: Report of a Formal Investigation into the Housing Department* (London: Commission for Racial Equality, 1989), 7.

91 Ibid., 9, 21–22.

92 The Black local historian Ray Costello, in an interview with Diane Frost and Peter North, notes Bond's lack of knowledge of the distinctiveness of Liverpool's Black population as particularly egregious. Forst et al., *The March of Militant*, 161.

93 Ibid., 148.

94 Some of these letters have been archived at LRO, ACC 6402, Box 32, Item 4.

95 For Sivanandan's critique of the liberal race relations establishment see, for example, A. Sivanandan, 'All that Melts into Air is Solid: The Hokum of New Times', in A. Sivanandan ed., *Communities of Resistance: Writings on Black Struggles for Socialism* (London: Verso, 1990, 2019), 19–61. For an intellectual history of more critical instances of radical Black non-nativist socialist movements in Britain see John Narayan, 'British Black Power: The Anti-Imperialism of Political Blackness and the Problem of Nativist Socialism', *The Sociological Review* 67, no. 5 (2019): 945–967.

96 'Liverpool's Race Relations Unit', LRO, ACC 6402, Box 32, Item 3.

97 Ibid.; Liverpool Black Caucus, *The Racial Politics of Militant*, 80–83.

98 Untitled collection of Liverpool Black Caucus letters and documents, LRO, ACC 6402, Box 32, Item 3.

99 'Black Caucus – Desperate Tactics', article in undated issue of *Militant*, LRO, ACC 6402, Box 32, Item 4.

100 'Disorders in Liverpool 8: Report of the County Solicitor and Secretary', 20 November 1985, Black Cultural Archives, RC/RF/16/17/E.

101 Ibid.

102 Merseyside Community Relations Council, Press Release, 3 October 1985, The National Archives, HO 287/3772; 'Will the Real Black People Stand Up', Leaflet, LRO, ACC 6204, Box 32, File 6.

103 Merseyside Community Relations Council, Press Release, 3 October 1985.

104 'Disorders in Liverpool 8: Report of the County Solicitor and Secretary'.

9. The Semi-Final

1 For subcultures among Liverpool fans in the 1980s see Ben Jones, 'Football Casuals, Fanzines and Acid House: Working Class Subcultures, Emotional Communities, and Popular Individualism in 1980s and 1990s England', *Modern British History* 34, no. 2 (June 2023): 299–323.

2 David Goldblatt, *The Ball is Round: A Global History of Football* (London: Penguin, 2007), 447–449.

3 A note on sources: For my account of the events of 15 April 1989 I have tried, where possible, to avoid using early press coverage, the first coroner's inquest and Lord Justice Taylor's two official reports, all of which have since been discredited to a greater or lesser degree by subsequent legal hearings. Instead, I draw heavily on the report of the Hillsborough Independent Panel published in 2012 and the writings of the lawyer Phil Scraton, one of the authors of the report and a scholar widely recognised as the authority on the disaster. I also make extensive use of the writings of the investigative journalist David Conn, who has been covering the aftermath of the disaster for more than twenty years for *The Guardian*. There are many accounts of the disaster by survivors. As well as those collected by Kevin Sampson in his edited collection, I have chosen to focus on Adrian Tempany's account from his 2016 history of the event for its clarity and urgency. I also draw in detail on the handwritten account of the tragedy compiled by the survivor Ed Doyle and deposited in the Liverpool Record Office in 2013. The late appearance of this account means that it has been left out of many histories of the event. I am extremely grateful to all of the campaigners and survivors whose research and documented memories make this chapter possible.

4 Edward Doyle, 'Hillsborough Script 2', handwritten account, Liverpool Records Office (henceforward LRO), ACC 7647 920 DOY/1, 1.

5 Phil Scraton, *Hillsborough: The Truth* (Edinburgh: Mainstream Publishing, 2016), 64.

6 Hillsborough Independent Panel, *Hillsborough: The Report of the Hillsborough Independent Panel* (London: The Stationery Office, 2012), 7.

7 Scraton, *Hillsborough*, 33–34.

8 Adrian Tempany, *And the Sun Shines Now: How Hillsborough and the Premier League Changed Britain* (London: Faber & Faber, 2016), 16.

9 Home Office of Great Britain, *The Hillsborough Stadium Disaster 15 April 1989: Enquiry by the Rt. Honourable Lord Justice Taylor Interim Report* (London: HMSO, 1990), 7.

10 Doyle, 'Hillsborough Script 2', 2.

11 Scraton, *Hillsborough*, 79–80.

12 Hillsborough Independent Panel, *Hillsborough*, 9; Scraton, *Hillsborough*,

76–77; Home Office of Great Britain, *The Hillsborough Stadium Disaster*, 4.

13 Tempany, *And the Sun Shines Now*, 6.
14 Ibid.
15 Scraton, *Hillsborough*, 76.
16 Tempany, *And the Sun Shines Now*, 5–6.
17 David Conn, 'Senior Hillsborough Officer Tells Inquest: I was the Best Man for the Job', *The Guardian*, 10 March 2015.
18 Doyle, 'Hillsborough Script 2', 3.
19 Tempany, *And the Sun Shines Now*, 20–22.
20 Ibid., 22. A clip of John Motson's commentary can be found in David Conn et al., 'Hillsborough: Anatomy of a Disaster – Video', *The Guardian*, 28 April 2016.
21 Peter Marshall, 'Hillsborough – How they Buried the Truth', *Panorama*, 20 May 2013.
22 Kevin Sampson in association with the Hillsborough Justice Campaign, *Hillsborough Voices: The Real Story Told by the People Themselves* (London: Ebury, 2017), 66.
23 Interview with Neil Fitzmaurice in Ella Hooton, dir., *Hillsborough – The Survivor's Story*. Hooton's film is accessible on YouTube at: www.youtube.com/watch?v=QlE-PwFGbKQ.
24 Tempany, *And the Sun Shines Now*, 26.
25 Ibid., 28.
26 Ibid., 29.
27 Doyle, 'Hillsborough Script 2', 3–4.
28 Scraton, *Hillsborough*, 99.
29 Ibid., 101.
30 Ibid., 102.
31 Doyle, 'Hillsborough Script 2', 6–7.
32 Scraton, *Hillsborough*, 108.
33 Ibid., 114.
34 David Conn in the *Guardian*, 'Hillsborough Inquest: Better Ambulance Response Could Have Saved Lives', 4 December, 2014.
35 Doyle, 'Hillsborough Script 2', 7–11.
36 The worst football disaster was a crush at the Estadio Nacional in Peru in 1964 that claimed the lives of 328. The second worst was a crush in the Accra Sports Stadium in Accra, Ghana, in 2001 that claimed the lives of 128. For typologies and quantifications of football disasters see Paul Darby, Martin Johnes and Gavin Mellor, 'Football Disasters: A Conceptual Frame', *Soccer & Society* 5, no. 2 (2004): 125–133.
37 Hillsborough Independent Panel, *Hillsborough*, 98.
38 In 2016, following a lengthy second inquest into the disaster, a judge

ruled that the Hillsborough victims were 'unlawfully killed due to gross negligence'.

39 Scraton, *Hillsborough*, 42–44.

40 Shane Ewan and Aaron Andrews, 'The Media, Affect and Community in a Decade of Disaster: Reporting the 1985 Bradford Stadium Fire', *Journal of Contemporary History* 35, no. 2 (2021): 258–283.

41 Scraton, *Hillsborough*, 47.

42 Goldblatt, *The Ball is Round*, 542.

43 Ibid., 576.

44 James Walvin, *Football and the Decline of Britain* (Basingstoke: Macmillan, 1986) 11.

45 For the historian see ibid. For a summary of contemporary sociological literature on hooliganism see Dick Hobbs and David Robins, 'The Boy Done Good: Football Violence, Changes and Continuities', *Sociological Review* 29, no. 3 (August 1991): 551–579. For a dissenting take on the sociological consensus on hooliganism as a pathology see Clifford Stott and Steve Reicher, 'How Conflict Escalates: The Inter-Group Dynamics of Collective Football Crowd "Violence"', *Sociology* 32, no. 2 (May 1988): 353–377.

46 Desmond Morris, *The Soccer Tribe* (London: Jonathan Cape, 1981). See, for example, 15–16.

47 Peter Marsh, 'Understanding Aggro', *New Society*, 3 April 1975.

48 Scraton, *Hillsborough*, 55.

49 Daniel Warner, 'When Saturday Comes: Football, Public Disorder and Liverpool's Urban Crisis, c. 1965–1985', *Urban History* 50, no. 2 (December 2021): 1–19.

50 Scraton, *Hillsborough*, 59.

51 Ibid., 101.

52 Shelia Coleman, Ann Jemphrey, Phil Scraton and Paula Skidmore, 'Hillsborough and After: The First Report', LRO, Hq 363 3497 HIL.

53 Scraton, *Hillsborough*, 170.

54 David Conn, 'Hillsborough Inquest: Police Memo "Attempted to Denigrate Fans"', *The Guardian*, 21 April 2015.

55 Hillsborough Independent Panel, *Hillsborough*, 154–155.

56 Even on its own terms, evidence of blood alcohol levels were highly suspect. Ibid., 174–176.

57 'Thatcher was Told "Drunk Liverpool Fans" Caused Hillsborough Disaster', *The Guardian*, 15 March 2012.

58 Scraton, *Hillsborough*, 136.

59 Ibid., 171.

60 Shelia Coleman et al., 'Hillsborough and After', 117.

61 Ibid.

62 Ibid., 208.

63 Ibid., 196–197.

64 Harry Arnold, 'The Truth', *The Sun*, 19 April 1989.

65 David Conn, 'Hillsborough Inquest: Police Admit Sun Report of Fans Looting Corpses was False', *The Guardian*, 10 October 2014; David Conn, 'Police "Got Away with" Hillsborough Safety Before Disaster: Inquest Told', *The Guardian*, 9 October 2014.

66 Scraton, *Hillsborough*, 173.

67 Florian Foos and Daniel Bischof, 'Tabloid Media Campaigns and Public Opinion: Quasi-Experimental Evidence on Euroscepticism in England', *American Political Science Review* 116 no. 1 (February 2022): 19-31.

68 Shelia Coleman et al., 'Hillsborough and After', 123.

69 Ibid., 166–167.

70 Ibid., 167–168.

71 Daniel Caradog Jones ed., *The Social Survey of Merseyside vol. 2* (Liverpool: Liverpool University Press, 1934), 390–403.

72 Andy Hunter, 'Everton Sign Contract to Complete New Stadium Construction', *The Guardian*, 13 April 2022.

73 Home Office of Great Britain, *The Hillsborough Stadium Disaster: Interim Report*, 40.

74 Ibid., 49.

75 Home Office of Great Britain, *The Hillsborough Stadium Disaster 15 April 1989: Enquiry by the Rt. Honourable Lord Justice Taylor Final Report* (London: HMSO, 1990), 6.

76 Ibid., 31.

77 Ibid., 44–45.

78 Ibid., 48.

79 Martin Johnes and Matthew Taylor, 'Football Ticket Prices: Some Lessons from History', *History and Policy*, Blog, 18 February 2016.

10. Redefining Care

1 Anne Case and Angus Deaton, *Deaths of Despair and the Future of Capitalism* (Princeton, NJ: Princeton University Press, 2020).

2 Lawrence King, Gábor Scheiring and Elias Nosrati, 'Deaths of Despair in Comparative Perspective', *Annual Review of Sociology* 48 (July 2022): 299–317, 300.

3 David Walsh et al., 'Deaths from "Diseases of Despair" in Britain: Comparing Suicide, Alcohol-Related and Drug-Related Mortality for Birth Cohorts in Scotland, England and Wales in Selected Cities', *Journal of Epidemiological and Community Health* 75 (2021): 1195–1201, 1197.

4 Sarah O'Connor, 'Left behind: can anyone save the towns the UK economy forgot?' *Financial Times*, 16 November 2017.

5 Port Health Authority of Liverpool, 'Report for the Year 1946 by the Medical Officer of Health', Liverpool Record Office (henceforward LRO), 352.4 POR, 26; Port Health Authority of Liverpool, 'Report for the Year 1947 by the Medical Officer of Health', LRO, 352.4 POR, 8–9.

6 Port Health Authority of Liverpool, 'Report for the Year 1948 by the Medical Officer of Health', LRO, 352.4 POR, 16.

7 Gareth Millward, *Vaccinating Britain: Mass Vaccination and the Public Since the Second World War* (Manchester: Manchester University Press, 2019), 82.

8 For example, Port Health Authority, 'Report for the Year 1948', 22.

9 See, for example, the exchange of letters regarding the seaman Ng King in September 1952, Liverpool Maritime Museum, OA 2342/2A.

10 Port Health Authority of Liverpool, 'Report for the Year 1951 by the Medical Officer of Health', LRO, 352.4 POR, 11. David F. Wilson, *Dockers: The Impact of Industrial Change* (London: Fontana Collins, 1972), 118.

11 Port Health Authority, 'Report for the Year 1947', 10–11.

12 Port Health Authority, 'Report for the Year 1946', 28.

13 Port Health Authority, 'Report for the Year 1948', 15–16.

14 Port Health Authority of Liverpool, 'Report for the Year 1949 by the Medical Officer of Health', LRO, 352.4 POR, 6; Port Health Authority of Liverpool, 'Report for the Year 1945 by the Medical Officer of Health', Liverpool Record Office LRO, 352.4 POR, 28.

15 Port Health Authority, 'Report for the Year 1948', 22; Port Health Authority of Liverpool, 'Report for the Year 1973 by the Medical Officer of Health', LRO, 352.4 POR, 7.

16 For a history of how deindustrialisation, sickness and healthcare relate to one another in a different context see Gabriel Winant, *The Next Shift: The Fall of Industry and the Rise of Healthcare in Rust Belt America* (Cambridge, MA: Harvard University Press, 2021).

17 John Ashton, *Health in Mersey: A Review* (Liverpool: University of Liverpool Department of Community Health, 1984), 31.

18 Ibid., 40.

19 Walsh et al., 'Deaths from "Diseases of Despair" in Britain', 1197.

20 Ashton, *Health in Mersey*, 41.

21 Douglass Black and Peter Townsend, *Inequalities in Health: Report of a Research Working Group* (London: Department of Health and Social Services, 1980), 68.

22 Mervyn Goodman, 'Unemployment in My Practice', *British Medical Journal* 282 (20 June 1981), 2020.

23 Ashton, *Health in Mersey*, 28.

24 Black et al., *Inequalities in Health*, 27.

25 Grace Redhead, '"A British Problem Affecting British People": Sickle Cell Anaemia, Medical Activism and Race in the National Health Service, 1975–1993', *Modern British History* 32, no. 2 (June 2021): 189–211.

26 Roberta Bivins, 'Picturing Health in the National Health Service, 1948–1988', *Modern British History* 28, no. 1 (March 2017): 83–109; Young Historians Project, 'Young Historians Project: African Women and the Health Service', *History Workshop*, 21 November 2019, www.historyworkshop.org.uk/Black-history/young-historians-project-african-women-and-the-health-service/#:~:text=In%20this%20project%20we%20have,of%20their%20lives%20in%20Britain; Andrew Seaton, *Our NHS: A History of Britain's Best-Loved Institution* (New Haven, CT: Yale University Press, 2023), Ch. 5.

27 Ntombenhle Protasia Khotie Torkington, *The Racial Politics of Health: A Liverpool Profile* (Liverpool: Merseyside Area Profile Group, 1983), 14.

28 Liverpool Black Caucus, *The Racial Politics of Militant in Liverpool: The Black Community's Struggle for Participation in Local Politics* (Liverpool: Merseyside Area Profile and Runnymede Trust, 1986), 61.

29 Ntombenhle Protasia Khotie Torkington, *Black Health: A Political Issue* (Liverpool: Liverpool Institute of Higher Education), 91–92.

30 Ibid., 128–129.

31 Ibid., 137–145.

32 Ibid., 123.

33 Beverley Bryan, Stella Dadzie, Suzanne Scafe, Lola Okolosie, *The Heart of the Race: Black Women's Lives in Britain* (London: Verso, 1986, 2018), Ch. 3.

34 'Black Health Workers Open Up New Health Project in Liverpool 8', *Black Linx*, September 1983.

35 William E. Nelson, *Black Atlantic Politics: Dilemmas of Political Empowerment in Boston and Liverpool* (Albany: State University of New York Press, 2000), 174–175.

36 These activities are all recorded throughout Torkington, *Black Health*. Torkington was also one of the founders of Mary Seacole House.

37 Torkington, *The Racial Politics of Health*, 10.

38 Howard Parker, Keith Bakx and Russell Newcombe, *Living with Heroin* (Milton Keynes: Open University Press, 1988), 18.

39 Geoffrey Pearson, 'Drug-Control Policies in Britain', *Crime and Justice* 14 (1991): 167–227, 178.

40 Ibid., 179.

41 Ibid., 184.

42 Ibid., 181–182.

43 Parker et al., *Living with Heroin*, 76.
44 Ibid., 19.
45 Ibid., 7.
46 Ibid., 6–7.
47 Tam Stewart, *The Heroin Users* (London: Pandora 1987), 14, 18.
48 Tony Gifford, Wally Brown and Ruth Bundey, *Loosen the Shackles: First Report of the Liverpool 8 Inquiry into Race Relations in Liverpool* (London: Kaira, 1989), 176–178.
49 John Belchem, *Before the Windrush: Race Relations in Twentieth-Century Liverpool* (Liverpool: Liverpool University Press, 2014), 29.
50 Pearson, 'Drug-Control Policies in Britain', 173–178.
51 Gerry V. Stimson and Edna Oppenheimer, *Heroin Addiction: Treatment and Control in Britain* (London: Tavistock, 1982), 33; Pearson, 'Drug-Control Policies in Britain', 197.
52 For ways that US drug policy has been racialised see Helena Hanson, Jules Netherland and David Herzberg, *Whiteout: How Racial Capitalism Changed the Color of Opioids in America* (Oakland: University of California Press, 2023).
53 Pearson, 'Drug-Control Policies in Britain', 196–197.
54 Patrick Minford et al., 'The Liverpool Macroeconomic Model of the United Kingdom', *Economic Modelling* 1, no. 1 (January 1984): 24–62.
55 Larry Elliot, 'Patrick Minford: Maverick Economist who Inspired Truss and Thatcher', *The Guardian*, 6 September 2022.
56 Michael Johnson, 'Professor's "Policy of Despair" on Drugs', *Liverpool Daily Post*, 24 September 1988.
57 '"Muckspreader" Prof Comes in for Bashing', *Liverpool Echo*, 24 September 1988.
58 Caroline Storah, 'Lashing for Boffin Over "Legal' Drug"', *Liverpool Echo*, 3 November 1988.
59 Editorial, *The Mersey Drugs Journal* 2, no. 5 (1988), 2.
60 For example, in 1986 a brief spectacular battle with heroin dealers in Toxteth involved a showdown between armed police and dealers hurling bricks: 'Seven Held in Toxteth Raids', *The Times*, 15 May 1986. For complaints about appeasement of dealers see Gifford et al., *Loosen the Shackles*, 176–178.
61 Gifford et al., *Loosen the Shackles*, 179–180.
62 Pearson, 'Drug-Control Policies in Britain', 187.
63 Parker et al., *Living with Heroin*, 16.
64 Peter Burton and Chris Kirk, 'Liverpool: Living on the Front Line', *Gay News*, 30 August – 13 October 1982. For a longer overview of Liverpool's gay history see Mike Homfray, *Provincial Queens: The Gay and Lesbian Communities in the North-West of England* (Oxford: Peter Lang, 2007).

See also forthcoming work by Khalil West on queer life in post-war Toxteth.

65 Burton et al., 'Liverpool: Living on the Front Line'.

66 Ibid.

67 'Second UK "Gay Compromise" Death', *Gay News*, 5 August – 18 August 1982.

68 For the political context of AIDS in Britain see Jeffrey Weeks, 'AIDS and the Regulation of Sexuality', in Virginia Berridge and Philip Strong, *AIDS and Contemporary History* (Cambridge: Cambridge University Press, 1993): 17–37; Matt Cook, '"Archives of Feeling": The AIDS Crisis in Britain 1987', *History Workshop Journal* 83, no. 1 (March 2017): 51–78; Matt Cook, 'AIDS, Mass Observation, and the Fate of the Permissive Turn', *Journal of the History of Sexuality* 26, no. 2 (May 2017): 239–272; Lucy Robinson, *Gay Men and the Left in Post-War Britain: How the Personal Got Political* (Manchester: Manchester University Press, 2007), 152–183. See also forthcoming work by Tom Ward. For the AIDS crisis in the context of the declining Fordist household see Christopher Chitty, *Sexual Hegemony: Statecraft, Sodomy, and Capital in the Rise of the World System* (Durham, NC: Duke University Press, 2020), 167–193.

69 Cook, '"Archives of Feeling"', 58.

70 Weeks, 'AIDS and the Regulation of Society', 28–29.

71 Cook, '"Archives of Feeling"', 52.

72 Quoted in Nigel Evans, dir., *The End of Innocence*, BBC, 1995.

73 Gill McMinn, 'AIDS – Special Survey', *Wirral Globe*, 19 February 1987.

74 Val Woan, 'Killer that Sails in with the Tide', *Liverpool Echo*, 28 August 1987.

75 Peter Sherlock, 'Danger Point', *Liverpool Echo*, 6 October 1987.

76 Monica O'Hara, 'AIDS Hoax Agony', *Liverpool Echo*, 13 August 1987.

77 Peter Oldham, 'Mersey AIDS Cases Lowest in the Country', *Liverpool Daily Post*, 14 July 1988.

78 For an excellent recent oral history of the syringe exchange see Ella Glover, 'How "Smack City" Liverpool Halted an HIV Epidemic', *Huck Magazine*, 18 March 2021. Ashton and Seymore outlined their philosophy of public health and harm reduction in several places. For example, John Ashton and Howard Seymour, *The New Public Health* (Milton Keynes: Open University Press, 1996); John R. Ashton and Howard Seymour, 'Public Health and the Origins of the Mersey Model of Harm Reduction', *International Journal of Drug Policy* 21 (2020): 94–96.

79 Pat O'Hare, 'Harm Reduction in the Mersey Region', *International Journal of Drug Policy* 18 (2007): 152.

80 Ashton and Seymour, 'Public Health and the Origins of the Mersey Model of Harm Reduction', 95.

81 Glover, 'How "Smack City" Liverpool Halted an HIV Epidemic'.

82 Ibid.

83 Russell Newcome, 'The Liverpool Syringe Exchange Scheme for Drug Injectors: Initial Evidence of Effectiveness for HIV Prevention', *The Mersey Drugs Journal* 1, no. 6 (1987): 4–5, 4.

84 Harry Shapiro, 'Guerrilla Public Health', *Wellcome Collection*, 21 November 2017, https://wellcomecollection.org/articles/WgsiQiEAABXB1KCS.

85 Russell Newcome, 'The Liverpool Syringe Exchange Scheme for Drug Injectors: A Preliminary Report', *Mersey Drugs Journal* 1, no. 1 (1987): 8–10, 8.

86 Ibid., 8.

87 Alan Parry, 'HIV and Drugs: Outreach Work in the Mersey Region', *The Mersey Drugs Journal* 2, no. 3 (1988): 7–9, 8–9; Chris Lightbrown, 'The Battle to Control AIDS: Arming the Street People in Liverpool's Red Light District', 8 August 1989, LRO, 362 SAH 1/5/1; 'Syringe Exchange Scheme: The Liverpool Experience', Information Pack, 15, Wellcome Collection Archives, SA/DRS/B/1/265.

88 'Syringe Exchange Scheme: The Liverpool Experience', 16; Parry, 'HIV and Drugs: Outreach Work in the Mersey Region', 8.

89 Untitled statement beginning 'How do you reply…', LRO, ACC 6204, Box 16, Item 3.

90 O'Hare, 'Harm Reduction in the Mersey Region'.

91 'Syringe Exchange Scheme: The Liverpool Experience', 2.

92 Lightbrown, 'The Battle to Control AIDS'.

93 Mersey Body Positive, 'Annual Report: May 1993', LRO, 362 SAH 2/1/1/2, 7.

94 Peter Saunders, 'AIDS Patients "Should not be Isolated"', *Liverpool Daily Post*, 5 February 1987. Virginia Berridge has argued that 1986 was when an ad hoc bottom-up approach to the AIDS was crisis was replaced nationally with a state of 'war time emergency' in Britain. Virginia Berridge, 'The Early Years of AIDS in the United Kingdom 1981–6: Historical Perspectives', in Terence Ranger and Paul Slack, *Epidemics and Ideas: Essays on the Historical Perception of Pestilence* (Cambridge: Cambridge University Press, 1992): 303–329.

95 Ron Carrol, 'The Day I had to Tell My Family I Could Die of AIDS', undated newspaper cutting from *Wirral Globe*, LRO, 362 SAH 1/5/1.

96 Monica O'Hara, 'Helping in Any Way They Can', *Liverpool Echo*, 2 March 1987. For grassroots responses to the AIDS epidemic in England see George Severs, *Radical Acts: HIV/AIDS Activism in Late Twentieth-*

Century England (London: Bloomsbury, 2024). Severs covers the formation of three Merseyside AIDS support groups on pp. 21–23.

97 Merseyside AIDS Support Group, 'Annual Report: 1990–1991', LRO, 362 SAH 1/2/1/4 10, 15.

98 Ibid., 11; Margaret Kitchen, 'A Knock that Says Someone Cares', *Liverpool Daily Post*, 17 November 1987.

99 Merseyside AIDS Support Group, 'Annual Report: 1990–1991', 11.

100 Mersey Body Positive, 'Annual Report: May 1993', 8.

101 Ibid., 12.

102 'The Positive Times: September 1993', LRO, 362 SAH 2/2, 32.

103 Mersey Body Positive, 'Annual Report: May 1993', 26–27. For alternative spiritualities as healing practices in Mersey Body Positive see Severs, *Radical Acts*, 128–129.

104 Melinda Cooper, *Family Values: Between Neoliberalism and the New Social Conservatism* (Cambridge, MA: MIT Press, 2017), 183.

105 Mersey Body Positive, 'Annual Report: May 1993', 50–51.

106 Ibid., 52–53.

107 '3.06 – The Moment', *Liverpool Echo*, 28 April 1989.

108 Thomas W. Laqueur, *The Work of the Dead: A Cultural History of Mortal Remains* (Princeton, NJ: Princeton University Press, 2016), 1.

11. The History Factory

1 'Just Like the Old Days…', *Liverpool Daily Post*, 22 February 1984.

2 Vladimir Nabokov, 'Lance', *The New Yorker*, 25 January 1952.

3 Anna Lowenhaupt Tsing, *The Mushroom at the End of the World: On the Possibility of Life in Capitalist Ruins* (Princeton, NJ: Princeton University Press, 2015).

4 By the early twenty-first century, Liverpool had an officially designated 'Knowledge Quarter', a 'Cultural Quarter', a 'World Heritage Site' and was a UNESCO-recognised 'Creative City'.

5 Barbara Metcalfe, 'A Mecca for Tourists', *Liverpool Echo*, 4 July 1986.

6 'City's Tourism Sector Continues to Bounce Back', *Liverpool Express*, 8 August 2023.

7 Quoted in Tony Lane, *Liverpool: City of the Sea* (Liverpool: Liverpool University Press, 1997), xiii.

8 For a full account of these events see Brian Marren, *We Shall Not Be Moved: How Liverpool's Working Class Fought Redundancies, Closures and Cuts in the Age of Thatcher* (Manchester: Manchester University Press, 2006), 177–200. Birkenhead has seen a minor revival in shipbuilding and repairing since 2008.

9 Anne Jones, 50,000 *Bluebells: The Story of Liverpool's International Garden Festival* (Leicester: Windward, 1984), 48–49.

10 Daniel T. Rodgers, *Age of Fracture* (Cambridge, MA: Harvard University Press, 2011), 223. For a similar argument see Andreas Huyssen, *Present Pasts: Urban Palimpsets and the Politics of Memory* (Palo Alto, CA: Stanford University Press, 2003). Debates over the politics of 'heritage' raged in Britain in the 1980s and 1990s. For some of the most significant interventions see Patrick Wright, *On Living in an Old Country: The National Past in Contemporary Britain* (London: Verso, 1986); Robert Hewison, *The Heritage Industry: Britain in a Climate of Decline* (London: Methuen, 1987); Raphael Samuels, *Theatres of Memory* (London: Verso, 1996); Stuart Hall, 'Whose Heritage? Un-settling "The Heritage", Reimaging the Post-nation', *Third Text* 13, no. 49 (1999): 3–13. For an overview of these debates see Jessica Moody, 'Heritage and History', in Emma Waterton and Steve Watson eds., *The Palgrave Handbook of Contemporary Heritage Research* (Basingstoke: Palgrave, 2015).

11 Michael Brocken, *The Twenty-First Century Legacy of the Beatles: Liverpool and Popular Music Heritage Tourism* (Abingdon: Ashgate, 2016), 37.

12 Sara Cohen, *Decline, Renewal and the City in Popular Music Culture: Beyond the Beatles* (Abingdon: Ashgate, 2007), 189.

13 Ibid., 175.

14 Mike and Bernadette Byrne have recently published their own history of the creation of the museum: Mike Byrne and Bernadette Byrne, *Birth of the Beatles Story: Our Time With the Beatles and How We Became Founders of the Most Successful Beatles Exhibition in the World* (New Haven Press, 2022).

15 Ibid.; Brocken, *The Twenty-First Century Legacy of the Beatles*, 128–130.

16 Simeon Yates, Richard Evans, Mike Jones, Gerwyn Jones, Martin Hudson and Stephen Crone, 'Beatles Heritage in Liverpool and its Economic and Social Cultural Sector Impact: A Report for Liverpool City Council', November 2015, https://iccliverpool.ac.uk/wp-content/uploads/2016/02/Beatles-Heritage-in-Liverpool-48pp-210x210mm-aw.pdf, 14.

17 Ibid., 22.

18 Ibid., 16.

19 Cohen, *Decline, Renewal and the City in Popular Music Culture*, 180.

20 Jacqueline Nassy Brown, *Dropping Anchor, Setting Sail: Geographies of Race in Black Liverpool* (Princeton, NJ: Princeton University Press, 2005), 18, 23.

21 Julia Rampen, 'Liverpool's Forgotten Columbus Day Celebrations Once Revolved Around Controversial Sefton Park Statute', *Liverpool Echo*, 12 June 2020.

22 Nassy Brown, *Dropping Anchor, Setting Sail*, 18.

23 Chris Eakin, 'Mersey to Mark Age of Discovery', *Liverpool Daily Post*, 14 November 1986.

24 The best account of the political consequences of the Columbus Quincentennial remains Michel-Rolph Trouillot, *Silencing the Past: Power and the Production of History* (Boston, MA: Beacon Press, 2015), 108–141. In 2021, Joe Biden became the first US president to issue a presidential proclamation on 11 October celebrating Indigenous Peoples' Day.

25 Lynda Baril and Kevin McCoy, 'City Police Arrest 26', *New York Newsday*, 3 July 1992.

26 Ian Herbert, 'US Firms Drawn to Tall Ships Regatta', *Liverpool Daily Post*, 1 August 1992.

27 For example, 'Invitation to Visit the Mersey: Transatlantic Sailing Races 1992', Liverpool Record Office (henceforward LRO), HQ 797.14.

28 'Return of Tall Ships to the Mersey: Official Mersey Programme', LRO, 797.14 RET, 7.

29 'Festival "Highlights Problems"', *Liverpool Daily Post*, 11 August 1992.

30 Nassy Brown, *Dropping Anchor, Setting Sail*, 168–169, 204.

31 Merseyside Dock and Harbour Company, "Annual Reports and Accounts for the Year Ended 1966," Liverpool Maritime Museum Archive, MDHB/FIN/1/2/26, 7.

32 For a full list see: https://whc.unesco.org/en/list/.

33 Liverpool World Heritage Liaison Group, 'Nomination of Liverpool Maritime Mercantile City for Inscription on the World Heritage List' (Liverpool: Liverpool City Council, 2003), 39.

34 Ibid., 28.

35 Peter de Figueiredo ed., *Liverpool: World Heritage City – The Official Guide to the City of Liverpool* (Liverpool: Blue Coat Press, 2014), 6.

36 World Heritage Liaison Group, 'Nomination of Liverpool Maritime Mercantile City', 16.

37 Ibid.

38 Marco D'Eramo, 'Unescocide', *New Left Review* 88 (July/August 2014), 49.

39 Liverpool World Heritage Liaison Group, 'Liverpool Maritime Mercantile City: Draft Management Plan', 2003, LRO, Hq 363.69 LIV.

40 The Council produced its own supplementary planning document that laid out restrictions for development in and near the Site: Liverpool City Council, 'Liverpool Maritime Mercantile City: Supplementary Planning Document, Consultation Draft', 2009, LRO, Hq 363.69 LIV.

41 The decision was adopted at the 36th Session of the UNESCO World Heritage Committee. For a full list of resolutions adopted at WHC

12/36 COM 19 including Liverpool's new designation see https://whc.unesco.org/archive/2012/whc12-36com-19e.pdf.

42 The decision was adopted at the 44th Session of the UNESCO World Heritage Committee. For a full list of resolutions adopted at WHC 21/44 COM 18 including Liverpool's revocation see https://whc.unesco.org/archive/2021/whc-21-44com-18-en.pdf.

43 For a succinct account of Liverpool's involvement in the trans-Atlantic slave trade see Kenneth Morgan, 'Liverpool's Dominance in the British Slave Trade, 1740–1807', in David Richardson, Suzanne Schwarz and Anthony Tibbles, *Liverpool and Transatlantic Slavery* (Liverpool: Liverpool University Press, 2007).

44 Jessica Moody, *The Persistence of Memory: Remembering Slavery in Liverpool 'Slaving Capital of the World'* (Liverpool: Liverpool University Press, 2020), 35.

45 Ibid.

46 Murray Steele, 'Confronting a Legacy: The Atlantic Slave Trade and the Black Community of Liverpool', in Alyson Brown ed., *Historical Perspectives on Social Identities* (Newcastle: Cambridge Scholars Publishing, 2009), 138–139.

47 Moody, *The Persistence of Memory*, 113–114.

48 Ian Gronback, 'What a Sight to See as the Ships Sail In', *Liverpool Daily Post*, 20 June 1984.

49 Phyllis K. Leffler, 'Maritime Museums and Transatlantic Slavery: A Study in British and American Identity', *Journal of Transatlantic Studies* 4, no. 1 (2006): 55–80, 58.

50 Tony Gifford, Wally Brown and Ruth Bundey, *Loosen the Shackles: First Report of the Liverpool 8 Inquiry into Race Relations in Liverpool* (London: Kaira, 1989), 26.

51 Alison Taubman, 'A Preliminary Assessment Survey of Visitors to the Merseyside Maritime Museum Regarding a Proposed Exhibition of the Atlantic Slave Trade', Report, 1993, Liverpool Maritime Museum Archive, D/KUYA/13/1/4/4, 9.

52 Moody, *The Persistence of Memory*, 160.

53 For a partial list of objects held in the collection see Anthony Tibbles ed., *Against Human Dignity: Transatlantic Slavery* (Liverpool: Liverpool University Press, 1994, 2007), 143–177.

54 Steele, 'Confronting a Legacy', 143.

55 Stephen Small, 'Slavery Colonialism and Museums Representations in Great Britain', *Human Architecture: Journal of the Sociology of Self-Knowledge* 9, no. 4 (January 2011): 117–127, 123; Moody, *The Persistence of Memory*, 161–163

56 Small, 'Slavery, Colonialism and Museums Representation', 123.

57 This dissonance has been described by Alice Mah, *Port Cities and Global Legacies: Urban Identity, Waterfront Work and Radicalism* (London: Routledge, 2014), 95–99.

58 Moody, *The Persistence of Memory*, 180.

59 Figueiredo ed., *Liverpool: World Heritage City*, 8.

60 Sven Beckett, *Empire of Cotton: A Global History* (New York: Knopf, 2014), 260.

61 Michael Parkinson, *Liverpool Beyond the Brink: The Re-Making of a Post-Imperial City* (Liverpool: Liverpool University Press, 2019), 172.

62 Figueiredo ed., *Liverpool: World Heritage City*, 3.

63 The plaque is part of a list of inspirational quotes. The line 'Liverpool's Story is the World's Glory' was a slogan used by the early twentieth-century Society of Lovers of Old Liverpool. In this context it likely refers to the title of John Belchem's contribution to John Belchem ed., *Merseypride: Essays in Liverpool Exceptionalism* (Liverpool: Liverpool University Press, 2000).

64 For two recent examples see Hannah Rose Woods, *Rule, Nostalgia: A Backwards History of Britain* (London: W. H. Allen, 2023); Charlotte Lydia Riley, *Imperial Island: A History of Empire in Modern Britain* (London: Penguin, 2023).

65 Hall, 'Whose Heritage?' 5.

66 Jenny Kirkham, 'Hundreds Sign Petition to Mayor Joe Anderson over Sefton Park Christopher Columbus Statue', *Liverpool Echo*, 11 June 2020.

67 Comedia Consultancy, 'The Cultural Industries in Liverpool: A Report to the Merseyside Taskforce – Volume 1: Main Report', January 1991.

68 Charles Landry, *What a Way to Run a Railroad* (London: Comedia, 1985).

69 See, for example, Jeff Mulgin and Ken Worpole, *Saturday Night or Sunday Morning? From Arts Industry to New Forms of Cultural Policy* (London: Comedia, 1986). For accounts of the emergences of the 'cultural industries' as a means of arresting urban decline see Hazel Atashroo, 'Beyond the "Campaign for a Popular Culture": Community Art, Activism and Cultural Democracy in 1980s London' (PhD diss., University of Southampton, 2017); Franco Bianchini and Michael Parkinson eds., *Cultural Policy and Urban Regeneration, The West European Experience* (Manchester: Manchester University Press, 1994); Justin Lewis, *Art, Culture and Enterprise: The Politics of Art and the Cultural Industries* (London: Routledge, 1990, 2014); David Hesmondhalgh, *The Cultural Industries* (London: Sage, 2018). For critical histories of this practice see Richard Hewison, *Cultural Capital: The Rise and Fall of Creative Britain* (London: Verso, 2014); Oli Mould, *Against Creativity* (London:

Verso, 2018); Justin O'Connor, *Culture is Not an Industry: Reclaiming Art and Culture for the Common Good* (Manchester: Manchester University Press, 2024).

70 Indeed, Mulgin and Worpole wrote, 'what was once thought of as the ideological superstructure has now become a significant part of the economic base'. Mulgin and Worpole, *Saturday Night or Sunday Morning?*, 14.

71 Peter Booth and Robin Boyle (eds), 'See Glasgow, See Culture', in Bianchini and Parkinson, *Cultural Policy and Urban Regeneration*, 22–47.

72 Lewis, *Art, Culture and Enterprise*, 132–134.

73 Greater London Council, *The London Industrial Strategy* (London: Greater London Council, 1985), 169.

74 Lewis, *Art, Culture and Enterprise*, 131–134.

75 Liverpool City Council, 'An Arts and Cultural Industries Strategy for Liverpool', November 1987, LRO Hq 700. 942753 CIT.

76 'Fringe '84', *Trident*, February 1984, LRO, MDC 8/2.

77 See, for example, Phillip Key, 'The Minister for Anxiety', *Liverpool Echo*, 14 February 1986.

78 Comedia Consultancy, 'The Cultural Industries in Liverpool', 9–11.

79 Michael Parkinson and Franco Bianchini, 'Liverpool: A Tale of Missed Opportunities?' in Parkinson and Bianchini eds., *Cultural Policy and Urban Regeneration*, 155–177.

80 Liverpool's application document noted that the city 'Lives on the edge of Europe, the edge of America, the edge of Africa, on the fault-lines of culture… built on the foundations of imperialism, economic migration and the Industrial Revolution.' Liverpool Culture Company LTD, 'Liverpool: The World in One City', 2002, LRO, Hf 700 942.753 LIV. For some critical reflections on Liverpool's year as capital of culture see Paul Jones and Stuart Wilks-Heeg, 'Capitalising Culture: Liverpool 2008', *Local Economy* 19, no. 4 (November 2004): 341–360; Phillip Boland, '"Capital of Culture, You Must be Having a Laugh!" Challenging the Official Rhetoric of Liverpool as the 2008 Capital of Culture', *Social & Cultural Geography* 11, no. 7 (September 2010): 627–654.

81 Boland, 'Capital of Culture, You Must be Having a Laugh', 629.

82 Ibid., 628.

83 For a full list of events see 'Liverpool 2008 Timeline', www.cultureliverpool.co.uk/liverpool-08-timeline/.

84 The data was gathered by the Impacts 08 European Capitals of Culture Research Programme. The full report is available online: Beatriz Garcia, Ruth Melville and Tamsin Cox, 'Creating an Impact: Liverpool's Experience as European Capital of Culture', www.a-n.co.uk/research/impacts-08-11/.

85 Chris Couch, *City of Change and Challenge: Urban Planning and Regeneration in Liverpool* (Abingdon: Routledge, 2003, 2018), 183–184.
86 David Taylor and Terry Davenport, *Liverpool: Regeneration of a City Centre* (Manchester: Building Design Partnership, 2009), 46.
87 David Littlefield, *Liverpool One: Remaking a City Centre* (Chichester: Wiley, 2009), 11.
88 Taylor and Davenport, *Liverpool: Regeneration of a City Centre*, 44–48. For out-of-town shopping malls and the privatisation of public space in Britain see Sam Wetherell, *Foundations: How the Built Environment Made Twentieth-Century Britain* (Princeton, NJ: Princeton University Press, 2020), 137–164; Alistair Kefford, *The Life and Death of the Shopping City: Public Planning and Private Redevelopment in Britain since 1945* (Cambridge: Cambridge University Press, 2022).
89 Taylor and Davenport, *Liverpool: Regeneration of a City Centre*, 116.
90 Anna Minton, *What Kind of World Are We Building? The Privatisation of Public Space* (London: Royal Institute of Chartered Surveyors, 2006), 14–15.
91 Sean Griffith, 'Empire State', *The Architectural Review*, January 2008.
92 Surviving copies are held at LRO, Hq 092 QUI.
93 David Ward, 'Liverpool to Build on Hope for Future', *The Guardian*, 20 May 2004.
94 'Global Financial System on Brink of Meltdown', *Reuters*, 11 October 2008.
95 Larry Elliot and Jill Traynor, 'Week in which Global Catastrophe was Averted', *The Guardian*, 17 October 2008.
96 Centre for Cities, 'Cities Outlook 2009', 2009, www.centreforcities.org/wp-content/uploads/2014/09/09-01-26-Cities-Outlook-2009.pdf; Robert Book, 'Red Alert for Capital of Culture in Thinktank's Recession Report', *The Guardian*, 26 January 2009.
97 Centre for Cities, 'Cities Outlook 2009', 41.
98 Tony Dolphin, 'The Impact of the Recession on Northern City Regions', *IPPR North*, October 2009, 27.
99 Patrick Butler, 'Deprived Northern Regions Worst Hit by UK Austerity, Study Finds', *The Guardian*, 28 January 2019.

Epilogue: Liverpool Waters

1 Historic England, 'Historic Textile Mills of Greater Manchester: Survey Review and Heritage Audit: Executive Summary', 2017, https://historicengland.org.uk/images-books/publications/historic-textile-mills-greater-manchester/greater-manchester-textile-mills-survey-exec-summary/.
2 Ibid.

3 'The Sunday Times Rich List 2023', 19 May 2023.

4 For Peel's early history see Alistair Ross Goobey, *Bricks and Mortals: The Dreams of the 80s and the Nightmare of the 90s: The Inside Story of the Property World* (London: Century Business, 1992), 178–184.

5 Guy Shrubsole, 'Who Owns the Country? The Secretive Companies Hoarding England's Land', *The Guardian*, 19 April 2019.

6 Ibid.

7 Ibid.

8 Mark Tran, 'Port Companies in £770 Merger', *The Guardian*, 9 June 2005.

9 At the time of writing, much of Liverpool Waters is still being reviewed and contested by planning authorities. For the clearest sense of the current proposals see www.liverpoolwaters.co.uk/about/.

10 Dan Whelan, 'Goodison Park Legacy Project Back in Spotlight', *Place North West*, 25 April 2022.

11 For IPCC's latest projected range of different sea level rise scenarios see Intergovernmental Panel on Climate Change, 'Climate Change 2023 Synthesis Report: Summary for Policy Makers', www.ipcc.ch/report/ar6/syr/downloads/report/IPCC_AR6_SYR_SPM.pdf, 17; for worst-case scenario sea level rises see Karen McVeigh, '"It's Absolutely Guaranteed": The Best and Worst Case Scenarios for Sea Level Rise', *The Guardian*, 26 June 2023.

12 Peel Holdings have produced a fourteen-page 'sustainability plan' in which a single paragraph is used to refer to various defences in the event of sea level rises. Peel L & P, 'Liverpool Waters: Sustainability Plan', https://peellandp.co.uk/media/4009/sustainability-plan-liverpool-waters-1.pdf.

13 James A. Boggs, 'The Outsiders', in Stephen M. Ward ed., *Pages from a Radical's Notebook: A James Boggs Reader* (Detroit, MI: Wayne State University Press, 2011), 114.

Acknowledgements

I arrived in Liverpool as a stranger – an outsider who had spent much of his adult life living overseas. Fortunately, I'm not sure that there is any other city in the world that would have been more welcoming or more kind to someone in my position. Some clichés really are true. While much of Britain can be cold and at times illegible, Liverpool does feel different. I am deeply grateful to the city for being so open-hearted, so generous with its history, so thoughtful and accepting of my work and so tolerant of my presence. I am truly lucky that the city I have chosen to spend the last five years writing about is such a wonderful place to spend time.

I have benefitted from a network of Scouse friends, academics, archivists and interlocutors. Thanks to Tom Ward for answering my interminable questions about Liverpool's geography and for his enthusiasm for the project from the outset. Thanks to Jack Shepherd for reading the manuscript and offering thoughts on everything from the composition of Bill Shankly's Boot Room to the colour of the bins in Speke. Laura Gutiérrez and Eoghan Ahern, as well as baby Liam, have been wonderful and supportive hosts and friends over the years. I hope I have sufficiently repaid them in lasagnas. Jimi Jagne was kind enough to share his thoughts and memories about Liverpool's recent Black history and to read parts of my manuscript. Our meeting was followed by a fascinating email exchange in which we tried to make sense of Britain's present political conjuncture. Michael Parkinson was kind enough to share his ideas, enthusiasm and contacts over several brunches. I am also grateful to John Belchem, Sam Caslin, Emma Copestake, Derek

Edwards, Tony Lane and Kerrie McGiveron. I was lucky enough to meet and pick the brains of both Derek Hatton and Michael Heseltine. They will profoundly disagree with the contents of this book, but I am grateful to each for sharing their memories.

Anyone who has ever worked in the Liverpool Record Office will be able to testify to the kindness, competence and diligence of the archivists who work there. In particular, my thanks go to Vicki Caren, who allowed me advance access to the Liverpool 8 Law Centre Archive and talked me through various other collections. Thanks also to the staff at the Liverpool Maritime Museum Archives, the National Archives, the Black Cultural Archives and the Schomberg Centre for Research in Black Culture. I am indebted to the diligence and competence of my research assistant Luke Cashmore. I am also grateful to four truly magnificent former students who I briefly employed at different times to visit archives when I was living overseas: Megan Hayton, Katie Shine, Olivia Wyatt and Tom Ward. Thanks also to Eoghan Ahern and Akosua Sarpong for their additional research.

This book evolved in conversation with a group of friends who are writing about very different topics but who are all responding in different ways to the tempestuous politics of the last five years. Many ideas were worked out over dozens of lunches with Trevor Jackson in Washington DC, where I basked in the distinctive glow of his dark humour, scholarly brilliance and steadfast enthusiasm. This book benefitted enormously from my friendship with Tom Johnson – a trans-Atlantic comradeship stitched together by WhatsApp voice notes, long emails and phone calls as we tried to figure out new ways to read and write about history. It is not an understatement to say that these discussions with Tom rejuvenated a flagging interest in intellectual life on my behalf. Two reading groups, 'HPC' and the Red Deer Collective, were the political and intellectual eco-system in which this book germinated. The Collective were kind enough to host a full manuscript workshop for this book and I am immensely grateful to Emily Baughan, David Huyssen, Tom Johnson, Erin Maglaque, Chris Millard and Simon Stevens for being such diligent and thoughtful readers. Venus

Bivar, Joey Kellner and Tehila Sasson also read some or all of this manuscript and have been sources of inspiration and friendship through the years. Thanks to Robbie Shilliam for some wonderful early advice and for persuading me to read James Boggs. Thanks also to Chris Casey, Jeannette Estruth, Alma Igra, Erica Lee, Robbie Nelson, Mircea Rainu, Sarah Stoller and Claire Wrigley, all of whom will, to a greater or lesser extent, see imprints of their ideas in this book. As always, my gratitude to James Vernon for his friendship, advice and willingness to read early drafts is boundless. I am impossibly lucky to have him on my side.

The Department of History at the University of York continues to be a wonderful home. This book was made possible by a year of research leave in 2019–20 and a Leverhulme Research Fellowship which my department helped me secure. It has not been an easy few years. Many working relationships have been forged and tested on picket lines and with marking boycotts under the shadow of redundancies and fiscal retrenchment. I am grateful for the solidarity of friends and colleagues during these difficult times, especially those in the darkest recesses of Vanbrugh's A Block — Lawrence Black, Eliza Hartrich, Hannah Jeans, Edd Mair, Shaul Mitelpunkt, Emilie Murphy and Eskandar Sadeghi-Boroujerdi. Thanks to Chris Renwick for his advice on how to write a trade book and for telling me about Daniel Caradog Jones. Finally, I'd like to thank the extraordinary students in my year-long 2023–24 Black British History seminar as well as the students who participated in York's Palestine encampment for offering hope that the university can be re-made, if fleetingly, on different terms.

I am grateful to Neil Belton at Head of Zeus for taking on this project, as well as for his advice, care and mentorship. My agent, Andrew Gordon, saw the potential in this idea from its first inception. I am deeply grateful for his experience, his reassurance and his ability to help me realise what I wanted to say in these pages.

It remains to thank my complex and internationally dispersed family. My Mum, Margaret Wetherell, and her partner, Pete Williams, tore themselves away from their home in rural New

Zealand to start a new life in freezing North Yorkshire. I hope it was worth it in the end; we are eternally grateful that you came out to join us here. My Dad, Jonathan Potter, and his partner, Alexa Hepburn, have propped up this project on both sides of the Atlantic with their love, support and little bowls of delicious crisps. Love also to Marion, Stephen, Kasper and Rosa, Simeon, Amy, Hazel and Graham, as well as Jane and Chris Jewell. I'm hoping that Jane Jewell can find the typos in this one *before* it goes to press.

My daughter, Charlie, was born in 2022. Readers may not be able to tell, but she was a constant invisible presence throughout the second half of this book. I wrote the best part of two chapters with her asleep on my chest. Many of the book's ideas were puzzled through over miles and miles of 'trundles' with the pram while she napped or pointed at dogs. She will get her book dedication one day, but this one is for my wife, Hannah Jewell, with love. It speaks to her extraordinary talent as an author and a journalist that Hannah is always one book ahead of me, and I'm left playing catch-up with acknowledgements and dedications. Our life together is perfect and she will always be the funniest, kindest, most loyal person I know.

Image Credits

p.22 RIBA Collections
p.27 Photo by Bert Hardy/Picture Post/Hulton Archive/Getty Images
p.57 Photo by Staff/Mirrorpix/Getty Images
p.72 Photo by Staff/Mirrorpix/Getty Images
p.80 Photo by Daily Mirror/Mirrorpix/Mirrorpix via Getty Images
p.89 *Liverpool Echo*
p.103 Photo by Western Mail and Echo/Western Mail Archive/Mirrorpix via Getty Images
p.126 Photo by Eric Piper/Mirrorpix/Getty Images
p.144 Photo by Staff/Mirrorpix/Getty Images
p.189 Photo by John Davidson/Liverpool Echo/MirrorpixGetty Images
p.190 Photo by Stephen Shakeshaft/Mirrorpix via Getty Images
p.204 Photo by Staff/Mirrorpix/Getty Images
p.221 Photo by Geoff Roberts/Mirrorpix/Getty Images
p.242 Photo by Staff/Mirrorpix via Getty Images
p.276 Photo by Derek Hudson/Getty Images
p.287 Photo by Stephen Shakeshaft/Mirrorpix via Getty Images
p.316 Photo by Staff/Mirrorpix/Getty Images
p.320 Photo by Derek Wright/Liverpool Echo/Mirrorpix/Getty Images
p.338 Sam Wetherell

Index